Concentrationary Cinema

Concentrationary Cinema

Aesthetics as Political Resistance
in Alain Resnais's
Night and Fog (1955)

Edited by
Griselda Pollock and Max Silverman

berghahn
NEW YORK · OXFORD
www.berghahnbooks.com

First published in 2011 by
Berghahn Books
www.berghahnbooks.com

©2011, 2014 Griselda Pollock and Max Silverman
First paperback edition published in 2014

Library of Congress Cataloging-in-Publication Data

Concentrationary Cinema: Aesthetics as political resistance in Alain Resnais's
Night and fog (1955) / edited by Griselda Pollock and Max Silverman.
    p. cm.
  Includes bibliographical references and index.
  ISBN 978-0-85745-351-8 (hardback) -- ISBN 978-1-78238-498-4
(paperback) -- ISBN 978-0-85745-352-5 (ebook)
  1. Nuit et brouillard (Motion picture) 2. World War, 1939-1945--Motion
pictures and the war. 3. Holocaust, Jewish (1939-1945), in motion
pictures. 4. Resnais, Alain, 1922--Criticism and interpretation. 5. Motion
pictures--Aesthetics. 6. Memory in motion pictures. I. Pollock, Griselda.
II. Silverman, Maxim.
  D804.3.N853A48 2011
  791.43'658405318--dc23

2011020657

British Library Cataloguing in Publication Data
A catalogue record for this book is available from the British Library
Printed in the United States on acid-free paper.

ISBN: 978-0-85745-351-8 hardback
ISBN: 978-1-78238-498-4 paperback
ISBN: 978-0-85745-352-5 ebook

Contents

List of Plates from *Night and Fog*

(All the plates are taken from Alain Resnais *Night and Fog* (1955). They are reproduced courtesy of Argos Films, Paris)

List of Figures

Foreword

This new book, illuminating Alain Resnais's *Night and Fog* from a number of perspectives, is essential not only in that it helps to enrich our understanding of one of the most important documentary films ever made, but also because it calls fresh attention to a film designed to warn against the emergence of new forms of racism. And unlike other representations of the Holocaust which position audiences in a self-exempting stance of righteous indignation, *Night and Fog* calls upon its viewers to ask difficult questions of themselves and to search their own souls for tell-tale signs of the racist 'contagion'.

This is one of the reasons why *Night and Fog* was shown on six French TV channels at midnight on 14 May 1990, as a symbolic response to the desecration of the Jewish cemetery at Carpentras. This simultaneous broadcast of the film on numerous channels was an unprecedented event in the history of television, and a confirmation of the utterly unique status occupied by *Night and Fog* in contemporary culture.

The final words of the film's narration, written by Jean Cayrol and spoken by Michel Bouquet with no melodramatic throb in his voice, are well worth considering once again. As the camera moves one last time over the terrain and relics of what was once a concentration camp, we are cautioned that this abandoned village is still heavy with peril and that new executioners, with faces like our own, may soon be among us.

And here we are, earnestly looking at these ruins as though the old monster of the camps lay dead beneath the rubble,

we who pretend to regain hope before this image that recedes into the distance, as if one could ever be cured of the plague of the camps,

we who pretend to believe that it is all confined to a single epoch and a single country, and who don't think of looking around ourselves, and who don't hear that people are crying out without end.

Richard Raskin
Aarhus, Denmark 2010

Acknowledgements

This book is the product of a four-year research project, *Concentrationary Memories: The Politics of Representation* (2007–11) funded by the Arts and Humanities Research Council of England. We gratefully acknowledge their financial support for this research. We would also like to thank Francesco Ventrella for unstinting administrative support on the project. We are also grateful to the many students and participants in the seminars through which this book was developed.

We acknowledge Faber and Faber and Farrar, Straus and Giroux, LLC for permission to reproduce the poem *Shemà* (1946) by Primo Levi from *Primo Levi: Collected Poems* translated by Ruth Feldman and Brian Swann (London: Faber and Faber, 1992).

We acknowledge *New German Critique* for their permission to reprint Andrew Hebard, 'Disruptive Pasts: Towards a Radical Politics of Remembrance in Alain Resnais's Night and Fog', *New German Critique* 71 (Fall, 1997).

Strenuous efforts have been made to contact copyright owners of the images and stills reproduced in this volume. We encourage any copyright owner to contact us if this has not been achieved.

Concentrationary Cinema

GRISELDA POLLOCK AND MAX SILVERMAN

Night and Fog made a decisive contribution to the way we regard the
concentration camp system, while apprehensively inventing a gesture
of cinema in order to face it. By assembling archival footage – some of
it known, some of it revealed to French audiences for the first time –
Resnais shaped our images of the camps.
Sylvie Lindeperg[1]

Remember that the concentration camp system even from its origins
(which coincide with the rise to power of Nazism in Germany) had as its
primary purpose the shattering of the adversaries' capacity to resist.
Primo Levi[2]

The extermination camps appear within the framework of totalitarian
terror as the most extreme form of concentration camps ... Concentration
camps existed long before totalitarianism made them the central
institution of government.
Hannah Arendt[3]

The anxiety can hardly abate in view of the fact that none of the societal
conditions that made Auschwitz possible has truly disappeared, and no
effective measures have been undertaken to prevent such possibilities and
principles from generating Auschwitz-like catastrophes.
Zygmunt Bauman[4]

A *concentrationary* cinema disturbs the slumber induced by post-war
reconstruction by showing us the novel message of the *concentrationary* system
in which we have to *see* what it means that 'everything is [now] possible'. It is
a cinema utilizing radical techniques of montage and disorientation, camera

movements and counterpointed commentary to expose invisible knowledge hidden by a normalized, documentary presentation of a real that could become bland and opaque unless agitated by disturbing juxtapositions and prolonged visual attentiveness. It connects the living to the dead, past to present, here to there in order to shock us out of comforting dichotomies that keep the past 'over there'. It uses the travelling shot and shocking montage to expose us to contamination. It is a cinema of hauntings, 'in-betweens' and warnings heavy with a menace revealed under sunny skies and harsh colour. Concentrationary cinema embraces other films of the era that work in a similar way (for example Resnais's *Hiroshima mon amour* (1959) and *Muriel* (1963), and Chris Marker's *La Jetée* (1962)). *Night and Fog* is, in our eyes however, the classic commentary on the *concentrationary* universe.

Night and Fog (1955)

When the producer of Argos Films, Anatole Dauman, first watched the final cut of the film he had commissioned from Alain Resnais in 1955, *Nuit et Brouillard* (henceforth *Night and Fog*), he declared it a work of art ('un beau film'). He added, however, that it would never be widely seen.[5] Dauman was convinced that the film was a major aesthetic achievement, and not a straightforward documentary history. At the same time, the film was both so deeply shocking and so profoundly made that Dauman could only imagine a brief exposure followed by a forgotten life of remembered renown on the shelf.

In fact, the politicizing scandal that erupted around the film in 1956 because of the attempt to censor two scenes (Plates 11 and 40) and to prevent its exhibition at the Cannes Film Festival ensured a much wider engagement with both the film itself (regarded by fellow filmmakers as worthy of the highest acknowledgement for its cinematic originality – it was awarded the Prix Jean Vigo in January 1956) and with its politics of the representation of history and the production of cultural memory.[6] *Night and Fog* has since come to be acknowledged by film historians and scholars in general as not only the first French film offering a commemorative analysis of the events 1933–45 but perhaps the most influential, significant and certainly the most widely shown film on these events ever made. But what was the film about? What was its purpose? What are the effects of its self-consciously formal strategies – what Resnais called his *recherches formelles*, that is his formal experiments – in representing the recent past in the film's present? How do its politics and its aesthetics interface? In what ways did Resnais's 'gesture of cinema' to confront the concentration camps create an aesthetic of resistance to political terror, a terror epitomized by the concentration camp but presented as seeping beyond its spatio-temporal origins? Thus where and how should this film be positioned in the history of cinema, in the history of a politics of representation, and in the creation of cultural memory of the horrors of the twentieth century? How, indeed, should its self-conscious aesthetic strategies of the use of the shot and the gaze, the relations between words and images, the intercutting of present and past and its imaging of the dead, be read?

Resnais's short but potent film has undoubtedly shaped the cultural imaginary of generations, not because of its (relatively limited) commercial distribution, but because of its pedagogical exhibition in schools and synagogues, university courses and festivals, and in museums and at conferences.[7] For many people worldwide, however, the film's selection of photographs, its combination of documentary and fiction-film footage, its montage of still and moving images, its compellingly haunting commentary combined with charged discordant music, its cutting between pans across abandoned ruins filmed in colour and swiftly-edited montages of fearful images in black and white, have established in their memories an iconic imagery of what they understand now as 'the Holocaust'. We can trace this connection in anecdotal evidence, and in the regular referencing of *Night and Fog's* images in later films, and even in what has become an unconscious visual memory of the event of the attempted destruction of European Jewry.[8]

But what does it mean to name the film a 'Holocaust' film? Does it concern the specificity of its content? Could it indicate the emergence of a new rhetoric for memory? Are we sure that we know to what we are referring by using this name for several historical events?

The name Holocaust, deriving from the Greek *holokauston*, meaning burnt whole, originates in the Hebrew word *olah*. *Olah* was the most sacred sacrifice in which, exceptionally everything, was wholly consumed by fire so that the scented aroma could rise to serve the deity. Freighted, therefore, with problematic religious and specifically sacrificial overtones that are utterly inappropriate to a modern crime of mass genocide, the term became a widely used name for the attempted destruction of European Jewry between 1941 and 1945 only after the mid-1950s. Capitalized, the Holocaust was effectively consolidated in Euro-American popular cultural memory by its use as the title of an American TV series about the destruction of Jewish Germans, *Holocaust*, created by Gerald Green in 1978, and watched by millions of people in the United States and across Europe.[9] Yet, as Jon Petrie has shown, uncapitalized 'holocaust' had as varied a semantic life, and as completely a secular range, before 1933 as it continued to have after 1945. Promiscuously it can signify both the Nazi persecutions in general and the threat of nuclear disaster. This breadth of reference is also exemplified, for instance, in the fact that when the United States Holocaust Memorial Museum was founded, President Carter and his Commission were pressed to ensure that the memorial was dedicated not only to the six million Jewish victims of the genocide, a strong meaning of Holocaust, but also to the five million other victims of Nazism in Germany and its occupation of many countries.

We do not propose to enter into a calculus of suffering or comparative victimization. We wish to clarify how it arises through the confusions now created by this common term, the Holocaust, that, in common parlance, often conflates several different aspects of the violence and terror of the Third Reich under Nazism. Here we wish to explore *Night and Fog* through the prism of a different term – the *concentrationary* – in order to bring into view a politico-aesthetic dimension of cinematic representation that is at once historical, relating to the period 1945–55 in Europe, and theoretical and conceptual, reflecting retrospectively on the political novelty represented by the *concentrationary* system whose implications and dangers go well beyond commemoration of a specific atrocity, its time and its places.

This book aims, therefore, to offer a series of textual readings of Resnais's film through the prism of *Concentrationary Cinema*. *Concentrationary Cinema* is not a synonym for Holocaust film. We are not concerned directly with the debates about the representation or representability of the Holocaust (understood either narrowly as the Judeocide or, more broadly, as Nazi persecutions and atrocities inflicted on many peoples and communities). In order to avoid often sterile, and potentially anti-Semitic, arguments about whether or not there has been an excessive focus on the Holocaust as Jewish suffering compared with that of other persecuted minorities, we are proposing the term *concentrationary cinema* to refer both to a historically-created and realized system of terror that took place in real locations and to a theoretical concept that emerges from this state of affairs as a new political possibility.[10] *Concentrationary cinema*, understood as a cinema of critical reflection on both these aspects of modern life, therefore, constitutes what we will call a new politics of representation.

Night and Fog has been typically placed by film scholars at the very inception of the history of *Holocaust* film, namely films that represent the specificity of the attempted destruction of European Jewry (even though it has often been claimed that the event is beyond the limits of representation).[11] Thus, for instance, in 2006, Ewout van der Knapp edited *Uncovering the Holocaust: The International Reception of Night and Fog.*[12] Van der Knapp's collection studied the reception of this film in France, Germany, Israel, the United States and Britain. This book provides subtle and textured analyses of the cultural politics of memory and forgetting in the countries both most deeply affected by the attempted genocides of Jewish and Romany peoples and engaged in the Second World War. It emerges that, in the aftermath of the war, each country had anxieties about its own role, actions – or lack of action and complicity – in the persecution and attempted destruction of European Jewry. Thus a study of uneven and locally-determined receptions of a single film such as *Night and Fog* mirrors back to each nation both the emergence and formalization of the concept of the Holocaust to designate a specific historical occurrence, and the deeply anxious and contested series of variegated rather than single histories of nationally created cultural memories for this event.

In this book, however, we ask how we would read *Night and Fog* if we do *not* approach it as a Holocaust film. No one can doubt the use that is made of *Night and Fog* for educational, cultural and political purposes in reconsidering the terrible events of attempted genocide of European Jewry (and, of course, the Romany peoples, although no mention is directly made of the Romany persecution in the film and to our knowledge no protest has been made for that failure). Yet, paradoxically, one of the key criticisms of the film has often been that it did *not* identify, specify, or directly address the central horror of racially targeted genocide and the systematic process of the attempted industrial extermination of these two peoples. For instance, in the first substantial documentary study of the making and reception of *Night and Fog,* published in 1987 (which included a dossier of reviews and responses to the film), film historian Richard Raskin reprinted a well-known essay by Robert Michael, published in 1984, dissenting from the general acclaim of *Night and Fog* and its celebrated place in the study of the Holocaust by means of film.[13] Stating that '(w)e are now approaching the thirtieth anniversary of the most powerful documentary film on the Holocaust, *Night and Fog*', Michael reviews the way in which the film has been praised for its historical accuracy and unremitting confrontation with radical evil and then observes:

> An otherwise historically and morally valid work, *Night and Fog* omits the particularity of the Jewish Holocaust and, in doing so, it emphasizes the universal at the expense of the particular ... it silently buries six million Jews in universal genocide. It sinks the specific case of the central victims in a sea of generalities, and the Jews vanish with hardly a trace.[14]

How do we make sense of this paradox? Although the film has become the foundation stone of studies of cinema and the Holocaust, and of pedagogical programmes about the Holocaust, in a very important dimension it only obliquely considers what is now understood by that term as denoting a racist and targeted genocide.[15] If the film did indeed universalize the genocide by not particularizing its racialized victims, why do we talk of *Night and Fog* as a Holocaust film? Perhaps the film was not centrally about the genocide at all? If so, are we looking at it in the wrong way? Without avoiding the question of Nazism's exterminatory racism, might there be other ways to understand the film's 'peculiarities'? Was it attempting to disclose a systemic logic within which such 'destruction' could have occurred alongside other variants of the same economic and political logic?

In its original and final edited form, *Night and Fog* is at best oblique in its acknowledgement of Jewish suffering and the attempted extermination. The designation 'Jewish' occurs once in the commentary when it speaks of Stern, the Jewish student of Amsterdam (shot 23), although there are visible identifiers of Jewish victims in the image track. In this volume the film historian Sylvie Lindeperg, who has written a major historical study of the making of the film, carefully analyses this problematic through close reading of the archives of the film's production process. She tracks the multiple influences on its final form so that we can better understand the conditions under which its particular set of representations was constructed. She shows how its starting point in a French commemoration of political deportation was eventually brought to the encounter that disclosed to the research team the fuller impact of the mass murder by the filming on its sites in Poland and the visits to Polish archives; this was, however, deflected in the editing of the final commentary (and not simply omitted in the way suggested by Michael) towards a different interpretation of its place within the *concentrationary* system that the film plotted out through its combination of visual montage and laconic commentary.

Lindeperg's reading of the archives for what she calls a micro-history is contexualized by two further chapters that also stress the film's place in the history of an understanding of the varied horrors perpetrated under the Third Reich. Film archivist for the Imperial War Museum, Kay Gladstone researches and analyses the making of a documentary film in spring to summer 1945 by the British and Americans, based on the materials filmed and photographed by the two armies in the large and small concentration camps that the Allies encountered and liberated in the spring of 1945. This footage was to be used immediately to make a propaganda film in the early summer of 1945 about what was then termed the 'Nazi atrocities' as witnessed in German concentration camps by the American and British forces. The joint Allied film was not, however, completed in 1945; the Americans rushed through their own, directed by Billy Wilder, titled *Death Mills* ('mills' being the American term for factory). The original rushes of the joint venture waited thirty years for an American broadcasting company to commission a recording of the commentary from Trevor Howard to be read over the newly-assembled footage that appeared in 1985 under the title *Memory of the Camps*. Like *Death Mills*, however, these initial film projects were never to be seen by their domestic publics. They were neither commemorative nor critically investigative in intent; their purpose was to overwhelm German viewers with the accumulation of the evidence of atrocity. They wanted to shock the German public with what had been perpetrated in their name. These films are, therefore, relentless; their imagery repetitive; their effects desolating and numbing. When Kay Gladstone screened *Memory of the Camps* for our seminar on this project, the audience was 'crushed' into silence by the unbearable structure that simply moved from one camp to another to another. Beyond the psychological assault, there was one relevant effect for this project that became clear on viewing *Memory of the Camps* as it had been compiled as a journey through Germany: namely that there were so many camps. They were everywhere across Germany, in town after town, holiday resort after holiday resort. This in itself was a crucial disclosure of the sheer extent of the *concentrationary* system.

Also returning to film footage created in 1945 and reviewed in the 1980s, French art historian Georges Didi-Huberman casts a theoretical light on the history of understanding the encounter with what was disclosed to Allied soldiers when they entered concentration camps across Europe and were asked to film what they saw. Didi-Huberman 'reads' a fragment of black and white film created by a young American GI in the First Infantry Division of the United States Army, known as the Big Red 1, when his company liberated a small concentration camp at Falkenau, in what was formerly Czechoslovakia. The soldier was Samuel Fuller who later became a major Hollywood film director. Fuller recreated his historical experience in his film about his war experience called *The Big Red One* (1980). At a time when it has become possible to commemorate with great pomp the liberation of Auschwitz, historical knowledge about concentration camps still stumbles upon a methodological problem: the problematic of articulating the legibility of history through what the recorded documents make visible but not self-evidently intelligible, whether photographs or films about this period, from July 1944 (the liberation of Majdanek by the Soviet army, filmed by Roman Karmen) to May 1945 (the liberation of Falkenau, filmed by Samuel Fuller). The theoretical framework set up by Walter Benjamin regarding historical knowledge, however, enables us to better articulate statement with narrative, 'spirit of the place' with 'spirit of the time', image with 'legend'. The film made by Samuel Fuller in Falkenau was re-contextualized by Emil Weiss in 1988 when a now elderly Fuller was both interviewed about his fragmentary film at Falkenau and taken back to the site on which he had filmed an extraordinary event when the Sergeant of his unit ordered the dressing and formal burial by civilians from the adjoining village of inmates' abandoned bodies. This double moment of original documentation and retrospective reading exemplifies how images of horror can be transmitted under certain – aesthetic and ethical – conditions of legibility so that the indignity of men can be rendered with dignity. Highlighting an age-old coalescence between *imago* and civil *dignitas*, Didi-Huberman provides a critical reading of 'a twenty-one-minute brief lesson in humanity' of quivering images that touches on the moment of encounter between the place – the concentration camp – and cinematic representation. Radically retheorizing notions of document, archive material, representation and interpretation of the image, Didi-Huberman asks the question: what did Fuller film? What does a study of this fragment reveal about the complex relations between visibility and legibility?

The Concentrationary I: History and Political Philosophy

Our aim is to reframe the reading of the showing and the writing that is the film *Night and Fog* and to explore its complex relationships through the concept of the *concentrationary*. The *concentrationary* is both a historical and a conceptual tool. Historically, it relates to a specific space and to the problems relating to both the representability of that space and the legibility of the images created as its witnessing and archiving. The scholars in this collection were commissioned to develop extended, critical and theoretically diverse readings of the political and aesthetic complexity of the film in order to enquire into its specific 'gesture of cinema' in the face of the 'image' and the construction of memory for, and from, the *concentrationary* space. Conceptually, however, the *concentrationary* also refers to a system, enacted in a historically specific time and space, but not identical with that moment alone. We will now explain the sources for the term the *concentrationary* and indicate its potential value as a heuristic device for revisiting the politics of representation.

Night and Fog, declares Sylvie Lindeperg, is a 'gesture of cinema' addressing the *concentration* camps. This terminological precision matters. For many, and perhaps for cultural memory in general, the concentration camps – *Konzentrationslager* in German – have become simply the epitome of the Holocaust. They were not only where it took place; 'concentration camps' are synonymous with it. In general conversation and talking with students on courses about the Holocaust, it is not uncommon to hear the phrase: 'the Jews were sent to concentration camps.' But this is not accurate.

Systematic industrial genocide of Jewish and Romany peoples did not take place in *Konzentrationslager*. It took place in a specialized locus named *Vernichtungslager*: the extermination camp or *Todeslager*: death camp. Under the Third Reich there were also *Arbeitslager* – sites of slave labour as well as re-education camps. All part of the same totalitarian system, these different sites need to be distinguished practically and theoretically.

Existence in any of the camps created by the Third Reich was desperate and likely to end in death as a result of starvation, overwork, torture or brutality. But some prisoners in concentration camps survived from 1933 to 1945. American CBS reporter Edward R. Murrow's famous and horrified report on Buchenwald in April 1945 included interviews with inmates who had been there for over ten years.[16] Extermination camps, on the other hand, were small, few in number (only four, in fact, with two additional mixed sites at Auschwitz-Birkenau and Majdanek) and only about 340 people survived their relentless daily production of death. They operated between December 1941 and late 1943 (with the exception of Auschwitz-Birkenau whose death factory operated until October 1944). Most people, almost all Jewish or Roma and Sinti, transported to an extermination camp did not survive the day or sometimes the hour of their arrival.

Concentrationees [*Inmates of the concentration camps*] did indeed die. Immediate death was not, however, the purpose of the concentration camp, unlike the extermination camp, where it was the sole function. The concentration camps created a physiological and psychological mode of existence where men and women were intended to suffer until they gave in to its agonizing deprivations and/or its psychological destruction or were 'polished off', having thus been drowned by it, in the terms of Primo Levi. In his late reflections written in 1986, *The Drowned and the Saved,* Primo Levi concluded that whether it was planned or merely emerged through experience, in the concentration camps there was a systematic assault whose purpose required the living to experience their own psychological disintegration and human degradation before a death that was neither any longer a natural destiny (death as the normal punctuation to a life-time) nor a welcomed relief from suffering. Something worse than death had been created.[17] This does not mean that the *concentrationary* was worse than being horrifically murdered on arrival. It does indicate that in the *concentrationary* existence, men and women were forced to experience another kind of destruction that made death a preferable outcome even while death was, however, denied to them. Dying was planned as a prolonged deferral of release from torture, while being killed permanently overshadowed and menaced every moment. Living in the permanent anxiety of its unpredictable imminence infected all obligatory living – that is *concentrationary* life – with anguishing terror that changed the very meaning of living and dying.

The populations of concentration camps were diverse, in terms of nationalities and reasons for their incarceration. It is vital, therefore to disentangle the confusion between two sites of terror: concentration camps and their expanding and multi-formed populations on German soil and the extermination camps on Polish soil, which were few, short-lived, single-purpose and genocidal. Let us, therefore, put some necessary historical information in place.

The system of concentration camps began in 1933 with the conquest of the German political system by the National Socialists that led to the suspension of the Weimar Republic's constitution and the creation of a one party state and a dictatorship. Camps were opened following the initial political victory to destroy all political opposition. Their populations had contracted by about 1935, only to grow again between 1937 and 1939 with the beginning of the persecution of German Jews following the Nuremberg Laws (1935). Between 1939 and 1941 there was a significant expansion of concentration camps. Their populations increased with the military occupations of surrounding countries and expanded progressively over the war years. After December 1941, the SS, already having taken over the concentration camp system from the SA in the later 1930s, was charged with the secret creation of hidden and dedicated sites of extermination for two peoples designated for total annihilation by the enactment of the Final Solution, minuted at the infamous conference at Wannsee, outside Berlin, on 20 January 1942.[18]

Thus, we need to grasp the fact that a vast network of concentration camps, ultimately numbering over 10,000, was built across Greater Germany, housing German political prisoners, common criminals, social undesirables, homosexuals, Jehovah's Witnesses and the deported political prisoners from countries occupied by the Germans as a result of the Second World War. The fluctuating population of these camps rose from about 4,000 in 1933, when the incoming National Socialists aimed to eradicate all domestic political opposition, to over 700,000 by January 1945. The names of major camps include Sachsenhausen, Ravensbrück (for women), Oranienburg, Struthof, Neuengamme, Dachau, Flossenburg, Gross-Rosen, Mittelbau (Dora), Buchenwald, Bergen-Belsen and Mauthausen.[19] Historian Wolfgang Sofsky calculates that 1.6 million people were admitted into the *concentrationary* system between 1933 and 1945, and that 1.2 million died in the frightful conditions of starvation, overwork and brutality that characterized its regime.[20] Some of the concentration camps were small. Others were vast, rising to the size of a small city. Many had satellite camps radiating from them. Some were linked with industrial installations, munitions factories and were essentially places of slave labour. Some, like Auschwitz I, had been built for Soviet prisoners of war and housed the persecuted intelligentsia of what had formerly been Poland.

The concentration camps that have been etched into European cultural memory, and which have, therefore, wrongly come to be confused with the actual sites of the extermination – the genocidal face of the Holocaust – are those that were photographed and filmed when the Allies invaded Germany in 1945 and found the vast network of the camp system in its final horrific condition. It was from the selective elements of this chaotic archive that Resnais would, ten years later, attempt to construct his film as a representation of *the concentrationary system*. As the Allies advanced, camps were abandoned by the SS or were no longer being resourced or even minimally maintained. Thus, their thousands of inmates were discovered by the invading British and Americans in advanced states of starvation and suffering rampant disease, having had no food or medical services provided for several weeks following often years of systematic malnutrition. These camps had huge international populations. For instance, liberators found 33,000 inmates alive in Dachau in a suburb of Munich from 34 different nations, including 1,000 Germans. Some of the German camps, such as Bergen-Belsen, Buchenwald and Dachau, included Jewish prisoners who had not generally formed part of the normal concentration camp populations in Germany, with some minor exceptions such as notables kept for potential prisoner exchanges. Jewish prisoners were present in concentration camps in 1945 as a result of the forced death marches in early 1945 from camps such as Auschwitz in Poland, evacuated as a result of the advancing Soviet forces or late transfers of slave labour to the ailing German economy.[21]

The other site of Nazi terror and deadly violence is a very small number of four dedicated camps, *Vernichtungslager* or *Todeslager*, created after 1941 for one purpose only: industrialized murder of targeted populations of Jewish and Romany peoples. These were at Chelmno (1941–43, 225,000 killed), Treblinka (1942–43, 974,000 killed), Sobibor (1942–43, 250,000 killed) and Belzec (1942–43, 600,000 killed). Most of these small camps required merely a railway spur off a main line in rural Poland, gas chambers and crematoria, and barracks for some prisoners selected to run the death machine or do other work for the SS who controlled the camp and lived outside its barbed wire enclosures. A tiny inmate population serviced a daily system of death inflicted on thousands per day. These special details (*Sonderkommando*) were regularly killed and replaced with fresh incomers. At Chelmno, the camp was merely the site for the disposal of bodies of those murdered by being gassed by carbon monoxide in mobile gas vans that travelled from the site of collection to the site of disposal. Treblinka killed its victims by the same exhaust fumes, using a tank engine attached to the gas chambers. These small sites were closed as early as 1943 and were destroyed by the Nazis, planted over with small forests, or abandoned in the hope of erasing all traces of the mass murder. All members of the final *Sonderkommando* were executed. The few witnesses were survivors of these final executions. The extermination sites were never 'liberated', and thus they were neither filmed nor photographed, nor known to the Allies from direct experience. It was to these empty, almost obliterated and hidden sites in the Polish countryside that French filmmaker Claude Lanzmann returned between 1973 and 1985, with the two or three escapees or chance survivors of the final massacres or revolts and escapes when he made his epic film, titled *Shoah* (1973–85) exclusively about the destruction of Europe's Jewish communities in these places.[22]

Some Jewish people were also the temporary inmates of the initially KZ (*Konzentrationslager*) camps of Auschwitz (near Krakow and on the Polish/ German border) and Majdanek (outside Lublin south of Warsaw). These were both hybrid camps in Poland, although Auschwitz was officially part of Greater Germany at the time. Auschwitz, nowadays the name that is almost synonymous with the Holocaust, was in fact a network of 48 camps around a Polish garrison town Oswiecim. Auschwitz I (*Stammlager*, original camp) was established as a camp for Soviet prisoners of war in February 1940. Political prisoners from Germany began arriving in May 1940 and the camp was subsequently filled with Polish prisoners as the persecution of the Polish intelligentsia and political resistance intensified. Auschwitz II was begun in October 1941 at the nearby site of a Polish village whose name translates into German as *Birkenau* to ease the pressure on the original camp, but following the Wannsee Conference on 20 January 1942 that determined a 'Final Solution to the Jewish Question', namely mass extermination, parts of Auschwitz-Birkenau were progressively transformed during the spring of 1942 into a dedicated *Vernichtungslager*: a killing centre, using Zyklon B pesticide in vast specialized gas chambers and needing multiple, multi-ovened crematoria to deal with over a million bodies of those murdered between 1942 and 1944.[23] The height of its operation was between April and July 1944, when 475,000 Hungarian Jews, half of the pre-war population, were deported to Auschwitz and murdered at a rate of 12,000 a day for a considerable part of that period. It is now believed that out of 1.1 million who died in Auschwitz, 900,000 Jewish people were murdered at Auschwitz-Birkenau. This represents almost one sixth of the total number of Jewish victims of Nazism, and it indicates the vast scale of the industrialized process of mass murder at Auschwitz-Birkenau. It also reminds us of the equally massive scale of the extermination process in other Polish death camps, and of the direct mass killings undertaken by shooting by the *Einsatzgruppen* (taskforces) attached to the invading German army during *Operation Barbarossa* begun on 22 June 1941, as it moved into the Soviet Union and special squads systematically annihilated the rural Jewish populations in the Ukraine, Lithuania, Latvia and beyond, village by village. These paramilitary death squads were responsible for over one million deaths, the largest of their killing operations taking place at Babi Yar outside Kiev, Ukraine, on 29–30 September 1941, when 33,771 people were shot in two days.

Industrial installations around Auschwitz, such as I G Farben at nearby Monowitz (to which Primo Levi was sent) required slave labour. As a result of the pressure from industrialists given the war-time labour shortage, the SS relented from their programme of total and immediate destruction of all Jewish deportees to Auschwitz-Birkenau; by July 1942 the SS had introduced selection of fit-for-work prisoners from the ramp at Auschwitz II. The last selection took place on 30 October 1944. About 60,000 prisoners were in the Auschwitz system as the Soviet Army pressed into Poland in late 1944 and most were death-marched westwards to Germany to the concentration camps.

The Red Army liberated about 7,500 prisoners in Auschwitz I, II and III on 27 January 1945.

In his periodization of the history of the KZ, the *concentration* camp, historian Nikolaus Wachsmann notes that, far from declining as defeat loomed, the population of the camps rose to their highest number by January 1945, 714,211, and that this number had been swelled by the forced death marches of surviving prisoners in the hybrid and slave-labour camps in Poland back into the German territories.[24] It is for this reason alone that some Jewish survivors were found in the concentration camps inside Germany when the Allies liberated and made infamous sites such as Dachau, Buchenwald and Bergen-Belsen. These names that resonate in cultural memory as Nazi camps were in fact the largest of the concentration camps inside Germany, not the real sites in the East of the massacre of European Jewry and Romanies.

Thus, the *concentrationary* system in Germany was vast. Camps were everywhere outside cities and towns, in the countryside, beside famous resorts and picturesque villages. Wachsmann also makes clear that while the camps as a whole formed a system of terror created and run by the SS under Himmler, they exhibit a dynamic history of changing functions and improvised processes which run counter to the confused and abstracted 'idea' of the concentration camp that circulates in post-war, media-formed public memory. So we can ask what is the relation between the 'Final Solution of the Jewish Question', code named *Operation Reinhard* (*Aktion Reinhard* or *Einsatz Reinhard*) undertaken in Poland (then named the General Government) after 1942 by the SS, and the vast network of concentration camps that had been set up slowly across Germany after 1933 whose populations continued to expand? Historians do not agree about the inevitable trajectory of Nazism towards exterminatory genocide.[25] There is considerable debate amongst them about its long-term planning or its emergence as another contingent adjustment to unforeseen events, such as the conquest of vast territories in the Soviet Union, and the problem of feeding the growing ghettoized populations 'concentrated' in the East. Although the SS had taken over the concentration camps from the SA in the late 1930s, and although the SS were also in charge of the extermination operations in the six key sites of mass murder, we must not conflate the two systems nor assume a direct relation between the two.

If historians have increasingly turned their attention recently to detailing the system and particular histories of the concentration camps between 1933 and 1945, political philosophers have analysed the meaning of the concentration camp as a '*nomos*', that is to say as a socially constructed ordering of experience which achieved an explicit realization in the actual camps of the Nazi epoch, but which exceed that historical actuality, having both precedents before 1933 (the infamous British concentration camps for the Boers during the Second Boer War of 1899–1902) and subsequent incarnations that infiltrate contemporary social experience globally. Italian philosopher Giorgio Agamben is best known for the following controversial proposition: 'The camp, which is now securely lodged within the city's interior, is the new biopolitical *nomos* of the planet.'[26] Taken seriously by political theorists and human geographers, Agamben's arguments have troubled some Holocaust scholars.[27] Many appear to be uncomfortable with Agamben's proposition because they read it as effacing the historical specificity of 'Auschwitz' (standing in for the genocidal Holocaust despite its ambiguity as a signifier) by suggesting that aspects of what occurred there might, or even do, recur in more normal conditions of contemporary society, for example, in our sporting stadia and television spectacles.

We would like to clarify this debate by distinguishing between the *historical* reality and specificity of the camps such as Auschwitz I, II or III, and Agamben's identification of a *logic of the camp* which can, and did, occur historically in one form, but which also informs and translates into other instances. The distinction between the *concentrationary* and exterminatory, furthermore, may facilitate a better understanding of Agamben's political-philosophical reading of the import of Primo Levi's writing about his experiences in the *concentrationary* dimension that he, a Jewish prisoner, selected for slave labour in Auschwitz III, witnessed in both Auschwitz II and III. Instead of a misinformed and certainly dangerous conflation of two distinct sites (an actual soccer match played between SS and Sonderkommando representatives at Auschwitz II and contemporary sporting events), Agamben is using Levi's analysis of the system to disclose a more recurrent logic of power that reveals itself as a logic of annihilation hidden within certain 'normal' social rituals and modern spaces. Of course, industrial mass murder is not taking place at the Olympics. Nor is Agamben reducing the reality of Auschwitz to a mere metaphor, a promiscuous figure for unrelated events. Neither is he generalizing nor universalizing a specific historical phenomenon, the Holocaust, which should be recognized for its unique horror.[28]

Agamben places that horror – but also the larger system of the *concentrationary* to which Levi, as an observer and participant of the camps for selected slave labour, gave his analytical witness – within a historical development of a political-legal event, namely the normalization of *the state of exception*. He traces a historically developed relationship between State (sovereign) power and the human body (its living and dying). Agamben notes that, historically, all States claim the right to a state of exception in which the normal legal protocols protecting the rights of citizens and limiting the power of the sovereign State over the body, and hence the life and death of the subject or citizen, may be suspended in confrontation with a national emergency. Under the *concentrationary* system created for real during the Third Reich, however, the typical legal boundaries that define the power of the former over the latter become blurred, or even undone, creating a novel scenario in which law ceases to exist as the law that attempts to adjudicate on facts and actions and determine the legality of political acts of State according to a jurisprudential theory of the state. Under the totalitarian regime created by Nazism, *the state of exception* became a norm, eradicating the distinction between legality (often separated in democratic systems from executive political power and functioning as a court of appeal to monitor political action) and what the regime did. Once law is suspended, what is done itself becomes the law of the place, hence the camp becomes the emblematic site of the political system that creates it as its instrument. The camp becomes a model for a society in which law and fact are blurred. What happened historically within the Nazi and indeed the Soviet camps gives rise not only to a historical event we hope remains utterly unique, but to a paradigm that we must recognize can and does recur in other configurations because of a common logic. The nature of these other sites and moments of totalitarian or absolute power can then be read through their being traced, logically, rather than historically, to these Nazi camps: the concentration camp and the extermination camp, that in Levi's case lay side by side but were not identical. Survivor and witness to the system he so brilliantly anatomized as a system, Levi also rightly declared that he was not a true witness to the core horror – the gas chamber.[29] But Agamben argues that in writing of the physical and psychological destruction of human life *qua* humanness that was the *concentration camp's* systematic function, and whose epitome is the living corpse, the so-called *Muselmann*, Levi's writing bears witness to a political-legal event that has repercussions in other modern spaces in which an everyday normalcy co-exists with deadly violence and violation of the human which is not confined behind barbed wire. Hence, Agamben writes that 'the essence of the camp consists in the materialization of the state of exception and in the subsequent creation of a space in which bare life and the juridical rule enter into a threshold of indistinction.' Where this becomes the case, 'we find ourselves virtually in the presence of a camp every time such a structure is created, independent of the kinds of crime that are committed there and whatever its denomination and specific topography.'[30]

Agamben's reflections on the profound significance of the camp for understanding both a specific historical event and a more general logic in contemporary society can best be grasped as politically and historically necessitated extensions of Michel Foucault's earlier theses about the novel logic of modern power as disciplinary, and modern States as those which extend, via disciplinary measures, power over the bio-political sphere of people's lives. In his analysis of distinctive modern forms of power, Foucault had identified key spaces through which to track the intricate relations between modern disciplinary power and its prime object, the body, which typify Modernity: the hospital, the asylum, the school, the family and the prison. The camp is not merely a new form of prison, a carceral space that sets apart the criminal from the citizen after due process of law. Agamben's reading of Primo Levi's writings on his experience in and, more importantly, his analytical observations of Auschwitz II and III enabled him to identify a novel space of bio-political power relations through which historical events associated with the Third Reich become emblematic of a widespread political condition, never as heinous, but still necessitating our knowing vigilance and political resistance. This space and its *nomos* Agamben calls 'the camp'. Radical dehumanization extending to industrialized extermination of human life were features of the historically realized camps of the Third Reich. Rather than focus on the specificity of the extreme crime that is industrial extermination of selected human groups in specialist sites, Agamben alerts us to the *logic* that, having made that crime possible within a system of the camp (even if the specification of the racialized targets for extermination derived from a different logic within Modernity and specifically Nazism), exceeds that specificity and indicates that we may now live in a world in which what was once an exceptional 'state of exception' could, by the erosion of law that protects democratic polity, be enacted on many scales as a 'normal' procedure of contemporary societies, and to which we have become inured or inattentive.[31] The exception becomes a normal fact of management of certain kinds of populations, from economic migrants to untried political opponents. Looking away, failing to notice, tolerating what should be resisted, create conditions of complicity with logics that have within them both a dreadful historical past and a contemporary capacity to poison the world with 'campness', which is at once an actual zone or space within the polity and a mental structure disabling the kinds of political anxiety and resistance that should revolt against any instance of the camp logic utilized by contemporary social or political authorities.

This intersection of historical precision and politically structural argument about the spaces of modern power and its object, the human body, defines the first dimension of the *concentrationary* with which we are working. It opens up analyses of Resnais's film to new readings. Taking up the question of not looking away but attending to what it might be that Resnais's film presented to be seen, encountered, and even felt, as an ethical or a political response to the *concentrationary*, two chapters differently address Resnais's *aesthetic* strategies for effecting an encounter via film with this *concentrationary* that has ethical or political effects.

Film and literary scholar Emma Wilson has long studied Resnais's cinema in general and has identified some of its recurrent concerns with materiality rather than vision. Wilson argues that *Night and Fog* first gives form to a concern, felt through the decades of Resnais's feature filmmaking, with the possibility of (physical) contact with the dead. This concern can be read as an ethical gesture of refusal to forget or to deny. Wilson suggests that for Resnais, the attempt to find a mode of response to the camps encompasses a move to conjure the dead as animate, physical and tangible. This is effected through the use, on the one hand, of still photographs and moving images, and, on the other, through attention to material objects, clothing, personal effects and even physical remains. The film depends on attention to effigies of the dead, their imprint on film, to the material items with which they have come into contact, and, most excessively, to the items into which their remains have been transformed. Touch, tactility, the desire to hold the dead still animate, give way, in the underworld of the film, to abject, obscene contact with inanimate and disintegrating matter. As Resnais pushes his film towards tactility, investigating film as medium of sensation and contamination, Wilson suggests that he draws his viewer to question any possibility of sure purchase or contact. Yet the aesthetics of such cinematic 'contact' bring the viewer to an ethical as well as political attentiveness to the threshold between human life and human death and an inhuman domain that produced death as it produced things from personal remains.

Libby Saxton, author of a major study of French film and ethics in relation to the Holocaust, raises the issue of attention through considering the act of witnessing. She suggests that one of the recurrent motifs in the archive photographs and footage used in *Night and Fog* is that of the observer, bystander or witness. Like the censored French *gendarme* at Pithiviers, these figures often lurk at the edges of the frame, yet their presence marks them as actors in, rather than simply spectators at, the events depicted. Simultaneously inscribed in the images are the looks of another set of actors, those of the Nazis, Allies and, in certain cases, deportees operating the cameras, alongside Resnais's own. In representing onlooking as an inherently political act, whether of collaboration or resistance, Saxton argues that the film implicitly questions the possibility of neutral bystanding in the face of the *concentrationary* and positions its viewers as both responsible and complicit. Saxton argues that *Night and Fog* was one of the first films to ask what it means to 'regard the pain of others' (in Sontag's phrase) and to view such spectatorship in political and ethical terms, issues which gain urgency as our culture becomes increasingly mired in unprocessed images of abjection. While the film has been canonized as a monumental injunction, its dialectical, rather than didactic, form implicates viewers differently at different historical moments (Algeria, Carpentras, the Balkans, Rwanda, Iraq). While it has been instrumentalized as an ethical touchstone, a model of virtuous filmmaking instructing in virtuous viewing, its elisions and blind spots hint at a strategic prioritization of political agency over ethical reflection. Resnais's film poses, according to Saxton, prescient questions about the relationship between a politics and an ethics of spectatorship: to what extent does politically engaged viewing lead to an evasion of ethical responsibility? Conversely, to what extent does a properly ethical response entail a retreat from politics in the face of atrocity perpetrated as a political tactic?

The Concentrationary II: Aesthetics and Politics

Having outlined the political and philosophical basis of the *concentrationary* system and its emergence as a new possibility of shaping the human, we need to define the politico-aesthetic roots of the term *concentrationary* that informs our notion of *concentrationary cinema*. In terms of a conjunction of aesthetics and politics the phrase *concentrationary* derives from articles first composed and printed in Paris in 1945 but published as a book in 1946 by David Rousset (1912–97) under the title *L'Univers concentrationnaire*, 'the *concentrationary* universe' variously translated as 'The Other Kingdom' referencing Albert Jarry's Dadaist play or 'A World Apart' – thus losing the visibility and acoustic force of *concentrationnaire*.[32] David Rousset was a French political prisoner held in the German concentration camp of Buchenwald, outside Weimar. A Trotskyist at the time of his imprisonment, in his post-war writing Rousset aimed to produce a political anatomy – literally a disclosure of the hidden structure – of the novel political space of systematic terror that Agamben, following Foucauldian analysis of the novel spaces of Modernity, would later elaborate as the camp. Rousset named this space and its system *the concentrationary universe*, arguing that the place was itself symptomatic of an extended political logic not confined within it. Rousset's notion of a *concentrationary universe* invokes a political system of terror whose aim was to demolish the social humanity of all its actual and potential victims within and beyond the actual sites. Enclosed within the camp, the concentrationees experience its brute violence and pain directly in their bodies. They directly witness the terrifying novelty where 'everything is possible'. As the laboratory of limitless possibility the camp functions, paradoxically, as the heart of the totalitarian society that creates it at once as a 'world apart', utterly other to the everyday world beyond its barbed wire enclosures and as an emblem of total domination infecting and destroying all political life in the apparently 'normal' world around it. From experience inside the camp, Rousset argues that the camp is symptom of the *concentrationary* as an infection of the entire social fabric.

For Rousset, the *concentrationary* is not, therefore, a moment of extreme atrocity that occurred only in one place and at one time to be revealed by the liberators and thus cleaned up and cleared away. The concentration camp system marks the inception and initiating actualization of a new political possibility in modern political life of a form of terror that, as a result of this realized experiment under the Third Reich, will always be with us now that it has been unleashed on the world. While the fully realized actualization of such terror had been unprecedented in this form until the 1930s, now that it has happened, become real, made into fact, it is a precedent and hence a constant menace. Not reducible to a term that signifies an event, such as the Holocaust, the *concentrationary* is the inception of a modern 'anti-political', anti-democratic political possibility that must be opposed by understanding its realized configurations, not only in Nazi Germany but also in Stalin's Soviet Union. Rousset used his own experience in Buchenwald to alert the French public to the gulag system in the Stalinist Soviet Union:

> The existence of the camps is a warning. German society, both because of the strength of its structure and the violence of the crisis that demolished it, underwent a decomposition that is exceptional even in the present state of affairs. But it would be easy to show that the most characteristic traits of both the SS mentality and the social conditions which gave rise to the Third Reich are to be found in many sectors of world society – less pronounced, it is true, and not developed in any such scale as in the Reich. But it is only a question of circumstances. It would be blindness – and criminal blindness, at that – to believe that, by reason of any difference of national temperament, it would be impossible for any other country to try a similar experiment. Germany interpreted with an originality in keeping with her history, the crisis that led her to the *concentrationary* universe. But the existence and the mechanism of that crisis were inherent in the economic and social foundations of capitalism and imperialism. Under a new guise, similar effects may reappear tomorrow. There remains therefore a very specific war to be waged.[33]

In Rousset's *writing*, however, we can note that his analysis of the political innovation – totalitarianism – is created by constructing an *aesthetic* counter-representation of the camps. The text is not a dry political treatise. His book is not, however, anaestheticizing representation. Rather, it becomes clear that aesthetic effects of figurative language and stylistic devices are needed to convey as horrifyingly real what was hitherto only imagined. As literature rather than simple political documentation, Rousset sought to create a warning to contemporary cultures, by means of an affective and poetic representation, of the ever-present danger of what is no longer unprecedented because what was brought about in the camps themselves is the very sign of the novel forms of totalitarian societies that now exist. Although Nazism shattered the existing limits to, and hence terms of, representation of violence and dehumanization, as a result, we have to acknowledge that such violence is now no longer unprecedented. The reality of what the Nazis enacted has created a model. It has left a memory. It could become a resource. It has become part of history and its representations are part of culture; equally as important, its real sites continue even if in different forms.

The *concentrationary* is, therefore, also part of the politics of representation – of thought, memory and imagination. Given the importance of Rousset's post-war writing to an elaboration of this politico-aesthetic idea of the *concentrationary*, in contradistinction to the more familiar contemporary Holocaust paradigm, let us look more closely at Rousset's text as both the initial analysis of the *concentrationary universe* and itself an aesthetic operation of (anti)*concentrationary* art.

In France a particular way of perceiving the concentration camps had emerged in the immediate aftermath of liberation, as many of the returnees were not 'Holocaust survivors' – that is, racialized survivors of the exterminatory programme of the Final Solution with which some parts of French society had sympathized, if not collaborated – but political deportees (including Rousset himself). Of the 115,000 political deportees from Occupied France, about 35 per cent returned. Hence there was a considerable constituency to bear witness to the *concentrationary*. Of the 390,000 French Jewish citizens, about 80,000 were deported and killed in the extermination camps; only four per cent returned. Of the 7,500 Jewish men and women rounded up during the notorious Vel' D'Hiv' *rafle* on 16 July 1942, 811 alone survived.[34] Under the Occupation, the resistance movement led to many thousands of political prisoners being transported to the concentration camps of Germany rather than the extermination camps in Poland specializing in killing Jewish Europeans to the East. Many deportees died in camps from the harshness of the regime; but also some (one third) came back and several wrote influential texts about the world they had endured, but also what they had observed as the system or logic of these other worlds.

The political deportees of occupied nations were sent to the *concentrationary* universe under a particular decree, conceived by Hitler and formalized by Field Marshal Keitel, dating from 7 December 1941 (which was, coincidently, also the date of the first mass gassing of Polish-Jewish people in Chelmno, Poland). The purpose of the decree was not to kill but to 'disappear' the deported. They were to be cut off completely from any contact with the outside world, ensuring that their relatives and friends could find no trace of them. Handed over to the SS, they would effectively 'cease to exist' as civil or juridical subjects while living on in that knowledge of effaced existence through the regime of *Vernichtung durch Arbeit* (annihilation through work: slave labour). The decree that brought about this regime was the *Nacht und Nebel Erlass*, translating as *nuit et brouillard* (night and fog), and marked on its prisoners by the letters N N painted on their jackets.[35] Some of those who survived this regime returned and produced (almost immediately) a compelling literature that was, it must be emphasized, written by intellectuals accustomed to writing political analysis, literary prose or poetry. These authors gave highly crafted and morally reflective testimony to their experience of *l'univers concentrationnaire*. Survivor of Mauthausen-Gusen *Nacht und Nebel Häftling*, Jean Cayrol (1911–2005) published a book of poems under the title *Poèmes de la Nuit et du Brouillard* also in 1946, while the resistance fighter Robert Antelme (1917–90), sent first to Buchenwald and then to a slave labour camp at Gandersheim before being discovered at the liberation on the verge of death from typhus and starvation in Dachau outside Munich, wrote *L'Espèce humaine*, which was published in 1947 by Gallimard.[36]

Thus, although the Jewish population of France suffered imprisonment and then deportation through French camps such as Gurs, Pithiviers, or Drancy, and then destruction in Auschwitz-Birkenau, or lived in hiding or escaped through Marseilles and crossing the Pyrenees, the public memory of the war in France was largely written as a memory of Resistance to the occupying German forces.[37] The experiences of the deported political prisoners substantiated this comforting narrative. The literature ranged from a study of the resilience of human solidarity even *in extremis*, offered by the defiantly optimistic Antelme, to Rousset's Trotskyist analysis of the *concentrationary* universe as a perverted (anti)political system, whose effects were not confined to those who suffered incarceration, but remained as a permanent threat to humanity.

Like Hannah Arendt after him, Rousset linked the *concentrationary*, therefore, with the larger political logics of capitalism and imperialism. But he also wanted to stress the novelty of its actual forms. In introducing his readers to this *concentrationary* universe, however, Rousset had to create a montage from the existing cultural repertoire of metaphors for 'other' worlds, both ancient and modern. For instance, if we look at his chapter headings which function as cryptic, poetic markers for the *concentrationary* universe, we find a strange mixture of imagery falling between surreal parody and Dadaist sarcasm:

Les portes s'ouvrent et se ferment: The Portals Open and Close
Although *porte* in French means both door and gateway, in English a portal is both an architectural term for an entryway and one used in science fiction as a magical or technological doorway to other worlds. The literary connotation of portal is with the entrance to Hell.

First-Born of Death
This evokes the tenth Biblical plague from the Book of Exodus.

And God Said Let There be Night and Day
The reference here is to the creation story in the Book of Genesis.

In My Father's House are Many Mansions
This is a citation from the Christian Gospels: John 14:2.

What Shall it Profit a Man if he Gain the Whole World
This is also from the Christian Gospels: Mark 8:36.

Man does not live by Politics Alone
A variation on the more famous phrase about that man cannot live by bread alone: Deuteronomy 8:3.

The Dead Stars Pursue their Courses
A corruption of an ancient text, Aesculapius III 24–25 *Hermetica* translated by Walter Scott and quoted in John Anthony West, *The Traveller's Key to Ancient Egypt*, p. 439.

The Realm of King Ubu
A reference to Alfred Jarry's play *Ubu Roi* (1896), a precursor of the Surrealist movement and the theatre of the absurd. Jarry's play *Ubu Enchaîné* also provides Rousset with his opening epigraph that concludes 'You will see very far into hunger, cold and emptiness. It is time for our nap. The jailer will show you out.'

Faced with the task of rendering the extreme experience more accessible, therefore, Rousset depicts the *concentrationary* universe through mixing Biblical metaphors with avant-garde French absurdist literature. Rousset thus frames the 'otherworldliness' of the *concentrationary* universe in culturally-coded visions of heaven and hell and uses the legacies of the trauma of the imperialist Great War of 1914–18, as well as the proto-Surrealist Dada theatre, that was itself a cultural response to the civilization that produced that industrial slaughter. How do we make sense of this dependency on literary images? It might well be critiqued were we to be considering what Rousset described in terms of a Holocaust narrative, as the horrifying novelty of the experience would preclude both metaphorization and comparison. Many writers on the Holocaust, however, do not place it beyond all representation, but rather, in Saul Friedlander's words, at its very limits, because the limits of historical precedent had been breached by industrialized, racialized mass murder.[38] Yet, we are suggesting, the *concentrationary* falls under a different rubric from the debate on the Final Solution and thus it is possible to search for precedents without in any way compromising the uniqueness of the Holocaust. On the other hand, in a move that was focussed on the chronotope of Auschwitz that often blurs the distinctions between mass killing and systematic brutality, Theodor Adorno, in his essay on 'Commitment' (1962), returned to his 1949 statement about the barbarism of poetry or art 'after Auschwitz'. Adorno not only pointed to the exemplary work of Samuel Beckett as a decent and just response to that which comes 'after', but paradoxically to Franz Kafka, whose vision precedes the bureaucratic administration of a new kind of species killing.[39] Adorno demonstrates, in effect, how Kafka's texts are imaginatively coincident with what became real in the *concentrationary* system. Thus the Surrealist poet Jean Cayrol, who wrote the spoken text to accompany *Night and Fog* (and to whom we shall turn shortly), also called upon Kafka to convey his first impression of the *concentrationary* universe: 'As I arrived, I exclaimed immediately "It is Kafka! It is *The Penal Colony!*" I entered Mauthausen with Kafka under my arm, so to speak.'[40]

A possible explanation for the potency of the anachronism lies in the prescience with which a pre-war Kafka fashioned a literature disclosing in imaginative and fictional form some of the decisive features of Modernity itself. In his major sociological intervention *Modernity and the Holocaust*, Zygmunt Bauman later came to identify the same features as the conditions within Modernity that could make possible racist, bureaucratically administered and systematic genocide.[41] In arguing this, there is, however, a risk of confusion. We have again invoked the Holocaust even while we are aiming to shed light on the *concentrationary*, not as a totally independent or separate dimension, but as a specific site within the network of terror and violence unleashed by Nazism after 1933. For our purposes here, however, the coincidence between the horrific reality of the actualized *concentrationary* universe – the Mauthausens and Buchenwalds rather than Auschwitz-Birkenau – and the specifically modernist literary projections of Jarry or Kafka created decades before 1933, suggest that the *concentrationary* universe's extremity, and its extension into death factories, should not mask the fact that both depended on possibilities present not only in sociological Modernity (identified by Bauman following Weber as instrumental reason, bureaucracy and fear of ambivalence), but, as Rousset and later Arendt will stress, in capitalism and notably racist imperialism, where there were undoubtedly precedents inflicted on non-Europeans for what was later done in Greater Germany to Europeans.[42] Thus, the invocations by Rousset and Cayrol of absurdist or Kafkaesque modernism recognize in the *concentrationary* universe a political reality that was at first only allusively identified in imaginative disclosures, but for which these anticipatory metaphors and scenarios, like *The Penal Colony*, acquired the power of prescience that finally matched the experience concentrationees now carried 'in their muscles'.

> Normal men do not know that everything is possible. Even if the evidence forces their intelligence to admit it, their muscles do not believe it. The concentrationees [*concentrationnaires*] do know.'[43]

If Rousset drew on metaphors from the past to convey the horrific otherness of the world from which he only partly returned, he equally wanted to insist that it had not disappeared: 'The *concentrationary* universe shrivels away within itself. It still lives on in the world like a dead planet ladened with corpses.'[44] What remains incomprehensible to those who never entered the actual camps but which is known by the survivors: *in the muscles* is not the immediacy of being murdered, but living with the absolute knowledge of a new kind of dying being 'carved' into the muscles on a daily basis. This radical possibility is the alteration of the course of human life and death:

> Death lived among the concentrationees at every hour of their existence. She showed them all her faces. They came to know all her exigencies. They lived dread (*inquiétude*) as an ever-present obsession.[45]

Not confining the *concentrationary* universe to the encampment itself, Rousset then also names it a *disease* that infiltrates the entire social fabric in which it occurs: 'The decomposition of a society … in a fetid stench of destroyed social values … a gangrene of a whole economic and social system. Its contamination spreads far beyond the ruins of cities.'[46]

Rousset's final chapters, however, belie the dark vision of a pestilent and death-bearing hell that now infests the planet: 'On the positive side, it is still too soon to reckon on the value of our experiences as concentrationees, but already it promises to be a rich one.'[47] What is the value? 'Dynamic awareness of the strength and beauty of the sheer fact of living, in itself, brutal, entirely stripped of all superstructures.'[48] Faced with relentless hunger, dread and pain, Rousset places the concentrationee beyond all existing social and economic structures. Yet Rousset's Trotskyist idealism, punctured by the *concentrationary* reality, discovers an unexpected humour which reminds him of the absurdist visions of Alfred Jarry and Franz Kafka whose surreal images, created before the *concentrationary* universe came into being, now 'cease to be literary fantasies and become component elements of a living world'.[49] Through the discovery of humour as an objective pattern of the universe, Rousset reclaims his politics: the German experiment is not exceptional; other countries share the components of the crisis that led to the *concentrationary* universe; it may re-appear under a new guise; thus all anti-fascists must unite internationally against an enemy within.[50]

In the epigraph to her first essay 'The Concentration Camps', published in the American leftist cultural periodical *Partisan Review* in 1948, Hannah Arendt cites David Rousset to assert the political significance of the camps: 'The SS made the concentration camp the most totalitarian society in existence up to now.'[51] Both central instrument and exemplary encapsulation of a terrifyingly total exercise of power – not merely over a political system but over the life and death of all it touched – the camps needed not only to be revealed for the dreadful legacy of suffering and atrocity exposed to view when they were found abandoned by the retreating Germans, but also to be studied for the meaning of this novel system, however perverse or insane it appeared. Hence, Arendt follows Rousset in suggesting that it was necessary both to expose what had happened in the camps and to evaluate that knowledge in terms of analysis of now 'current' political possibilities. The camps introduced into the modern world a face of Modernity that politically demands the constant work of resistance to the totalitarianism the camps both enacted and emblematized but did not confine to their singular historical moment. Recognition of the existence of the camp therefore also demands the concomitant work of active reconstruction of the democratic and post-camp humanist project 'after Auschwitz', that is, after the radical deconstruction of democracy's deepest principles and European humanity's Enlightenment aspirations.

In the same essay Arendt recognized the difficulty the *concentrationary* writers faced in communicating their visceral experiences to the world to which they returned which necessitated a certain management of the reality they had endured. Hence she declares:

> There are numerous such reports by survivors; only a few have been published, partly because, quite understandably, the world wants to hear no more of such things, but also because they all leave the reader cold, that is, as apathetic and baffled as the writer himself, and fail to inspire those passions of outrage and sympathy through which men have always been mobilized for justice, for 'misery that goes too deep arouses not compassion but repugnance and hatred' (Rousset).[52]

Thus to move the world for social justice, it is not sufficient to bear tales of atrocity alone. Arendt observes that Rousset and a German Communist prisoner from Buchenwald, Eugen Kogon (who wrote *Der SS Staat*, in 1950 which was translated as *The Theory and Practice of Hell: The German Concentration Camps and the System Behind Them*), write 'assimilated recollections' for 'the world of the living'. They try to communicate not only an understanding of the camps but also an examination of 'the totalitarian regime as a whole'.[53] Yet Arendt impatiently dismissed Rousset's desire to find 'consolation of an "extreme experience" in a kind of suffering which, strictly speaking, no longer permits of experience, and thus arrives at a meaningless affirmation of life that is extremely dangerous because it romanticizes and transfigures what must never under any circumstances be repeated on this earth'.[54] In a difficult move, therefore, Arendt appears to be arguing that an exclusive commemorative focus on the suffering inflicted in the camps – ultimately too difficult adequately to convey justly – would distract the political theorist from understanding the full import, for the future, of the political novelty, and hence the continuing menace, represented by the camps *qua* products of a now realized totalitarian system beyond law. Arendt came to recognize the extreme danger in clothing Nazism's horrors in past metaphors that might adorn it as demonic or infernal. Too grandiose would be as dangerous as too atrocious. So how could any form of cultural response, written, theorized, filmed or imaged, mobilize resistance to this assault on the human condition?

For Arendt, then, the importance of the analyses offered by political prisoners such as Rousset or Kogon, combined with the evidence assembled for the Nuremberg trials of the Nazi regime and its perpetrators she studied so astutely, was to enable us to understand what had been tried out in the political laboratory for a new imperial world order in the camps of the Third Reich.[55] Not a Marxist like Rousset and Kogon who explicitly linked the *concentrationary* with capitalism, Arendt, none the less, also argued that what this laboratory tested out was nothing less than the destruction of the human being *qua* human individual:

> The supreme goal of all totalitarian governments is not only the freely admitted long-range ambition to global rule but also the never-admitted and immediately realized attempt at the total domination of man. The concentration camps are the laboratories in the experiment of total domination, for human nature being what it is, this goal can be achieved only under the extreme circumstances of a human-made hell. Total domination is achieved when the human person, who somehow is always a specific mixture of spontaneity and being conditioned, has been transformed into a completely conditioned being whose reactions can be calculated even when he is being led to certain death.[56]

Having been experimentally destroyed in this *concentrationary* system, what is *human* in a human being emerges into theoretical clarity for Arendt. The horror of the *concentrationary* system was to find a means to detach organic life from human life in the person by means of three levels of destruction: of the individuality, the plurality and the spontaneity that, she concluded, fundamentally defines the human being. The camp system firstly erased all traces of the juridical person – identity, civil rights and access to the world. Secondly, it assaulted and aimed to destroy the moral person, creating a situation that removed all meaning from resistance, including martyrdom (that is, making dying have any social or individual meaning). Thirdly, the regime aimed at destroying spontaneity and individuality by 'the permanence and institutionalizing of torture' so that the human being was so reduced that s/he was forced to respond, in a conditioned manner, to basic organic functioning, thus further reducing both choice and personality.[57] Driven by agonizing thirst and hunger, life was only the struggle for any kind of existence, which rendered normal forms of sociality, connection, affection and solidarity positively dangerous and irrelevant. Of course, we have testimonies of concentrationees to the necessity for such connections and human solidarity as the condition of any survival at all. Primo Levi reports precisely on his shock on arrival at Auschwitz of the complete absence of solidarity between inmates and incomers.

From her study of what happened in the *concentrationary* universe, Arendt redefines what constitutes 'the human condition' but not in the form of some generalizing universality. She defines what each person must uniquely enjoy as spontaneous action and what each person must actively practise as the thoughtfulness of our fundamental plurality as human beings. Plurality arises from natality. Natality is Arendt's term for the creative significance of the event of every human birth, which initiates the utterly novel beginning of an unpredictable singularity: 'the new beginning inherent in birth can make itself felt in the world only because the newcomer possesses the capacity of beginning something anew, that is, of acting.'[58] The *concentrationary* systematically assaulted and in practice erased plurality, singularity, spontaneity and the capacity for action. From her study of the totalitarian eclipse of human history, therefore, Arendt created her larger political theory about 'The Human Condition', which is, therefore, a text we could propose as an example of (anti-)*concentrationary* art and thought.[59]

As a result of the Nazi experiment, it was now clear to Arendt that, for the very first time in history, the very concept of the human could not be taken for granted; it has to be specified and defended in this new confrontation with a political experiment in which the human condition could be, and was experimentally and for real, systemically eradicated, not only through swift and horrific extermination of specific racially othered populations, but precisely through the prolonged torment of the *concentrationary* existence that functioned to experimentally erode the civil identity, the emotional and intersubjective meaning and finally the possibility of anything beyond instinctual, organic bare life which the human individual had to endure and witness in those others around him or her already succumbing to this living death that was the sustained torture of the *concentrationary* universe.

The emaciated, starved and brutalized concentrationee so often imaged by Allied liberator footage and photography, and burned into public consciousness and cultural memory by repetition, becomes a terrifying figure of a living being who is, and yet is no longer fully, human. S/he is reduced to the body's dehumanized struggle for existence. Starvation has eroded brain functions, eyesight and hearing and worse; the starving organism consumes its own organs to maintain life to the bitter end. This is the systematic erosion of human life by reducing people to just-still-living corpses that would be epitomized by the infamous *Muselmänner*, as they were named in Auschwitz slang, encountered by the liberators and taken up in Primo Levi's writings (and later in Agamben's study, *The Remnants of Auschwitz*).[60]

Although Arendt would depart from what she saw as Rousset's sentimentality, between her desire to analyse what happened so that it can never happen again and Rousset's contradictory blend of romanticism and clear-sighted recognition of a new *concentrationary* plague, there was, nevertheless, a conclusion that both shared. The specific novelty that will be the core of Arendt's thesis about concentrationary totalitarianism is Rousset's insight (previously quoted) that hereinafter 'everything is possible'. This is the menacing potentiality, the unimaginable and the exceptional made normal having crossed the threshold into actualization.[61] The purpose of trying to know the *concentrationary* is thus monitory rather than memorial. Agamben himself comments on this when he writes:

> Hannah Arendt once observed that in the camps, the principle that supports totalitarian rule and that common sense obstinately refuses to admit comes fully to light: this is the principle according to which 'everything is possible.' Only because the camps constitute a state of exception – in which not only is law completely suspended but fact and law are completely confused – is everything in the camps truly possible.[62]

The analyses of Rousset and Arendt are fundamental in shaping the post-war idea of the *concentrationary* as this new potential for the destruction of the human, and the monitory warning to guard against its reappearance. This – the *concentrationary* – is, therefore, the context within which we would like to situate *Night and Fog*.

To this political-theoretical vision of the *concentrationary*, however, we must add another perspective derived from the poetic and aesthetic writings of a French camp survivor who was not a political theorist but the Surrealist poet and resistance fighter, Jean Cayrol, whom we quoted above. In a number of essays written after the war, Cayrol elaborated the idea of a *concentrationary art*: this refers to an aesthetic and poetic form of resistance to that which had come into existence as the *concentrationary* universe and from which he had 'returned from the dead', like a modern Lazarus, having died in some dimension without being actually killed. Cayrol's concept of a *concentrationary art* is not an art about the camps; it involves recognition of this new state of affairs (which contains both historical specification and general theoretical import) that then demands a response to what has been created by the *'concentrationary* universe'. This aesthetic response is a political resistance to that universe through aesthetic affectivity and poetic formulation. Why aesthetic? Why not purely intellectual, rational, factual, political or philosophical? *Concentrationary* art both embodies affecting commemoration of the suffering and the dead and incites active resistance in the viewing or reading subject to the novel persistence of the *concentrationary* universe. This is now slumbering in the aftermath of the war but has the potential to be re-activated at any moment and anywhere, including within nations such as France. The legacy of the *concentrationary* universe is a political disease that can infect a whole society, allowing violation of human life and rights that are not seen as such, but are accepted under conditions of 'emergency', politically permitted states of exception. *Concentrationary* art is the art made by the returnees from this universe of death, who have in some ways already died as human beings, having lived with death daily, but must arise from this 'death' of their humanity to be constantly alert, creating what Cayrol named a *dispositif d'alerte*: a warning system, addressed to the present.[63] Cayrol thus uses Lazarus (in the Christian Gospels, Lazarus is the brother of Mary and Martha whom Jesus raised from the dead) as the emblematic figure of *concentrationary* art. The Lazarean hero is the returnee who has experienced in his or her body and mind that other planet in which political terror became a system, and must now warn us of the reality that 'everything is possible'.

We suggest that this specific French politico-aesthetic context around the formulation of the *concentrationary* for the making of *Night and Fog* has been obscured by a different history of the emergence of the cultural memory of the event, one which was itself initially obscured by the focus on deportation, namely the exterminatory dimension of Nazism, now named the Holocaust. This version of cultural memory has, over time, screened out the specific conjugation of politics and aesthetics in the period between 1945 and 1955. The year 1955 – the year of the making of the film to mark the tenth anniversary of the end of the war – should be seen in its contemporary context: it was the occasion for both public commemoration and an 'unconscious return of the repressed'.

It has been suggested that the belated emergence of a memory of a catastrophic event might be understood through the metaphor borrowed from medicine and psychology: trauma. On the level of the individual, trauma is an extreme event that overwhelms the psyche, which cannot assimilate what has happened according to the imagination's available fantasies or the intellect's known concepts. Thus, the event, that has really impacted the person affectively, becomes a latent, unformulated 'thing', a presence haunting the psyche it occupies without being known or remembered. Secondary incidents that share something with the original trauma can, however, trigger the unbound affective freight associated with it, endowing the new occasion with the latter's frightful charge while also enabling the secondary event to discharge some of the originary terror that returns to supercharge this secondary staging. Can the psychological concept of trauma be translated into cultural terms? There is no such thing as collective trauma because there is no collective psychic mechanism. But we can point to the magnification of individually experienced trauma that can lead to collectively shared experience. But we can also use the model of trauma to understand a cultural phenomenon of initially willed amnesia or resistance to the integration of a difficult or excessive historical event into cultural memory not for psycho-mechanical reasons, but for the cultural lack of representational resources adequate to the novelty that then functions as if traumatic: a ghostly disturbance without full registration according to available terms or tropes. Without positing a trans-individual psyche or collective unconscious, we can observe that the overwhelming and extreme historical event – traumatic because it happens but culture has no adequate representational precedents through which to know it – emerges, like psychic trauma, into cultural elaboration *belatedly*. Events such as anniversaries, or other politically traumatic events that themselves cannot yet be confronted but which share something with the originary traumatic event are often the trigger for delayed re-engagement with unprocessed pasts.[64] This is not to say that a detention camp or political torture is identical with Auschwitz, but similarities inject into the lesser or later evil the freight of anxiety because of possible, even tenuous, connection and because of a sense generated by political discourse of potential affinities.

Thus some of the authors in this collection move beyond close analysis of the specific dynamics of the film as text and situate Resnais and Cayrol's project as one that evokes the pressing questions of other politics in its own moment of production. The possibility for considering the film's work in relation to other instances of atrocity, troubled memory, or failed remembrance is explored through comparative studies.

In her chapter entitled 'Auschwitz as Allegory in *Night and Fog*', Debarati Sanyal reminds us that *Night and Fog* closes with a disquieting admonition: the narrative voice declares that we who have watched these images of atrocity fail to see the ongoing reality of *concentrationary* terror as it unfolds in different times and places, just as we fail to hear the endless cry of human suffering. The film's final gesture breaches the limits of historical documentary and opens up an allegorical reading of its testimony. In so doing, it also positions the spectator as a deaf and blind witness – if not accomplice – to contemporary iterations of the post-Nazi terror. The intersection of allegory and complicity upon which the film closes, indeed through which it *refuses* closure, might well explain the enduring force of its critique across historical horizons and geopolitical sites. Sanyal's essay hence probes *Night and Fog*'s role in constructing an allegorical topography of the *concentrationary* experience. More specifically, it proposes that the dialectical force of allegory, along with the film's visual and verbal positioning of the audience as a potentially complicitous witness, open *Night and Fog* out to alternative historical projects, specifically in a colonial and postcolonial context. As examples of such projects, Sanyal puts *Night and Fog* into dialogue with subsequent allegorizations of the *concentrationary* experience. At the same time, she takes up the troubling ethical questions that such allegories raise even as they mobilize political action at various historical junctures.

Joshua Hirsch also tracks the *concentrationary* potential across different moments of racialized violence. Hirsch's concept of 'posttraumatic cinema' (of which *Night and Fog* is an initiation), elaborated in his major study *After-Image: Film, Trauma and the Holocaust*, allows for just such an extrapolation from the *concentrationary* aesthetic of *Night and Fog*. Hirsch revisits some of the major arguments for this concept while setting its work in a relation with the film *Sankofa* (Haile Gerima, 1993) in which an African-American model, shooting a fashion spread in a former slave fortress in Ghana, 'falls' through time back to the historical moment of enslavement in an allegorical study of repressed memory and historical witnessing.

Max Silverman proposes that the concept of memory that we can derive from the film necessitates a reading that links one time and place with another. He argues that *Night and Fog* exemplifies Arendt's notion of 'fearful imagination' proposed in her essay 'The Concentration Camps' – that is, a way of seeing the absolute novelty of totalitarian rule unleashed on the world – through its invention of what Silverman names '*concentrationary* memory'. This is a concept of memory as the haunting (and hence a disturbance) of the present, a site of the in-between, of doublings and overlappings, of an uncanny superimposition of the visible and the invisible, the here and the elsewhere, and the living and the dead. Silverman draws out some of the implications of *concentrationary* memory to suggest that, for Resnais and Cayrol, 'fearful imagination' in the wake of the camps is one that must permanently unsettle all normalizing assumptions that, in the words of the film, 'all this happened only once, at a certain time and in a certain place'.

We believe that allegorical readings of *Night and Fog* are both a crucial part of the idea of the *concentrationary* (as elaborated by Rousset, Arendt and Cayrol) and are built in to the political aesthetic of the film itself. Our larger research project entitled *Concentrationary Memories: The Politics of Representation*, of which this collection of essays on *Night and Fog* is the first part, attempts to re-establish the context and importance of this focus alongside 'Holocaust studies'. It does not aim to displace the central horror of exterminatory racism and its instrument: the extermination camps. It does, however, seek to create analytical space between the exterminatory system and the larger and older *concentrationary* system beside which the genocide came to be enacted, in order to draw attention to the specific political meaning of the *concentrationary* universe and the idea of *concentrationary* art to challenge it, both of which have received less cultural analysis. Our aim is to reinstate the historical and cultural understanding of that which seemed, to those who returned from the German concentration camps, the larger significance of the camps as the instrument of a novel totalitarian system that could morph under other political necessities in so-called democratic states and be enacted by other regimes of anti-democratic repression. Thus, without diminishing the necessity to research and analyse the horror of racism that led to the attempted genocides of the Final Solution, our project aims to explore the intersection of the politics and aesthetics of resistance in relation to the new possibility created in modern society by the totalitarian systems whose instrument and privileged site was the camp.

The Making and Reception of a Film

By 1948 deportee literature had dried up. Thus, when Henri Michel and Olga Wormser, of the *Comité d'Histoire de la Deuxième Guerre mondiale*, completed their book *Tragédie de la déportation 1940–1945: Témoignages de survivants des camps de concentration allemands* (published by Hachette in 1954) and prepared a historical exhibition of the same name in November 1954 at the Pedagogical Museum at 29 Rue D'Ulm in Paris, they were already re-engaging with a past that had become dormant, but a past already shaped by images. Their pedagogical exhibition was greeted as a monument to the history of resistance, deportation and liberation. From this exhibition, the proposal to make a film about that history of the deportees and the system they endured was conceived and taken up by Argos Films produced by Anatole Dauman.[65] Although Sylvie Lindeperg will re-examine the film's genesis in her chapter, a short résumé is necessary here.

The film was commissioned in May 1955 and research began with a trip to Poland and attempts to gather further documentation, including from military archives. This is significant in so far as visiting Auschwitz and Majdanek took Resnais and his film crew to hybrid sites of both *concentrationary* and exterminatory terror, and also gave them access to archive materials of perpetrator imagery found by Polish and Soviet liberators of these complexes. Relatively less 'notorious' than Bergen-Belsen for the British or Buchenwald and Dachau for the Americans, Auschwitz, liberated by the Red Army, enters into representation. Because of his known left political position as a filmmaker, Resnais it appears experienced difficulties in accessing official French materials on the concentration camps, and he had been denied access to materials collected by the British (Gladstone explores the reasons in his chapter). He had visited the Netherlands and found the footage of the departure of a train from Westerbork deportation camp. As a whole, Resnais's film draws extensively on Polish/Soviet documents and even fiction films made after 1945.

At the end of November, Jean Cayrol watched in excruciating silence Resnais's mute montage. Fearfully transported back to the *concentrationary* universe by this all too vivid encounter with its visual traces, he withdrew to write a script from memory. The difficult challenge of matching his beautiful, mournful but autonomous poetic composition to the reworked montage of the film was only effected with the intervention of Resnais's former collaborator Chris Marker, who reconfigured Cayrol's initial text and brought him back to work with Resnais's carefully calibrated rhythms of editing and sequencing of past and present images.[66] Cayrol had the final say over the words spoken in the commentary and excluded certain phrasings planned by Resnais.

In *Night and Fog*, the gas chambers and crematoria and the selections at Auschwitz, recognized by Resnais and his team when they consulted the archives in Poland and notably at Auschwitz as 'the final solution', are 'contained' by the briefest of Cayrolian phrasings: Himmler says 'We must destroy, but productively.'[67] It would be easy to read this as Cayrol's overlaying of the exterminatory system he did not know personally with the *concentrationary* experience he knew all too well 'in his own muscles'. It is also possible to read this phrasing as an acute if compressed registration of what Resnais's film specifically brings into vision. If there is so little direct visual evidence of the mass genocidal destruction for which there is so little cinematic documentation, there was plenty more, if one could see it, of a cynical, capitalist mentality in which remnants of the destroyed and the murdered were systematically harvested for varied uses: not only recycling of clothes and possessions, but women's hair woven into blankets, bones for fertilizer and so forth. Some of the grisliest scenes in Resnais's film intimate other unspeakable experiments with skin and body parts that remain almost too painful even to watch. Cayrol himself in the commentary allows words to fail before the sights.

The German-Jewish composer Hanns Eisler was brought to Paris to watch the film and, in the space of two weeks, he reworked existing compositions and created new material to complete a musical score for the film. The film was then sent to the French censors who demanded, however, the removal of the images of bulldozers pushing bodies into mass graves at Bergen-Belsen and a scene in which a '*képi*' (the distinctive cap) clearly identifies a *French* policeman surveying a *French* concentration camp for foreign-born Jewish men and women at Pithiviers. The scene remained in the film, but the offending képi was blocked out by the addition of a black bar across the frame. Resnais received the Prix Jean Vigo in January 1956. This award brought the film into public debate through newspaper reviews and commentaries. The film was then nominated as a French entry for the Cannes Film Festival of that year. After a private screening of the film, representatives from the German Embassy wrote to the French Minister of Foreign Affairs

requesting that the film be withdrawn from official French submission to
Cannes, under the rule that 'if a film is deemed offensive to the national
sensibilities of a participating country, that country's representatives may
request that a film be withdrawn from the competition, though compliance
with such requests is not obligatory'.[68] Following this complaint, the film was
indeed withdrawn from competition but the scandal resonated across the
media. Cayrol wrote an excoriating article objecting to the notion that the
film renewed German-French hostilities and calling for a Franco-German
democratic alliance against the repression of the film's non-judgemental, non-
nationalist, anti-fascist '*dispositif d'alerte*'.[69] The film was finally shown outside
the competition at the Palais du Festival in Cannes, under French government
sponsorship. The organizers of the Berlin Film Festival immediately expressed
their desire to show the film in Berlin in June. *Night and Fog* was finally
released for public exhibition in France on 22 May 1956. When the film
appeared one month later at the Berlin Film Festival, the Chairman of the
Bundestag Committee on Press, Radio and Film suggested that the government
of West Germany should commission a German language soundtrack to
ensure the widest distribution of the film in cinemas and youth organizations.[70]

This brief study of the film's genesis and initial exhibition reveals three
important issues. First, the film's making and chequered reception was part and
parcel of the intense but variable sensitivity within Europe about the *national*
identities of perpetrator and victim in relation to post-war narratives about
wartime national experience. Thus the debate circled around questions of the
film itself appearing anti-German, while events of June 1956 revealed that it
could equally be used by the new West Germany as part of its campaign of
democratization and de-Nazification to distinguish the Bundesrepublik
Deutschland from the National Socialist Third Reich. There the film was being
read as less about the war between nations, and more about the specificity of
National Socialism or the Fascist Third Reich between 1933 and 1945 now
being disowned by a reconstructed Germany rapidly welcomed back into
European nationhood as a democratic bulwark against the new totalitarian
threat posed by the Soviet Union and its now satellite states in the East.

Second, the complex manoeuvrings between government agencies,
cultural agencies, the press, and the producers of the film index the intensely
'political' climate in which a committed film about the recent past was being
received and disputed in France. Ostensibly concerned with managing both
French sensitivities about disavowed collaboration (the *képi* incident that
implicated French police in round-ups of Jewish men and women) and
German sensibility about its horrendous recent past, the attempted censorship
of this film also registered, if indirectly, heated political issues within the
actual moment of distribution in 1956, to which the film's specific cinematic
argument openly gestured in its final question about responsibility and the

merely slumbering *concentrationary* monster. Thus, the immediate reception crisis surrounding the film during the emergence of the Algerian anti-colonial struggles and the French use of camps for its colonial rebels exposes the politics engendered by its critical aesthetic practice as a film that was clearly intervening in the still uncharted minefield of unprocessed memory of an event that was itself sufficiently relevant to the current moment to crank up heated debate. Yet by virtue of not being much debated before, there was as yet no consensus as to how the troubled histories of Europe and Nazism and still questioned responsibilities might be finally contained.

Third, the arguments indicate that there was no dominant narrative about the past by which to judge the film. The defence of the film against censorship (French or German), and the attempts to censor its content or displace it from being a French entry at Cannes seem to circle around contested issues of national sovereignty versus international, anti-fascist solidarity. Concerned with how French policemen and Germans in general might be viewed, the debate in 1956 shows no indication, however, that anybody was then too much concerned with the representation, or rather the lack of specific representation, of the Jewish, Roma and Sinti victims of genocide.

We feel that it is important to remind ourselves of some of the contemporary debates framing the making and reception of the film because we wish to approach the film in relation, precisely, to the politico-aesthetic particularities of its moment of production. As we have mentioned, these pre-date the dominance of the interpretation of this past through the prism of the term 'the Holocaust', which rightly centres on the dark exterminatory core of Nazi racism. Without in any way seeking to minimize or displace the absolute centrality of the destruction of European Jewry and Romany peoples, we want to think about what we would learn if we could reconfigure the moment before such knowledge was publicly shaped by the eventual emergence of the literature of testimony. The image produced across the Eichmann trial (1961) and the many events since that have fostered theoretical, historical and cultural analysis of the genocidal project, have superseded the focus on the *concentrationary* that dominated in France during the 1950s and have made us view this earlier focus as a failure rather than a historico-political contingency that has relevance for the understanding of the work and the effects of Resnais's film.

Primo Levi's seminal testimony *If This is a Man*, originally composed and published in a limited edition in 1946, was reissued in 1958 by Einaudi and translated into English in 1959. Elie Wiesel's *Night* was written in Yiddish in 1954, published in 1955 in Buenos Aires and was only rewritten in French later that year as the slim volume that has now become celebrated throughout the world. Returning to the historical moment of *Night and Fog's* production and reception before these major literary forms of testimony had shaped the event in their different visions specifically of Auschwitz II and III allows us to see Resnais's film not as the first major film about the Holocaust as such. Rather, we can read it as an effort to disclose and, at the same time, to incite resistance through a knowledge of, the *concentrationary* universe by means of self-consciously aesthetic cinematic techniques and strategies (image, word, music) that resonated with a range of political and aesthetic cinematic experiments for which Resnais was already notorious. In 1953, working with Chris Marker, Alain Resnais had made a 30-minute anti-colonial film entitled *Les Statues meurent aussi* (*Statues Also Die*) which was censored for eight years after its making. Ostensibly a film about the sculptural art of the African continent, its deeper question as to why the arts of Africa were found in European anthropological museums and not in art museums served to expose the effects of colonialism as culturally murderous not only of the historical art of Africa but also of its living creators of today. The film shows how the vitality and cultural foundations of African sculptural imagination were being crushed by colonization, forcing African artists to become mere replicators of colonial trophies. Music, a dramatic means of filming the sculptures so as to animate their aesthetic force, and a voice-over that underscored the tension between the liveliness of the works and their colonial fate, identified Resnais and Chris Marker as not only anti-colonialist in politics, but filmmakers capable of finding a cinematic form that itself could visually, aurally and critically indict colonial violence. Montage, poetic voice-over and dramatic juxtaposition had also defined Resnais's film *Guernica* (1950), which violently denounced the fascist, military assault on a defenceless Basque town and offered a poetic lament for the dead through Picasso's images, from his paintings of the urban poor through to the violent torsions of his painted homage to suffering and denunciation of fascism. Thus, when speaking of the new commission for *Night and Fog*, Resnais's already formulated politicized '*recherches formelles*' (formal researches) will generate a specifically cinematic mode of encounter – a 'gesture of cinema' – between past and present, the moment and history that presents not a monument to the dead but a political questioning of the present and an exploration of *concentrationary* memory.[71]

Included in this newly commissioned collection are, however, two previously published articles which demand to be placed within this study of *concentrationary cinema* because they are benchmarks for the critical analysis of both the production and reception of the film and the politics and logics of its 'formal researches'.

First published in *New German Critique* in 1997, Andrew Hebard's 'Disruptive Histories: Toward a Radical Politics of Remembrance in Alain Resnais's *Night and Fog*' challenges a predominantly psychoanalytic reading not only of this film in relation to Freud's concept of mourning, but its use as a means of 'working through' the trauma of the Holocaust. Looking carefully at the film's distribution and reception in Germany after 1956, Hebard resists the later memorial interpretation of *Night and Fog*, and proposes instead a political reading by invoking another Freudian aesthetic concept: the uncanny. Hebard argues that the film set out not to commemorate but to generate anxiety in the spectator. After a critique of the new vocabulary of 'trauma studies' (trauma, mourning, acting out and working through), Hebard states that 'a politics of the uncanny … asks what aspects of the history can and do possess us?' Hebard's use of a politics of the uncanny thus demonstrates how the temporal ambivalence created in *Night and Fog* is a sign of a return of history and, hence, the politico-aesthetic creation of a permanently anxious present.

On the other hand, we might also have to ask: What place might cinema as a visual technology and a mass medium itself have had in creating and sustaining the *concentrationary* imaginary and massified aesthetics of Nazi totalitarianism? What treacherous and compromised aspects of the cinematic might *Night and Fog* have had to, or failed to, negotiate as a political and historical work that would have to use materials created by the perpetrators – both perpetrator imagery as well as the spectacular use of cinema as a means to document this universe? We invited John Mowitt to participate in this volume precisely because he had been the first scholar to raise this troubling question in his critical study of Resnais and cinema. At the same time we wanted to acknowledge the historicity of the discourse on *Night and Fog*. Thus we asked Mowitt to revisit a text he had originally composed in 1988, critically examining its own genesis and politics in the changing context of debate and reception. Mowitt here reframes his own work in a new conversation with our work. In 'showing' (a term used in US English to designate the act of walking through a commercial space, typically a home) his text within the context of our initiative to think about the cinema and the *concentrationary*, Mowitt investigates the role of the cinematic itself in making possible not only fascist aesthetics of spectacle but the imagining of mass movements and mass violence. Where and how does an attempt at a counter-*concentrationary* art practice become complicit with the aesthetic technologies of that which is being resisted?

Concentrationary cinema: a politics of representation

We are not proposing that *Night and Fog* was in any way a cinematic treatise in political theory. Nor are we suggesting that Resnais read Arendt's *The Origins of Totalitarianism*, first published in 1951, with a full third of the volume being dedicated to the concentration camp. It was not available in French.[72] Arendt's contemporary political focus on totalitarianism, however, is a significant element of the context within which the film was produced, since it also drew on the largely political analyses offered by French and German deportee literature and itself represented a context of political reflections.[73] We want to stress the presence of a *political* reading of the camp as a systematic weapon for the destruction of human life – a fine distinction from the mass production of non-human death that was the horror of the extermination camp. We wish to offer a range of new readings of *Night and Fog* by placing the film in the context of this complex terrain of emerging and contested political and cultural narratives, memorializations and political anxieties. By focusing on the nature of the political terror of the system rather than the suffering and identity of the victims, we do not minimize that suffering, nor ignore the racialization of genocide. No longer placing *Night and Fog* at the beginning of a history of cinema and the genocide we know now as the Holocaust, we are viewing it as a politics of representation, situated in, but not confined to, the 1950s, and as a representation of politics in relation to an event we might consider the most politicized instance of attempted eradication of the political, the *polis*, the sphere of social action. This means inviting the scholars assembled here to assess the film's aesthetic strategies and their political consequences beyond the limits of existing debates that have either eulogized the film or critiqued it as a brilliant or flawed documentary about the Holocaust. We would, therefore, like to ask what the film does and how it has become a benchmark for a political poetics in cinema that transcends classification as documentary, compilation or fiction. We will call this political poetics arising from a cinematic reflection on the *concentrationary* system *concentrationary cinema*, hence distinguishing it from 'Holocaust film' and the different politics, aesthetics and ethics that has raised.

If one reason for returning to *Night and Fog* is to detach it from the debates about 'representing the Holocaust' and the focus on trauma that were to develop later (especially with the appearance of Claude Lanzmann's *Shoah* in 1985 and his 'resistance to representation', that is, the refusal, and in fact debarring, of the use of archive photographs and footage) and to reinsert it into the immediate post-war context of an aesthetic resistance to *concentrationary* terror, it is, none the less, necessary to address what has become a major tendency to pit *Shoah* against *Night and Fog*.

Night and Fog's distinctive operations have, perhaps, not only been disfigured by the critique of its failure to focus on the destruction of European Jewry, but also by the implicit critique by Lanzmann of Resnais's aesthetic strategies. Lanzmann's film is important for the precise fact that *Shoah* revisited and disclosed the hidden or forgotten history of two of the specialist extermination camps at Chelmno and Treblinka. An offshoot of Lanzmann's huge project led to a free-standing film about the revolt at Sobibor. To recreate traces and memories of these short-lived death camps, Lanzmann filmed only in the present, and hence reaffirmed Resnais's opening gesture, the often empty landscapes of erased extermination camps now punctured only by belated memorial monuments desolately keeping watch over places few tourists visit. But he also filmed bystanders such as signalmen, railway workers, local farmers, German colonists and a handful of survivors of these places. Lanzmann went to the sites, spoke to the bystanders and filmed the survivors some of whom he took back. Faces, places and words became a means of signifying the central meaning of the project: absence – the almost obliterated traces of the camps and the millions of people disappeared from the Polish and European world.

Resnais's film, however, is not about absence and absenting. It is about terror and the systematic operations of its specific experimental sites: the concentration camps. Thus the debate about the impossibility of representing the nature of extermination by means of the image, which has led to a critique of *Night and Fog* precisely as a compilation film utilizing compromised archive footage (and, let it be said, pioneering the return to the forlorn and dismal actuality of the site of Auschwitz II in a self-conscious gesture that marks the gap in memory between past and present) can, in our opinion, be displaced by a more precise focus on the politics of representation in the moment of making of the film.

It is, therefore, necessary to distinguish the two projects (*Night and Fog* and *Shoah*) in terms of their different premises and rationales. In confronting the unimaginable project of State-sponsored, industrial mass murder, Lanzmann has consistently argued for a 'resistance to representation': an acceptance of the limits of representation of an event that goes beyond any previous event or crime or experience, such that there is no convention through which it can be comprehended and represented. He goes further in his refusal to rescreen perpetrator images of violence. Indeed, he has even claimed that were he to discover actual footage of a gas chamber in action he would destroy it.[74] Lanzmann, therefore, created a different cinematic process involving duration, repetition, rhythm and the intensive, affecting, phenomenological encounter with the places, the faces and the voices of survivors, bystanders and perpetrators who are all encouraged to put into words experiences that still have the traumatic capacity to undo the speaker in the vividness with which the unprocessed event still 'happens' in the present moment before the relentless camera. Thus Lanzmann's film contains no archive photography, no archive footage, nothing except that which could be filmed in the present as he and his crew pursued the handful of survivor-witnesses of the extermination camps of Poland or Lithuania and of Auschwitz in its various forms, taking them sometimes to 'the place', as in the case of Simon Srebnik and Chelmno, sometimes interviewing them in their new relocated lives.

Between the photograph-rich exhibition of 1954 about German deportations and torture of French resistance fighters organized by Henri Michel and Olga Wormser, which returned to visibility an archive of documents which led to Resnais's film, and Lanzmann's anti-archival position lie more than two decades in which the relatively little-known images used in Resnais's film had acquired a different status and even charge, precisely as a result of the film and the further memorializations that subsequent events and anniversaries set in motion. The progressive production of an iconography that often confused the Holocaust and the *concentrationary* universe – that is, a consolidation of the historical memory of the event through the selective but repeated use of certain photographs and certain extracts of the Allied liberation footage, often without specification and detailed identification of place, date, photographer, function and so forth – would indeed alter the power of any image over time. No better analysis of this fading of affect exists than that provided by Susan Sontag, one of the first cultural critics to theorize photography:

> One's first encounter with the photographic inventory of ultimate horror is a kind of revelation, the prototypically modern revelation; a negative epiphany. For me, it was the photographs of Bergen-Belsen and Dachau which I came across by chance in a bookstore in Santa Monica in July 1945. Nothing I have ever seen – in photographs or in real life – ever cut me as sharply, deeply, instantaneously. Indeed it seems plausible to me to divide my life into two parts, before I saw those photographs (I was twelve) and after, though it was many years before I understood fully what they were about.[75]

What was once the overpowering impact of a reality transmitted by the photograph may, however, be de-realized by the repeated exposure of the image. Sontag continues:

> To suffer is one thing; another thing is living with the photographed images of suffering, which does not necessarily strengthen conscience and the ability to be compassionate. It can also corrupt them. Once one has seen such images, one has started down the road of seeing more – and more. Images transfix and images anaesthetize. An event becomes more real than it would have been if one had never seen a photograph. But after repeated exposure to images it also becomes less real.[76]

Thus Sontag also suggests that even the most shocking images of atrocity cannot retain their initial power, while, none the less, she affirms that her first impressions leave her eternally grieving for a loss of innocence before the sight of such pain. In her more recent study of *Holocaust Memory through the*

Camera's Eye, Barbie Zelizer documents an important discovery in her research. When the first journalists reported the *concentrationary* horror, they struggled with the inadequacies of language to describe what they were seeing as they followed the Allied troops into concentration camps on German soil. 'Words fail me', was their repeated refrain. Readers in the United States or Britain could not fully appreciate the nature of the horror these men and women were witnessing. Zelizer then argues that this changed as soon as a stream of photographic images began to accompany the written word and appeared in daily newspapers and illustrated weeklies (the like of which Sontag encountered, possibly in *Life* or even *Vogue*, for which Margaret Bourke White and Lee Miller respectively worked as war photographers). It appears that the photographs and newsreels were necessary for any sense at all of the extremity to be conveyed to the outside world. This shock of the first time may happen for individuals as they too come across this archive. But as a culture, the archive cannot hold this terrible rupture for us any more. It has become part of the possible; it has made the unimaginable knowable as the photographic images of it. It has a look. Repeated exposure of these images also risks other dangers of being misused, allowing for sadistic voyeurism or even pornography.

Thus, by the mid-1980s, Lanzmann's critique of the use of the archive of photographic and film imagery can be granted some validity; to document again is to repeat and thus destroy what should remain challenging rather than becoming banal and over-familiar. In this sense, Lanzmann's decision to create another cinematic strategy that disavows repetition is both an ethical and political move of great importance. But it would be wrong to use this necessary reconfiguration of cinematic encounters with the unremembered past by the 1980s to make *Night and Fog* the fall-guy in a critique of an unthinking, unethical, pernicious use of archive footage.

Inevitably, our revisiting the moment of *Night and Fog* takes place in the aftermath of Lanzmann's work. It is mindful of the debates to which his position on the resistance to representation has given rise, rightly. Our project is an informed and self-aware return to *Night and Fog* in order to reconsider not so much the brute differences between the two classic films, as to re-contextualize and identify what Resnais named his *formal researches*. What can we make of the calculated and self-conscious, modernist cinematographic aesthetic as the very ground for a means to re-encounter the *concentrationary* universe in all its radical otherness? How did the formal choices represent the complexity of that universe and make the gap between the past and the present vivid for an outsider, a non-participant viewer, irrespective of the time or moment at which that viewing takes place.

Thus the debate about the validity of the archive and representation which has emerged following Lanzmann's film often fails to take into account both the alteration of the ability of the image (often the same images) to shock and disturb over time and the power of Resnais's film to sustain the ability to shock and disturb, not because of the images he used, but because of the cinematic construction he created with his collaborators Cayrol, Eisler and Marker.[77] We believe, however, that by recontextualizing these images as *concentrationary* images rather than as Holocaust images, and therefore defamiliarizing our normalized view of the iconography of the Holocaust, these images can be released from their entrapment within an anaestheticizing aesthetic and rediscover their power to shock or to provoke analysis.

In 2001, Jacques Rancière contributed a long reflection on representability and extremity to a special edition of the journal, *Genre Humain*, relating to an exhibition on *Art and the Memory of the Camps: Representation and Extermination*.[78] Refuting those who have claimed that the *concentrationary* and exterminatory universes are 'beyond' representation (he has in mind both Lanzmann and philosopher Jean François Lyotard), Rancière makes a telling comparison between a moment in Gustave Flaubert's seminal modernist novel, *Madame Bovary* (in which Charles Bovary's burgeoning love for Emma is linked with a play of dust animated by a draught under the farm kitchen's ill-fitting door) and the literary language used by deportee Robert Antelme in *L'Espèce Humaine*. Attempting to describe, paratactically, a momentary human experience, Antelme links the steam rising from the flow of urine as the prisoners pee together in the night with a momentary and exhilarating experience of human solidarity. The texts by both Flaubert and Antelme exhibit a distinctively modernist mode of literary writing, associated with what Rancière defines as the 'aesthetic regime' that characterizes modern culture, in which there is a momentary, paratactic conjunction of a human pathos and a tiny detail of material existence:

> Thus Robert Antelme's experience is not unrepresentable in the sense that a language for conveying it does not exist. The language exists and the syntax exists. Not as exceptional language and syntax, but on the contrary, as a mode of expression peculiar to the aesthetic regime in the arts in general ... The language that conveys the experience is in no way specific to it. The experience of programmed dehumanization finds itself expressed in the same way as the Flaubertian identity between the human and inhuman, between the emotion uniting two beings and a little dust stirred up by the draught in a farm kitchen.[79]

Rancière contrasts Antelme's Flaubertian prose with Lanzmann's *Shoah* which, he argues, attempts to deal with both the fact of extermination having happened and the elimination of the traces of extermination: a material event and an absent one. Rancière thinks both 'perfectly representable' but not by means of creating equivalents in fictional embodiments of executioners and victims. 'It is through a confrontation between the words uttered here and now about what the place was and the reality that is materially present and absent in this place.' But this confrontation exposes an abyss haunted by a hallucinatory dissonance so that:

> the impossibility of adequate correspondence between the place and the speech and the very body of the witness goes to the heart of the elimination that is to be represented. It touches the incredible character of the event, programmed by the very logic of extermination … This is what the speech of the witness framed by the camera responds to. It avows the incredible, the hallucinatory, and the impossibility that words could fill this empty place.[80]

Thus Rancière concludes that there is nothing in the event that proscribes art/ representation. Even when dealing with the extreme or the inhuman or even the absent, it is a matter of choices: the present against historicization, or a focus on the means as opposed to the causes and so forth.

More recently Lanzmann's position has been deployed in a polemic against art historian Georges Didi-Huberman who published an article in the catalogue to an exhibition in Paris in 2001, *Mémoire des Camps: Photographies des camps de concentration et d'extermination Nazis 1933–1945*. The focus of Didi-Huberman's article is the only *four* photographs, out of an archive of half a million images from the Nazi era, of the extermination process at Crematorium V at Auschwitz II, taken surreptitiously by members of the Sonderkommando – the Jewish prisoners selected to work in the gas chambers and crematoria before themselves being gassed. Didi-Huberman argued that images of the unimaginable exist 'in spite of everything' (*malgré tout*). He also insists that we need to *see* these photographs not merely as images purveying information but as material traces of an act of witnessing bearing the marks of their own moment of production. These photographs have a physical materiality as photographs taken in spite of terrible danger of extreme punishment by those desperate to ensure a witness record of the killing process. Their distinctive features – the lack of focus, or oblique framing, or even capturing only the trees above the site of killing or burning – are read by Didi-Huberman not as elements which diminish the value of the photographs as documents but rather as the very indices of the conditions under which the photographs were taken which are their meaning. They are thus marked with their historical moment even as these characteristics make the images *difficult* to read as images. What, therefore, should we be looking at them for? Didi-Huberman wants to make us see the photographs *per se* and in so doing come to see history. That means that the photographs are not to be *used* as images, as an image of x or y, or for a documentary value for any information these four photographs might yield. History, and their function as its inscription, lie in the fact that they exist at all, *despite* everything militating against their having been made and surviving. Their materiality and the specific forms of the images are the traces of the dangerous constraints under which 'Alex', the Greek prisoner who took the shots and his colleagues who stood guard or smuggled the negatives out, fought to find a means of bearing witness to the killing process that would be otherwise 'unbelievable' without such indexical, evidential, visual testimony which incorporates in what is shown the will to make this seen. Didi-Huberman is arguing a case for the value of the very existence of the photograph itself.

In this light, the notion that *Night and Fog* opted for historicization by means of a simplistic belief that the incredible and unimaginable might be 'represented' by indexical documents can be dismissed as a radical oversimplification. The opening sequence of the film *Night and Fog* produces a shocking collision between two worlds whose physical proximity belies their incommensurability.[81] This is effected by tracking shots: the camera tilts down, and then, in a second sequence, pans from left to right, both shots traversing the once electrified barbed wire fence from a camera positioned inside the camp perimeter. The accompanying text by Jean Cayrol enacts the poet's Surrealist reworking of a Proustian concept of memory. As we argue above, this formal technique produces an aesthetic vision that Cayrol formulated as *art concentrationnaire* or *art lazaréen*. *Concentrationary* art is premised on the confusion of *l'invraisemblable et le naturel* (the extraordinary and the ordinary): 'Objects will be central to this vision for they will be shown to have a secret life alongside their familiar appearance which will capture that tension between familiarity and strangeness.'[82]

Our collection of 'readings' of the film as a 'writing' – *écriture cinématique* – focuses precisely on the choices Resnais and his team of collaborators made in order to produce the disturbing quality of Rousset's *univers concentrationnaire*. Uncanniness effected by estranging juxtapositions infects what cannot be reproduced or re-presented. The *concentrationary* universe, however, left material traces in the form of places, buildings, objects, documents and (as importantly) images – filmed and photographed – which function both as evidence but also phenomenologically beyond evidence because they were made within the very system itself. Though not 'images despite everything', as is the case of the *Sonderkommando* photographs, what remains is perpetrator image-making, inscribing their 'will' to show, their will to record. In their ordinariness touched by the horror of extremity, these images enact the uncanniness of the proximity between the everyday and the horrific that is indeed the deepest horror of the systematicity of *the concentrationary* (Plate 41). Disclosing this required a profoundly aesthetic gesture that is at once deeply thought cinematically.

As many readers of the film have already stressed, the central logic of the film *Night and Fog* is the logic of alternation between the 'present' filming in the sites of Auschwitz and Majdanek – the abandoned, not yet musealized and fully touristic sites of commemoration – and the montage of found imagery, the ready-mades of history, to plot out what Rancière has helpfully named the necessary 'logic of fictions'. Here again we return to the politics of the aesthetic. Rancière claims that '[t]he real must be fictionalized in order to be thought'. In a difficult and theoretically paradoxical move, Rancière favours art as a means to access understanding over a simplistic notion of history as the mere telling of fact or event. He argues that what he calls the historical is 'condemned to presenting events according to their empirical disorder' in which actual history often chaotically happens, while the poetic, a structured and structuring representation, creates for the historical an order of intelligibility.[83] Actual occurrences are often a seemingly chaotic jumble of coincident events whose patterns of meaning and significance are not self-evident as they occur. To discern meaning is to find an order that seeks it, investigates it and discloses it. Thus Rancière displaces the notion of fiction as a falsification, while the notion of documentary as truth is also undermined. In this surprising inversion, self-consciously aesthetic or formal film creates a *machine for understanding*:

> The poetic 'story' or 'history' henceforth links the realism that shows us the poetic traces inscribed directly in reality with the artificialism that assembles complex machines of understanding. This connection was transferred from literature to the new art of narrative, film, which brought to its highest potential the double resource of the silent imprint that speaks and the montage that calculates the values of truth and the potential for producing meaning. Documentary film, film devoted to the 'real', is in this sense capable of greater fictional invention than 'fiction' film, readily devoted to a certain stereotype of actions and characters.[84]

Thinking about this paradox, in her chapter Griselda Pollock places *Night and Fog* in conversation with a problematic fiction film about the *concentrationary* universe, *Kapò*, directed by Italian filmmaker Gilles Pontecorvo in 1958. Using *Night and Fog* as his benchmark of thoughtful cinema, French film critic and director Jacques Rivette attacked *Kapò* not so much for being a fictionalizing recreation with actors and built sets of the *concentrationary* universe as for the misuse of a cinematic device: one tracking shot. Rivette considered abject Pontecorvo's decision to create a tracking shot moving in to restage, in medium shot, a woman who has killed herself on the electrical wires, an act already filmed once. What were the politics of Rivette's revulsion at Pontecorvo's tracking shot when the larger issue of any fictional reconstruction and romanticization of the *concentrationary* experience already begs a profound question after the work done by *Night and Fog*?

Rivette's article became the resource for French critic Serge Daney who was formed as a critical *cinéphile* through exposure to *Night and Fog* as exemplary of what thinking, engaged and ethical cinema could be. Revisiting this now famous intertextual moment in French film studies, Pollock critically interrogates Resnais's own ethics of the shot and the encounter with the dead, noting his repeated cropping of close-ups and reframing and decontextualization of archive images. Confronting the few frames in which Resnais did attempt to use his gesture of cinema to face the extermination process, Pollock examines the unexpected incursion of potentially eroticized images of naked women that serve Resnais when he has to confront mass death. Does the film falter here? Is it reclaimed, like *Kapò* by existing tropes? What do we do when the killing process is confusingly displaced and rendered treacherously pornographic by troubling images of naked *women*, using archive images that are not to do with murder by gassing in the extermination camps but from the Einsatzgruppen murders? Drawing on psychoanalytical readings of the deep mythic linkage of the feminine, the aesthetic and death, Pollock exposes the way the film stutters politically at this point by using such embedded and gendered tropes that typically serve to deflect the confrontation with mortality irrespective of the cultural or racialized identity of the victims.[85]

Rivette disowned Pontecorvo and praised Resnais because the former abused camera movements. Pollock questions Resnais's selection, editing, cropping and montage of images of the dead in order to re-open this classic debate in French film studies. Circling back to Emma Wilson's reflections on Resnais's confrontation with the dead, Pollock asks if Resnais's film is compromised by its thoughtless insertion of the erotic image. Reworking the problem with the help of Arendt, on the meaning of the *concentrationary* system, and Adorno, on how the self-conscious modernist artwork might for a moment still the inevitable cultural reification of suffering, Pollock makes a connection with Mowitt's chapter. She poses the question of Resnais's aesthetic effects at the level of the politics of technology. If aesthetics can be both political and ethical, does this operate at the level of the shot – the technologies of cinematic representation – or at the level of the authorial decision about what shots to create, or at the level of a spectatorial reading of the effect generated between the two? Who is to blame for the failure of ethics in representing death: cinema, the desire of the spectator to see everything, the auteur who sets up the scene/seeing?

Daney used Rivette to develop an ethics of viewing the other and dying across classic cinema after 1960; but, approaching the 1990s, he sensed that new digital technologies enabled forms of image manipulation that could become as dangerously thoughtless as Pontecorvo's tracking shot appeared to

Rivette. Daney, formed critically by exposure to *Night and Fog* in the 1960s, thus brings the question of a *dispositif d'alerte* directly into the politics of the contemporary image and our responsiveness of the mediatized 'camp' *nomos* of our image culture in the present.

This collection emerged out of our decision to devote 18 months to a standing seminar on 32 minutes of film. It is not in any way conclusive. Through a historical, theoretical, cinematic, literary and political engagement with the *concentrationary*, we seek to re-invigorate the debates about aesthetics and the politics of representation in the light of the ethical obligations to see and know a historical violence and the political necessity to recognize that which was then initiated. The final phrases of Cayrol's text declare over the contemporary filming in colour of the monumental ruins of the crematoria at Auschwitz-Birkenau a message to a 'we' that comes 'after' who must know not the comfort of ruined empires but the menace of a merely sleeping pestilence. This knowledge shatters the silence of our complacency by means of an endless cry that, in Cayrol's wording (*'qu'on crie'*) specifically leaves entirely open to any time and any place and any suffering:

> Who amongst us is still watching in this strange observatory to warn us of the coming of new executioners? Are their faces really so different from our own?

> Somewhere, amongst us, live on the lucky Kapos, the reinstated leaders, the unknown informers.

> And there are some of us who sincerely gaze upon these ruins as if the *concentrationary* monster lay dead beneath its rubble, who pretend to take up hope again as the image recedes into the past, as if we could be cured once and for all from the *concentrationary* plague, we who want to believe that all this belongs to one time and one country, and are failing to look around ourselves and hear the unending cry. (*qu'on crie*).[86]

Concentrationary Cinema is a response to Resnais's and Cayrol's political vision for aesthetics in 1955, a making visible that seeks continually to reveal the monster beneath its ruins, the past in the present, echoing with continuing sound of the haunting cry. The metaphor of the contaminating disease that spreads beyond one time and one place functions beyond figuration, for it is monitory: we must see and we must hear the unending cry of violated humanity. Thus, we hope that this critical exploration of cinematic *concentrationary* memory will maintain some fidelity with the concept elaborated by Rousset and Cayrol of the *concentrationary* universe that knows no limits.

Notes

1. Sylvie Lindeperg, '*Night and Fog*: Inventing a Perspective', in *Cinema and the Shoah: An Art Confronts the Tragedy of the Twentieth Century*, ed. Jean-Michel Frodon, trans. Anna Harrison and Tom Maes (New York: SUNY Press, 2010), p. 63.
2. Primo Levi, *The Drowned and the Saved*, trans. Raymond Rosenthal (New York: Random House Vintage Books, 1989), p. 38.
3. Hannah Arendt, 'Social Science Techniques and the Study of Concentration Camps', *Jewish Social Studies* 12:1 (1950), reprinted in *Essays in Understanding 1930–1954: Formation, Exile, Totalitarianism* (New York: Schocken Books, 1994), p. 226.
4. Zygmunt Bauman, *Modernity and the Holocaust* (Cambridge: Polity Press, 1989), p. 11.
5. Richard Raskin, Nuit et Brouillard *by Alain Resnais: On the Making, Reception and Functions of a Major Documentary Film, Including a New Interview with Alain Resnais and the Original Shooting Script*, Foreword by Sascha Vierny (Aarhus: Aarhus University Press, 1987), p. 54. Like all scholars working on this film, we are deeply indebted to the pioneering research undertaken by Richard Raskin.
6. The French censors objected to the horrifying images of the corpses being bull-dozed at Bergen-Belsen and to the visibility of a French policeman watching over prisoners in a French concentration camp at Pithiviers. For the discussion of the furore around the Cannes Film Festival, see later in this chapter (plate 11).
7. For detailed studies of the film's distribution and reception, see Ewout van der Knapp, ed., *Uncovering the Holocaust: The International Reception of Night and Fog* (London: Wallflower Press, 2006); Sylvie Lindeperg, *Nuit et Brouillard: Un Film dans l'Histoire* (Paris: Odile Jacob, 2007); primary source documents are printed in Richard Raskin, Nuit et Brouillard *by Alain Resnais*.
8. For instance, film analyst Joshua Hirsch attests to this in his Preface to *Afterimage: Film, Trauma and the Holocaust* (Philadelphia: Temple University Press, 2004), pp. ix–x.
9. Capitalized, the Holocaust is an interesting linguistic phenomenon in naming a real historical event figuratively with a term already loaded with both secular and religious meanings. Alternative namings of the destruction within the Jewish world include Hebrew terms such as *Churban* or *Shoah*, which mean catastrophe or destruction. In German, the event was generally named *Vernichtung der Juden* (Annihilation or Extermination of the Jews). The most extensive study of the currency of the term in secular pre- and post-war American, French and Israeli contexts is Jon Petrie, 'The Secular Word "HOLOCAUST": Scholarly Myths, History, and Twentieth Century Meanings', *Journal of Genocide Research* 2:1 (2000), 31–63. Petrie challenges many historians by documenting the varied secular uses of the term 'holocaust' before 1939 and after 1945 when it was often associated with the threat of nuclear war and other catastrophes. Petrie notes the significance of the gradual emergence of the term in American writing, firmly established in the 1978 TV series *Holocaust*. See also Gerd Korman, 'The Holocaust in American Writing', *Societas*, 2 (1971), 250–70, which traces the uses of the capitalized term in American literature to the mid-1950s. Elie Wiesel, wrongly associated with its widespread dissemination, notably in Germany, first used the term in August 1963: *The New Leader*, 5 August 1963, p. 21. See also James Young, 'Names of the Holocaust: Meaning and Consequences', *Writing and Rewriting the Holocaust: Narrative and the Consequences of Interpretation*

(Bloomington: Indiana University Press, 1988), 83–98. Young examines the effects of the metaphor for an event whose dreadful reality cannot be metaphoric.

10. For historical precision to which we hope also to contribute, we can spell out some of the sources of confusion. Only two peoples were designated by documented means for a 'final solution' – mass destruction by increasingly industrialized means: the Jewish and the Roma–Sinti peoples. Nazism's designation of a range of persons as socially undesirable led to persecution, but not extermination, of sexual and religious minorities. Political resistance also led to extreme punishments. In addition the euthanasia programme initiated in Germany itself was directed at physically disabled persons, while some within that community were subjected to forced sterilization.

11. For major studies of film and the Holocaust, see Judith Doneson, *The Holocaust in American Film* (New York: Jewish Publication Society, 1987), Annette Insdorf, *Indelible Shadows: Film and the Holocaust* (New York: Random House, 1983), Ilan Avisar, *Screening the Holocaust: Cinema's Images of the Unimaginable* (Bloomington: Indiana University Press, 1988), Joshua Hirsch, *Afterimage: Film, Trauma and the Holocaust.*

12. Ewout van der Knapp, ed., *Uncovering the Holocaust.*

13. Richard Raskin, Nuit et Brouillard *by Alain Resnais.*

14. Robert Michael, 'A Second Look: *Night and Fog*', *Cinéaste*, 13:4 (1984), 36–37, reprinted in Raskin, *Alain Resnais's* Nuit et Brouillard, p. 159.

15. According to Annette Wieviorka, 'the film has nothing to say regarding the genocide of the Jews' (*Déportation et genocide*, Paris: Plon, 1992, 223).

16. Edward R. Murrow, 'They Died 900 a Day in "the Best" Nazi Death Camp', *PM*, 16 April 1945. http://www.jewishvirtuallibrary.org/jsource/Holocaust/murrow.html, accessed 8 September 2009.

17. Primo Levi, *The Drowned and the Saved*, p. 39. See also Sarah Kofman, *Smothered Words*, [1987], trans. Madeleine Doby (Evanston: Northwestern University Press, 1998): 'Since Auschwitz, all men, Jews (and) non-Jews die differently; because what took place – back there – without taking place, death in Auschwitz, was worse than death.' Kofman in turn quotes Theodor Adorno, *Negative Dialectics*, trans. E.B. Ashton (New York: Seabury Press, 1979), p. 362.

18. Mark Roseman, *The Villa, The Lake, The Meeting: Wannsee and the Final Solution* (London: Penguin, 2002).

19. Wolfgang Sofksy cites the calculations by G. Schwartz in his *Die nationalsozialistischen Lager* (Frankfurt: Campus, 1990, 221–2), that taking into account all forms of camps (including ghettoes, labour-education, labour, forced labour and special detention camps) across the German Reich and its territories there were about 10,006 (Wolfgang Sofsky, *The Order of Terror: The Concentration Camp* [1993], trans. William Templer (Princeton: Princeton University Press, 1997), p. 292). See also Jo Reilly, David Cesarani, Tony Kushner and Colin Richmond, eds, *Belsen in History and Memory* (London: Frank Cass, 1997) for a documentation of the impact of the liberation of Belsen on British cultural memory. They write 'Although Nazi camps of a far more murderous nature were liberated before Belsen, the scenes recorded at Belsen by soldiers, journalists, photographers, broadcasters and film crews were perhaps the most gruesome images of all relating to the Nazi atrocities,' p. 3.

20. Sofsky, *The Order of Terror*, p. 43.

21. Anna and Margot Frank were sent from Auschwitz to Bergen-Belsen in October 1944 where Anna encountered a former schoolmate, the Berlin-born Hannah Goslar,

whose family had been deported from Westerbork transit camp in the Netherlands to the Albalallager at Bergen-Belsen, a special sub-camp that held prominent Jewish people who could be used in exchanges for prisoners of war.

22. Two men survived Chelmno. Following the revolt at Sobibor on 14 October 1943, 300 prisoners escaped, of whom between 50 and 70 survived beyond 1945. Possibly 40 people survived Treblinka following an uprising on 2 August 1943.

23. Scholars accept the figures compiled from train transport lists of 960,000 Jewish deaths and 140,000–150,000 ethnic Polish victims, along with 23,000 Roma and Sinti. Franciszek Piper, 'Ilu ludzi zginęło w KL Auschwitz. Liczba ofiar w świetle źródeł i badań 1945–1990 ['How many people died in Auschwitz Concentration Camp? The number of victims in the light of sources and research,' 1945–1990] (Oświęcim, 1992); German version: Die Zahl der Opfer von Auschwitz Aufgrund der Quellen und der Erträge der Forschung 1945–1990 (Oświęcim, 1993).

24. Nikolaus Wachsmann, 'The dynamics of destruction: the development of concentration camps, 1933–1945' in *Concentration Camps in Nazi Germany*, ed. Jane Caplan and Nikolaus Wachsmann (London and New York: Routledge, 2010), 17–43.

25. For the functionalist account in contrast to the intentionalist model of the decision to exterminate the Jewish population, see Christopher Browning, *The Path to Genocide: Essays on Launching the Final Solution* (Cambridge: Cambridge University Press, 1998, 1992) and *The Origins of the Final Solution: The Evolution of Nazi Jewish Policy, September 1939–March 1942* (Lincoln: University of Nebraska Press, 2004).

26. Giorgio Agamben, *Homo Sacer: Sovereign Power and Bare Life*, [1995] trans. Daniel Heller-Roazen (Stanford: Stanford University Press, 1998), 176.

27. Richard Ek, 'Giorgio Agamben and the Spatialities of the Camp: An Introduction', *Geografiska Annaler B Human Geography* 88:4 (December 2006), 363–86.

28. Many scholars have critiqued Agamben's propositions. Debarati Sanyal offers a sustained criticism in her 'A Soccer Match in Auschwitz: Passing Culpability in Holocaust Criticism', *Representations* 79 (2002), 1–27. She also references Claudine Kahan and Philippe Mesnard, *Giorgio Agamben à l'épreuve d'Auschwitz* (Paris, 2001). All criticisms aim at the problematic relation between the historical reality and specificity of the camps such as Auschwitz and the identification of a logic which can occur historically in one form but also inform and translate into other instances.

29. 'I must repeat: we, the survivors are not the true witnesses ... We the survivors are not only an exiguous minority but also an anomalous minority: we are those who by their prevarication or abilities or good luck did not touch bottom. Those who did, those who saw the Gorgon, have not returned to tell about it or have returned mute, but they are the "Muselmänner", the submerged, the complete witnesses, the ones whose depositions would have general significance. They are the rule and we are the exception.' (Primo Levi, *The Drowned and the Saved*, pp. 83–4).

30. Agamben, *Homo Sacer: Sovereign Power and Bare Life*, p. 174.

31. In his study *States of Exception*, [2003] trans. Kevin Attell (Chicago: University of Chicago Press, 2005), p. 3, written after the invasion of Iraq, Agamben extends his thesis to the study of the order for 'indefinite detention' declared by President Bush on 13 November 2001.

32. David Rousset wrote a series of articles in 1945 for Maurice Nadeau in *La Revue Internationale* which appeared as a volume, *L'Univers concentrationnaire* (Paris: Editions de Pavois, 1946); translated as *The Other Kingdom*, trans. Ramon Guthrie

(New York: Reynal and Hitchcock, 1947), and reissued in 1951 as *A World Apart*. He was the first to use the term 'Gulag' in French to introduce the Stalinist labour camps to French public awareness. In 1949 he instituted with other survivors of the Nazi concentration camps the *International Commission Against Concentrationary Regimes*.

33. David Rousset, *The Other Kingdom*, p. 173.
34. Hirsch, *Afterimage*, p. 28, citing Charles K. Krantz 'Alain Resnais' *Night and Fog*: a Historical and Cultural Analysis', *Holocaust Studies Annual* 3 (1985), p. 109 and David Weinberg, 'France' in *The World Reacts to the Holocaust*, ed. David S. Wyman (Baltimore: Johns Hopkins University Press, 1996), p. 15.
35. Raskin, Nuit et Brouillard, pp. 15–17.
36. Charlotte Delbo's trilogy of writings, which were collectively published as *Auschwitz et après* were written immediately after her return from Ravensbrück but were not published until 1970. They were translated by Rose C. Lamont for an English edition: *Auschwitz and After* (New Haven: Yale University Press) in 1995. See also Geneviève de Gaulle-Anthonioz, *La traversée de la nuit* (Paris: Editions du Seuil, 1998), a memoir about de Gaulle's niece, who was deported to Ravensbrück, written only 50 years later.
37. Henry Rousso, *The Vichy Syndrome: History and Memory in France since 1944*, trans. Arthur Goldhammer (Cambridge, MA: Harvard University Press, 1994).
38. Saul Friedlander, *Probing the Limits of Representation: Nazism and the 'Final Solution'* (Cambridge, MA: Harvard University Press, 1992).
39. Theodor Adorno, 'Commitment', in *The Essential Frankfurt School Reader*, ed. Andrew Arato and Eike Gebhardt (Oxford: Basil Blackwell, 1978), pp. 313–15. 'Even the most extreme consciousness of doom threatens to degenerate into idle chatter. Cultural criticism finds itself faced with the final stage of the dialectic of culture and barbarism. To write poetry after Auschwitz is barbaric. And this corrodes even the knowledge of why it has become impossible to write poetry today. Absolute reification, which presupposed intellectual progress as one of its elements, is now preparing to absorb the mind entirely. Critical intelligence cannot be equal to this challenge as long as it confines itself to self-satisfied contemplation,' 'Cultural Criticism' [1949] is reprinted in *Prisms*, trans. Samuel and Shierry Weber (Cambridge, MA: MIT Press, 1997), p. 34.
40. Jean Cayrol, 'Les rêves concentrationnaires', *Les Temps Modernes*, 36 (September, 1948). In Kafka's short story *The Penal Colony* published in 1914, a visiting researcher is told about a machine, no longer in use in the colony, which brought about the death of the condemned by carving the script of his sentence onto his skin over a period of 12 hours.
41. Zygmunt Bauman, *Modernity and the Holocaust* (Cambridge: Polity Press, 1989).
42. The most careful exploration of the links between colonial-imperial racism and Nazism is offered in Paul Gilroy, *Between Camps; Nations, Cultures and the Allure of Race* (London: Allen Lane, 2000). See especially Chapter 4: 'Hitler wore Khakis.'
43. Rousset, *The Other Kingdom*, p. 168.
44. Rousset, *The Other Kingdom*, p. 168
45. Rousset, *The Other Kingdom*, p. 169.
46. Rousset, *The Other Kingdom*, p. 169.
47. Rousset, *The Other Kingdom*, p. 171. This is one of the challenges also posed by Imre Kertesz in his *Fatelessness*, written between 1960 and 1973, finally published in 1975 and translated in 1992. In this semi-autobiographical novel of the author's

experiences as a fifteen-year-old Hungarian Jewish boy sent first to Auschwitz and then to Buchenwald, Kertesz remembers moments of 'happiness' experienced by inmates just before sunset, between exhausting work and minimal rations and dreadful sleep. He mourns the intensity of that experience when he returns and cannot communicate why this is the abiding memory. Such experiences as those that Rousset and Kertesz report indicate the impossibility of the non-concentrationnee fully grasping this other world.

48. Rousset, *The Other Kingdom*, p. 171.
49. Rousset, *The Other Kingdom*, p. 172.
50. Rousset, *The Other Kingdom*, p. 173.
51. Arendt, 'The Concentration Camps' *Partisan Review,* XV (1948), p. 743.
52. Arendt, 'The Concentration Camps', p. 744.
53. Arendt, 'The Concentration Camps', p. 744.
54. Arendt, 'The Concentration Camps', p. 744.
55. Eugen Kogon, *Der SS Staat* [1950] translated by Heinz Norden as *The Theory and Practice of Hell: The German Concentration Camps and the System Behind Them* (New York: Farrer, Strauss and Giroux, 1950). Arendt also drew on United States Office of Chief of Counsel for the Prosecution of Axis Criminality, *Nazi Conspiracy and Aggression*/Office of United States Chief of Counsel for Prosecution of Axis Criminality. Washington, DC: US GPO, 1946.
56. Arendt, 'Social Science Techniques and the Study of Concentration Camps', p. 240.
57. Arendt, 'Social Science Techniques and the Study of Concentration Camps', p. 240.
58. Hannah Arendt, *The Human Condition* (Chicago: University of Chicago Press, 1958), p. 9.
59. Hannah Arendt, *The Human Condition*.
60. Giorgio Agamben, *The Remnants of Auschwitz*, trans. Daniel Heller-Roazen (New York: Zone Books, 1999).
61. The phrase 'everything is possible' is widely known from Arendt's *Origins of Totalitarianism* (1951), although it was first used by Rousset. On the significance of the phrase in Arendt's elaborated political theses about totalitarianism as opposed to its precedent, imperialism, see Patricia Owens, 'Humanity, Sovereignty and the Camps', *International Politics* 45 (2008) 522–30 in which Owens emphasizes the difference between camps created with the imperialist justification 'everything is permitted' and Nazi concentration/extermination camps that put into practice 'everything is possible'.
62. Agamben, *Homo Sacer: Sovereign Power and Bare Life*, p. 170.
63. Michel Pateau, 'Avant-propos' to Jean Cayrol, *Nuit et Brouillard* (Paris: Librairie Fayard, 1997), p. 9. *Dispositif* means a contrivance or device: a warning device.
64. The linking of trauma to culture has generated heated debate amongst historians. For a critical rebuke, see Wulf Kansteiner, 'Genealogy of a Category Mistake: A Critical Intellectual History of the Cultural Trauma Metaphor', *Rethinking History* 8:2 (2004), 193–222.
65. For the fullest and most recent historical analysis of the making of this film, see Sylvie Lindeperg, *Nuit et Brouillard: Un Film dans l'Histoire* (Paris: Odile Jacob, 2007).
66. Sylvie Lindeperg, *Nuit et Brouillard: Un film dans l'histoire*, pp. 119–21.
67. Christian Delage, '*Nuit et Brouillard*: a Turning Point in the History and Memory of the Holocaust' in *Holocaust and the Moving Image: Representations in Film and Television since 1933*, ed. Toby Haggith and Joanna Newman (London: Wallflower

Press, 2005), p. 134: 'The last cut was made without any modifications to the images and on the sole initiative of Cayrol, who was the final arbiter in the chain of collective decisions in the making of the film.' Delage tracks the text of the screenplay to the final spoken commentary, noting the removal, on Cayrol's poetic initiative, of Resnais's initial synoptic reference to ' "the definitive solution to the Jewish problem" decided upon in 1942'.

68. Raskin, *Nuit et Brouillard by Alan Resnais*, p. 35.

69. Jean Cayrol, *Le Monde*, 11 April 1956, reprinted in Raskin, *Nuit et Brouillard*, p. 38. See also Jean Cayrol, 'Nous avons conçu *Nuit et Brouillard* comme un dispositif d'alerte', *Les Lettres françaises* 606 (9 February 1956), Richard Raskin, *Nuit et Brouillard*, p. 137.

70. The film was commercially exhibited in France and then distributed in Germany with a translation of Cayrol's text by the poet Paul Celan. The film was screened in Britain at the National Film Theatre in December 1956 but was not distributed commercially until 1960. In the United States it was first screened on 7 December 1960 (the anniversary of both the *Nacht und Nebel* decree and the first murders by gassing of Jewish Europeans at Chelmno) by the film society Cinema 16, which was slated to show *Les statues meurent aussi* by Resnais and Marker. This was withdrawn because of its political interpretation of colonialism and *Night and Fog* was screened instead. The film was not finally commercially screened in the USA until 1962. See essays by Judith Peterson, 'A Little-known Classic: *Night and Fog* in Britain' and Warren Lubline, 'The Trajectory of *Night and Fog* in the USA', both in Van der Knapp, *Uncovering the Holocaust*: 106–28 and 149–64, respectively.

71. Richard Raskin, 'Interview with Alain Resnais', 18 February 1986, in Raskin, *Nuit et Brouillard*, p. 53.

72. Arendt's three volumes which compose *The Origins of Totalitarianism* were not translated into French until 1972 (Vol. 3: *Le Totalitarisme*), 1973 (Vol. 1: *L'Anti-Sémitisme*) and 1982 (Vol. 2: *L'Impérialisme*).

73. Alfons Söllner, 'Hannah Arendt's *The Origins of Totalitarianism* in its Original Context', *European Journal of Political Theory* 3:2 (2004), 219–38.

74. Claude Lanzmann, 'Seminar with Claude Lanzmann', *Yale French Studies* 79:96 (1991), 82–99; see also 'The Obscenity of Understanding: An Evening with Claude Lanzmann', in *Trauma: Explorations in Memory*, ed. Cathy Caruth (Baltimore: Johns Hopkins University Press, 1995), 200–20.

75. Susan Sontag, *On Photography* (London: Penguin Books, 1977), pp. 19–20.

76. Susan Sontag, *On Photography*, p. 20.

77. For an excellent overview of this debate in France, see Libby Saxton, *Haunted Images: Film, Ethics, Testimony and the Holocaust* (London and New York: Wallflower Press, 2008).

78. Jacques Rancière, 'S'il y a de l'irreprésentable?', *Genre Humain* 36 (2001), 81–102; reprinted as 'Are Some Things Unrepresentable?' in Jacques Rancière, *The Future of the Image*, trans. Gregory Elliott (London: Verso, 2007), 109–38.

79. Jacques Rancière, *The Future of the Image*, p. 126.

80. Jacques Rancière, *The Future of the Image*, p. 128.

81. For a fuller discussion of this point, see Max Silverman, 'Horror and the Everyday in Post-Holocaust France: *Nuit et Brouillard* and Concentrationary Art', *French Cultural Studies* 17:1 (2006) 5–18.

82. Max Silverman, 'Horror and the Everyday in Post-Holocaust France', p. 9.

83. Jacques Rancière, 'Is History a Form of Fiction?' in *The Politics of Aesthetics: The Distribution of the Sensible* [2000] trans. Gabriel Rockhill (London: Continuum, 2004), p. 36.
84. Jacques Rancière, 'Is History a Form of Fiction?', p. 38.
85. For a comparative study of gender and representation in Lanzmann's *Shoah*, see Marianne Hirsch and Leo Spitzer, 'Gendered Translations: Claude Lanzmann's *Shoah*' in *Gendering War Talk* ed. Miriam Cooke and Angela Woollacott (Princeton: Princeton University Press, 1993), pp. 3–19. See also Griselda Pollock, 'Photographing Atrocity: Becoming Iconic?', in *Photographing Atrocity*, ed. Jay Prosser, Nancy Miller and Mick Gidley, (London: Reaktion Books, 2011).
86. Authors' translation. For another version, see Robert Hughes, ed., *Film: Book 2: Films of Peace and War* (New York: Grove Press, 1962), p. 255.

CHAPTER 1

Night and Fog:
A History of Gazes

SYLVIE LINDEPERG

Writing a historical analysis of the film *Night and Fog* presents several challenges
to the film historian – developing the ideas on the fate and migration of
archives which I broached in my book *Clio de 5 à 7*, implementing a 'history
of gazes', and gaining a historian's understanding of the question of the work
of art.[1] In my book-length study of Resnais's film, published in French in
2007, I resolved these challenges through the manner in which I structured
the presentation of material and through the conclusions I was able to draw
from my extensive examination of the archives, documents, and visits.[2] In this
chapter, in which I wish to present the main lines of my model of historical
film analysis, I will retrace that structure and present the key conclusions at
which I arrived. What I set out to produce is not so much a monograph on
Alain Resnais's documentary film as a 'micro-history in movement', which
consists in slowly and carefully observing the film and then displacing it in
space and time.[3]

In a stimulating text on Michelangelo Antonioni's *Blow-up* (1966),
Jacques Revel establishes an analogy between the process of micro-history and
that of the main character's investigation, which is set in motion by some
seemingly insignificant photographs taken in a London park. Thus, the
historian tells us, 'is constituted a corpus that makes a story, or rather several
stories, possible, since every time a photograph is printed anew, it discloses a
different, hitherto invisible, reality that engenders a new plot'.[4] My book is
marked by these dynamics of stories generated by images being printed,
re-framed and enlarged, and meanings and interpretations branching off into
different directions, led by the interplay of many different gazes.

The main historical question is how did *Night and Fog* come into being. It is necessary to explore the mysteries of its creation and penetrate the 'black box' of its production. Once the film was completed, the questions to be addressed are how *Night and Fog* was seen, how perceptions of the film were brought into play in different national contexts, and how they have shifted with time. The film's longevity and the international scope of its distribution have made it a 'portable *lieu de mémoire*' (site of memory), in the strongest sense of the term, or, to borrow the expression of Ruth Klüger, a 'timescape', intersected by the many issues at stake.[5]

In writing a historical study of this film's production and reception, questions of writing and narrative construction I was confronted with. The study of the film evolved into a two-part portrait of the historian Olga Wormser-Migot, who served as Resnais's adviser and his inspiration in all the questions related to the history of the deportation. I followed the thread of Olga Wormser-Migot's perception of the historical events while pondering the oft-debated question of how the film was written, what historical knowledge underpinned the writing, and what issues of memory formed it. I was unable to solve what seemed puzzling to me at the time: the way the scenario fluctuated, the changes in point of view, and above all, the gap between what some of the images *seemed* to mean and what the commentary of the film, written by Jean Cayrol, did not say. The bird's-eye view approach of drawing up an inventory, as it were, of the body of historical knowledge existing at the time and the domination of memory did not work. So I went back to look at the problem from the inside, trying to penetrate the heart of what Michel de Certeau calls 'the historiographical operation'.[6]

It was while studying Olga Wormser-Migot's personal and professional background at closer range – her first confrontations with the deportation, her discoveries and assumptions about the concentration camp system – that I began to understand. Olga Wormser-Migot's knowledge and reading had nourished *Night and Fog*, but her hesitations and contradictions had also filtered into the film. My initial thinking was wrong then; I had assumed that *Night and Fog* conformed to the principle of most historical films: as a rule, when historians are brought in to act as advisers to filmmakers, they arrive with a finished, solidly constructed work which they put at the service of the staging and construction of a filmed account. In the case of *Night and Fog*, however, the film was not the fruit of an accomplished work; it was actually the rough draft and first summary of a still-evolving history.

In *Blow-up* it is the desire and the gaze of the female partner of the couple *in* and *on* the photograph that give the investigation its momentum. The woman's need to recover the film raises a question. The point from which she observes within the photograph reveals another scene, the scene of a crime at which the photographer was present without seeing. It is because the thread of Olga Wormser-Migot's perception allowed me to see *Night and Fog* differently that I decided to construct my book with her portrait as its core.

Creation: the film as palimpsest

It was important to trace the creation of the film, laying particular emphasis on certain discoveries and on the archival documents that made them possible.

The plan for a film about the deportation was launched in November 1954 by Olga Wormser together with Henri Michel, secretary of the *Comité d'Histoire de la Deuxième Guerre mondiale*, a government commission assigned to document and study the history of the Second World War. The two historians made the announcement at the inauguration of '*Résistance, Libération, Déportation*', an exhibition organized in Paris on the tenth anniversary of the liberation. This exhibition played an important role to the extent that it served as a documentary collection for the film *Night and Fog*.

My first discovery had to do with the role played in the launching of the project by an agency that remained very discreet and as a result was either unknown or ignored. The initiative behind the film was, in fact, essentially due to the *Réseau du Souvenir* (network of remembrance), an association of former deportees belonging to the French Resistance, founded in 1952 for the purpose of promoting the memory of the deportation. During the 1950s the *Réseau* was behind many initiatives: it established a national Deportation Day, made the decision to erect the Memorial to the Martyrs of the Deportation in Paris, and published *Tragédie de la Déportation*, an anthology of first person accounts of former deportees collected by Henri Michel and Olga Wormser.[7] In 1954 the *Réseau*'s priority was to reach the generation of young people who had not lived through the occupation and seemed to know nothing about it. For the members of the association, film was the ideal medium through which to reach the young, and they considered it logical to ask the state education system to participate in funding the film and to be partly responsible for distributing it.

Discovering the role of the *Réseau du Souvenir* gave me a better grasp of the origin and characteristics of the commissioning of the film. Three points stand out: first, the issues of history and memory were interwoven; second, the definition of the Deportation established the hegemony of the figure of the deportee-patriot-resistance fighter, as can be seen by the film's working title, *Résistance et Déportation*; and lastly, the association's members advocated a conception of art as monumental and commemorative that was at odds with Resnais's work.

This brings me to the point where Argos producer Anatole Dauman was contacted by Henri Michel and became involved in the project. This marked the emergence of the project as art. Dauman stressed that if the film was to reach the public it had to be sustained by a lofty formal artistic ambition. Dauman first approached Nicole Vedrès (1911–65); when she declined, he offered the film to Alain Resnais. After the ensuing negotiations, the terms of which are now well known, Resnais accepted.

Three cinematic techniques were recommended in the terms of the contract signed with the filmmaker: an iconographic part created from documents, illustrated by diagrams or items constituting authentic souvenirs from the deportation; a second part consisting of editing from shots borrowed from the French film institute or foreign film libraries; and a third part created from shots taken directly on the site of the deportation.[8] The first two components refer back to a tried and tested model of the historical film. The reference to memorabilia can be explained by the desire to make use of the collection in the Resistance-Liberation-Deportation exhibition in Paris; it confirms the relic-like aspect of the work commissioned by the *Réseau du Souvenir*.

The shooting *in situ*, on the other hand, establishes the originality of the project. Resnais went even further by suggesting to Dauman that the sequences shot on location be filmed in colour, which would be more expensive. In February 1954 Henri Michel informed the members of the *Réseau* of the shooting locations. Shooting would be done in Struthof, Mauthausen (to which the poet Jean Cayrol had been deported), Auschwitz-Birkenau and Majdanek.[9]

Shooting in Auschwitz-Birkenau and Majdanek, however, required substantial financial aid from Poland. This support was acquired after lengthy negotiation. When I examined the budgets and financial documents of Argos Films, I discovered that the Poles had funded close to half of the cost. This substantial contribution went unnoticed because the co-production was disguised as an advance on the distribution rights in Eastern European countries.[10] The Polish aid was absolutely decisive: contrary to the initial intentions, all the filming ended up being done in Auschwitz-Birkenau and Majdanek; in addition, the Polish central cinematography institute lent the filming team many archival documents which profoundly altered the face of the film.

Crossing over to the East: documentary research and screenplay

The process of collecting archival documents had begun in the spring of 1955 using exhibition catalogues, photograph and film collections of associations of former deportees, and the resources of the *Centre de documentation juive contemporaine*, the contemporary Jewish documentation centre of the Paris Holocaust memorial museum. The filmmaker and his two advisers, Michel and Wormser, then viewed the footage on the liberation of the camps that the news firm *Actualités Françaises* had edited in the spring of 1945. But the French military film service refused to grant them the use of the shots they had selected,[11] and the Imperial War Museum of London barred them from access to its archives.[12] Resnais, Michel and Wormser then went to the Netherlands Institute for War Documentation, where they found footage filmed by the British during the liberation of Bergen-Belsen. These sequences provided the bulk of the shots in the last part of the film. Their most significant find was footage shot in the Dutch transit camp of Westerbork on 19 May 1944, showing the convoy of Jews, Roma and Sinti boarding the trains and leaving for Auschwitz.[13]

The progressive opening up of the question of genocide can be seen more confusedly in the stages of the screenwriting, which was taking place at the same time. The first synopsis was written by the two historians starting in February 1955, even before Resnais became involved.[14] This first version was copied from the table of contents of the anthology *Tragédie de la Déportation*. It followed the ordeal of a deportee from France step by step and put the emphasis on survivors' accounts. In conformity with the commissioning of the film, it is the concentration camp model and the figure of the deported resistance fighter that predominate in this synopsis and the subsequent ones. In July 1955 Resnais drafted a screenplay based on these outlines, working in close collaboration with Wormser.[15] The new text introduced the role of the camera and outlined the form of the future film; it also had a more pronounced historical ambition: to explain the concentration camp system and relate its history.

The successive ordeals of the deportee were now punctuated by the insertion of chronological markers about the birth and development of the concentration camp system. The screenplay begins in 1933 with the construction of the first camps in Nazi Germany; then the story's centre of gravity shifts to Auschwitz-Birkenau. Drawing from Olga Wormser's research, the script underscores the turning point of 1942 that marked a new phase in the history of the concentration camp system: using camp prisoners as slave labour in the service of the war economy. This measure also had significant consequences for the destruction of the Jews of Europe. From that point on, 'selections' were carried out and only those Jews who were declared fit for work entered the camps, while the majority went straight to the gas chambers. In 1942 the hitherto unconnected worlds of concentration camps and killing centres met in one place, Auschwitz-Birkenau. The combined camps were mentioned in one paragraph of the July screenplay that turns on Himmler's inspection of Auschwitz in the summer of 1942: the SS Reichsführer first toured the I G Farben factory in Monowitz and then watched the gassing of Dutch Jews in Birkenau.

The extermination of the Jews is explicitly mentioned in this passage. But this important development in the script was thwarted by Jean Cayrol's commentary, which describes this same sequence in very allusive terms, omitting any mention of the victims' Jewish identity and blotting out the explicit reference to the Final Solution. The marginal but very real place given in the screenplay to the account of the genocide of the Jews was doubly reinforced by the stay in Poland.

Shooting in Poland: the experience of perception

The filmmaker and the two historians arrived in Warsaw in September 1955. There they researched the collection of the Jewish Historical Institute and chose some photographs, including the one from the Auschwitz Album depicting the 'selection' of the transport of Hungarian Jews in Birkenau (Plate 32), the now iconic photograph of the little Warsaw ghetto boy being arrested, a few shots of the camps under construction and several photographs of executions, by the *Einsatzgruppen* in particular.

At the Documentary Film Studio they viewed Soviet and Polish films pre-selected by the filmmaker Wanda Jakubowska, a former Auschwitz inmate who in 1947 had made the film *Ostatni Etap (The Last Stage,* aka *The Last Stop)*, the first fictional work filmed in Birkenau.[16] The documentary research ended in the collections of the camp museums, in particular the one in Auschwitz, where they found the series of photographs of Himmler's visit in July 1942 and the four taken clandestinely by the members of the *Sonderkommando*. The research done in Poland thus considerably reinforced the presence in the film of shots and photographs referring to the extermination of European Jewry.

The filming began on 28 September in Auschwitz and continued in Majdanek from 7 to 10 October. The main stages may be reconstructed thanks to the correspondence of the Argos firm, production documents, first-person accounts of production team members, and the script notes kept by assistant director André Heinrich. The discrepancies between the film and the July screenplay, which was based on the idea that all Nazi camps were interchangeable, allow us to gauge the impact the visit to the sites had on Resnais.

For the filmmaker the filming was indeed an initial phase of elucidation; it further reinforced the centrality of Auschwitz-Birkenau and inaugurated a form – tracking shots in colour moving at walking pace inside the camps and along their peripheries. On site, Resnais gauged the extent of the differences between Auschwitz I and Birkenau, between the well-maintained blocks of the museum-camp at Auschwitz I and the desolate site overgrown with weeds and cluttered with motley objects at Birkenau.[17] As a result of his reassessment, Resnais altered the screenplay and the filming plan and opted to shoot the epilogue entirely in Birkenau, which in the film becomes a trenchant metaphor for oblivion.

But when I myself made the trip to Auschwitz, I was able to confirm my intuition that Resnais had also filmed certain sequences in the museum blocks in black and white: the pan of the Kapo's room, the vertical tracking shot of a puppet and the long bleak shot of the huge pile of women's hair preserved in Block 4 (Plate 39).[18] These shots, which for years were thought to be archival images, are precious indications of Resnais's vision and his desire to divert the commission he had been given. The *Réseau du Souvenir* had entrusted the artist with the mission of 'transforming remembrance into a monument and memory into a memorial'.[19] By filming objects and relics in black and white, thus placing them in the layer of an impenetrable past, Resnais expressed his rejection of the museographical approach to art and history, an attitude he would convey in his film *Hiroshima Mon Amour* several years later with a *mise en abyme* in the opening sequences.

To these shots of objects, which corresponded to the iconographic component of the film, Resnais added other shots, also in black and white, filmed outside Auschwitz and Birkenau, such as the long tracking shot on the main entrance to Auschwitz I (Plate 19). This sophisticated shot with its expressionist lighting belongs to an imaginative cinematographic world inspired by Czech filmmaker Alfred Radok's fictional work on the ghetto-camp of Theresienstadt, *Daleka Cesta* (1949: *The Long Journey*, aka *The Distant Journey*), and by Jakubowska's *The Last Stage*, from which Resnais selected two shots for *Night and Fog*.

The follow shot acquired its full meaning when it came time for editing. It was placed at the point in the film when the narrator mentions the 'night-time scenes the Nazis so loved to stage', after the ground had been prepared for it by stock footage of the Westerbork camp and the first extract from *The Last Stage* showing the arrival of a transport at night (Plate 17). This night-time follow shot fleetingly becomes part of another category of the visible. There is a striking contrast with the colour shot that precedes it; a dolly in along the train tracks revealing, in the distance, the porch entrance of Birkenau standing out against the emptiness. The editing of this footage expresses, even to the very composition of overflow and emptiness, the contrast between the sites of Auschwitz I and Birkenau which gripped Resnais during his stay on the site. Perhaps through this contrast he sensed, without being clearly conscious of it, the difference between two events – the phenomena of the concentration camps and the destruction of the Jews of Europe. This remark brings us to the question of editing.

The editing darkroom

Analysing this essential stage of Resnais's work gave me the opportunity to revisit the solutions he adopted for reducing the heterogeneity of his source materials – the heterogeneity between photographs and filmed shots, between different generations of archives (the Nazi period and the liberation), and between different categories of images (stock shots, shots filmed by Resnais in black and white, fictional shots borrowed from Jakubowska). By opting for a strongly pronounced alternation of rhythm to intensify the chromatic alternation between colour shots and black and white images, Resnais made the black and white shots homogeneous, assigned them uniformly to the layer of the past, and fitted the whole movement of the film into the present, in perfect harmony with the spirit of Jean Cayrol's commentary.

In my analysis of these aesthetic decisions, I focussed on a precious document – the editorial script.[20] This is a text that, for each of the film's shots, gives the location where research was done, a caption and often a description of the image. Not only does this document enable us to find the origin of the different shots that were edited, it also offers a revealing look at the state of knowledge about images of the camps at the time of the film's making. The editorial script tells us how the production team viewed the assembled shots and photographs. It helps us understand the questions the team members asked – and those they did not ask but that we ask today.

I shall take just one example, which concerns the series of now famous photographs taken clandestinely in August 1944 by the members of the *Sonderkommando* in Birkenau. One of the two photographs depicting the process of gassing and cremation is edited into *Night and Fog* (Plate 38). In the editorial script the caption reads '*Sonderkommando*: clandestine photograph Schmoulewski Auschwitz Museum.' This means that in 1955 the essential information was known, even if the photograph is attributed to David Szmulewski and not to a Greek Jew named Alex, which is the current historical attribution. Yet the photograph is not given the value that we attach to it today. Resnais does not by any means consider it in its absolute rarity and uniqueness. To do so would have required making a clear distinction between concentration camps and killing centres, thinking out these two events in their similarities and their radical differences, and detecting the contrast between the substantial corpus of images taken in the concentration camps and the virtual absence of images of the killing centres. The gesture of the clandestine photographer had to be endowed with a symbolic and testimonial value, as it was by Georges Didi-Huberman, and it had to be considered an act of resistance to the policy of secrecy and the invisibility of the genocide of the Jews.[21] Finally, attention had to be paid to the question of the victims' viewpoint. These questions were not asked in 1955, so for the production team the *Sonderkommando*'s photographs seemed interchangeable with other images, such as those taken by the *Einsatzgruppen*. Resnais chose the cremation photograph only for what it *showed* – an open-air pyre that enabled him to recall the final stage of the killing of the deportees.

Another equally rich source was the film rushes that were left at the *Comité d'histoire* and later transferred to the *Institut d'histoire du temps présent* (Institute of the History of the Present). An examination of these shots reveals

Figure 1.1 Rushes for *Night and Fog*: two of Resnais's experimental reframings of one of the four photographs taken clandestinely by 'Alex', a Greek-Jewish member of the Sonderkommando of Auschwitz-Birkenau, August 1994, showing naked women being driven into a gas chamber – the original is in Auschwitz Museum, Poland (Collection Argos Films)

that Resnais had selected a second photograph in the series of four that were taken by the *Sonderkommando* – the photograph of the naked women in the woods of Birkenau being driven towards the gas chamber from inside whose doorway the photograph was secretly taken. In the rushes one discovers the director's unsuccessful attempt to reframe and re-centre this photo that had been shot by guesswork because of the immense danger of taking any photograph during this process (Fig. 1.1). This insight into the filmmaker in action helps us understand the very prosaic reasons that led him to forego this photograph that he could not manage to reframe and to which, moreover, he attributed no particular uniqueness.

The editing was carried out in symbiosis with the drafting of the commentary, which came up against the weakness of Jean Cayrol, who at first was incapable of looking at and confronting the archival images collected by Resnais. Chris Marker then lent his support by rewriting the poet's first text, which was not in sync with the images. This intermediary version of the commentary helped Cayrol return to the editing room. The final commentary of *Night and Fog* bears the traces of this dual paternity: the structure is definitely Marker's but the words and thoughts are Cayrol's. It is at the very end of my research that I found an intermediary version of the commentary that had not been contributed to the Cayrol archives and bore the trace of this plural writing, in which Wormser also took part.[22]

The German voice of the music

There are two points I should like to make regarding the score. The first is the fact that the famous string prelude that is the film's musical signature, as it were, is not an original piece. It was composed by Hanns Eisler in 1954 for

East German playwright Johannes Becher's tragic play *Winterschlacht*. As Albrecht Dümling has shown, the prelude was composed by Eisler in reference to Horatio's soliloquy in *Hamlet*.[23] I found this information all the more interesting since in his book on the memory of Nazism in Germany, Michael Schneider uses the theme of Hamlet's melancholy to analyse the conflict of generations that emerged in West Germany in the late 1960s.[24] It is no coincidence that the musical theme now associated in audiences' minds with Resnais's film is heard in the opening of Alexander Kluge's film *Die Patriotin* (1979, *The Patriotic Woman*), a counter-history of Germany in which the main character, a young history teacher, tries to unearth the concealed episodes of the German past using a metaphorical shovel.

This German voice of the music of *Night and Fog*, which examines the Nazi past and the question of German guilt, is found in another passage of the film's score, in the Westerbork sequences. Over the images of the transport being boarded the composer offers a pastiche of the German national anthem. He purposely breaks the melodic line of the '*Lied der Deutschen*' and eliminates the string accompaniment, keeping only the rhythmical structures.

With this passage Eisler offered an intentional caricature of a song that had been banned in 1945 by the Allied Occupation Forces and was later reinstated, minus its first two couplets, as the national anthem of West Germany. The pastiche could refer not only to the song perverted by the Nazis but also to the song belonging to West Germany, where the economic requirements of reconstruction had outweighed the political requirements of denazification. The East German composer's rough handling of '*Lied der Deutschen*' was not to Bonn's liking: in the West German copies of *Night and Fog* distributed by the *Bundeszentrale für Heimatdienst*, the musical passage that opens the Westerbork sequence was deleted, giving way to silence. This pastiche was all the more irritating to the West as Eisler had composed the music of the East German national anthem to lyrics by Johannes Becher.

Passages and migrations

I shall now introduce several examples that underscore the process of reinterpretation, sometimes distortion, of the original work, carried out in different countries and in different times.

The translation battle in Germany

How was the film used and screened following its displaced appearance at the Cannes Film Festival? What can we learn from the test screenings organized in Bonn and Berlin in 1956, and the three German versions of *Night and Fog*?

Paul Celan's translation of Cayrol's commentary for West Germany has already been analysed in depth.[25] We know that the translator subtly reintroduced the genocide of the Jews, which had been erased in Cayrol's text: for example he transformed the phrase 'old concentration camp monster' into *Rassenwahn*: 'racial madness'. Celan refused to re-use certain expressions in the language of the Third Reich in his translation. Finally, he made additions to the text to denounce the unfinished work of denazification in West Germany.

But this version was not released in East Germany: Veb-Defa decided to have it retranslated, this time by Henryk Keisch in 1958. In the first versions of this commentary, we notice glaring distortions.[26] The most obvious one was the translation of the epilogue in which Cayrol's last lines warning his contemporaries of the coming of new perpetrators and the 'endless cry' of the victims were intentionally mistranslated to read: 'In one part of the world [implying the Eastern bloc] the dead have ceased crying out because the chaff has been uprooted.' This translation distortion made it possible to divert attention from the Soviet camps and at the same time to fit the text into the context of the Cold War and the conflict between the two Germanies by presenting East Germany as the heir to the struggle against fascism. The *Night and Fog* team rejected this translation and Veb-Defa was forced to back down.

But Veb-Defa had its revenge in a second version – the third in the German language.[27] This version is a clandestine 1974 remake produced by East German television as part of a programme entitled '*Filme contra Faschismus*'. Cayrol's text was translated this time by Evelin Matschke. It is a vague plagiary and a very short summary of the original text. For one thing, the new commentary brings back the distorted epilogue, which is mistranslated as: 'Nine million dead wander in this landscape; their cries will defy oblivion.' Furthermore, the text makes a point of establishing that fascism is in collusion with capitalism. Matschke weaves the metaphor of industrial death, which is reinforced, this time intentionally, by the lack of synchronization between image and commentary. This is the case for the British images of the bulldozer pushing corpses towards the ditches of Bergen-Belsen. In *Night and Fog* these unbearable images are placed in their context, the liberation of the camps by the Allies. In the East German version, however, the use of the bulldozer is attributed to the Nazis and the British images are accompanied by a sentence that does not appear in the original: 'The perpetrators produce mountains of corpses.' Thus the image is twisted into a metaphor of the industrialization of death and reinforces the interpretation of Nazism and fascism as the ultimate stage of capitalism.

But East Germany was not the only country that distorted the work of Alain Resnais in the context of the conflict between East and West.

The film in kit form in the US

In 1959 the filmmaker and producer Nico Papatakis tried in vain to have *Night and Fog* distributed in the US. In 1960 he received a rather unusual offer from an independent chain, the Metropolitan Broadcasting Corporation, which wanted to use *Night and Fog* in fragments for an hour-long television programme about the deportation and the Nazi camps. The result was quite surprising: the director, Arnee Nocks, actually proceeded to re-edit all the shots in *Night and Fog* and some of the passages of Eisler's musical score.

This hybrid programme was called *Remember Us*.[28] Presented by the well-known journalist Quentin Reynolds, it borrowed the narrative and formal codes of television shows and edited documentaries. *Night and Fog* was reassembled as a kit using two procedures. In the first part of the programme Nocks appears as the announcer of a kind of TV news magazine and introduces four extracts borrowed from Resnais's film to illustrate the accounts of four witnesses. He abundantly recycles Eisler's music in a redundant fashion that is totally unfaithful to the spirit in which the composer worked. The second part lasts 20 minutes and is made up exclusively of the reassembly of all the shots of *Night and Fog* accompanied by a commentary by Reynolds which repeats entire passages of Cayrol's text (who does not feature in the credits, any more than Resnais or Eisler do). At the very end of the film this re-editing reaches a function of pure padding: on the closing credits the director just jumbles together all the shots of the film he had left.

The recycling of the Resnais film, as disastrous as it is, does enlighten us on the use of the images from *Night and Fog*. The method stems from an illustrative documentary approach that does not grant any existence of their own to visual documents and the context in which they were recorded, and thus sanctions the loss of their historical quality.

Arnee Nocks draws on *Night and Fog* as he would take from a collection of archives, even though the extracts from the film are sequences that were already edited from shots and photographs of different origins assembled on the basis of precise formal choices that make the relation to the archives a 'tertiary' one. Doing away with this gesture, the American director confers on the fragments of *Night and Fog* the status of primary sources which, as such, can be recycled in his own editing. This levelling-out also concerns Resnais's colour shots that are reproduced in the TV show in black and white. They are thus shifted in time and change status, entering the generic category of 'archival images'.

Another injustice done to the film is the transformation of this restive, fragile work into a propaganda film hurling out messages and certainties. Re-using several elements of Jean Cayrol's epilogue, Reynolds transforms the spirit of the text into a long anti-Communist diatribe:

Grass has now grown in the ...pits of Auschwitz ... but new regimes are building new camps elsewhere...Those who don't learn by history may live to see it repeated......Those who refuse to look around and not see the cruelty of new crimes, those who refuse to recall and ponder the past and the present for the sake of the future. Communism is the productive murder. Lenin, revered today as the saviour of Russia, liquidated millions and allowed millions more to starve. During the purges Russia's population fell twelve and a half per cent as late as 1954, 8 to 14 million were in Soviet labour camps ...

A last feature of *Remember US*, which was broadcast soon after Israel announced the arrest of Adolf Eichmann, is its clear refocusing on the question of the extermination of the Jews of Europe. This emphasis is illustrated by the choice of witnesses, all Jewish survivors of persecution and genocide, and the readaptation of the commentary on the turning point of 1942 and the use of gas chambers. I stressed earlier that this passage was the cause of much wavering: the reference to the Final Solution explicitly mentioned in the July screenplay had been erased by Jean Cayrol. Taking up this passage of *Night and Fog*, the commentary of *Remember US* first translates Cayrol's commentary word for word and then introduces, in the gas chamber sequence, an extract from the memoirs of Auschwitz commander Rudolph Hoess that clearly identifies the assassinated victims as Jews.

This reintroduction of the genocide of the Jews leads me to a last example of the migration of the film – precisely at the Eichmann trial which opened in Jerusalem in April 1961.

Screening in Jerusalem

Night and Fog was used again in fragments, without its musical score but with sub-titles of the American version, in the edited document that was screened in Jerusalem during the hearing of 8 June 1961. Jean-Louis Comolli suggests that in 1945 the Allied operators had filmed 'without knowing' and 'without understanding' what would be revealed in an 'after-effect of history'.[29] In Jerusalem, the 'as yet unrevealed meaning' of the films about the camps was disclosed for the first time during a silent showing, punctuated by the prosecutor's explanations, that emphasized the images relating to the extermination of the Jews.

This viewing session had been preceded, at the request of the defence, by a pre-screening of *Night and Fog* that was shown to Eichmann in its entirety. The screening was filmed by the American documentary maker Leo Hurwitz, who was in charge of recording the entire trial on video.[30] This exceptional document[31] reveals the issues at stake for Hurwitz. The recording device favours shot/reverse shot sequences; the changes of camera and the variations in the length of takes shed light on the filmmaker's intentions. First Hurwitz constructs the play of looks – between victim and oppressor – by showing the wide-eyed stare of the inmate at Vaihingen in contraposition with a close-up of Eichmann's face; and then between oppressors, by showing the fictitious face-to-face confrontation between Himmler and Eichmann. Then Hurwitz links two trials in two different eras, turning the camera back on Eichmann just after he has seen the images of the accused on trial in the immediate post-war period, each claiming in turn, 'I am not responsible.'

But the rhythm and the changes of camera also reveal Hurwitz's desire to pay tribute to Resnais by re-filming certain long sequences on the projection screen and refusing to cut them. In this regard it is interesting to point out an astonishing particularity of this document: the filming of the screening session of *Night and Fog* has 120 shot/reverse shots; but the shots that Hurwitz filmed with the camera directed onto the projection screen most often contain several shots already edited by Resnais. Now if we move from these hyper-shots of Hurwitz's to the total number of shots contained in the recording, we get a total of 307 – the exact number of shots contained in *Night and Fog.*

This amazing coincidence, no doubt unintentional, allows the recording of the viewing session to be considered as a new version of Resnais's film: a documentary of 31 minutes of a film that has become silent again, with occasional sub-titles of the American translation, into which the look of the perpetrator has been integrated under the look of a second filmmaker.

I conclude with this last example dating from 1961; but the history of the film and how it is used is not over. The film continues to be shown in school systems and television stations in France and Germany. Then there are the issues of the gradual development of a cinéaste's critical view, and the harsh criticism levelled at the film during the 1980s. Thus we arrive as the idea of the 'micro-history in movement' mentioned in the introduction. The thrust of my work on *Night and Fog* is to write the history of a film, but even more, to write history with and through this film. I strove to follow the path opened by Walter Benjamin, the precursor of micro-history, as it were, when he invited historians 'to discover in the analysis of the small individual moment the crystal of the total event'.[32]

Translated by Pauline Haas Hammel, 2009.

Notes

1. Sylvie Lindeperg, *Clio de 5 à 7. Les actualités filmées de la Libération: archives du futur* (Paris: CNRS éditions, 2000).

2. Sylvie Lindeperg, *Nuit et Brouillard. Un film dans l'histoire* (Paris: Odile Jacob, 2007). See also Sylvie Lindeperg, '*Night and Fog*': Inventing a Perspective' in *Cinema and the Shoah*, [2007], ed. Jean-Michel Frodon, trans. Anna Harris and Tom Maes (New

York: SUNY Press, 2010), pp. 63–84. See also Christian Delage, 'Nuit et Brouillard: A Turning Point in History' in The Holocaust and the Moving Image: representations in film and television since 1933, eds. Toby Haggith and Joanna Newman (London: Wallflower Press, 2005) pp. 127–39.

3. See also studies of the international reception of the film in the collection Ewout van der Knapp, ed., Uncovering the Holocaust: The International Reception of Night and Fog (London: Wallflower Press, 2006).

4. Jacques Revel, 'Un exercice de désorientation: Blow up' in De l'histoire au cinéma, ed. Antoine de Baecque (Bruxelles: Éditions Complexe, 1998).

5. Ruth Klüger, Still Alive: A Holocaust Girlhood Remembered (New York: The Feminist Press, 2001), Pierre Nora, ed., Les Lieux de Mémoire, 7 vols (Paris: Editions Gallimard, 1984–92) and Pierre Nora, 'Between Memory and History: Les Lieux de Mémoire' [1984], Representations 26 (Spring 1989), 7–25.

6. Michel de Certeau, 'The Historiographical Operation' in The Writing of History (New York: Columbia University Press, 1988).

7. Olga Wormser and Henri Michel, Tragédie de la Déportation. 1940–1945. Témoignages de survivants des camps de concentration allemands (Paris: Hachette, 1954).

8. Contract dated 24 May 1955, archives of the Institut Lumière in Lyon (Argos Films collection).

9. General assembly of the Réseau du Souvenir, 5 February 1955, Archives nationales, 72AJ2147.

10. Institut Lumière, Nuit et Brouillard collection and Archives nationales, CAC (Centre of Contemporary Archives) of Fontainebleau 1989/0538 article 945.

11. The hostility of the French military is due mainly to Alain Resnais's nefarious reputation as co-director with Chris Marker of Les Statues meurent aussi. The authorities considered this 1953 film an anti-colonialist pamphlet and its release was banned by the committee for the classification of cinematographic works.

12. See also Chapter 2 by Kay Gladstone in this volume on this matter.

13. These are sequences to which Harun Farocki devoted his film, Respite (2007).

14. Archives nationales, CAC of Fontainebleau 1989/0538 article 945.

15. Archives of IMEC (Institute of Contemporary Publishing), Jean Cayrol collection.

16. See Chapter 11 by Griselda Pollock in this volume for a brief discussion of this film.

17. See Annette Wieviorka, Auschwitz, 60 ans après (Paris: Robert Laffont, 2005).

18. See Sylvie Lindeperg, Nuit et Brouillard, pp. 94–9.

19. Declaration by Jean Cassou at general meeting of the Réseau du Souvenir of 19 December 1953 (Archives nationales, 72AJ2147).

20. Document provided by Florence Dauman (Argos Films).

21. Georges Didi-Huberman, Images in Spite of All: Four Photographs from Auschwitz (Chicago: University of Chicago Press, 2008). Didi-Huberman's article, 'Images Malgré Tout' was first published in Memoires des Camps: photographies des camps de concentration et d'extermination Nazis 1933–1999, ed. Clément Cheroux (Paris: Marval, 2001).

22. Bibliothèque nationale, Performing Arts department MY1858.

23. Albrecht Dümling, 'Musikalischer Kontrapunkt zur filmischen Darstellung des Schreckens. Hanns Eislers Musik zu Nuit et Brouillard von Alain Resnais' in Kunst und Literatur nach Auschwitz, ed. Manuel Köppen (Berlin: Erich Schmidt, 1993), pp. 113–23.

24. Michael Schneider, Den Kopf verkehrt aufgesetzt oder die melancholische Linke (Darmstadt: Luchterhand, 1981).

25. See Thomas Heck and Peter Gossens, 'Nacht und Nebel. Ein Film wird übersetzt' in *Fremde Nähe. Celan als* Übersetzer, ed. Axel Gellhaus (Marbach: Deutsche Schillergesellschaft, 1997); Alexis Nouss, 'La traduction mélancolique' (on Paul Celan) in *Psychanalyse et traduction: voies de traverse*, ed. Ginette Michaud, Études sur le texte et ses transformations, Canadian Association for Translation Studies, McGill University, IX:2, second semester 1998, p. 201; Jean-Pierre Lefebvre, 'Paul Celan traducteur des camps (on five verses of the poem "Engführung")', in 'Les Camps et la littérature. Une littérature du XXe siècle', *La Licorne* 51 (1999); Andréa Lauterwein, 'Les deux mondes, Paul Celan et Anselm Kiefer', doctoral thesis, ed. Gerald Stieg, Paris III, Dept. of German, December 2002; Sylvie Lindeperg, *Nuit et Brouillard*, pp. 182–90.

26. Archives of the Institut Lumière. See Sylvie Lindeperg, *Nuit et Brouillard*, pp. 192–9; Jörg Frieß, 'Das Blut ist geronnen. Die Münder sind verstummt? Die zwei deutschen Synchronfassungen von Nuit et Brouillard', *Filmblatt* 28 (autumn 2005), pp. 40–57.

27. Deutsches Rundfunkarchiv, Potsdam, Babelsberg.

28. This was brought to my attention by Stuart Liebman.

29. Jean-Louis Comolli, 'Fatal rendez-vous', in *Cinema and the Shoah: An Art Confronts the Tragedy of the Twentieth Century*, ed. Jean-Michel Frodon, trans. Anna Harrison and Tom Mesand (New York: SUNY Press, 2010).

30. On the filming of the Eichmann trial, see Sylvie Lindeperg and Annette Wieviorka, *Univers concentrationnaire et génocide. Voir, savoir, comprendre* (Paris: Mille et Une Nuits, 2008).

31. The film was brought back to me from Jerusalem by Annette Wieviorka.

32. Walter Benjamin, *The Arcades Project* (Cambridge, MA: Harvard University Press, 1999), p. 461.

CHAPTER 2

Memory of the Camps:
The Rescue of an Abandoned Film

KAY GLADSTONE

'Discovery' of the film

Memory of the Camps is the title allocated by the Imperial War Museum (IWM) in 1984 to an officially commissioned documentary on the liberation of the German concentration camps which was assembled in London during 1945 but abandoned before completion.[1] Five of the film's intended six reels survive in the form of a fine-cut print without titles, credits or soundtrack. In 1952, these five reels were transferred from the film vaults of the War Office to the IWM's film archive, at the same time as the Museum assumed responsibility for the permanent preservation of all the record film shot by British combat cameramen during the Second World War.

Why this film suddenly attracted so much attention in late 1983 is due to the publicity generated by a short piece in the British newspaper, *The Times*, by a journalist who had been commissioned by the main figure behind the aborted project, Sidney Bernstein, to write his biography.[2] Under the banner headline 'What Hitchcock saw, filmed — and hid. Caroline Moorehead uncovers another missing Hitchcock', the daughter of the Australian war correspondent Alan Moorehead wrote that the five reels had been compiled by Alfred Hitchcock in the summer of 1945, then filed away in the archives of the IWM and never shown.[3] What the article failed to mention was that these compiled reels, as well as the raw unedited camera rushes from which they were derived, had been accessible to historians and broadcasters ever since. Although this material was not consulted by Alain Resnais while researching *Night and Fog* (1955), it was extensively trawled by researchers working on *Genocide*, Episode 20 of the Thames Television series *The World at War* (1974).[4]

Not surprisingly the IWM was deluged with enquiries about this missing Hitchcock masterpiece, and requests from around the world to screen the film immediately followed. At that time the film had no title, being simply referred to under its file reference (F3080) or by the name of this file held at the The National Archives at Kew, *Films for Liberated Territories – Investigation of War Atrocities – Factual Film Report on German Concentration Camps*.[5] This documentation covered its production history and was as incomplete as most other Ministry of Information (MOI) files covering wartime film projects. The fact that the film had never been given a title was additional indication that the film had never been finished.

As suited a film that had originally been intended for screening to German audiences, *Memory of the Camps* was first shown at the Berlin Film Festival, on 27 February 1984. The neutral title was designed to be both commemorative and to reflect the fact that thanks to the passage of time the impact of the film on modern audiences would inevitably differ from that originally intended by the production team; commemoration of the Second World War remained, moreover, a difficult subject in Germany, a country then still strongly divided by distinct generational and ideological differences in its recollections of the war years.

The currently available digital video is a version of the intended film which was completed by WGBH Boston for the Public Broadcasting Service in the US for screening on 8 May 1985, to commemorate the fortieth anniversary of the end of the war in Europe. WGBH selected the British actor Trevor Howard to narrate the script, an undated and unsigned commentary which exactly matches a shotlist (dated 7 May 1946), both held by the IWM.[6] His measured delivery of the extraordinary text, ironic or accusatory towards the German bystanders, compassionate to their victims, appalled by the succession of atrocities authenticated beyond possibility of denial, notionally recreates for the modern viewer some of the reactions in 1945 to the discovery of the camps.

Production history

The project to compile a documentary film on German atrocities originated in February 1945 in the Psychological Warfare Division (PWD) of SHAEF (Supreme Headquarters Allied Expeditionary Force). The chief of PWD's 'Film Section, Liberated Areas' was Sidney Bernstein, who also headed the Liberated Territories Section of the Films Division within the Ministry of

Information (MOI); this had earlier been set up to show in the liberated countries of North Africa and Europe freed from Axis control British documentaries recounting the military and political struggle of the Allies against the Fascists and Nazis, as well as mainstream features.

Bernstein had since 1940 been Honorary Films Advisor to the MOI's Films Division, where he played a vital role on behalf of British propaganda by successfully promoting the distribution of documentaries in the US. As the owner and chief executive of the Granada cinema chain in the pre-war period, he had a thorough understanding of film distribution and was a man of wide cultural interests and sympathies, extending, rather unusually among Britons of the period, to a liking for Americans. He was an energetic and persuasive force, well suited to leading the joint British–US Allied project which began as an investigation into the possibility of producing a film using material already shot by the service and newsreel cameramen accompanying the British, US and Russian armies. 'This material is being collected with a view to preparing a film which will show the German atrocities committed in many parts of the world. The basic idea of the film is to present an objective report, almost like a criminal investigation report.'[7] During this initial film archival research phase, the target audience was that covered by the two sections (Allied SHAEF and British MOI) headed by Bernstein which oversaw screenings via non-theatrical or theatrical distribution to audiences in the liberated territories who had been exposed during the preceding four or five years to Nazi propaganda.[8]

This plan was suddenly transformed in early April when film of the first camps liberated by US forces advancing across Central Germany was screened in London to shocked officials.[9] Their determination to have this material publicly exhibited must have been strengthened by the subsequent British footage from Belsen, which Bernstein visited on 22 April. In filming terms, this was already 'Belsen Day 7'. British forces had liberated the camp one week previously, and the small team of cameramen and photographers of the Army Film and Photographic Unit (AFPU) were nearing the end of recording the first ten days of Belsen's freedom. Their mute film had already covered the interrogation of the commandant Josef Kramer and bulldozers burying the dead. The mass burials continued, though now the cameramen were also filming some of the survivors, bathing and delousing scenes suggesting the first steps of their slow rehabilitation.

Bernstein instantly realized the need to authenticate the date and place of these almost incredible background scenes and on the spot requested the British Movietone News sound cameraman Paul Wyand to film sound interviews with British officials and members of the German SS.[10] Bernstein was aware that two British newsreel editors had initially hesitated to screen the first American camp footage on the grounds that 'pictorially it was not entirely convincing', so his intervention at Belsen marks the start of his quest to prove beyond the possibility of all future denial the existence of the camps.

Bernstein's visit to Belsen transformed the German Atrocity Film Project. What had been initially conceived as a retrospective compilation now became a project to make a definitive film based not only on archive material but also on new and specially shot sequences. Its production basis and new main target audiences, as well as its Allied status, were promptly agreed. The film was to be made by the MOI as a combined Anglo-American production on German concentration camps on behalf of PWD SHAEF, with production work being carried out in conjunction with the US Office of War Information (OWI) Films Division. It was now primarily intended to be shown in Germany and to German prisoners of war. Other versions commentated in English and other languages would probably be prepared for showing in neutral and liberated territories, as well as in Great Britain and the United States.[11]

Bernstein himself prepared a nine-page document titled 'Material Needed for Proposed Motion Picture on German Atrocities'. He listed the main subjects to be covered as: (a) victims of German atrocities, (b) the criminals themselves, (c) testimony given by witnesses and victims, (d) physical conditions inside the camps, and their surroundings, and (e) reactions exhibited by German civilians when confronted with the evidence. Detailed notes instructed the Allied film units on the type of material required under each of these headings.

The psychological warfare purposes of the version for German audiences were defined:

(a) By showing the German people specific crimes committed by the Nazis in their name, to arouse them against the National Socialist Party and to cause them to oppose its attempts to organize terrorist or guerrilla activity under Allied occupation.

(b) By reminding the German people of their past acquiescence in the perpetration of such crimes, to make them aware that they cannot escape responsibility for them, and thus to promote German acceptance of the justice of Allied occupation measures.

The document continued that it was 'essential that the film should be factual and documented to the *n*th degree … It will have to be assumed … that in several years time the Nazis will either try to disprove the evidence or suggest that only a minority was responsible.' Cameramen were specially asked to photograph any material which would show the connection between German industry and the concentration camps – e.g. name plates on incinerators, gas chambers – and which firms built the camps.[12]

Bernstein's warnings against future Holocaust deniers were prescient, his instructions to Allied cameramen meticulous and comprehensive. Many of the instructions were, however, too late to be acted on. In the final days of the war in Europe, British and American combat cameramen had other stories to cover and for both sanitary and humanitarian reasons the camps were being cleared as rapidly as conditions allowed.

Work now began urgently within the MOI on the collation and rough-cutting of the material already available, mainly the AFPU's coverage of Belsen. Progress on the whole film, however, was held up throughout May by the slowness of the US Army Pictorial Service in providing the British with duplicate prints of American film, by bottle-necks and trade disputes in the London film laboratories, and even by the search for an editing machine.[13] So the project was hampered by severe practical difficulties at the same time as changing conditions on the ground in Germany, regularly monitored by PWD SHAEF, began to affect Allied policies towards the defeated Germans.

By June, eyewitness accounts from the western zones of occupation showed that German civilians (as well as captive audiences of German prisoners of war) had already been made fully aware via the press and radio of Nazi atrocities long before the date on which the film being specially prepared to educate them on the subject was likely to be completed; they also indicated that well before the reopening of the cinemas where the film could be screened, both German civilians and occupation officials were worried by more pressing practical matters.

The British documentary film director Basil Wright, travelling through the ruined landscape of the British Zone of Occupation to make *A Defeated People* for the MOI, could already foresee the food and other domestic difficulties the Germans were likely to face in the coming winter. He described the entrance to the military government building at Wesel which had 'a large panel covered with photographs from Belsen, which no German coming to the building can avoid seeing'. Wright noted:

> It is quite clear the sudden removal of the Nazi machine has left the Germans dazed and stupid … The colonel told me his only object is to avoid actual starvation setting in before the harvest; in his opinion the next two months are the danger points.[14]

Reporting from Berlin in June about public opinion in this city under quadripartite control, an American serving in PWD who had been in Germany since the end of March, Harry J. Schneiders, noted the changing sentiments among Berliners to their occupiers. After he had highlighted the popular appeal of the Russians' Berlin Radio Station – interesting, excellent musical selections, Russians' altruistic donation of foodstuffs – he noted that 'opinions in the past few weeks have turned against America.'

The average German is horrified about the bestial and sadistic crimes committed in the concentration camps but he does not feel that he is responsible, nor does he feel himself as a criminal ... After Mr and Mrs Kraut have enjoyed the nice program from Berlin, they turn the dial (to Radio Luxembourg, London or Voice of America) and what do they hear? All about concentration camp crimes, which at first they listened to attentively, but repeated every time it became nauseating.

Schneiders ended his Progress Report by advising PWD not to stress hunger but to 'hold out hope of better things to come'.[15]

The most significant eyewitness report was that by Davidson Taylor, the American head of PWD SHAEF's Film Theatre and Music Control Section (FTCMS), written after a week-long reconnaissance trip through the American Zones in Germany and Austria in late June in the company of the film director Billy Wilder, recently arrived from OWI Films Division in London. The inhabitants of Germany's devastated cities were so stunned by the terrors they had undergone that it might 'prove difficult to move them by showing them the miseries of the concentration camps'. The relative priorities of PWD's propaganda lines should change radically to take account of actual conditions.[16]

By June 1945 there was growing impatience between the partners in this Anglo-American project. London had not yet appointed a director, producer or writer when the Americans suggested that Billy Wilder complete the film in Munich. Nor had any completion date been fixed, even provisionally, although the first licensed cinemas were due to open in the US zone in July. The project was still being slowed down by the constant determination of Bernstein to build up a quasi-legal case proving German guilt and to authenticate the evidence beyond any possibility of future denial. It is not entirely surprising that the Americans eventually withdrew from the film on 9 July 1945, a few days before the dissolution of SHAEF and the PWD.[17]

The project was apparently now the full responsibility of the British Ministry of Information, although following the dissolution of its official Allied sponsor, the film was actually in a state of political limbo. Stewart McAllister and Peter Tanner, the two experienced editors who had respectively been working since late April on assembling the Belsen material and the film from the camps liberated by the Americans, now became part of a larger though still informally structured production team, hastily assembled by Bernstein to complete the whole film.

Alfred Hitchcock, who was named director, and who had arrived in London in late June, after the Belsen material had been assembled, left in late July, two months before work on the film appears finally to have stopped. An Australian journalist from the *News Chronicle*, Colin Wills, who had visited Belsen, had provided a treatment and commentary by 16 July. Eight days later a second treatment was provided by Richard Crossman, who had been in charge of German propaganda in PWD and who had also visited Belsen. Professor Solly Zuckerman was appointed scientific and medical advisor.

Production team

Alfred Hitchcock

Speaking in 1984, Peter Tanner recalled the details of Hitchcock's contribution, describing him as the advisor on the film, and certainly not the director.[18] He considered Bernstein had made a very clever choice, to use his considerable film and technical knowledge to make the film as interesting and telling as possible, cinematically shaping the material.

He clearly recalled his first meeting with Hitchcock in his suite at Claridge's Hotel. Although not all the material had yet come in,

> he'd probably seen some of the material. And anyway he had Sidney Bernstein's ideas for what was wanted. And he did outline to me at considerable length the kind of form he thought the material should take.

> Hitchcock had made a great point that the material would be disbelieved by many people, and that the Allies would be accused of faking a film. And it must try to be made as clear as possible that this was actual material, actually filmed by a reliable army film cameraman at the time. Not propaganda. It was absolutely factual film and therefore every endeavour in the editing must be made not to do any tricky editing that would give the impression that it was contrived or faked in any way. And he did suggest as far as possible using long shots and panning shots with no cuts, which panned from say guards onto the bodies and so on. And tied up the various things to make sure that the atrocities that went on were seen to be genuine. A good example of that was, all the inhabitants in the nearby village were forced to come out and see for themselves what went on inside the camp because they all denied any knowledge of knowing it was an extermination camp.

> Another of Hitchcock's specific suggestions was the sequence in the last reel covering the possessions of the dead people [Auschwitz], their hair cut off, pathetic shots of wedding rings, even spectacles and toothbrushes – and these somehow were more moving, more harrowing sometimes than the actual bodies.

Based on this testimony, and in order to avoid the misleading implication that the great British director may have played any part in filming concentration camp scenes, the Imperial War Museum has preferred to credit Hitchcock as 'Treatment Advisor' rather than as Director. While it is true that Hitchcock was appointed director for the project, he actually had little chance to exercise any directorial role. The bulk of the film had been shot by service cameramen long before his appointment or his arrival in London in late June 1945 (so he could have had no control over the material filmed), and work on the project continued after he had again left London in July 1945.

During his hurried month's stay in London, Hitchcock worked initially with the Australian-born journalist Colin Wills who prepared the first draft treatment (or 'outline') and first commentary, then with Richard Crossman, who had been PWD Chief of German propaganda. Both men had first-hand knowledge of the camps (which Hitchcock, of course, lacked).

Colin Wills

Wills had been at Belsen since the start of filming on 16 April 1945 ('Day 1') as war correspondent for the *News Chronicle*, and had over the next week filed daily reports to his London paper about the clearing and rehabilitation of the camp.[19] Already an experienced commentary writer and speaker for many MOI sponsored films, Wills had the first treatment (or 'outline') and first commentary for 'the Concentration Camp film' ready by 16 July, when his participation was cut short by his departure for Paris the next day, evidently before the final shape of the film was agreed.

Richard Crossman

Crossman (inaccurately transcribed as 'Grossman' on the WGBH video version), who was Assistant Editor of the *New Statesman and Nation* (1938–55) and Assistant Chief of the Psychological Warfare Division of SHAEF (1944–45), was 'valued for his knowledge of German propaganda, German mentality and German language'.[20] Crossman appears to have taken over from Wills, after the latter left for Paris on 17 July. Even before Germany's surrender, he had been directly concerned with how photographs of Belsen should be captioned and selected for publication in Germany, urging for example that any text be written 'as though they [OWI's German translators] were writing not a brochure, not a moving story, but an official military report'.[21]

Professor Solly Zuckerman

The British scientist, who had been attached to the Deputy Supreme Commander of SHAEF, was commissioned early on to act as advisor to ensure the scientific and medical accuracy of the film. After a visit to Germany in May, he listed a number of points for further investigation for the 'MOI Concentration Camp Picture' but could in 1984 recall no further involvement in the project. Had the film ever been completed he would presumably have been invited to vet the final treatment.[22]

Sergei Nolbandov

A graduate in law from Odessa University, Nolbandov was a gifted linguist and production manager at Ealing Studios as well as a friend of Bernstein. He was already working in the Liberated Territories Section of the MOI Films Division, so was the natural choice to manage the project.

Stewart McAllister

An experienced editor who had worked on many of the wartime films of Humphrey Jennings, McAllister shaped the first half of the film consisting primarily of the film shot by the cameramen of the AFPU at Belsen.[23]

Peter Tanner

Tanner had been working within the Liberated Territories Section of the MOI Films Division, cutting as well as recutting documentaries in French and Dutch and other languages for local exhibition in the liberated nations of Europe, when he was appointed to work on the German Atrocity Film, 'with every urgency', on 21 April 1945.[24] His main role was to assemble and cut the material shot by combat cameramen of the US Army Signal Corps Photographic Units of the camps liberated by American forces.

In 1984 he recalled how the camera rushes were processed at Denham Laboratories, the site of his cutting room. The material was considered too horrific for any of the young workers to view, while the elderly projectionists were so horrified that they wouldn't watch the film at all. If the reel went out of focus, or out of rack, Tanner had the greatest difficulty attracting their attention to come and put it right. It seemed to him that 'even the film was contaminated with this terrible thing that was going on – the terrible persecution of the Jewish people in these camps.'

There was much discussion as to what could be released to the newsreels and even to the Allied project, although the only sequences which Tanner recalled actually being ordered deleted by the censor were of a British sergeant kicking a German guard, and American film of a guard being stabbed by an inmate with a concealed knife just after the leading vehicle had smashed open the gates of a concentration camp.

Army Film and Photographic Unit (AFPU)

How this record was made is a matter of more than mere technical interest as documentary filmmakers were inevitably constrained by the nature of the actuality material available, which can be illustrated by reference to the typical experience of British wartime filming.

Combat cameramen of the AFPU were experienced soldiers, who volunteered for training as cine cameramen and photographers at Pinewood Studios, where they learned over eight weeks the elementary principles of cine and still photography, including how to edit in camera, how to shoot a story and how to complete a 'dopesheet' (camera reports marked 'Secret' which recorded the subject, location and date of each roll of film shot). Soldiers who passed the end of course test were posted with the rank of sergeant, as either cameramen or photographers, to one of the four units based overseas (Cairo, Italy, South East Asia Command or North West Europe). Cameramen and photographers were paired, then attached to military formations and provided with a jeep and driver and sufficient supplies and film stock to afford them the mobility and independence they needed to carry out their task. This was primarily to shoot film of the activities of the British Army for the historic record, and/or for publicity purposes, meaning material suitable for inclusion in the five British newsreels and other Allied film outlets. Cameramen were expected to accompany their fighting comrades in the front line, and to 'cover everything possible'. Whatever taboos they may have later consciously or unconsciously applied during their filming of certain subjects, each cameraman carried a pass which authorized him to film unrestrained by senior personnel, as all material was subject to War Office censorship after processing.[25]

Film was shot on black and white 35 mm rolls lasting one or two minutes, using spring clockwork driven cameras which exposed approximately 30 seconds of film per winding. All film was recorded mute, apart from a small amount of material specially taken by British Movietone News at the request of Bernstein at Belsen, and certain Army Signal Corps units tasked with recording sound interviews for War Crimes Investigation Team purposes at camps liberated by the US Army.

Abandonment of the British film project

Despite this flurry of activity in July, the film was still unfinished when Bernstein's project came to the attention of an official in the German and Austrian Division of the Political Intelligence Department (PID) of the Foreign Office in early August. Having 'accidentally' discovered that work had 'begun again' on a project which clearly fell within its own territory,

Commander McLachlan asked Bernstein who now had political responsibility for the film being made by the MOI. He simultaneously informed Bernstein:

> policy at the moment in Germany is entirely in the direction of encouraging, stimulating and interesting the Germans out of their apathy, and there are people round the C-in-C [Commander-in-Chief] who will say 'No atrocity film'. I would say that the atrocity film, if really good and well documented, would be shown willingly and successfully in nine months' time when the difficulties of the winter have been tackled. There may therefore be no hurry for it, and rawstock and technical personnel could perhaps for the moment be spared from it for the needs which the C-in-C has stated as urgent and of which you have been informed.[26]

Work on completing the film was therefore halted, leaving in place, however, most of the elements which would be needed to complete the film one day according to the intentions of the production team, apart from the selection of a composer to write a score and commentators to deliver the script in German (and possibly other languages too). Only the final intended sixth reel, to be based on Russian coverage of the liberation of Majdanek and Auschwitz which had already been viewed by Hitchcock and Peter Tanner, remained in its raw form, pending editing according to the shotlist. At the end of September Bernstein, about to leave the MOI to return to peacetime activity as a film producer (in association with Hitchcock), before going on to create Granada Television, wrote to thank Tanner for his work on the film, adding 'One day you will realise it has been worthwhile.'[27]

Realization of the American project

In the meantime the Americans had appointed Billy Wilder to direct their own two-reel concentration camp film *Die Todesmühlen (Death Mills)*, which was released in their zone in January 1946.[28] It should be remembered that much of the material used in the British compilation and shown in the American film had already been prepared for exhibition to German audiences as issue no. 5 of the joint Anglo-American newsreel *Welt im Film*, scheduled for release on 15 June 1945 (although in fact this issue was not widely distributed in Germany). Other ad-hoc compilations were shown to German prisoners of war, and to civilians in certain locations in Germany.

MEMORY OF THE CAMPS (Allocated title) UK, 1945 (unfinished)	
CREDITS	
Executive Producer:	Sidney Bernstein
Producer:	Sergei Nolbandov
Editors:	Stewart McAllister
	Peter Tanner
Treatment Advisor:	Alfred Hitchcock
Treatments:	Colin Wills
	Richard Crossman
Commentary:	Colin Wills
Proposed Scientific Advisor:	Professor Solly Zuckerman
Length of surviving print:	55 minutes

Notes

1. The uncompleted film, previously referred to by its MOI File Number F3080, was given this title by the author for its Berlin screening.
2. Caroline Moorehead, *Sidney Bernstein A Biography* (London: Jonathan Cape, 1984).
3. *The Times*, 12 December 1983.
4. Christian Delage, '*Nuit et Brouillard*: a Turning Point in the History and Memory of the Holocaust', quoting interview given by Alain Resnais to André Heinrich for the radio programme '*Nuit et Brouillard* au-delà de la censure', broadcast 6 August 1994 on France Culture, in *Holocaust and the Moving Image – Representations in Film and Television since 1933*, Toby Haggith and Joanna Newman (eds) (London: Wallflower Press, 2005), p. 130.
5. TNA INF1/636 Films for Liberated Territories. Investigation of War Atrocities. Factual Film Report on German Concentration Camps.
6. IWM Film and Video Archive Documents.
7. TNA INF1/636 Memo, German Atrocities, Sergei Nolbandov to Sidney Bernstein, 8 February 1945.
8. Moorehead, *Sidney Bernstein*, p. 164.
9. TNA INF1/636 Cecil W. B. Matthews Film Censor to E. A. Adams (MOI), 10 April 1945.
10. TNA INF1/636 Sidney Bernstein to Paul Wyand, 22 April 1945.
11. TNA INF 1/636 Sidney Bernstein to Lt Colonel W. A. Ulman, Army Pictorial Service, 33 Davies St, London, 2 May 1945.
12. IWM Documents, Sidney Bernstein Collection. Material Needed for Proposed Motion Picture on German Atrocities, Sidney Bernstein, 30 April 1945.
13. TNA INF1/636 Report on German Concentration Camp Material, Sergei Nolbandov to Sidney Bernstein, 29 May 1945.

14. IWM Documents 83/10/1 Basil Wright Diary Extracts (31 May, 6 June, 8 June) for German Visit, 28 May–10 June 1945.
15. NARA RG 319.1 Progress Reports, Box 17, June 1945.
16. NARA RG 331 319.1 Progress Reports, Box 17 Report on Trip to Munich of 20 June through 26 June 1945, Davidson Taylor to Brig. Gen. Robert McClure et al.
17. TNA INF1/636 William D. Patterson to Sidney Bernstein, 9 July 1945.
18. IWM Sound Archive 7379/03 Peter Tanner interview with Kay Gladstone, 1984.
19. IWM Film A700/304/1-2 shot by Sgt Mike Lewis on 16 April 1945 shows Colin Wills speaking to a prisoner.
20. TNA INF 1/636 German Concentration Camp Film, Sidney Bernstein to MOI Finance, 23 July 1945.
21. NARA RG 331 Box 7 062, Photographs and Photography, Richard Crossman to Barney Barnes, 3 May 1945.
22. IWM Film and Video Archive Correspondence between Lord Zuckerman and Kay Gladstone, February–March 1984. Note headed MOI Concentration Camp Picture, 17 May 1945.
23. Dai Vaughan, *Portrait of an Invisible Man: Working Life of Stewart McAllister, Film Editor* (British Film Institute, 1983).
24. TNA INF1/636 F3080 German Atrocity Film, Sergei Nolbandov to Archibald, 21 April 1945.
25. Kay Gladstone, 'The Origins of British Army Combat Filming during the Second World War', *Film History* 14 (2002), 326–8.
26. IWM Documents Sidney Bernstein Papers 65/17/1-12 [9], Donald McLachlan to Sidney Bernstein, 4 August 1945.
27. IWM Sound Archive 7379/03 Peter Tanner interview with Kay Gladstone, quoting from a letter from Sidney Bernstein to Tanner, 30 September 1945.
28. Brewster S. Chamberlin, 'Todesmühlen. Ein früher Versuch zur Massen-"Umerziehung" im besetzten Deutschland 1945–1946', *Vierteljahrheft für Zeitgeschichte* 3 (July 1981), 420–36.

Chapter 3

Opening the Camps, Closing the Eyes: Image, History, Readability

Georges Didi-Huberman

As the hand cannot let go of the burning object to which its skin melts and sticks, so the image, the idea which drives us mad with pain, cannot be torn away from the soul, and all efforts and attempts to put it out of one's mind drag it away with them.

Paul Valéry, *Mauvaises pensées et autres* (1941), p. 812

The image and the readability of history

The 60th anniversary of the liberation of Auschwitz was commemorated in 2005. Pilgrimages were made and minutes of silence observed. Numerous speeches were made by political figures. People gathered together. Some books were republished. Certain images were seen again. For several weeks, magazines put the horror of the camps on their covers, as though this horror could be used as a 'cover'– and to cover what in any case? Some films and archival documents were seen again, which are in fact always good to see again. The television depicted a multitude of 'subjects' and 'panels' with the kinds of time constraints, questions and formal vulgarity which are said to govern their work, or perhaps, non-work. More seriously, new memorials and museums with their adjoining libraries were inaugurated.

Why, in the midst of all this, are we left with a double impression of, firstly, political necessity (because this kind of thing unsettles the firm denials of those with the best intentions, and, for a moment, silences the negation adopted by those with less good intentions) and, secondly, a sense of the terrible disjunction as to the desired aim of these memory rituals ('never again')? Annette Wieviorka speaks, quite rightly, of a 'saturated memory', and of the host of suspicions which accompany any attempt nowadays to do yet *more* work on this part of history: 'a perverse fascination with horror, a deadly hunger for the past, a political instrumentalization of victims'.[1] This rejection, this desire to forget, was already noticeable when the camps had only just been opened: '*More!* the indifferent will say, those for whom the words "gas chamber", "selection", "torture" don't belong to living reality but only to the vocabulary of years gone by', Olga Wormser-Migot would write in 1946.[2] So, what was this memory so quickly saturated with? Annette Wieviorka responds: 'Auschwitz is more and more disconnected from the history which produced it … More importantly, Auschwitz has practically been set up as a concept, that of absolute evil [so that] the "it" of Auschwitz-Birkenau, saturated with morals, is crammed full of too little historical knowledge' – a knowledge, never complete, which consists in 'making Auschwitz as readable as possible.'[3]

It is easy to see that a saturated memory could well be memory whose very effectiveness is under threat.[4] It is more difficult to know what must be done to de-saturate memory – with anything other than forgetting. In short, to reinvent a work of memory capable of making the camps *readable*, specifically by using a variety of sources together – written sources, survivors' testimonies and visual documentation, to which historians now understand must be given specific, as well as contextual attention, even though this material is disconcerting and the obvious evidence it presents can increase the danger of its misinterpretation.[5] To make readable could be to re-ask universal questions, for example when Florent Brayard interrogates the 'Final Solution' from the point of view of the techniques and time-frames it employed in decision-making.[6] Or, more modestly, it could come from a local or 'micrological' principle – promoted by Aby Warburg, theorized by Walter Benjamin, and implemented in his own way by Carlo Ginzburg and his 'evidential paradigm' – by studying a singular object in order to discover how, by its intrinsic complexity, it re-asks all the questions which it has come to crystallize.[7]

The *readability* of an historical event as considerable and as complex as the Shoah depends, to a great extent, on the way in which one views the innumerable *singularities* which run through this event, one of which, for example, would be when Raul Hilberg decided to dissect the railway organization used for the deportations and the great massacre.[8] If memory of the camps can seem 'saturated', it is because it is no longer capable of linking up historical singularities, and, when not simply denied, memory settles on being what Annette Wieviorka calls a 'concept' – that is, when the Shoah as an historical event becomes 'the Shoah' as an abstraction and as the absolute limit of the nameable, the thinkable and the imaginable. 'Saturated memory' is simply the effect of spontaneous philosophy which, at little expense, has reached its peak of historical transcendence. As for history's complexities and exceptions, they find themselves reduced to simple slogans, as 'radical' as is possible to be. But, let us remember Bergson's great methodological lesson: wanting to discern what he called 'false problems', he started by saying that thought 'lacks precision' when formed by 'conceptions so abstract and consequently so vast that they maintain in themselves all that is possible and even that which is impossible right next to that which is real', whereas a true *readability* suggests that a well thought-out notion 'is one that adheres to its objective' – therefore to its singularity and complexity.[9]

It was probably Walter Benjamin who, within the domain of history, articulated what readability means with the most finesse and precision. Above and beyond the great structural and universal interpretations that used to characterize orthodox historical materialism, Benjamin argued that history's 'readability' (*Lesbarkeit*) should be linked to its concrete, immanent and singular 'visibility' (*Anschaulichkeit*). As this is not just about *seeing* but also about *knowing*, to do this we must 'carry over the principle of montage (*der Prinzip der Montage*) into history'[10]: a literary principle adopted by the surrealists and by the writers of *Documents*, a review created in 1929, like *Les Annales*; it is, above all, a cinematographic principle like those developed in the same period by Eisenstein, Dziga Vertov, Abel Gance or even Fritz Lang.

Benjamin specifies from the beginning that this principle is simply to favour thinking about singularities in terms of how they relate to each other, how they move and the intervals between them: in short, montage is to 'to assemble large-scale constructions out of the smallest and most precisely cut components. Indeed, to discover in the analysis of the small individual moment (*in der Analyse des kleinen Einzelmoments*) the crystal of the total event (*Kristall des Totalgeschehens*)'.[11] It is on the basis of such a reflection that Benjamin characterizes the readability of the past, not making any claims to general concepts or to 'essences' of *bildlich* – contrary to what has been said against Heidegger, but also contrary to Jung's archetypes. We then understand that the past becomes readable and therefore knowable when singularities appear and are dynamically connected to one another, by means of montage, writing, cinema – like *images* in motion:

What distinguishes images (*Bilder*) from the 'essences' of phenomenology is their historical index. (Heidegger seeks in vain to rescue history for phenomenology abstractly through 'historicity.') ... For the historical index of the images not only says that they belong to a particular time; it says, above all, that they attain to legibility (*Lesbarkeit*) [readability] only at a particular time. And, indeed, this acceding 'to legibility' constitutes a specific critical point in the movement (*kritischer Punkt der Bewegung*) at their interior. Every present day is determined by the images that are synchronic with it: each 'now' is the now of a particular recognizability (*Erkennbarkeit*). In it, truth is charged to the bursting point with time … It is not that what is past casts its light on what is present, or what is present its light on what is past; rather, image is that wherein what has been comes together in a flash with the now to form a constellation. In other words, image is dialectics at a standstill. For while the relation of the present to the past is purely temporal, the relation of what-has-been to the now is dialectical: not temporal in nature but figural (*bildlich*). Only dialectical images are genuinely historical – that is, not archaic – images. The image that is read (*des gelesene Bild*) – which is to say, the image in the now of its recognizability – bears to the highest degree the imprint of the perilous critical moment (*des kritischen, gefährlichen Moments*) on which all reading (*Lesen*) is founded.[12]

This wonderful fragment, this crystal-like text, compact, enigmatic and luminous, tell us a lot about conditions of historical 'readability' (*Lesbarkeit*) and 'knowability' (*Erkennbarkeit*). Firstly let us note that this text is situated above and beyond eternal quibbles about the primacy of the readable over the visible or *vice versa* which have too often consumed historians, iconologists, or even structuralists, and all those who are still seeking to establish an order of ontological hierarchy between the 'symbolic' and the 'imaginary', for example. Here, Benjamin's point of view finds its source in Aby Warburg's undertaking, not only because the question of the 'afterlife' (*Nachleben*) of cultural images is explicitly recognized as being central to any historical knowledge,[13] but still more because Warburg's iconology was already asserting this system of historicity that will only be grasped 'if we do not back away when faced with the effort of restoring the natural link, the coalescence (*Zusammengehörigkeit*) between the word and the image'.[14] Today, the best attempts at rebuilding an historical anthropology of culture recognize the notion of 'readability' as being the very principle of their methodology.[15]

What does this fragment, this crystal, say to us? That historical knowledge is not in any way, as historians at work spontaneously experience from time to time, the act of going back to the past to describe it and bring it back 'just as it was'. Historical knowledge only comes about through the 'now', that is, through a state of our present experience from which emerges, from amongst the immense archive of texts, images or testimonies of the past, a moment of memory and readability that appears, and this is essential in Benjamin's conception, as a *critical point*, a symptom, a sense of uneasiness within tradition, which up until then painted a more or less recognizable picture of the past.

Benjamin calls this critical point an *image*: not a gratuitous extravagance, of course, but a 'dialectical image' described by the way in which 'what has been comes together in a flash with the now to form a constellation'. In this phrase, the *flash* portrays the lightning speed and the fragility of this apparition, that must be seized upon quickly because it is so easy to miss seeing it pass by; the *constellation* portrays the profound complexity, the depth, as it were, the over-determination of this phenomenon – as it would be with a fossil in motion, a fossil made up of a little light that passes by, like the photogramme of an enormous film. It also speaks to us of the need for *montage*, so that the flash – this monad – does not remain isolated from the multi-faceted sky from which it temporarily detaches itself.[16] In 1940, shortly before taking his own life, fleeing Nazism, Benjamin would develop these ideas in 18 theses 'on the philosophy of history'. Here, we discover, and this is an essential supplement to his work, that 'knowability' appears as an ethical and political question within history, even within history's very motion:

> The true picture of the past *flits by*. The past can be seized only as an image which flashes up at the instant when it can be recognized and is never seen again ... For every image of the past that is not recognized by the present as one of its own concerns threatens to disappear irretrievably ... To articulate the past historically does not mean to recognize it 'the way it really was' ... It means to seize hold of a memory as it flashes up at a moment of danger (*im Augenblick der Gefahr*) ... The danger affects both the content of the tradition and its receivers. The same threat hangs over both: that of becoming a tool of the ruling classes. In every era the attempt must be made anew to wrest tradition away from a conformism that is about to overpower it ... Only that historian will have the gift of fanning the spark of hope in the past who is firmly convinced that *even the dead* will not be safe from the enemy if he wins. And this enemy has not ceased to be victorious.[17]

The proof: opening the eyes to the space

Five years later, Nazism, the principal enemy, had been defeated by the Allied armies. The camps were then discovered and opened – if not liberated. And so were people's eyes – the eyes of the so-called 'civilized world' were suddenly opened, horrified, to the site of the camps. Even those who had known about the 'terrifying secret', as Walter Laqueur called it, many of whom worked in political and military spheres, could not believe their eyes.[18] Like an individual who, when faced with the ordeal of confronting the unimaginable wants to pinch himself to make sure he's not in the middle of a nightmare, so officials systematically called on visual techniques, cinema and photography to convince themselves, to convince the entire world, and to produce irrefutable 'exhibits' to use against the guilty parties that showed the enormous cruelty of the Nazi camps.

At the end of July 1944, the Red Army, which had joined elements from the Kosciuszko division of the Polish army, entered the town of Lublin and for the very first time took control of a German camp situated on Polish territory, Majdanek, where nearly a million and a half victims had been put to death. Although the Germans had burned down the crematoria on 22 July, the Russians found themselves faced with the terrible evidence of piles of ashes mixed with human bones, 820,000 pairs of shoes, and huge warehouses full of clothes.[19] Almost immediately, two teams of film-makers, a Russian one led by Roman Karmen from the Central Studio for Documentary Cinema in Moscow, and a Polish one led by director Aleksander Ford, were given the task of capturing images, which were quickly edited towards the end of that autumn, so that the film could be shown on time in Lublin in November 1944, where they had already commenced putting the camp's guards on trial.[20]

Other examples are better known: in Auschwitz, four cameramen from the Soviet army were present in the days and weeks following the camp's liberation on 27 January 1945. Most visual documentation of the state of the camp as it was opened comes from the film *Chronique de la libération d'Auschwitz*.[21] As Western armies advanced, they experienced the same series of events: opening, discovering, photographing and filming, editing images and showing them all together, whether they be for a magazine layout or for a documentary film. Our knowledge of the camps, even before the publication of the first major survivors' testimonies or historians' analyses, was first and foremost a visual knowledge, one that was filtered through journalism, politics and the military, a visual knowledge of the camps seen in their state of *destruction* by the Nazis and in that of their *opening* by the Allies. These images none the less caused a realization of this phenomenon: a 'negative epiphany' of the camps' existence, as Susan Sontag wrote, and Clément Chéroux remarked in his analysis of the reception of this appalling iconography.[22] Think of General Eisenhower's visit to the Ohrdruf camp on 12 April 1945 with his horde of journalists; of the famous photographers dispatched to places that had barely been 'liberated' by the American, British or French armies: Lee Miller and Margaret Bourke-White to Buchenwald, Éric Schwab to Dachau, Germaine Krull to Vaihingen, George Rodger to Bergen-Belsen ...[23]

When speaking of a 'negative epiphany', Susan Sontag wanted to point out the double impulse provoked when such a horror is brought out into the light: images of the camps 'paralysed' us with fright when we faced their *visibility*, but they also marked the beginning of an impulse of the soul indissociable from any of our existential, moral or political expectations, 'the beginning of tears', she writes, 'that I continue to shed'.[24] But, in watching these films today, we are arrested by something else – their lack of intrinsic *readability*, that is, the difficulty with which we understand these images as 'dialectic images', as images capable of implementing their own 'critical point' and their field of 'knowability'. Today, we must therefore look twice in order to extract an historical readability from this visibility which is so hard to bear.

For example, when we know that both film crews at Majdanek were led by Jewish filmmakers (and the cameramen Stanislaw Wohl, Adolf and Wladyslaw Forbert were also communist Jews – they had been part of *Start*, a group representative of the cinematographic avant-garde of the 1930s) and yet the edited results clearly minimize the place of Jews in the camp's organized massacres, the film's images grow heavy with a new readability – over the top of the readability of *acknowledgement* is superimposed the readability of an implicit *contract*, or even constraint, where of course what was at stake was the political instrumentalization of Nazi camps in Poland being opened by the Soviet powers in this territory.[25] Another example: we know that at Auschwitz 'the misery in the sheds could not be filmed immediately [because] the prisoners had to be transferred as quickly as possible [as they were] practically dying of cold'.[26]

We also know that at Mauthausen, where the opening of the camp had been a confused, appalling and sinister affair, the 'liberation' of the camps was subsequently re-enacted in order to fix this glorious photographic memory, with prisoners waving flags, smiling and cheering as the American tank passes by.[27] Finally, we know to what point images of Bergen-Belsen have served to crystallize the visibility of horror (even in Alain Resnais's *Night and Fog*) on the basis of a genuine historical misinterpretation concerning the corpses being shown in the belief that they would 'illustrate' the phenomenon of mass gassing. The opening up of camps thus liberated a whole horde of these images, where 'education by horror' never came without a meticulous filtering of information – so that Sylvie Lindeperg could class all news production filmed in 1945 as possessing what she calls a 'blind screen' quality.[28]

In short, the historical readability of images produced at the camps' liberation seems to have been permanently undermined by the construction, manipulation of, and exchange values related to photographs and films taken at the time. The image of the camps rapidly found itself wrestling with tiresome paradoxes: the desire for memory and the desire to forget; culpability and denial; the desire to *assemble* history and to simply take pleasure from *showing* stories: an 'unfilmable history' was thus talked about, and Claude Lanzmann, when faced with this situation radically resorted, in his great film *Shoah* (1985), to a refusal of any visibility of Liberation archival material, in order to construct a readability of this historical phenomenon based on attentively listening to survivors.[29]

But, if Walter Benjamin is right to affirm that 'the historical index of the images not only says that they belong to a particular time; [but] it says, above all, that they attain to legibility [readability] only at a particular time', then we must not hold on to the reasoning that says that because they have been manipulated (don't all human signs, images or words undergo some sort of manipulation – for better or worse?), all images of the Liberation should be rejected from our reading of history. Rather, we should assume the double task of making these images readable in making their very construction visible.

An essential element of this construction lies in the *legal aim* of a large number of images taken at the time of the camps' opening. It is perfectly understandable: if the camp, as Giorgio Agamben defines it, really is this 'space of exception', this 'piece of territory that is placed outside the normal juridical order'[30] in which prison law no longer applies, then the first reaction at the opening of the camps would logically be to reaffirm the law, and therefore to want to legally establish guilt within this monstrous criminal organization. Discovering the camps, describing them and starting to write their history first of all went hand in hand with putting them on trial.[31] This is why the first images of the camps, like the first written descriptions or first statements made, see themselves first and foremost as visual testimonies.[32] This is why Allied personnel, among others on the American side, the heads of the Signal Corps and of the Office of Strategic Services whose film section was headed up by John Ford, quickly wrote up protocols relating to the film destined after the war to play a juridical role:

> In the execution of their normal duties, officers and soldiers are frequently faced with exhibits and testimonies relating to war crimes and atrocities, which have to be kept for later examination. As human memory is fallible and as objects being used as exhibits can be susceptible to decomposition, alteration or loss, it is important to record what happens at the time so that, where possible, one can acceptably prove its reality, identify participants and offer a way of tracing perpetrators of crimes as well as witnesses at any point in the future. In order to record such testimonies in a consistent manner and so that they will be acceptable to the military courts, it is essential to carefully follow the attached instructions. Please consult them with care and keep this manual as reference with you at all times in the field.[33]

The Nuremberg Tribunal was the first in history to use a cinema projector and large screen which would be used to place the accused in front of their crimes, images for the most part taken by the Soviet, American and British armies. They were 'included in the bundle' as they say, as evidence for the charges brought, or at the very least, they were used as exhibits.[34] The American film in particular was accompanied by various 'certificates of origin and affidavit' signed by the soldiers in charge, as well as by the director and editor of the film, George Stevens and E.R. Kellogg:

> These images have in no way been altered since they were taken. The commentary that accompanies them faithfully exposes the facts and circumstances surrounding the capturing of these shots. Signed: George C. Stevens, Lieutenant Colonel, United States Army. Made under oath on 2nd October 1945 ... I have meticulously examined the negatives which you are going to be shown. I certify that this documentary is made up of extracts of film taken by the Allies and that the images contained in it have not been retouched, distorted or modified in any way, and that they conform with original negatives contained in United States Signal Corps safes. These extracts represent 2,000 metres of film. They come from 25,000 metres of original negatives that I have viewed and are similar in nature to the extracts you are going to see. Signed: E.R. Kellogg, Lieutenant, United States Marines.[35]

The ordeal: opening the eyes to time

These films are overwhelming. We want to shut our eyes. But we just stare wide-eyed. How is it though, that with time, their value as testimony and even more so their value as proof has been called into question, up to the point where sometimes they are purely and simply revoked from any memory of the Shoah? Without needing to go to Claude Lanzmann's extremes,[36] it can be said that the historian will often view these images not with a feeling of being overwhelmed, but with that of suspicion: it is then preferable to question whether these images *betray* rather than to start by questioning what they *show*.[37] If not, due to the rhetorical processes inherent in the very destination of these images, one will doubt their usefulness to history – in short, their readability.[38]

Perhaps all one can ask of these images is to provide a kind of inventory of the space, already a considerable task, viewed through the lens of the (often difficult) progress, the kind of organization, the technical limitations and the available time of an army seeking first and foremost to win the war. Many testimonies speak of the intrinsic difficulty of producing visual testimonies of this hell that had only just been 'opened', where no one could yet know who among the victims would be lost and who would survive. Each situation had its own specific set of cruelties, impossibilities and decisions to be made. One Soviet army sergeant evoked this kind of situation at Auschwitz:

> In the late afternoon, some of those who were still crying started taking us in their arms, whispering words to us in languages we did not understand.

They wanted to talk, they started to tell. But we had no time left. Night was already starting to fall. We had to go.[39]

This one example helps us to understand an important aspect of the malaise inevitably caused by these images: if their readability remains problematic, it is not because their visibility is illusive or is hiding something from us; on the contrary, everything is shown as it was, but it is because their *temporality* itself is untenable or, rather, out of sync with the tragic experience it documents. If military films of the camps' liberation obliterate something, it is firstly, and inevitably, the passage of time: a camp is not opened like a door; prisoners are not released from a camp like birds liberated from a cage. These films open the eyes to an *inventory of the space*; they make readable the army's response to the victims' situation, but also to that of the perpetrators when they are recognized and arrested, and to that of the citizens of the neighbouring village when they are forced to come and see what they still denied having known about, etc. But these films were not shot, edited or shown to make readable the paradoxical *time zone* that they nonetheless document, that is, the experience of a camp in the process of opening.

We will continue to close the eyes to these images for as long as it takes us to find their 'critical point', as Walter Benjamin calls it, from which will arise the possibility of their being 'read' or placed in time, reunited, even if not entirely, with the experience itself. This critical point is still to be achieved. To construct readability for these images would not therefore be to content oneself with the voiceover of a commentator appointed by the American army. Rather, it would be to re-situate, to re-contextualize these images within a different kind of *montage*, with a different kind of text, for example, the accounts of survivors themselves as they speak of what the opening of their camp meant for them.

Opening the eyes to the camps' opening would thus be to watch images from these terrible archives whilst continuously making testimonies left to us by survivors themselves heard – ones which speak of this moment that at the same time was so decisive and so complex.[40] For example, we must know how to watch Russian soldiers' faces at Auschwitz whilst re-reading Charlotte Delbo's account of the appearance of the 'liberator':

The Morning of Our Freedom. The man who appeared before our eyes was the most handsome man we'd ever seen in our lives. He was looking at us. He was looking at these women who looked at him, without knowing that, as far as they were concerned, he was so perfectly handsome, handsome by having human handsomeness.[41]

We must also watch the face of the Kapo who had only just been denounced whilst re-reading the very last sentence of David Rousset's book *Les Jours de notre mort*: 'So they decided to stone him'.[42] We must know how to watch images of Buchenwald whilst remembering what Élie Wiesel tells us about it: 'Our first act as free men was to throw ourselves on to the provisions. We thought only of that. Not of revenge, not of our families. Nothing but bread.' and who ends *Night* by describing the first time he sees himself in a mirror: 'I had not seen myself since the ghetto. From the depths of the mirror, a corpse gazed back at me. The look in his eyes, as they stared into mine, has never left me.'[43]

This gaze is therefore like a period of time. Opening the eyes to an historical event is no more to seize upon a visible aspect of it which would summarize it like a photogramme – like a still, a frozen picture as they say in English – than it is to give it a meaning that would forever oversimplify it. Opening the eyes to history is to start by placing images that are left to us *in time*. Moreover, the opening of the camps is the subject of many survivors' accounts, who have meticulously placed events in time, something which should form our point of departure, the platform from which we should view archives of this period. Hermann Langbein noted how the opening of the camp, which was, it goes without saying, a miraculous event that gave life back its very possibility, does not liberate all things for a physically and psychologically broken prisoner. His description of Auschwitz's liberation consists mainly of solitude ('Meeting human society did not awaken profound feelings in me ... Sad and empty, I was still alone'), lack of feeling and 'unhealable wounds' mixed with 'feeling of guilt'.[44]

Primo Levi and Robert Antelme's testimonies are even more specific. We know that Primo Levi, along with his companion Leonardo De Benedetti, was required by the Red Army, which had just liberated the Auschwitz complex, to write a report about the organization of the camp at Monowitz. This text was written in 1945–46, the first by Primo Levi about his concentrationary experience, and can be compared to military images of the camp's opening which it in fact mentions in the first sentence:

> The photographic evidence, and the already numerous accounts provided by ex-internees of the various concentration camps created by the Germans for the annihilation of the European Jews, mean that there is perhaps no longer anyone still unaware of the nature of those places of extermination and of the iniquities that were committed there. Nevertheless, in order to make better known the horrors of which we too were witnesses and very often victims throughout the course of a year, we believe that it will be useful to make public in Italy a report which we submitted to the government of the USSR on the request of the Russian Command of the concentration camp for Italian ex-prisoners at Katowice. We were inmates

of this camp ourselves after our liberation by the Red Army towards the end of January 1945. We have added some information of general nature to the account given here, since our original report was required to concentrate exclusively on the operation of medical services in the Monowitz Camp. Similar reports were requested by the government in Moscow from all doctors, of whatever nationality, who had been liberated in the same way from other camps.[45]

What follows is a veritable *inventory of the space* – implacable, objective, concise, and of documentary nature.[46] He evokes the protocols for texts and images destined by Allied armies to constitute exhibits in the Nuremberg Tribunal. Levi's *If this is a man* the following year fulfilled an even more profound need (although the historian would be wrong to disregard it under the pretext that its aim is more directly 'literary') – the need to establish the (difficult) *state of time* related to this experience. Where legal protocol, from which the documentary films and military photographs stem, seeks to *establish facts* and their *proof*, witness literature, even in its poetic content, seeks to *represent the event* in terms of its most profound temporality – the temporality of the *ordeal*.[47] We can only give images of the camps a 'readability in spite of all' by adhering to a literary ethics which, when faced with the unnameable, says we must *continue* – we must relentlessly place things in time.[48]

Primo Levi, in *If this is a man*, devotes a total of over 20 pages to an unbearably slow epilogue about the camp's opening between 17 and 27 January 1945, to be precise.[49] The Russians are approaching. But this news is not good news in the hell that is Auschwitz, because following SS logic, it was accompanied by the total liquidation of the camp: on the morning of 18 January, 'the last distribution of soup took place ... [no] Jew seriously expect[ed] to live until the following day.'[50] The night of 18 January was filled with the sound of bombings. The following morning brought something unprecedented: 'The Germans had disappeared. The watchtowers were empty.' And, in the same breath, Primo Levi puts this 'miracle' in perspective as he describes the prisoners' reaction to this extraordinary vision of unmanned watchtowers:

> Today I think that if for no other reason than that an Auschwitz existed, no one in our age should speak of Providence. But without doubt in that hour the memory of biblical salvations in times of extreme adversity passed like a wind through all our minds.[51]

On that day, Primo Levi observes how the hope inspired by the vision of empty watchtowers inspires several prisoners to share their food for the first time, a concrete sign that humanity was capable of recovering its rights:

Only a day before a similar event would have been inconceivable. The law of the Lager said: 'eat your own bread, and if you can, that of your neighbour', and left no room for gratitude. It really meant that Lager was dead. It was the first human gesture that occurred among us. I believe that that moment can be dated as the beginning of the change by which we who had not died slowly changed from Häftlinge [inmates] to men again.[52]

But things don't end without any hitches: on 22 January, some SS return and methodically shoot any prisoners they can find 'lining up their twisted bodies in the snow on the road; then they left ... [the bodies which] nobody had the strength to bury.'[53]

Two days later, 24 January seems to be the day of 'liberty':

The breach in the barbed wire gave us a concrete image of it. To anyone who stopped to think, it signified no more Germans, no more selections, no work, no blows, no roll-calls, and perhaps, later, the return. But we had to make an effort to convince ourselves of it, and no one had time to enjoy the thought. All around lay destruction and death.[54]

And here we see the difficult task of establishing the time of the camp's opening: there is Somogyi, the Hungarian Jew who, experiencing 'a last and interminable dream of acceptance and slavery' in his agony murmurs *Jawohl* 'with every breath', and who yet again shows 'how laborious is the death of a man.'[55] There is the interminable delay in the Russians' arrival, who do not arrive until the perpetrators have deserted the camp. But '[l]ike joy, fear and pain itself, even expectancy can be tiring. Having reached 25 January, with all relations broken already for eight days with that ferocious world that still remained a world, most of us were too exhausted even to wait.'[56]

The camp is open; there are no more watchmen in the towers, no more SS guards, there are holes in the barbed wire, but everything remains as it was, everything continues to die while 'thousands of feet above us, in the gaps in the grey clouds, the complicated miracles of aerial duels began'.[57] On 27 January, at dawn, Primo Levi sees '[o]n the floor, the shameful wreck of skin and bones, the Somogyi thing ... The Russians arrived while Charles and I were carrying Somogyi a little distance outside. He was very light. We overturned the stretcher on the grey snow. Charles took off his beret. I regretted not having a beret.'[58] Even before the survivors' liberty the open camp would therefore allow what had not been possible under the camp's SS law: taking time to close the eyes of the dead and lie him down in the snow, if not bury him, in order to respect the dignity of he who had passed away.

Primo Levi's account finishes characteristically with this gesture, a funeral-like ritual, albeit feeble and pitiful, yet because of this all the more necessary. In fact, this gesture takes on a paradigmatic value when questioning what historical and ethical responsibility must be assumed once the camps have been liberated. A short while ago, Imre Kertész, during his Nobel Prize reception speech on 10 December 2002, repeated how Auschwitz remains with us like an 'open wound'.[59] The fact, therefore, that the camps were opened has not resolved or 'closed' the question of the camps, if only because the very idea of the camps, as Primo Levi very quickly understood 'is certainly not dead, like nothing ever dies'.[60] Even once opened, the camps therefore left *open* the historical, anthropological and political question posed by their very (past, present and future) existence. Robert Antelme, who similarly described Dachau's opening in a long chapter of *The Human Race* entitled 'The End',[61] ends his account by writing about the unreadability which, as soon as the camp is opened, closes in again inexorably when faced with the survivors' words, like eyes closing when faced with the evidence:

April 30 … For the first time since 1933 soldiers have entered here without harmful intent. They give out cigarettes and chocolate. You can talk to the soldiers. They answer you. We don't have to take off our caps in front of them. They hold out a pack, and we help ourselves and smoke the cigarette. They don't ask questions. We thank them for the cigarettes and the chocolate. They have seen the crematorium, and the dead bodies in the railroad cars. … The men have already got back in contact with civility, with pleasantness. They look at the American soldiers from close on, look at their uniforms. They are happy to see planes passing low overhead. They can walk about the camp, if they so desire. But should they wish to leave it, they would – for now – be told it's not allowed. 'It's not allowed. Kindly go back.' … Dead bodies lie on the ground amidst the trash, and guys just walk past them. Some guys eye the soldiers sullenly. There are also some lying on the ground who have their eyes open but who aren't looking at anything any more … There isn't a great deal to be said to them, the soldiers may perhaps think. We liberated them. We're their strong arms and their rifles. But nobody has anything to talk about. It is frightful. Yes, these Germans really are worse than barbarians. *Frightful, yes, frightful!* Yes truly frightful. When a soldier says something like that out loud, a few guys try to tell him about what it was like. The soldier listens at first, but then the guys go on and on, they talk and they talk, and pretty soon the soldier isn't listening any more.[62]

And Antelme concludes his account by writing of the ease with which already the word *unimaginable* could be used by those who had just opened their eyes to the proof, but who closed them quickly to the ordeal, those who could not yet manage or find the time to locate a readability for the experience of those who were nevertheless before their very eyes, those who were already trying in vain to tell them about their experience:

All the stories that the guys are telling are true. But it requires considerable artfulness to get even a smidgen of truth accepted, and in the telling of these stories there wants that artfulness which must vanquish necessary disbelief. In all this, everything must be believed, but truth can be more tedious to listen to than some fabulation. Just a piece of the truth would be enough, one example, one idea; but nobody here has only one example to offer, and there're thousands of us. These soldiers are strolling about in a city where all the stories should be added end to end, and where nothing is negligible. But no listener has that vice. Most consciences are satisfied quickly enough, and need only a few words in order to reach a definitive opinion of the unknowable...*Unimaginable*: a word that doesn't divide, doesn't restrict. The most convenient word. When you walk around with this word as your shield, this word for emptiness, your step becomes better assured, more resolute, your conscience pulls itself together.[63]

Indignation: opening the murderers' eyes

How does one behave in the face of the unimaginable? History is undoubtedly made up of rules, but there are almost as many exceptions. It is likely that at the beginning of the month of May in 1945, whilst discovering the Falkenau Camp in Czechoslovakia, men from the American army's first infantry division, the famous 'Big Red One', would probably – stupefied – have uttered the same words heard by Robert Antelme a few days earlier in Dachau: *Frightful, yes, frightful!* The Americans had entered Falkenau during the night of 7 May, while thousands of disarmed German soldiers – maybe 40,000 or 45,000 – were crossing the region to give themselves up to western forces, rather than the Russians who were stationed just a few kilometres away. It was there that men from the 'Big Red One' discovered the sign for the *Konzentrationslager Falkenau*. A short-lived battle ensued against the remaining members of the camp's SS, who did not realize, or did not want to believe, that the German surrender was in the process of being signed. It was then, in the very last hours of the war, and in the very first hours of peace, that the camp was 'opened'.

There was, among the soldiers of this infantry division, a certain Samuel Fuller who, although already defining himself as a Candide or Don Quixote figure before history, was still far from imagining the great cinematographic destiny that he would later fulfil.[64] He had forgotten the sinister warning given to him in 1942, that to enter such an infantry division was to come back dead, injured or at best, mad.[65] He had joined up to fight against Nazism, but also, as he would later write, to serve as an eyewitness who would be given the opportunity to 'cover the biggest crime story of the century.'[66] Fuller had been a journalist for the New York tabloid press in the early 1930s. 'I was a reporter trained to track down the truth. At that time, I wasn't interested in fiction. All I could think of was travelling across the country, banging out articles about the people and places I ran across. Real people and real places [and as for myself, confronting that, was a] real eye opener.'[67]

He had also discovered the power of images used in conjunction with accounts he had written about violence before the war, which he had already witnessed close-up, like mafia or Ku Klux Klan crimes: 'I was beginning to realize that I could better convey emotions with words *and* images. And not just any image that captured a multitude of emotions in a frozen instance.'[68] And that's when he started a scriptwriter's life in Hollywood – 'zigzagging between journalism and fiction',[69] a charmed life brutally interrupted by the war and his first traumatic experiences: the severed head of a comrade cut down by a mortar shell – a vision 'imprinted on my mind', Fuller would write 'like a leaf in a fossil, never to fade',[70] the Arab woman battered, as though an enemy, with her baby still at her breast,[71] and the water at the shore reddened with blood on 6 June 1944 at Omaha Beach[72]... But at Falkenau, another thing altogether would loom up on him, something that Samuel Fuller, who had a whole war behind him – one lived on the front line, closest to the worst – defined as *impossible*, beyond the frightful:

> Then we discovered the horrible truth about the camp ... What had been happening in that concentration camp was beyond belief, beyond our darkest nightmares. We were overwhelmed to come face to face with all the carnage. I still tremble to remember those images of the living hunkered down with the dead ... I vomited. I wanted out of there at any cost, but I couldn't stop myself from looking into the second oven, the third, mesmerized by the impossible.[73]

In an interview in the 1980s with Jean Narboni and Noël Simsolo, Samuel Fuller talks about what he calls the impossible at more length:

> Now the impossible happens. We advance. We feel someone catch our feet. The prisoners could not believe they were free. They didn't know what was going on. They only knew one thing: the guards were dead. For them, that meant freedom. But they had had to see it with their own eyes. No one could just say to them: 'It's alright'. That would have meant nothing to them. The Germans had also said to them 'It's alright', or told them to go to this or that building, and that's where they were going to die. The impossible is when everything had been taken out into broad daylight and all of us had to hold our noses. Do you know what

'concentration camp' means? It means the smell! That was what it was for all of us. We used handkerchiefs. Anything. To tie around our faces. The smell. Appalling! It is not horror. It's something that's not there! You can't see *it*. But at the same time you see it and it's impossible, unbelievable. It's more than horror. It is the impossible. We had never had this feeling of the impossible when we were fighting.[74]

And yet, this *impossible* coexists with a very precise historical and juridical situation: Germany had just surrendered; and that meant that from then on it was a crime to kill a German. The impossible perhaps also comes in part from the impossibility in which these hardened soldiers found themselves – here more indignant than they had ever before been on a battlefield – unable to respond by gunfire to the atrocious crimes to which they were witness. The impossible comes from the fact that in these soldiers' minds, a war could not finish just like that, at a place worse than all the combat already endured. The impossible comes from the fact that before the reality of this opened up camp, nobody, at first, knew exactly *how to react*. Fuller would later sum up the situation precisely in terms of witnessing: 'How could we tell the world about what we'd experienced? About what we'd witnessed. How could we live with it ourselves?'[75]

They therefore had to respond to this impossible with something other than weapons. On the one hand there was the *tragedy* that opening the camp had in no way 'resolved'. It was not enough just to feed the survivors: their physical state was such that they continued to die – like the young girl whom the sergeant of the garrison tried in vain to nurse for several days – Fuller would remark, here, how the dead were lighter than anywhere else.[76] On the other hand there was the soldiers' *indignation* when faced with the *baseness* of the Nazis, and almost as bad, that of the neighbouring village's population: some blaming one another, the rest pretending to know nothing, even though the camp was only a few metres away from the nearest houses in the town, and, more importantly, an unbearable smell of death reigned over all the surrounding area.[77] Fuller tells of Captain Kimble R. Richmond's indignation when faced with all of this denial. The only response was therefore to create a situation appropriate for judging, not the crime itself (the time for the great trials had not yet come) but at least this lie. And to perform some kind of gesture of dignity, in the face of such baseness.

This gesture of dignity would be a double and dialectic one. A *death ritual* accompanied by his meticulous *visual testimony*. A gesture to *close the eyes* of the dead, and to stand before them, keeping *one's eyes open* for a long time during this very charged moment. Captain Richmond ordered everyone who denied having known about the camp's activities – among them 'the mayor, the butcher, the baker and other respected townspeople'[78] to publicly pay their last respects to the dead: the living were to dress them again, put each one in shrouds and delicately bury them together. At the same time, Samuel Fuller was asked to fix a visual trace of this funeral ritual, in its simple solemnity, using his little 16mm Bell & Howell camera.

Over a year before Fuller had written to his mother from the battlefields of North Africa to ask her for his camera, which had only reached him a short while previously in Bamberg. The shots taken by Fuller in Falkenau therefore constitute his first as a filmmaker, 'my first amateur film about professional killers', as he would later say with his particularly black sense of humour.[79] It is a 21-minute silent film, painstaking and unsophisticated. Fuller never ordered it chronologically so that the sequences followed one another in the order it had been shot – although he did hastily scribble some credits on sheets of white paper.

We see men walking, armed with shovels. We see barbed wire, prisoners, soldiers. We see men standing in silence (as though the 'technical' silence in Fuller's film is intensified by a much more fundamental silence). We see naked corpses being taken out of a building with *Leichenkammer* written on it, and then being dressed with difficulty by civilians. We see Soviet army uniforms. We see dressed corpses laid down in lines on white sheets or even on the ground, heads straightened, arms crossed over stomachs. We see, in a single shot, the camp's barbed wire and the houses in the village close by. We see groups of men crouching, then standing in line before the corpses and on the promontory. We see a single man speaking, he is probably making a speech. We see military salutes. Then, about 15 bodies are loaded onto two carts that the civilians then push through the village. When the carts pass by, the camera films the wheels and the walkers' feet, as though the gaze spontaneously lowers at the passing of the dead. We see the funeral cortège stretch out. A child plays on the road with his wooden rifle. In the corner of the image, a man takes off his hat. We see the springtime countryside, the road leading to the cemetery, then, in a large grave at the top of the hill, more corpses stretched out, one next to the other. We see the civilians again – among them a blond adolescent boy in shorts – laying a large shroud made of sheets and assembled pieces of material over the corpses. The film ends with clods of black earth being thrown by the living onto the white shroud of the dead. We see the shadows of the living moving over the graves' mounds.

It is 'raw material', as they say. We see movement, but we do not detect any affect. The film's silence seems to intensify the sense that all expressiveness is exhausted when faced with the gravity of the situation and the act to be accomplished. Although we immediately understand these movements to be a collective funeral ceremony, we are missing the whom, the why, the before, the after, the elsewhere, the context, the destiny of all that we see. And yet, there were hundreds of camps like this one in German-dominated territories, and most of them were more extensive and even more horrifying than this one.[80] The film showed in Nuremberg by the American army is made so unbearable by its length and its endless litany of atrocities discovered all over the place, offering all possible varieties of Nazi inhumanity ... This is probably the reason why, other than the fact that Falkenau quickly fell under the Soviet military occupation zone, soldier Fuller's faint and trembling film was not retained in the mass of visual exhibits used in the coming trials for crimes against humanity. Thus, the film stayed in this state on the director's shelves for over 40 years – mute, silent, and in one sense blind. Unreadable, in fact.

Unreadable because too close. And yet irrefutable in its value as testimony. *Too far away, one loses sight* (like when one talks about camps in general or about the Shoah as a purely dumbfounding notion), *too close, one loses one's own sight* (one's capacity to work out a point of view, this working-out only being possible by relating, editing and interpreting things). That is to say that an image is only readable when *dialecticized*, in the precise sense that Walter Benjamin wanted to give this word. The Falkenau experience, nevertheless, was decisive in, and even in one sense foundational to, the life and work of Samuel Fuller. The director would attempt to lend a readability to his experience at all available opportunities: the Falkenau episode dominates almost all of the main interviews he gave to cinema enthusiasts, especially to journalists at *Cahiers du cinéma* who were great admirers of his films.[81] Jean-Luc Godard admired the 'brutal', 'political' and 'pessimistic' filmmaker in Fuller, as for him, the 'cinema experience' and the 'war experience' had never been disconnected.[82] 'Journalism, war, cinema ... these days, these three words are what make the world go round at a more dizzying pace than ever', the American director would say: War kills, journalism tells us about it, and 'cinema causes us to relive those emotions'.[83]

Fuller meticulously recounted the state of psychological breaking-point in which he remained for a long time after returning home from the war.[84] Having returned to the cinema, he would go on to devote no less than a dozen films to war-time events, whilst the subjects of racism and violence would run through all of his works. And what absolutely distinguishes them from other Hollywood films on this kind of subject is that the central figure is that of the *survivor* and not of the hero: 'There are no heroes in my films. They are war survivors, and they have just done what they had to in order to stay alive'.[85] This is also why Fuller's cinema – a cinema about survivors which was devoted to the dead and to those who survived violent death – can bring a precious contribution to the historian, in that it is ultimately a meticulous testimony, and one which has been impressively developed on screen.[86] As opposed to the sugar-coating he denounced in Hollywood cinema, Fuller, particularly in his famous exchange with Howard Hawks, called for cinema to be 'artistic' as much as 'truthful': 'Make it artistic, but show the truth.'[87]

I used my firsthand knowledge to create films that, I hope, showed the truth about people at war. ... I hate violence. That has never prevented me from using it in my films. It's part of human nature ... War is not about emotions. It's about the absence of emotions. That void *is* the emotion of war ... Hell, words just can't describe it.[88]

This is why, although having written a very long account of his experience in his novel *The Big Red One* – where naturally, the Falkenau episode takes up a whole chapter and part of the epilogue[89] – Fuller never abandoned the idea of remaking it visually into a fictional feature-film. The film *The Big Red One* would finally come out in 1980 in a version considerably cut down by the studios, which was of course against Fuller's advice, but a text at the beginning of the film stated very clearly his intention: 'This film is about fictional life but based on factual death.'[90] Significantly, Fuller had turned down the suggestion that John Wayne play the role of the sergeant, as he in no way wanted his actions to be portrayed as heroic or 'patriotic'.[91]

Rather, he wanted his film to contain a certain 'dry lyricism'[92] that was capable of showing 'the emotion of war' made up of a 'void' of all emotion, when one finds oneself in situations of extreme danger, where the body takes over almost automatically, and one is beyond the normal expression of emotions. The choice to have Lee Marvin play the role of the sergeant contributed to this – his emaciated and inexpressive face being for Fuller the impersonal face of death: 'His face was a face of the war, the most lined, tired and corpse-like as possible. But precisely because of this, he could not be reached by death.'[93]

Nevertheless, Fuller's film is also entirely built on a turbulent *pathos*, the *pathos of action*, a typically Hollywood aesthetic from which he constantly diverges but to which he continues to belong. We are therefore left poles apart from the inexpressive and ritualistic slowness of the 1945 footage – the exhausted gestures of Falkenau. And when he does actually come to filming the episode at the camp in the *The Big Red One*, Fuller will choose an economical approach (no more than four faces of deportees in the shadows), a paradoxical point of view (with the American soldier viewed from the crematorium's ashes), and finally a type of powerful musicality brought out by the tolling and repeated gunshots of Griff (played by Mark Hamill) who, shattered by what he has just seen, seems to want to endlessly destroy the SS guard, whom, absurdly, he has nonetheless killed again and again already. In a scene where the plot has lost all sense, all of this serves to bring out the *pathos of indignation* when faced with a reality that the war film, as a genre, doubtless fails to represent.

Dignity: closing the eyes of the dead

We cannot demand from a fictional film something it has never promised to give. *The Big Red One* is not a film about the camps but a film about war. Significantly, in the final episode at Falkenau, nothing that we saw in the images from 1945 is recounted – neither the civilians' denials, nor the ethical decision to organize the victims' solemn burial. The readability of the camps is therefore reduced – and this is also quite significant – to the temporal fracture in the plot, to the soldiers' mute stupefaction in the face of horror, to the refusal of any explanation, and to the hopeless conclusion of a child dying on the shoulders of the sergeant.[94] It is a readability that opens up the space of *indignation before the impossible*, as Samuel Fuller puts it. And one of the most beautiful things about this readability was to be the *silence* that Fuller created as images of deportees and crematoria come into view, even though the battle continues to rage in the story.[95]

Six years later, when the director recorded interviews with Yann Lardeau and Emil Weiss, the latter convinced him to think of a way of *making visible* the 16mm film shot at Falkenau in 1945. Obviously, it was necessary to create conditions in which it could be *made visible*. This was in Paris in 1986. Following in the footsteps of Marcel Ophuls' masterpieces, Claude Lanzmann's film *Shoah* had recently brought a new value to films about the camps: the value of testimony. At the same time, negationism was at a worrying level, so above and beyond pure indignation, it was important to continue fighting the historiographic battle itself.[96] If images 'attain to legibility [readability] only at a particular time' and if 'acceding "to legibility" [readability] constitutes a specific critical point in the movement at their interior', as Walter Benjamin writes, we can then say that this critical point for Emil Weiss took the form of a direct response to Jean-Marie Le Pen's very famous 'détail'.[97]

In order to make the 21 minutes of silent footage taken at Falkenau in 1945 readable, Emil Weiss would proceed much like Lanzmann did by filming Fuller at the (almost destroyed) sites of the 'original scene'.[98] But contrary to Lanzmann, he would not orientate the elderly man's testimony around planned questions, but around a direct and filmed face-to-face with images from the 1945 document. So, it is the images themselves which, although mute, interrogate the witness: in speaking, he would in return make it possible for them to really be 'watched', 'read' and even 'understood'. One can imagine the intrinsic difficulty of this anachronistic and reminiscent exercise (as more than 40 years separate the man who filmed Falkenau from the one who is seeing his own images in 1988, under the camera's watchful eye): 'it was painful to relive those terrible times so many decades old yet so fresh in my mind', Samuel Fuller would later write.[99] The critical point of any readability probably doesn't go without the pain this type of reminiscence brings up.

But this was the price that had to be paid so that beyond indignation, we could reconstruct a readability for the *gestures of dignity* present not only in the ritual organized at Falkenau by Captain Richmond, but also in the visual testimony conducted on site by Fuller the soldier, and, finally, in the young Emil Weiss's film, constructed on the basis of the elderly Fuller's images and words. The *ritual* that Richmond organized was the first response to the baseness of the camp's monstrous conditions, for which no one was prepared; the images captured by the infantry soldier's small camera remind us of the fundamental anthropological link, in western society and no doubt elsewhere, between *imago* and *dignitas*, or between the image and one's attitude when faced with someone else's death.[100] In this respect, Fuller's *words* in 1988 could logically be construed as the funeral eulogy that accompanies all rituals of this kind, but that, in May 1945, whilst the surviving prisoners continued to suffer, no one had the strength to utter. 'I felt [that in making this film with Emil Weiss] we were honouring the memory of the camp's prisoners'.[101]

The conditions of readability that the 1988 film provides for the 1945 images cannot be separated from what I have called (in relation to a fairly similar case – that of Jorge Semprun describing how, just after his liberation from Buchenwald, he watched images of the camp filmed by the American army during the Liberation) the ethical moment of the gaze.[102] This ethical dimension cannot be reduced to a purely moral or moralizing attitude: firstly, it is about *giving knowledge* to these images, whose 'mute' state at first just left us 'mute' – mute with indignation. It is only through the dialectical task of *montage* that dignity is built into the image – and in this way, the 1988 footage – which scrupulously follows the original edit, only repeating one shot (that of the prisoners standing on the mound) *makes us see* or *shows* the short 1945 film.

What are the main effects, or more importantly the *acts of readability* we can draw out from this *montage*? The first *act of readability* relates to the *author*: the name Samuel Fuller does not appear in the credits scribbled down in 1945; one can just read the following: 'Supervised by Captain Kimbal *[sic]* R. Richmond presented by the 16th infantry regiment commanded by Frederick W. Gibb, 1st infantry division, Falkenau, 9th May 1945.' In 1988, the director would comment 'Richmond is the real author of the film', in that he made the decision to organize this whole ritual; but, Fuller adds, 'you could say that history wrote itself'.[103] In short, there is no 'author', in the same way that the people whom we see in this film are not the characters or 'creations' of the person who films them. Here, the one being filmed does not belong to, and will forever resist the one filming him – there is therefore no contract or corrupt relationship present within the gaze being focussed on these events.

In this particular case, you could even say that those filmed at Falkenau left Fuller mute for 40 years.

The second *act of readability* concerns visual *proof*: the 1945 film was at first considered to be what the English language calls *evidence*, in the sense that proof is something that can be seen. It is this understanding of readability within which the long shot described here in 1988 should clearly be situated:

> This shot shows just how close the camp was to the village. Those are the houses, the camp is behind them. It hasn't been cut or edited. I just took a panoramic shot from the houses up to the camp. You see how close they are! I didn't cut it at all. I was right not to. Children playing on that hillock would surely have been able to see inside the camp.[104]

In *The Big Red One*, Fuller would use the contrast of multicoloured flowers against the barbed wire to symbolize the cruel proximity of the camp and the villagers' indifference. Filmed by Emil Weiss in Nuremberg, the director would clearly state his regret at not having been present for the trial. There were undoubtedly a number of close-up shots in the 1945 footage where those being filmed had been ordered to look at the camera, so that their faces would be recognizable during the course of any legal action.[105]

A third *act of readability* relates to the fact that this 'evidence' does not actually provide us with any direct access. For the ordeal itself exceeds proof, and the images' *atmosphere* (both *Atmosphäre* and *Stimmung*) exceeds visible evidence. The *Atmosphäre* relates to the fact that the corpses and bodies of the sick seen in the 1945 film emitted an unbearable smell that invaded the whole area (and this is what makes the villagers' denials so unbearable to the American soldiers): 'The stink of gangrenous flesh was everywhere ... The stink just got worse. Then came their time to leave the camp ... Captain Richmond refused to use vehicles to move the corpses. He wanted them to be pulled and pushed by the men who had denied the atrocious deaths that took place in the camp.'[106] When you look carefully at the document, you can see men protecting themselves from the unbearable smell with their handkerchiefs.

As for *Stimmung*: 'The tension was impossible to imagine: it was as if you were in a barrel of powder or a field full of mines. Just one objection voiced and all hell would have broken loose.'[107] More particularly, the most tragic event in Fuller's eyes is one that is in no way readable in the mute *montage* from 1945. But, thanks to the footage from 1988, it becomes clear that the Russian officer filmed alone facing the assembled prisoners not only pays homage to those who have already died, but makes the sinister announcement that people would continue to die in spite of the camp's 'liberation'.

They were brought together to listen to the most macabre words I had ever heard anywhere. Any soldier would rather have gone to battle than have to speak to these prisoners like that Russian soldier did. He must have had enormous courage! After the heroic courage needed to face gun-fire, he had to speak to them like a witch-doctor. He told the first group of men that they had suffered so much from malnutrition that it would be impossible to save them. He told the second group that they had incurable contagious diseases and that they had to stay in the prison and die. It wouldn't be possible to move them because of the risk of contagion. He told the third group that they would survive. But, as irony would have it, it was these unfortunate ones who had been stuck in the camp for I don't know how long, and then finally been freed, who would pass from a living death to a life of agony.[108]

Finally, in his interviews with Jean Narboni and Noël Simsolo, Samuel Fuller talks about this deeply moving subject – something that his 1945 film doesn't even touch on – although it formed an integral part of the visual experience of soldiers when opening up a concentration camp – 'You see living people with dead people and you can't tell the difference. People who are sprawled out. People who are dead. But are they dead? ... You see a man moving. He's not yet dead but he's dying. I couldn't use that ... At the end of war, the impossible.'[109]

As if in an attempt to construct, in spite of everything, an ethical position against the background of this hopeless lack of distinction, Fuller's camera, in 1945, attempted to focus on *faces*. This is the fourth 'act of readability', most apparent through the choice of frames and the camera's movements which suggest that the director, not happy with just observing the bare facts, lingers and tries to bring out the human dimension to these facts; it is as though he is seeking out their glances and being attentive to their gestures – apart from when it is *he* who gestures to lower his gaze as the funeral cart goes by. The fact that Fuller still remembers so many names in 1988 is linked to this ethical dimension – for example when he recognizes the back of the soldier who is saluting: 'That man who's saluting – I used to call him "Steely Mike" – he's saluting those who died in this camp, but also those who died in all the camps, in all the damned camps. A simple salute free from pathos or heroism. Just an acknowledgement.'[110]

Filming men in groups is an essential aspect of this cinematographic approach. There is, of course, the military hierarchy that isolates Captain Richmond, just for an instant, from his men. But, in general, the 1945 footage leaves each person in his own space, with his own pain, his own destiny, his own responsibility, his own shame. When Fuller states that there is no heroism present but instead just witnessing or acknowledgement, he is articulating, without perhaps being fully aware of it, the fact that his meagre and clumsy film succeeds where other Hollywood films fail – including his own. In contrast, he renders unbearable those films where some people's pain (that of the heroes or 'main characters') is portrayed to the detriment of others (that of the 'extras' or *figurants* in French – remember that the Nazis sometimes called the camp detainees *Figuren*), as we see in the films of Spielberg, Benigni and even Polanski, not to mention the television series *Holocaust*. This is why Falkenau's dead, as well as the villagers forced to bury them, are not filmed as a *crowd* but as a *community*, together but one by one, numerous but side by side, each one with his own dignity (that of the dead, whose names and even nationalities remain unknown) or unworthiness (that of the villagers who were undoubtedly still proud of their names).

This is where a fifth act of readability becomes clear. One where *dignity* emerges as the main subject and careful direction of the 1945 film, commented upon scrupulously in 1988. For example, when Fuller notes that the prisoners stand up together when the corpses arrive; or when conversely, he explains 'Richmond has just ordered someone to take off their hat' – a villager whom we see lurking on the side of the road.[111] Fuller's film shows how men – hardened soldiers – attempted to open up a camp by *opening up a space and a time for dignity amid the horror:* each one dressed, each one covered in a shroud, each one honoured by a clod of earth thrown into the communal grave by the living. This kind of dignity consists of both an ethical act and an act of memory: 'teaching a lesson' to the unworthy villagers and organizing this ritual 'so that [the victims] leave this world with dignity ... so that a dignified burial could be given to the dead'[112] as Fuller says again and again in his commentary. It is about asking the living to perform the *ancient gestures* which are summed up in the word 'burial': to hold the body round the waist – the gesture of *pietas*, to dress it, to cover it, to uncover oneself before it out of respect, to bury it, to mark the place where it lies ... Even Fuller's silences in the 1988 footage are like punctuations destined to make this dignity more readable. This is where, what he appropriately calls 'a brief lesson in humanity in twenty-one minutes', lies.[113]

History and the readability of the image

'A brief lesson in humanity in twenty one minutes': this expression assumes that, for Samuel Fuller, 21 minutes of mute images, as long as constructed and watched carefully and with precision (in the critical sense), refusing to come to hasty conclusions, would be capable of 'teaching a lesson', in terms of ethics as well as knowledge – in short in terms of the *humanism* that the director's vocabulary assumes. For Samuel Fuller, the last 'act of readability' is therefore a *pedagogical* task which images, in spite of all, are capable of achieving. Why 'in spite of all'? Because it has become so easy to make images without any kind of work going into them, and for the worst possible reasons. Because Fuller, who had found pornographic images of the horror perpetrated by the SS at the Falkenau site (photos of naked women being chased by dogs[114]) had to, in spite of all, take up his camera and film the horror – film the horror for a 'lesson in humanity', not for some perverse exercise in inhumanity; film the horror in order to learn, with dignity, about the kind of baseness of which men are capable.

To whom is this 'lesson' addressed? Fuller says that Captain Richmond wanted most of all to 'teach a lesson' to the 'bastards' who continued to deny what had nevertheless been right under their noses for years.[115] But the film itself is not at all addressed to them. It could be said that from then on, *it was addressed to children*, that is, to the future of memory. Fuller's cinema, in general, is obsessed with childhood. In *The Big Red One* in particular, children become, as it were, the principal parts in acting out History with a capital H (even though they play the secondary parts in the narrative). There are those who do want to learn the lesson and those who don't – whether it be the young Sicilian boy who drags his mother's dead body around behind him, the little girl who weaves flowers around the soldier's helmet, the Hitlerite boy who is smacked on the bottom instead of being shot, or the child at the camp who dies, eyes wide open, on the sergeant's shoulders. In the 1945 film, it was not only a child playing on the side of the road with his wooden gun whom we saw; we also see a very young man in shorts who covers up the dead with a white sheet in the communal grave, with Fuller recalling that Richmond threatened him with death if he dared to put one foot on the corpses ('If you walk on the corpses, I will kill you'). Later, in the 1988 footage, it is as though Fuller is speaking to children when he explains what the expression *Arbeit macht frei* means.

So, on the one hand, the 1945 film is an image of the past; on the other hand, it is like a 20 minute will or testament written in images, which as a film and especially as a testament 'doesn't lie'[116] when faced with its responsibilities towards history. Many, if not most, films doubtless lie. But a film thought-out and worked-out like a 'will' or a 'lesson' in history owes it to itself not to lie. This, at the very least, is the dignity which Fuller gave these images: to ensure that when looking at them one can know something truthful (even if this is something singular, local and lacunary) about Nazi camps, and better still, that one can 'revolt against what one sees'.[117] It is evidently even more complex than this: Fuller addresses children like an old man who has been at war tells future generations about the inhumanity men are capable of; but in return, he is also questioning children's gazes, their particular way of *looking at history in images*.

Fuller teaches a lesson because he has first-hand knowledge. But he is also seeking to learn something from childhood's gaze. Herein lie his greatness and his modesty: he knows that knowledge is not only limited to the master. One example clearly and simply demonstrates this: when looking at the road that leads to the camp, Fuller stops to film the child who is playing; when looking at the hillock on the outer edge of the camp, he imagines that children must have played there, and that they must have watched with curiosity: 'children playing on that hillock would surely have been able to see inside the camp … kids love climbing up and down hills.'[118] And this is why, in *The Big Red One,* Fuller would have multicoloured flowers carefully planted all around the edge of the camp, in stark contrast to the barbed wire and gunfire; he would say that only a child would be able to look at the contrast (which for adults would be morally unbearable) between blooming spring flowers and the death that reigned over it all regardless.[119] The question remains as to what the child would later go on to do with this gaze.

There is a fundamental relationship between childhood and history: because experience and imagination are indissociable, because children take the haunting capacity and the ghostly nature of images seriously.[120] Samuel Fuller includes cinema in this relationship, or even thinks of it in terms of cinema.[121] To go above and beyond summary typologies about relationships between cinema and history[122] and to put aside the contradictions that cinema evidently faces due to its double relationship with history and fable,[123] perhaps one should meditate on Serge Daney's writing about the *innocence of the gaze* in the first films that accompanied the opening of the camps (at least those which were on the whole amateur and not directly subject to the liberation armies' juridical protocols) – namely those of George Stevens[124] and Samuel Fuller:

> What I understand today is that the beauty of Stevens' film lies less in the justness of the distance found than in the *innocence* of its gaze. Justness is the burden of whoever comes 'after'; innocence is the terrible grace bestowed on the first to arrive, the first person who simply makes the cinematic gesture … not so much the not-guilty, but the one who, in filming evil does not think of evil … In 1945, it was perhaps enough just to be American and, like George Stevens or Corporal Samuel Fuller at Falkenau, to witness the opening of the real gates of the night, camera in hand. One had to be American (and therefore to believe in the fundamental innocence of spectacle) in order to be able to parade the German population in front of these open tombs, to *show* them what they had lived so easily and so terribly next to. It took ten years before Resnais sat down at his editing table … .[125]

The great force of this writing makes us understand that the gaze brought to bear on the camps should not just be judged according to a system of moral oppositions (Pontecorvo's 'abjectness' against the 'innocence' of Fuller's or Stevens' panoramas), but should also and especially be placed in time according to an *historical system relating to images*. So Daney assumes that filming a camp during its opening, and making a film about camps once they are just ruins or museums simply does not constitute the same cinematographic gesture. When a camp opens, the issue is about knowing how to bear and *direct the gaze*, to open the eyes with the 'terrible grace' of discovery, as Serge Daney dares to write. Afterwards, it becomes something altogether different: it is about *finding the point of view*, finding the 'appropriate distance'. When a camp opens, we just look, stupefied; we take in everything we can *without thinking of evil*. Afterwards, it is about choosing, understanding, *thinking about evil*. When a camp opens, the issue is just about filming as much as possible and 'carrying out cinematic gestures' which meant for Fuller *walking* on the site of horror, camera in hand – that small camera with its manual-wind which recorded images at varying speeds, giving the 1945 film its 'primitive' rhythm. Later, with Emil Weiss, it would be about *sitting* at the editing table in order to bring the value of historical readability to the original footage.

Finally, as Daney rightly points out, filming the space of a camp as it opens is only possible if the medium can be *trusted*, in the 'fundamental innocence' of its optical recording. Later it would be about how to use images according to a *critical* point of view, according to a concomitant analysis of the sight's 'non-innocence'. This is why, despite their proclaimed relationship to childhood (childhood relating to entertainment and not to the wide-eyed gaze when faced with the world's harshness), the cinematographic enterprises of Steven Spielberg or Robert Benigni cannot be credited as being innocent. It is significant that in 1959 Samuel Fuller broached this very subject in a film called *Verboten*, where after the war, a teenage Hitlerite finds himself confronted with images (and text from the evidence for the prosecution, read by Samuel Fuller himself) from the Nuremberg Tribunal. 'It was enough just to be American', as Serge Daney says, to still believe in 'the sight's fundamental innocence' in 1959, because the child, after opening his eyes wide, bursts into tears, slumps back into his seat, accepts the truth and enters the 'Good' camp.[126]

In a recent article in *Cahiers du cinéma*, Hubert Damisch mentioned a similar example, directed in 1946 by Orson Welles in his film *The Stranger*: here it is not a child, but a young wife (another figure of innocence) to which an investigator from the Interallied Commission on War Crimes shows images of the camps, so that she might recognize the enormity of the crime of which her husband is suspected of committing. This 'truth session' is directed and edited as follows:

The protagonists watch the unfolding film but the viewer is only permitted to watch flickers of light that the screen casts on their faces, apart from a few images which appear at the edges of shots, just a slight camera movement which is only just noticeable. This happens with the first image, as I said barely visible, showing a pile of naked corpses scattered across the ground ... After which the projection is suddenly interrupted as the film skips, the empty bobbin races on, and the broken end of film continues to turn, making a tapping noise.[127]

This off-camera narrative, incidentally omnipresent in all of Orson Welles' work, strangely provide Hubert Damisch with the opportunity to enter carelessly into what he calls the 'new quarrel over images', even though he denounces its pathetic and deceptive nature, after which he evokes the argument between Jean-Luc Godard and Claude Lanzmann about *Can and do images of the gas chambers exist?*. If he is to be believed, this argument can be equated with the argument opposing my own 'diatribe' about *Images in Spite of All* to Gérard Wajcman's 'critique' of images.[128] After making three or four hasty judgements backed up by some surprising untruths,[129] Hubert Damisch comes to his principal argument, that he articulates in the form of a psychoanalytical *credo* borrowed from Gérard Wajcman himself: 'Gérard Wajcman was right to remind us, contrary to those who are in favour of images *in spite of all*, that Freudian psychoanalysis has long professed that "problems with images" cannot in fact be solved by using images but by using words.'[130]

Despite his reference to *Studies on Hysteria*, this argument is as simplistic in relation to Freudian psychoanalysis as it is in relation to the notion of the image. It considers the former as simply a way of 'solving problems' and the latter as simply a 'problem to be solved', like a sort of sickness that should be gotten rid of. But Freud knew how to respond when faced with the image – even one of an hysterical convulsion – so that it could be questioned for what it was, and not 'solved' in some curative process thought of as the destruction of the image; he did not look at the smiles of people painted by Leonardo da Vinci in order to 'solve' them, but in order to let their own power speak while seeking to understand, if only partially, their unconscious motives. An 'analytical iconology' that in this way would attempt to cast out its own subject, to 'solve' it like a problem by replacing it with words or speech is not *iconological* in the sense that Aby Warburg was first to give this word, or *analytical* in the sense that Freud gave it when speaking of 'construction in analysis', for example.

At the limit of this argument is the eternal primacy of language over the image from which structuralist semiology, and especially the tendency to read Lacan only through the lens of language, has never succeeded in freeing itself completely. Hubert Damisch perhaps senses this *malaise* because in his analysis of Welles, a hesitation can be observed as to whether the *primacy of words* should be defended (psychoanalytical argument in line with the prosecutor's position in *The Stranger* as a subject revealing truth to his young 'patient's' conscience) or the *primacy of montage* (a more directly cinematographic argument in line with Orson Welles' own position when he says 'montage is not one aspect, *it is the aspect*[131]), which is not at all the same thing. It is indeed not the same thing to 'solve problems of images with words', i.e. to *reduce* images to words which could redeem them, as it is to *construct* their readability, their own anamnesis and knowledge using montage.

The example chosen seems to principally back up the first argument: Hubert Damisch notes that in the sequence directed by Orson Welles, the snatches of documentary images, which he fails to question in terms of history and to whose true provenance he is indifferent,[132] are only shown as flashes: images already reduced in terms of the time they have to appear, as well as in terms of the prosecutor's speech when he sums them up for the young Mary. If Welles is the first cinematographer to have used such documentary images of camps in a work of fiction,[133] his production remains entirely constructed around dialogue, or rather, around the kind of interrogation and prosecutor's summing up designed, as Wilson the prosecutor says, so that we 'hear the truth'. Moreover, what is mostly filmed is the *pathos* caused in Mary as she listens: the light from the projected images does indeed fall on her face, but she manages easily to extricate herself from seeing these documents by looking at the prosecutor as he speaks, reacting violently to his accusatory words (in her eyes the images themselves do not accuse her loved one) and seeming to find the words *clocks* or *Nazi* more horrible than any of the shots of dead bodies before her eyes. It is only when the film snaps that she really jumps with fright. The fact that she ends up running away, distressed, into the garden is not down to the terrible images she has just seen, but to the risk posed to her dearest love.

In short, this fiction does undoubtedly contain small pieces of documentary (Orson Welles would later tell Peter Bogdanovitch 'a step forward is made each time an opportunity arises to force the public to watch images of a concentration camp, whatever the pretext'[134]), but they are there for the purposes of the narrative, where images only constitute a kind of accessory to the film's ending. Mary will go on to understand that she has married a 'criminal' (without the help of images, which have no real destiny in this story, and are never again evoked in the film) at the same time as she realizes she will be his next victim, like in any good thriller. *The Stranger* therefore does not in any way, as Hubert Damisch believes, anticipate Resnais's, Godard's and Lanzmann's specific reflections on the central question of cinema when confronted with the question of the camps, as this question is quite simply not central to Welles' film.[135]

However, things are quite different in Samuel Fuller's *Verboten*: the young Franz, who after the war was a member of a group of young Hitlerites who sabotage Germany's reconstruction, is brought before the Nuremberg Tribunal by his sister, and while there, with a mixture of stupefaction and horror, is confronted full in face with filmed documentary of what was called in 1945 'Nazi atrocities', with Fuller organizing all his production and editing around the power of these images over the young man's conscience. Be that as it may, Welles' and Fuller's sequences both use the same historical model, which Damisch quite simply ignores: cinematographic showings from the Nuremberg Tribunal, with the faces of the accused lit up amid the darkness, while films of their 'atrocities' unfold on the screen. Journalists from all over the world would describe this extraordinary face to face between senior Nazis and images of their own crimes. A report of the Tribunal written by Joseph Kessel for 3 December 1945 issue of *France-Soir* is particularly eloquent in describing this dialectic of *faces* being 'watched while watching' and of 'watched and watchful' images:

> That's when, in the enormous darkened room, I noticed a second source of light. On my left, the beam of a projector lit up perfectly the two rows of seating on which, ten by ten, the accused found themselves. This lighting must have been adjusted in advance with extreme care: dim, clear, subtle and, as though aware of them, it lit up their faces at a diagonal angle, and in a way that didn't interfere at all with their vision, but at the same time, none of their expressions could escape the gazes of the public and the judges. This therefore was the real object of the exercise: it was not to show members of the Tribunal a document about which they no doubt had a profound knowledge. It was about suddenly putting the criminals face to face with their enormous crime … and catching the movements that this spectacle, this shock, forcibly provoked in them.

> Thus, only two beams of light were present in the whole of the darkened room. On one of them could be seen the bare horror of the concentration camps. On the other could be seen the exposed profiles of the faces of those who were responsible for it. Goering, viceroy of the Third Reich, clamped shut his livid jaws, so that it looked as though they would break. The commander in chief Keitel, from whom the armies had saved so many men destined for the mass graves, covered his eyes with a trembling hand. A grimace of abject fear deformed the features of Streicher, executioner of the Jews. Ribbentrop moistened his dry lips with his tongue. A dark red colour covered the cheeks of von Papen, a member of the *Herren Klub* and Hitler's servant, Frank, who had decimated Poland, burst into tears.

> And all of us, who, with tight throats watched this spectacle in the darkness, felt as though we were witness to a unique moment in the existence of mankind.[136]

This eminently dialectical situation opens up the possibility for *montage* where images are not separated, isolated or in hypostasis with regard to the faces who watch them and where, symmetrically, these faces will not place the images which gaze at them off-camera. If montage is a way of finding readability, it does not presume to reduce any of its constituent dimensions. Hubert Damisch describes montage as 'the truth of cinema, the *truth in cinema*'[137] and on this point I can only wholeheartedly agree with him.[138] It is also necessary to know what *writing* means when Damisch borrows this expression from Blanchot to say that montage is 'about writing'.[139] Writing, according to Blanchot, far from what Damisch's polemical position in the so-called 'quarrel over images' implies, is in no way there to 'solve problems of the image using words': quite the contrary, it is there to *unravel images* as a 'medium' for appearance and disappearance to which Blanchot continually returns.[140]

'Problems of images' are not 'solved' by writing and montage. Rather, writing and montage lend images a readability which assumes a double and dialectical standpoint (on the condition, of course, that along with Benjamin we understand that to dialecticize is not to synthesize, to resolve, nor to 'solve'): continually opening wide our childlike eyes before the image (accepting the ordeal, the not-knowing, the danger of the image, the flaws of language) and continually constructing, as adults, the image's 'knowability' (which assumes knowledge, a point of view, the act of writing, ethical reflection). To *read* is to *link* these two things – *lesen* in German means just that: to read and to link, to gather and to decode – just as in the life of our faces, our eyes continually open and close.

One of Freud's famous dreams speaks of this, and is even more exemplary in that it precedes a founding moment in psychoanalysis (the discovery that an unconscious memory exists outside of normal memory) and in that it articulates the ethical dimension of respect owed to the dead, along with the epistemological dimension of the past's readability. On 2 November 1896, Freud writes to Wilhelm Fliess about his pain and his mourning for his father who had died a few days before: 'in [my] inner self the whole past has been awakened by this event. I now feel quite uprooted'.[141] He then speaks of the dream which he 'had during the night following his burial' and where the following inscription could be read: 'You are requested to close the eyes.'[142] The *Traumadeutung* text follows with two variants:

The night before my father was buried I had a dream of a printed panel, a placard or notice nailed up, rather like the notices forbidding smoking in railway waiting rooms. Written on it is either:

> *You are requested to close your eyes.*

Or

> *You are requested to keep an eye closed.*[143]

Here, where a French reader would spontaneously take from this sentence a command to close one's eyelids, to turn away from the visible world (and who knows, to 'solve' once and for all 'the problem of images'), Freud uses a very specific expression (*die Augen zudrücken*) which is not an expression usually used to say that eyelids should be closed so as not to see (*die Augen schließen*). The verb *zudrücken* is much stronger: it is to close tightly, to clamp shut, as one closes one's eyes for a few instants after receiving a shock to the face – even the shock of an image. But, most of all, *die Augen zudrücken* commonly means 'to close the eyes of a dead person' and figuratively 'to *comfort* someone in their last hour'. To use the singular, the expression *ein Auge zudrücken* (literally to close an eye) means 'to use indulgence' which in Freud's dreams refers to the duty towards the dead, something which is often imperfectly carried out:

> The sentence on the sign has a double meaning: one should do one's duty to the dead (an apology as though I had not done it and were in need of leniency), and the actual duty itself. The dream thus stems from the inclination to self-reproach that regularly sets in among the survivors.[144]

But the expression that Freud dreams about, and which is made readable by him, has a more general meaning, in which we locate the motivation behind Samuel Fuller's short film at Falkenau (as an historian's undertaking when faced with the camps): in a single action, it is to *close the eyes of the dead* (an ethical action particularly necessary at a camp's opening) and to *keep our eyes open to their death* (an action relating to the knowledge and vigilance necessary 60 years later). This action perhaps fundamentally involves the act of writing: it is found in poetic writing like that of Gershom Scholem (in a biblical archaeology involving finesse, offering and lamentation[145]) in testimonial writing like that of Primo Levi,[146] and in historical writing like that of Aby Warburg, when he said he wanted, despite everything, to make suffering a 'treasure' for humanity.[147]

Closer to home, Michel de Certeau, extrapolating Michelet's expression according to which the shadows of the dead 'returned to their graves with less sadness', spoke of history writing being like a *statement of evidence*. He said that the historian 'weeps' for the dead and 'closes their eyes': 'This loss and this obligation generate writing.'[148] So that writing, as Benjamin implored in 1940, serves as much as possible to protect the dead themselves from the 'enemy [that] has not ceased to be victorious'.[149] So that, even where *survival fails* (I am thinking of the sick condemned to die in the liberated Falkenau camp) a bit of film, even though clumsy, lacunary and 'scratched to death' can all the same *start an afterlife* which sustains our memory.

Translated by Katie Tidmarsh, 2010.

Translated from the original French: 'Ouvrir les camps, fermer les yeux', *Annales, Histoire, Sciences sociales*, LXI, 2006, pp. 1011–1049; reprinted in Georges Didi-Huberman, *Remontages du temps subi: L'Oeuil de l'histoire* (Paris: Editions de Minuit, 2010), pp. 9–67.

Notes

1. Annette Wieviorka, *Auschwitz, 60 ans après* (Paris: Robert Laffont, 2005), p. 9.
2. Wieviorka: *Auschwitz, 60 ans après*, pp. 9–10.
3. Wieviorka: *Auschwitz, 60 ans après*, pp. 14 and 20.
4. See Régine Robin, *La Mémoire saturée* (Paris: Stock, 2003), pp. 217–375 ('Une mémoire menacée: la Shoah').
5. Robin: *La Mémoire saturée*, pp. 304–14 (where we see that Régine Robin has difficulty in drawing out a point of view from the so-called 'quarrel over images of the camps'). For an excellent – and incisive – summary of the use of history as memory, see Enzo Traverso, *Le Passé, modes d'emploi. Histoire, mémoire, politique* (Paris: La Fabrique, 2005).
6. Florent Brayard, *La 'Solution finale de la question juive': la technique, le temps et les catégories de la décision* (Paris: Fayard, 2004).
7. See Georges Didi-Huberman, 'Pour une anthropologie des singularités formelles. Remarque sur l'invention warburgienne', *Genèses. Sciences sociales et histoire* 24 (1996), pp. 145–63 (where Ginzburg's 'evidential paradigm' is discussed). It is from the point of view of this principle that I attempted to interrogate the four photographs taken in August 1944 by members of the Birkenau *Sonderkommando*. See Didi-Huberman, *Images malgré tout* (Paris: Minuit, 2003), English version: *Images In Spite of All: Four Photographs from Auschwitz* (Chicago: University of Chicago Press, 2008).
8. Raul Hilberg, *The Destruction of the European Jews* [1961] (New Haven, CT: Yale University Press, 2002).
9. Henri Bergson, *La Pensée et le mouvant. Essais et conférences*, ed. André Robinet, Œuvres (Paris: PUF, 1959 ed. 1970), p. 1253.
10. Walter Benjamin, *The Arcades Project*, trans. Howard Eiland and Kevin McLaughlin (London: The Belknap Press of Harvard University Press, 1999), p. 461.
11 Benjamin: *The Arcades Project*, p. 461.
12. Benjamin: *The Arcades Project*, pp. 462–3.
13. Benjamin: *The Arcades Project*, p. 460. On this matter, see Georges Didi-Huberman, *Devant le temps. Histoire de l'art et anachronisme des images* (Paris: Minuit, 2000); Didi-Huberman, *L'Image survivante. Histoire de l'art et temps des fantômes selon Aby Warburg* (Paris: Minuit, 2002); Cornelia Zumbusch, *Wissenschaft in Bildern. Symbol und dialektisches Bild in Aby Warburgs Mnemosyne-Atlas und Walter Benjamins Passagen-Werk* (Berlin: Akademie Verlag, 2004).
14. Aby Warburg, 'L'art du portrait et la bourgeoisie florentine. Domenico Ghirlandaio à Santa Trinità. Les portraits de Laurent de Médicis et de son entourage' (1902), trans. S. Muller, *Essais florentins* (Paris: Klincksieck, 1990), p. 106.
15. See Gerhard Neumann and Sigrid Weigel (eds), *Lesbarkeit der Kultur. Literaturwissenschaften zwischen Kulturtechnik und Ethnographie* (Munich: Wilhelm Fink, 2000).

16. In a subsequent section of *The Arcades Project*, Benjamin attempts to resume this notion of historical readability in five words: 'images' (*Bilder*), 'monad' (*Monade*), 'experience' (*Erfahrung*), 'immanent critique' (*immanente Kritik*) and, finally, 'rescue' (*Rettung*) of memory. Benjamin, *The Arcades Project*, p. 476.

17. Walter Benjamin, 'Theses on the Philosophy of History', in *Illuminations*, trans. Harry Zorn (London: Pimlico, 1999), p. 247.

18. Walter Laqueur, *The Terrible Secret: Suppression of the Truth about Hitler's 'Final Solution'* (New York: Henry Holt & Co., 1998).

19. *Soviet Government Statements of Nazi Atrocities* (London: Hutchinson, 1946), p. 222.

20. All this information comes from Stuart Liebman's very precise study: 'La libération des camps vue par le cinéma: l'exemple de *Vernichtungslager Majdanek*', trans. J.-F. Cornu, *Les Cahiers du judaïsme* 15 (2003), pp. 49–60.

21. See Renata Boguslawska-Swiebocka and Teresa Ceglowska, *KL Auschwitz. Fotografie dokumentalne* (Warsaw: Krajowa Agencja Wydawnicza: 1980); Teresa Swiebocka (ed.), *Auschwitz. A History in Photographs*, trans. Jonathan Webber and Connie Wilsack (Oswiecim/Warsaw/Bloomington, IN: Auschwitz-Birkenau Museum/Ksiazka I Wiedza/ Indiana University Press, 1993), pp. 190–215 and *passim*; Andrzej Strzelecki, *The Evacuation, Dismantling and Liberation of KL Auschwitz* (Oswiecim: Auschwitz-Birkenau State Museum, 2001); Wieviorka, *Auschwitz, 60 ans après*, pp. 23–37.

22. Clément Chéroux (ed.), *Mémoire des camps. Photographies des camps de concentration et d'extermination nazis (1933–1999)* (Paris: Patrimoine photographique-Marval, 2001), pp. 103–27.

23. Chéroux, *Mémoire des camps*, pp. 128–71.

24. Susan Sontag, *Sur la photographie* (1973), trans. Philippe Blanchard (Paris: Christian Bourgeois, 1983 ed. 1993), p. 34.

25. Liebman, 'La libération des camps vue par le cinéma', p. 55.

26. Alexandre Voronsov's testimony, in Wieviorka: *Auschwitz, 60 ans après*, pp. 27–8.

27. Ilsen About, Stephan Matyus and Jean-Marie Winkler (eds), *La Part visible des camps. Les photographies du camp de concentration de Mauthausen* (Vienna/Paris: Bundesministerium für Inneres/Editions Tiresias, 2005), pp. 130–41 (where the terrible shots from 5 May 1945 can be seen just before those of the re-enactment of the camp's liberation on 7 May).

28. See Marie-Anne Matard-Bonucci and Édouard Lynch (eds), *La Libération des camps et le retour des déportés* (Brussels: Éditions Complexe, 1995), pp. 63–73 ('La pédagogie de l'horreur') and pp. 163–75 ('Les filtres successifs de l'information'); Christian Delporte, 'Les medias et la découverte des camps (presses, radio, actualités filmées)', *La Déportation. Le système concentrationnaire nazi*, ed. François Bédarida and Laurent Gervereau (Paris: Musée d'Histoire contemporaine-BDIC, 1995), pp. 205–13; Dagmar Barnow, *Germany 1945. Views of War and Violence* (Bloomington, IN: Indiana University Press, 1996); Claudine Drame, 'Représenter l'irreprésentable: les camps nazis dans les actualités françaises de 1945', *Cinémathèque* 10 (1996), pp. 12–28; Sylvie Lindeperg, *Clio de 5 à 7. Les actualités filmées de la Libération, archives du future* (Paris: CNRS-Éditions, 2000), pp. 155–209.

29. See Annette Insdorf, *L'Holocauste à l'écran* (Paris: Le Cerf, 1985); Ilan Avisar, *Screening the Holocaust: Cinema's Images of the Unimaginable* (Bloomington, IN: Indiana University Press, 1988); Micel Deguy (ed.), *Au sujet de Shoah, le film de Claude Lanzmann* (Paris: Belin, 1990); Saul Friedlander (ed.), *Probing the Limits of Representation. Nazism and the 'Final Solution'* (Cambridge, MA: Harvard University

Press, 1992); Beatrice Fleury-Vilatte, *Cinéma et culpabilité en Allemagne, 1945–1990* (Perpignan: Institut Jean Vigo, 1995), pp. 21–52; Guy Gauthier, *Le Documentaire, un autre cinéma* (Paris: Armand Colin, 1995 (ed. 2005), pp. 224–8; Barbie Zelizer, *Remembering to Forget. Holocaust Memory Through the Camera's Eye* (Chicago, IL: The University of Chicago Press, 1998); Francesco Monicelli and Carlo Saletti (eds), *Il racconto della catastrofe. Il cinema di fronte a Auschwitz* (Verona: Società Letteraria-Cierre Edizioni, 1998); Philippe Mesnard, 'La mémoire cinématographique de la Shoah', *Parler des camps, penser les génocides,* ed. Catherine Coquio (Paris: Albin Michel, 1999), pp. 473–90; François Niney, *L'Épreuve du reel à l'écran. Essai sur le principe de réalité documentaire* (Brussels: De Boeck Université, 2000 ed. 2002), pp. 253–92; Vincent Lowy, *L'Histoire infilmable. Les camps d'extermination nazis à l'écran* (Paris: L'Harmattan, 2001), pp. 38–56; Omer Bartov, Atina Grossman and Mary Nolan (eds), *Crimes of War. Guilt and Denial in the Twentieth Century* (New York: The New Press, 2002), pp. 61–99; Waltraud Wara Wende (ed.), *Geschichte im Film. Mediale Inszenierungen des Holocaust und kulturelles Gedächtnis* (Stuttgart/Weimar: Metzler, 2002); Sven Kramer (ed.), *Die Shoah im Bild* (Munich: Text + Kritik, 2003).

30. Giorgio Agamben, 'What is a camp?', *Means without End: Notes on Politics,* trans. Vincenzo Binetti and Cesare Casarino (Minneapolis, MN: University of Minnesota Press, 2000), p. 39; Agamben, *Homo Sacer. Sovereign Power and Bare Life,* trans. Daniel Heller-Roazen (Stanford, CA: Stanford University Press, 1998), p. 169.

31. Florent Brayard (ed.), *Le Génocide des juifs entre procès et histoire, 1943–2000* (Paris/Brussels: IHTP/Éditions Complexe, 2000). About the relationship between history and law – that is between historian and judge, see Carlo Ginzburg, *The Judge and the Historian: Marginal Notes on a Late-Twentieth-Century Miscarriage of Justice,* trans. Antony Shugaar (London: Verso, 1999); Ginzburg, *History, Rhetoric, and Proof. The Menachem Stern Jerusalem Lectures* (London/Hanover: University Press of New England, 1999).

32. On the general question of visual testimony and images as proof, see Renaud Dulong, *Le Témoin-oculaire. Les conditions sociales de l'attestation personelle* (Paris: Éditions de l'EHESS, 1998); Peter Burke, *Eyewitnessing. The Uses of Images as Historical Evidence* (Ithaca, NY: Cornell University Press, 2001); François Niney (ed.), *La Preuve par l'image? L'évidence des prises de vue* (Valence: Centre de Recherche et d'Action culturelle, 2003).

33. Quoted by Christian Delage, 'L'image comme preuve. L'expérience du procès de Nuremberg', *Vingtième Siècle. Revue d'histoire* 72 (2001), 65.

34. See Lawrence Douglas, 'Film as Witness: Screening *Nazi Concentration Camps* before the Nuremberg Tribunal', (1995), *Memory of Judgement: Making Law and History in the Trials of the Holocaust* (New Haven, CT: Yale University Press, 2001), pp. 11–37. Christian Delage, 'L'Image photographique dans le procès de Nuremberg', pp. 63–78. Christian Delage has also published the text of the Nuremberg Tribunal hearing on 29 November 1945 in which the film *Nazi Concentration Camps* was shown. Commandant Donovan announces explicitly that 'the United States present a documentary about the concentration camps as evidence. This account comes from films taken gradually of the areas where the camps were found by military authorities during the liberation by allied armies.' 'L'Audience du 29 novembre 1945 du Tribunal militaire international de Nuremberg et la projection du film *Les Camps de concentration nazis*', quoted by Christian Delage, *Les Cahiers du judaïsme* 15 (2003), 81–95 (p. 84 here).

35. Christian Delage, *Les Cahiers du judaïsme*, p. 87. On films taken by the British army and Sidney Bernstein's unfinished project – for which Alfred Hitchcock advised on editing – see Sylvie Lindeperg, *Clio 5 à 7*, pp. 231–5; Benedetta Guerzoni, '*The Memory of the Camps*, un film inachevé. Les aléas de la dénonciation des atrocités nazies et de la politique britannique de communication en Allemagne', *Les Cahiers du judaïsme* 15 (2003), 61–70. See chapter 2 in this volume.

36. See Didi-Huberman, *Images malgré tout*, pp. 115–49.

37. See Laurent Gervereau, *Les Images qui mentent. Histoire visuel au XXe siècle* (Paris: Le Seuil, 2000), pp. 203–19.

38. See Martine Joly, 'Le cinéma d'archives, preuve de l'histoire ?', *Les Institutions de l'image*, ed. Jean-Pierre Bertin-Maghit and Béatrice Fleury-Vilatte (Paris: Éditions de l'EHESS, 2001), pp. 201–12 (about Sidney Bernstein's film).

39. Quoted by Christian Delage, 'L'image comme preuve', p. 69.

40. Today these testimonies form a corpus of considerable size. On more about their status and the way they demand the historian's attention, see Annette Wieviorka, *L'Ère du témoin* (Paris: Plon, 1998 and Paris: Hachette-Littératures, 2002). Among the most recent publications of testimonies about the opening of the camps, see *Les Derniers jours de la déportation* (Paris: Le Félin, 2005); Christian Bernadac, *La Libération des camps racontée par ceux qui l'ont vécue* (1995), new edition ed. É. Bernadac (Paris: Éditions France-Empire, 2005).

41. Charlotte Delbo, *Auschwitz and After*, trans. Rosette C. Lamont (New Haven, CT: Yale University Press, 1995), p. 219.

42. David Rousset, *Les Jours de notre mort* (1947) (Paris: Hachette-Littératures, 1993), p. 960.

43. Élie Wiesel, *Night*, trans. Stella Rodway (London: Penguin, 1981), p. 126.

44. Hermann Langbein, *Hommes et femmes à Auschwitz* (1972), trans. Denise Meunier (Paris: Fayard, 1975) (ed–1997), pp. 448–75.

45. Primo Levi with Leonardo De Benedetti, *Auschwitz Report*, trans. Judith Woolf (London: Verso, 2006), pp. 31–2.

46. Levi and De Benedetti, *Auschwitz Report*, pp. 32 ff.

47. See François Rastier, 'Primo Levi: prose du témoin, poèmes du survivant', *Formes discursives du témoignage*, ed. François-Charles Gaudard and Modesta Suárez (Toulouse: Éditions Universitaires du Sud, 2003), pp. 143–60; Rastier, *Ulysse à Auschwitz : Primo Levi, le survivant* (Paris: Le Cerf, 2005). Also see Claude Mouchard's beautiful text, ' "Ici"? "Maintenant"? Témoignages et œuvres', *La Shoah. Témoignages, savoirs, œuvres*, ed. Claude Mouchard and Annette Wieviorka (Saint-Denis: Presses Universitaires de Vincennes-Cercil, 1999), pp. 225–60.

48. See Samuel Beckett, *The Unnamable*, in *Molloy; Malone Dies; The Unnamable*, trans. the author, 1959), (London: Calder and Boyars, 1959), p. 418: 'you must go on, I can't go on, you must go on, I'll go on, you must say words, as long as there are any, until they find me, until they say me, strange pain, strange sin, you must go on, perhaps it's done already, perhaps they have said me already, perhaps they have carried me to the threshold of my story, before the door that opens on my story, that would surprise me, if it opens, it will be I, it will be the silence, where I am, I don't know, I'll never know, in the silence you don't know, you must go on, I can't go on, I'll go on.'

49. Primo Levi, *If This Is a Man*, trans. Stuart Woolf (London: Abacus, 1987), pp. 157–79. This final chapter is simply called 'The Story of Ten Days'.

50. Levi, *If This Is a Man*, p. 162.

51. Levi, *If This Is a Man*, pp. 163–4.

52. Levi, *If This Is a Man*, p. 166.
53. Levi, *If This Is a Man*, p. 171.
54. Levi, *If This Is a Man*, pp. 174–5.
55. Levi, *If This Is a Man*, pp. 176–7.
56. Levi, *If This Is a Man*, p. 177.
57. Levi, *If This Is a Man*, p. 178.
58. Levi, *If This Is a Man*, p. 178.
59. Imre Kertész, 'Discours prononcé à la reception du prix Nobel de littérature à Stockholm, le 10. décembre 2002', trans. N. and C. Zaremba, *Bulletin de la Fondation d'Auschwitz* 80–81 (2003), 169.
60. Primo Levi, 'Retour à Auschwitz', (1982), transcription Marco Belpoliti, in Primo Levi and Leonardo De Benedetti, *Rapport sur Auschwitz* (1945–1946), trans. Catherine Petitjean (Paris: Kimé, 2005), p. 108. We know that Giorgio Agamben radicalized this idea in going as far as saying the camp is 'the hidden matrix and *nomos* of the political space in which we still live'. Giorgio Agamben, 'What Is a Camp?', p. 36. Agamben, *Homo Sacer*, p. 166.
61. Robert Antelme, *The Human Race*, trans. Jeffrey Haight and Annie Mahler (Marlboro, VT: The Marlboro Press, 1992).
62. Antelme, *The Human Race*, pp. 287–9.
63. Antelme, *The Human Race*, pp. 289–90. For more about unbearable accounts of the deportation, see Annette Wieviorka, 'Indicible ou inaudible? La déportation: premiers récits (1944–1947)', *Pardès* 9–10 (1989), 23–59.
64. Samuel Fuller, *A Third Face. My Tale of Writing, Fighting and Filmmaking*, eds. Christa Lang Fuller and Jerome Henry Rudes (New York: Bantam Books, 1962). On Samuel Fuller, see: Lee Server, *Samuel Fuller: Film is a Battleground. A Critical Study, with Interviews, a Filmography, and a Bibliography* (London: McFarland, 1994).
65. Fuller, *A Third Face*, p. 110.
66. Fuller, *A Third Face*, p. 105.
67. Fuller, *A Third Face*, pp. 65 and 73.
68. Fuller, *A Third Face*, p. 73.
69. Fuller, *A Third Face*, p. 79.
70. Fuller, *A Third Face*, p. 114.
71. Fuller, *A Third Face*, pp. 118–20.
72. Fuller, *A Third Face*, pp. 162–75.
73. Fuller, *A Third Face*, p. 214.
74. Jean Narboni and Noël Simsolo, *Il était une fois … Samuel Fuller. Histoires d'Amérique*, transcription and trans. Dominique Villain (Paris: Cahiers du Cinéma, 1986), pp. 114–15.
75. Fuller, *A Third Face*, p. 218.
76. Fuller, *A Third Face*, p. 218. Also see Samuel Fuller's testimony in the film by Yann Lardeau and Emil Weiss, *A Travelling is a Moral Affair* (Paris: M.W. Productions, 1986).
77. Fuller, *A Third Face*, pp. 215–16.
78. Fuller, *A Third Face*, p. 215.
79. In Emil Weiss's film, *Falkenau, vision de l'impossible* (Paris: M.W. Productions, 1988).
80. The kind of funeral ceremony imposed on the civilians at Falkenau also happened in numerous other camps, for example in Vaihingen or in Buchenwald. See Marie-Anne Matard-Bonucci and Édouard Lynch (eds), *La Libération des camps et le retour des déportés*, pp. 68–71.

81. See Narboni and Simsolo, *Il était une fois*, pp. 114–18; Lardeau and Weiss, *A Travelling is a Moral Affair.*

82. See Jean-Luc Godard, 'Rien que le cinéma' (1957), *Jean-Luc Godard par Jean-Luc Godard*, ed. Alain Bergala (Paris: Cahiers du Cinéma, 1998), I, p. 96; Godard, 'Signal' (1957), *Jean-Luc Godard par Jean-Luc Godard*, pp. 115–16; Godard, 'Feu sur *Les Carabiniers*' (1963), *Jean-Luc Godard par Jean-Luc Godard*, p. 239; Godard, 'Trois mille heures du cinéma' (1966), *Jean-Luc Godard par Jean-Luc Godard*, p. 295. We know that Godard had Samuel Fuller play himself in *Pierrot le fou*, where cinema would be defined in six words: '*Love, hate, action, violence, death, emotion.*' See Godard, 'Parlons de Pierrot' (1965), *Jean-Luc Godard par Jean-Luc Godard*, p. 268.

83. Narboni and Simsolo, *Il était une fois*, p. 13.

84. Fuller, *A Third Face*, pp. 229–34.

85. Quoted by Server, *Samuel Fuller: Film is a Battleground*, p. 52.

86. See Christian Delage and Vincent Guigueno, *L'Historien et le film* (Paris: Gallimard, 2004), pp. 46–58 and 210–14.

87. Fuller, *A Third Face*, pp. 236 and 240.

88. Fuller, *A Third Face*, pp. 219, 234 and 291.

89. Fuller, *The Big Red One* (1980), trans. Géraldine Koff d'Amico (Paris: Christian Bourgois, 1991), pp. 515–31.

90. Fuller, *A Third Face*, pp. 122, 219, 382–3 (where Fuller recounts the thousands of pages of script, the problems with casting, etc.) and pp. 475–83. The film *The Big Red One* (Los Angeles: Lorimar, 1980) has recently been 'restored' – where numerous scenes that had been cut for its release were replaced (Los Angeles, Warner Bros. Entertainment, 2005).

91. Fuller, *A Third Face*, p. 383.

92. Fuller, *A Third Face*, p. 482.

93. Narboni and Simsolo, *Il était une fois*, p. 320.

94. The version in the novel is slightly different. See Fuller, *The Big Red One*, pp. 520–3.

95. As with all Hollywood films, this silence which Fuller wanted is attenuated by a musical composition which was made without his agreement (he had never even met the composer Dana Kaproff). So here, 'silence' means that the orchestra is reduced to a few oboes, flutes or cellos.

96. See Pierre Vidal-Naquet, *Les Assassins de la mémoire. 'Un Eichmann de papier' et autres essays sur le révisionnisme* (1980–1987) (Paris: La Découverte, 1991).

97. 'Today, there are people who say, like Le Pen, that all of this is a "détail"!' Fuller in E. Weiss's film, *Falkenau.*

98. For more about this return to the site, beyond simply its destruction, see Didi-Huberman, 'Le Lieu malgré tout', (1995), *Phasmes. Essais sur l'apparition* (Paris: Minuit, 1998), pp. 228–42.

99. Fuller, *A Third Face*, p. 511.

100. I am of course thinking of the Roman *imago* and its function in terms of genealogy, dignity and funerals. See Didi-Huberman, 'L'image-matrice. Histoire de l'art et généalogie de la ressemblance', (1995), *Devant le temps*, pp. 59–83.

101. Fuller, *A Third Face*, p. 511.

102. Didi-Huberman, *Images malgré tout*, pp. 110–13.

103. Fuller, *Falkenau.*

104. Fuller, *Falkenau.*

105. Christian Delage reminds us that because of this 'American military tribunals sentenced twenty five torturers from Flossenbürg and its satellite camps to death'. Delage and Guigueno, *L'Historien et le film*, p. 288.

106. Fuller, *Falkenau.*

107. Fuller, *Falkenau.*

108. Fuller, *Falkenau.*

109. Narboni and Simsolo, *Il était une fois*, p. 117.

110. Fuller, *Falkenau.* This is his way of showing the ethical dimension of 'acknowledgement', above and beyond the dimension relating to proof and knowledge.

111. Fuller, *Falkenau.*

112. Fuller, *Falkenau.*

113. Fuller, *Falkenau.*

114. Fuller, *A Third Face*, p. 215.

115. Fuller, *Falkenau.*

116. Fuller, *A Third Face*, p. 217. Fuller would repeat later on p. 511: 'Film doesn't lie'.

117. Fuller, *Falkenau.*

118. Fuller, *Falkenau.*

119. In the film by Yann Lardeau and Emil Weiss, *A Travelling is a Moral Affair.*

120. See Georgio Agamben, *Enfance et histoire. Destruction de l'expérience et origine de l'histoire*, trans. Yves Hersant (Paris: Payot, 1989), pp. 33–4 and 102–6. Let us remember how in 1929 Warburg defined his 'science of images': 'Histoire de fantômes pour grandes personnes' (*Gespenstergeschichte f[ür] ganz Erwachsene*).

121. Christian Delage's two essays should be read together: 'Cinéma, enfance et histoire', *De l'histoire au cinéma*, ed. Antoine de Baecque and Christian Delage (Paris/ Brussels: IHTP/Éditions Complexe, 1998), pp. 61–98 and C. Delage, 'Samuel Fuller à Falkenau : l'évènement fondateur', *L'Historien et le film*, pp. 46–58. Also see the article (that came out when this text had already been written) by Laurent Le Forestier, 'Fuller à Falkenau: l'impossible vision?', *1895. Revue de l'Association française de recherché sur l'histoire du cinéma* 47 (2005), pp. 184–93.

122. In Marco Ferro's nevertheless pioneering work *Cinéma et histoire* (1977), (Paris: Gallimard, 1993), pp. 144–52 ('Sur l'antinazisme américain, 1939–1943') and 217–26 ('Y a-t-il une vision filmique de l'histoire?').

123. See Jacques Rancière, 'L'historicité du cinéma', *De l'histoire au cinéma*, pp. 45–60. J. Rancière, *La Fable cinématographique* (Paris: Le Seuil, 2001).

124. For more on Stevens, see C. Delage, 'La couleur des camps', *Les Cahiers du judaïsme* 15 (2003), pp. 71–80.

125. Serge Daney, 'Le travelling de *Kapò*' (1992), *Persévérence* (Paris: P.O.L., 1994), p. 24. Translation adapted from: Serge Daney, 'The Travelling Shot in Kapò' in *Postcards from the Cinema*, trans. Paul Douglas Grant (Oxford: Berg, 2007), p. 23–24.

126. See Fuller, *A Third Face*, pp. 365–74. Narboni and Simsolo, *Il était une fois*, pp. 226–34. For a critique of this scene, see Sylvie Lindeperg, *Clio de 5 à 7*, pp. 258–60.

127. Hubert Damisch, 'Montage du désastre', *Cahiers du cinéma* 599 (2005), p. 76.

128. Damisch, 'Montage du désastre', pp. 73 and 78.

129. Damisch, 'Montage du désastre', pp. 76–7. First and foremost, Damisch wants to make out that I presented images of the Auschwitz *Sonderkommando* as previously

unpublished, 'known about for a long time' he writes, whereas I have in fact followed the history from 1944 up until their treatment in recent history books (Didi-Huberman, *Images malgré tout*, pp.11–56). He then disputes, in so many words, without arguments to back himself up, that two of these photos were taken from the gas chamber at the Birkenau V crematorium (Damisch, 'Montage du désastre', pp. 22–5 and 144–9). He infers from this that these images 'presumably taken from one of the gas chambers at Auschwitz … cannot in any case be considered [to be images of gas chambers] however hard one might try to imagine', thus attributing to me a confusion between images taken *from* a gas chamber and images *of* a functioning gas chamber, a confusion which I never make. Finally, he claims to trace in this pseudo-confusion an explicit call for a 'concept as suspect and overused as that of empathy' which supposedly supports an 'apology of the image' contrary to any language or words, where in fact I was simply trying, by means of historical research and writing, to reconstruct a point of view and a *readability* for these images.

130. Damisch, 'Montage du désastre', p. 76.

131. Damisch, 'Montage du désastre', p. 72.

132. However, Delage has already undertaken this task: Christian Delage, 'Les camps nazis: l'actualité, le documentaire, la fiction. À propos du *Criminel* (*The Stranger*, Orson Welles, USA, 1946)', *Les Cahiers de la Shoah* 7 (2003), pp. 87–109.

133. However, see Stuart Liebman, 'Les premières constellations du discourse sur l'Holocauste dans le cinéma polonais', *De l'histoire au cinéma*, pp. 193–216.

134. Orson Welles, *Moi, Orson Welles. Entretiens avec Peter Bogdanovitch* (1992), trans. Évelyne Châtelain (Paris: Belfond, 1993), pp. 213–14.

135. Hubert Damisch is also wrong when he writes that 'where the commentary from *Actualités françaises* has, with good or bad motives, systematically abstained from using the word 'Jew' … and where, eleven years later, silence was still the rule on this point in Jean Cayrol's commentary for Alain Resnais' *Nuit et Brouillard*, the few images of camps presented by Welles in *The Stranger* from the very beginning fall notably and unequivocally within the perspective of the 'final solution' and what would later be called the *Shoah*' (p. 74), because in his commentary about images of the camps, Wilson the prosecutor does not evoke Jews, but 'the populations of the defeated countries' as being the victims of the Nazi genocide. For other examples of this use of documentary in fiction at that time, see Christian Delage, 'L'image dans le prétoire. Usages du document filmé chez Fritz Lang and Stanley Kramer', *Études photographiques* 17 (2005), pp. 45–66.

136. Joseph Kessel, 'Image vues au tribunal de Nuremberg' (1945), *Les Cahiers du judaïsme* 15 (2003), pp. 97–9.

137. Damisch, 'Montage du désastre', p. 78.

138. See Georges Didi-Huberman, 'Montage des ruines', *Simulacres* 5 (2001), pp. 8–17. Didi-Huberman, *Images malgré tout*, pp. 151–87 ('Image-montage ou image-mensonge').

139. Damisch, 'Montage du désastre', p. 77.

140. See Didi-Huberman, 'De ressemblance à ressemblance', *Maurice Blanchot. Récits critiques*, ed. Christophe Bident and Pierre Vilar (Tours/Paris: Éditions Farrago/Léo Scheer, 2003), pp. 143–67.

141. Sigmund Freud, *The Complete Letters of Sigmund Freud to Wilhelm Fliess, 1887–1904*, trans. and ed. Jeffrey Moussaieff Masson (Cambridge, MA: The Belknap Press of Harvard University Press, 1985), p. 202.

142. Freud, *The Complete Letters of Sigmund Freud to Wilhelm Fliess*, p. 202.

143. Sigmund Freud, *Interpretation of Dreams*, trans. Joyce Crick (New York: Oxford University Press, 1999), p. 242.

144. Freud, *The Complete Letters of Sigmund Freud to Wilhelm Fliess*, p. 202.

145. See Sigrid Weigel, 'Scholems Gedichte und seine Dichtungstheorie. Klage, Adressierung, Gabe und das Problem einer biblischen Sprache in unserer Zeit', *Gershom Scholem. Literatur und Rhetorik*, ed. Stephen Mosès and Sigrid Weigel (Cologne/Weimar/Vienne: Böhlau, 2000), pp. 16–47.

146. Rastier, *Ulysse à Auschwitz : Primo Levi, le survivant*, pp. 192–8.

147. See Uwe Fleckner, ' "Der Leidschatz der Menschheit wird humaner Besitz". Sarkis, Warburg und das soziale Gedächtnis der Kunst', *Sarkis. Das Licht des Blitzes – Der Lärm des Donners* (Vienna: Museum Moderner Kunst-Stiftung Ludwig, 1995), pp. 33–46.

148. Michel de Certeau, *L'Écriture de l'histoire* (Paris: Gallimard, 1975), p. 327.

149. Walter Benjamin, 'Theses on the Philosophy of History', in *Illuminations*, trans. Harry Zorn (London: Pimlico, 1999), p. 247.

CHAPTER 4

Resnais and the Dead

EMMA WILSON

In an essay published in the *Cahiers du Cinéma* volume on Cinema and the Shoah, Marie-José Mondzain considers art's response to trauma and death. In thinking about the representation of the Shoah, and the dead matter of the archive, Mondzain emphasizes the importance of questioning through art, and the questioning of all the spectres of emotion conjured through the artistic process, both creation and reception. She suggests that we should speak not of the problem of the Shoah, but of the question of the Shoah, and that this should be a question we keep open, unanswered, like an anxiety. It is in the field of this anxiety, in its grip, that Mondzain envisages the construction of a perspective on the horror of the historical event. Art, for Mondzain, can let us believe there is a poetics of responsibility, or an ethics, informed by the emotions. In this force field we can seek to grasp what remains beyond our reach.[1]

In this chapter I am returning to *Night and Fog* and sensing the film as newly ungraspable.[2] In its ethos and organization, the film invites us not to let it rest. Laura Mulvey has discussed *Night and Fog* in an essay about compilation films; she reminds us of the specificity of compilation films and of the process of return and reorganization they depend on formally: 'Compilation films are made from pre-existing footage. Once selections are made from the raw material, a new narrative and a new consciousness emerge out of the old footage.'[3] Mulvey is interested in the ways in which the arrangement of footage allows a hidden story to become visible. She has recourse in particular to the Freudian notion of *Nachträglichkeit*:

As defined by Jean Laplanche and Jean-Baptiste Pontalis, 'deferred action' [...] implies that 'experiences, impressions and memory traces may be revised at a later date to fit in with fresh experiences or with the attainment of a new stage of development. They may in that event be endowed not only with a new meaning but also with psychical effectiveness.[4]

It is this association of rearrangement and revision with renewed psychical, affective and political effectiveness that informs this analysis. I am concerned with the psychical effects, if not effectiveness, of Resnais's film. I argue that it is not only in the film's rearrangements, but also in our rearrangements as viewers, as we turn back to this material, anxious, keeping its questions open, that its resonance and meanings may begin to be felt.

Influential in my re-encounter with *Night and Fog* has been the work of Griselda Pollock and Max Silverman. In her chapter, 'After Auschwitz: Femininity, Futurity', in *Encounters in the Virtual Feminist Museum*, Pollock writes:

> I am of the opinion that the archive of the photographic inventory of Nazi atrocities cannot and should not be publicly exhibited. Each image contains known or knowable individuals, not merely anonymous corpses or walking skeletons whose horrifying neglect and reduction to anonymous numbers is part of the profound horror of this event. If we wish to resist participating in fascism's rupture of the most ancient marker of humanity's self-consciousness, namely the consideration for the human dead, we must return to each body its status as a potentially known, beloved, valued, possibly brilliant, certainly mourned human being whose degradation and torture has served its first and immediate purpose as evidence and must now be sheltered in the decent obscurity of archival entombment not allowed to those who in being 'disappeared' remain unburied and worse.[5]

These important words trouble my viewing of *Night and Fog*. I want to ask how far viewing of the film can encompass or respond to the reminder that 'each image contains known or knowable individuals' and the injunction to 'return to each body its status as a potentially known, beloved [...] human being'. In his essay, 'Horror and the Everyday in Post-Holocaust France', Max Silverman illuminates the strategic uses made of the everyday object in Resnais's filmmaking and the importance of defamiliarization and reinvention in *Night and Fog* such that it is 'as if the thin veneer of everyday life is liable, at all times, to dissolve into the overwhelming trauma of genocide.'[6] I am concerned here with modes of response to images of pain and suffering, with the difficult questions the film raises about the exposure and defamiliarization of the bodies of once known and loved others.

In my earlier study of this film, I was interested in two particular tropes within *Night and Fog*: the moves between still images and moving footage; and the attention to the senses and to tactility. I want now to draw up and rearrange this argument. In looking at the moves between still and moving images, I examined the even pace of Resnais's editing – four seconds per still photograph held within the frame – and the way this sequencing anticipates a move towards moving footage. Looking at a sequence early in the film, I argued:

> The still photographs anticipate movement, looking towards the shock of the transition from shot 41 to 42. In the crucial moment towards which we have been moving, Resnais cuts from still photo to documentary footage [...] The figures in the footage are of the same size and scale as in the previous still photograph. They are also seen walking in the same direction. In this transition from stasis to movement Resnais fulfils the viewer's (painful) wish to see these figures as animate, as living and moving.7

I moved on to examine borders between living and dead in the film and those images which disturb the viewer's perception and grasp, evoking in particular Agamben's discussion of the *Muselmann*. My discussion culminated in evocation of the Allied footage from Belsen used by Resnais.

> [S]hock, the visceral register for the viewer is key, too, to Resnais's notorious use of Allied footage from Belsen (shots 272–292). While this material is taken from live footage, Resnais edits it at first in a manner recalling his use of still photos. We see each image for only a matter of seconds, again with a sense of the recrudescence of desecration and outrage with every image. The bodies, dead, in many cases decaying (we see an empty eye socket, fragilized and now putrid flesh) are still. The editing of the shots allows them to appear framed in still photographs. Yet Resnais pushes further, cutting from a woman's dead face in close-up to shots of the bodies moved by bulldozers. These images bring with them a fearful return of vulnerability as the flesh moved seems again fragile and pliable. Horror again arises, maximally from the subject of the images, yet also from their category disturbance.8

I continued:

> As we make category errors, mistaking the living and dying for the dead, mistaking live footage for still images, our relation to the images seen is disturbed. Fear insists in the inability to distinguish stillness from movement, living from dead matter. Resnais brings an uncanny hesitation to the viewing process where stillness and motion interrupt each other, where images and footage are interposed one upon another with an inexorability and rhythm which become nauseating and sick. These

images, and the formal play of stillness and movement created from them, do not claim to represent the *Muselmann* to us. Rather, in riskily imitating the cognitive disturbance and impossibility the *Muselmann* embodies, Resnais moves to make the images of his film unassimilable, ungraspable despite their attention to matter and brute materiality.[9]

In retrospect I find my moves to think category error and visual disturbance too far removed from the emotive context of the film's photographic evidence, from the questions about the knowable, lovable others of which Pollock reminds us. I risk reducing the human dead to matter and substance; I think this is not all that Resnais's film allows. In response to Pollock's work, I am drawn to retrieve my initial intimation of the viewer's painful wish to see the figures Resnais represents as living and moving.

In her book, *Nuit et brouillard: un film dans l'histoire*, film historian Sylvie Lindeperg writes that, for the orphans of the deportation, 'Alain Resnais's film functioned symbolically in revealing death and initiating a work of mourning.'[10] She writes of how the final sequences of the film mark out the end of a period of waiting, of a concerted desire for denial and the mad hope for restitution: now the orphan recognizes that his mother's hair, his father's bones are massed in the slaughterhouses Resnais represents. Lindeperg describes viewers looking for the visage of their murdered parents in the mass of falling corpses shot in movement. She sees the film achieving a symbolic act of unveiling and revelation. Some sense of the purchase or horror of this is felt in conjuring a search for recognition, for familiarity, for family, in the human remains the film reveals. Imaginary moves between the family photograph, memento or memory image and the nauseous, surreal, body images Resnais exposes in *Night and Fog* illustrate again the thin veneer of which Silverman has spoken. These are issues I pursue here.

My second trope, tactility and touch, again deserves revision. I argued previously:

As in his experimentation with still and moving images, so more broadly Resnais is concerned to unsettle his viewer (to irritate our senses in Bersani's terms) and, in particular, to bring us close to the matter, substance and affect of the images he manipulates. He seeks indeed to make the image distressingly manipulable, tangible, sentient, graspable. This is a paradoxical, even impossible task in the scopic medium that is cinema. Indeed one way in which *Night and Fog* works to remind us of the very ungraspability and invisibility of its subject is through its privileging, at points, of the haptic over the optic.[11]

Yet in thinking about the ungraspable, what cannot be mastered or held, in thinking about the textures and substances of the film, I missed a connection I want to bring through now, a connection between the grief of the viewer facing the wish for animation or familiarity in these desolate and desecrated images, and the trope of impossible tactility that Resnais traces through the film.

In the conversation with Bernard Stiegler published as 'Spectrographies', Derrida speaks about spectrality and the return of the dead. He makes particular connections between the privation we face confronted with a spectre and the privations of cinematic and televisual art:

> The very thing one is deprived of, as much in spectrality as in the gaze which looks at images or watches films or television, is indeed tactile sensitivity. The desire to touch, the tactile effect or affect, is violently summoned by its very frustration.[12]

For Derrida, the absence of tactility, the frustration of the desire to touch the spectral image, the departed other and his or her fleeting photographic trace, violently summons the will for contact, the wish to hold the dead and know them once again as sentient, tactile and animate. Griselda Pollock, looking at the beautiful mourning images of artist Bracha Ettinger, cites Ovid, and the image of Orpheus seeking in vain to hold the dead or dying Eurydice:

> Instantly she slipped away.
>
> He stretched out to her his despairing arms, eager to rescue her, or feel her form, but could hold nothing save the yielding air.[13]

The image in Ovid can be aligned with Virgil's image of Aeneas seeking to catch the shade of his father in the *Aeneid* as he journeys through the Underworld:

> Then thrice around his neck his arms he threw;
>
> And thrice the flitting shadow slipp'd away,
>
> Like winds, or empty dreams that fly the day.[14]

In the encounter with the dead father, unreachability is figured in this thrice repeated gesture of the son reaching to clasp the fleeting shadow, reaching to touch the dead. In his attention to the corporeal, in cinematic images of moribund flesh, Resnais summons this violent desire to touch and hold the dead, to rescue them and feel their forms. His attention is very literally to images of dead matter, not to the spectre as in Ovid or Virgil. But his medium, film, itself frustrates the desire for tactility. His manipulation of that medium, through a heightening of hesitations between life and death, further underscores his emphasis on desire and its frustration. I argue that the film exposes the human form, its fragility, its familiarity yet deadly ungraspability, in order to generate emotion. It summons the emotions of the relative seeking their lost loved one, and illustrates the frustration of desire in the most graphic forms. About whether this exposure is justified, in the name of politics or ethics, I remain uncertain.

Images of nudity persist in *Night and Fog*. At 7'50" we see a photograph, shot from a high angle, of massed, shaved, naked men. At 8'05" we see lines of naked men from behind. At 14'25" and 14'30" two shots in sequence show men at different stages of physical suffering, degradation and emaciation, evoking the duration of deprivation and its physical marks. Images I want to examine more closely are shots 225–233, shown at 21 minutes through *Night and Fog*. They appear as the film attempts to represent the first selection made at the camp: the division of those who will be put to work and those who will be murdered immediately. In synoptic manner Resnais edits in four images, two from the Institute of Jewish history in Warsaw, the third from the Institute of Jewish History in Trzebinia and the fourth a German photograph sourced at the Contemporary Jewish Documentation Centre. The soundtrack instructs that the images were taken a few instants before an extermination. Although the photographs have different sources, their apparent sequential editing in the film offers them a residual narrative function. In the images in sequence we see women undressed, sitting on the ground, lined up naked and then running forwards, under the gaze of SS officers. Compositional resemblances between the images – the lines of women creating a segmented image, the contrast of their dark hair and pale flesh, the shadow of features indistinct in the shots – seem further to attract a sequential reading. I am interested in pausing over them, resisting their narrative function and holding on to them as images which hold a trace of individuals in a moment in time.

Mondzain (and Silverman) have drawn attention to the tense relation between soundtrack and image track in the film. Mondzain encourages us to explore this inter-relation in our viewing. She argues that the voice-over speaks of the SS and not of their victims:

> The voice-over only speaks of the Nazi torturers even if the images mostly show the victims. So this voice does not speak of what is shown, on the contrary, it speaks of what one doesn't see.[15]

This seems right for this sequence. Shot 225 is accompanied by the words explaining that a selection is made. Those on the left will go and work. The fate of those on the right is left unspoken. In its clipped explanation of the system exposed, in its assumption of ellipsis and euphemism, the voice-over strategically imitates the inhuman logic of the torturer. For Mondzain: 'The archive images are not called on to "show" everything that happened, but to allow a *décalage* to be created between what is seen and what is said about the torturer.'[16]

Resnais's strategy here, revealed by Mondzain, looks forwards to the moments in the opening sequences of *Hiroshima mon amour* (1959) where Resnais edits together images of bodily horror from Hiroshima with words of recrudescence and rebirth gleaned from contemporary journalistic accounts. In the sequence of shots in *Night and Fog* the images work not to illustrate or narrate, but to exceed the words of the text, to stand in stark contrast to its ellipses, to the brevity of its evocation of extermination. Mondzain has said that it is the role of art to move, not to teach. This may be the function of the *décalage* between word and image, the over-reaching of the images. An aspect of this *décalage* here, its visceral as well as intellectual effect, is the exposure of the body. Resnais allows human flesh uncovered to connect us affectively to images of excess and desecration.

In *Family Frames*, Marianne Hirsch speaks of acts of imaginary identification with Holocaust photography, with those family photographs that create the Tower of Faces in the Holocaust Memorial Museum in Washington DC. She argues: 'We reanimate the pictures with our own knowledge of daily life, and we experience, emotionally, the death that took those lives so violently.'[17]

> We mourn the people in the photographs because we recognize them, but this identification remains at a distance marked by incomprehension, anger, and rage. They may be like us. But they are not us: they are visibly ghosts and shadows.[18]

Hirsch reminds us that these images are uncanny as well as familiar, that political and historical atrocity divides us from their subjects, that these figures caught on camera, so proximate, so familiar, are like ghosts and shadows untouchable however feelingly we reach for them.

How much keener our divide, then, from the images of nakedness and humiliation Resnais collages together in *Night and Fog*. What does he do in letting these images circulate? Can we respond to them? What about the viewer who, recalling Lindeperg's comments, looks for her parents in these images? In the first volume of her trilogy *Auschwitz and After*, Charlotte Delbo writes:

> My mother
> She was hands, a face
> They made our mothers strip in front of us
>
> Here mothers are no longer mothers to their children.[19]

Delbo's words summon the horror of the dichotomy the archive images represent. She summons a memory image of her mother, evoking her tactility and proximity, her hands, her face. This is a haptic, proximate economy of vision. From the archive image used by Resnais, such a moment of tenderness is retrievable. We see a woman holding her infant child, her hand encircling the baby's head. The child is nestled against her, her arm folded round it, the gesture expressing some attempt to shield the child and to protect it. In the image we glimpse maternal affection, its familiar tokens, and see them in fearful contrast to the surreal exposure of the women's bodies. We confront this estrangement and its savage, defamiliarizing force, caught elliptically by Delbo in her poetic prose, in Resnais's exposure of these images.

Resnais's will to make this savagery evident to us, to build his film around a logic of escalation and increment in shock, despite the lacunae of the film and its constant pointing to what is still not seen, is witnessed in the move from shot 229, the column of naked women in the grass to 230, with its view of four naked women in the foreground. The image is closer still before our eyes and excessive in its presence and in the brute fact of its having been taken. The horror of the revelation of these women's bare, vulnerable, sentient flesh is magnified for the viewer as we see the women closer in the foreground, with the same illusion of sequence and continuity from image to image. Unlike the naked Eve hiding her sex, these women's arms shield their breasts, they cradle themselves in a bare gesture of self-protection or shielding which is then belied by the unspeakable exposure of their pubic hair and of the pale weight of their bodies in contrast to the clothed, armoured surveillant figures behind them.

These images disturb me as I approach them. Their presence, and their demands on viewers, are startlingly different from the reparative work afforded in post-memory work with family photography. These are images that disarm and unsettle, which challenge us to question whether we can construct a work of mourning and love, a work of restitution. They are images which, the more I look at them, remind me of the choking, shocking presence of these women at this moment and of their soft, death-bound bodies. When Resnais returns to the subject of torture, the desecration of a woman's body and her murder in *Muriel ou le temps d'un retour* (1963), he uses only words to narrate this and absents any image from the screen. In *Night and Fog* the women's nudity, the indignity and inhumanity of their exposure, creates a shock for me as viewer. This itself has its full effect only in terms of what it points to beyond the frame. Marianne Hirsch reminds us:

> The Holocaust photograph is uniquely able to bring out this particular capacity of photographs to hover between life and death, to capture only that which no longer exists, to suggest both the desire and the necessity and, at the same time, the difficulty, the impossibility, of mourning.[20]

Retrospective knowledge that these women face death invests their image with the emotions attached to the conditional perfect (in Barthes's terms), the horrified knowledge that they are now dead, and their death was impending even as they were imaged alive. Their nudity insists as well, intrudes in the frame as a token of the tragic vitality of their charnel, sentient vivid presence. As an image placed here by Resnais, edited in a film of found footage to release new meanings, it reminds us as well of the horror, against nature, of the transition from living to dead flesh. This Resnais forces us to confront again in his use of the footage filmed by the Allies at Belsen.

Kristeva reminds us in *Powers of Horror* of how violently the cadaver upsets and disrupts our identity as we view it. She continues: 'If dung signifies the other side of the border, the place where I am not and which permits me to be, the corpse, the most sickening of wastes, is a border that has encroached upon everything.'[21] In speaking about Lazarean art, Cayrol imagines 'an art born directly from such a human convulsion';[22] he speaks of the need for writers 'who did not feel shame at encompassing corpses and desecration.'[23] Cayrol draws on images which have a particular physicality, that acquire some vibration, some quickness from the experience. Resnais appears to aspire to this extreme mimesis, this shudder of physical suffering, in his use of the footage from Belsen. In its last parts, as it confronts the physical traces of slaughter, *Night and Fog* brings us closer still to images of the dead. Shots of corpses are shown in close-up in the frame, their faces recognizable. The scale of the images is large enough for us to recognize, and come close to, the skin of a woman's arm, the back of her neck, the sweep of her hair. The soles of feet lie exposed. A hand lies rigid. We witness the fall and movement of the bodies, their distressing pliability and sinuousness. Resnais's attention to the images in close-up, with a haptic immediacy and presence, brings us as close as film can, despite its tactile deprivations, to feeling, touching, recognizing these falling bodies.

Sylvie Lindeperg states that: 'Michel Certeau used to say that doing history was going to visit the dead so that at the end of this "uncanny dialogue", they would return less despairing to their graves.'[24] In his brilliant volume *Haunted Subjects*, Colin Davis considers what it means to visit the dead or to be visited by them; he writes: 'the dead return not as adversaries, not to impose regret or remorse, not to possess us or to be possessed by us, but to communicate from their still-signifying secretiveness.'[25] He continues: 'Can the dead speak to us? Is it possible to envisage some sort of mediation between the worlds of the living and the dead without lapsing into mysticism and wish-fulfilment?'[26] He warns too: 'restoring speech to the voiceless risks becoming a theft or imposition of meaning rather than a response to radical otherness.'[27]

What Resnais seeks further in his late shots in *Night and Fog* is not speech with the dead, but tactile contact with them, as his film bristles with reminders of flesh as mortal and vulnerable, of the pathos of bodily acts of tenderness and self-protection, of the corpse as strangely fragile, physically present, inviting a haptic gaze despite the abject untouchability of the corpse. If restoring speech risks theft or imposition of meaning, in Davis's terms, then seeking to touch the dead, to feel their flesh, to clasp sensations of former vitality and sentience, seems to court further risks of violation or exposure. Yet may there also be ethical gains in this commerce with dead flesh, the matter that Resnais uses in his art, the haptic gaze he invites? For Davis, 'in the process of attending to the words of the dead [...] our own subject position is disturbed.'[28] Through Levinas he reminds us that 'the other is always with us. Because the other is susceptible to death, she or he may of course die; but this does not mean that the other ceases to impinge on the world of the living.'[29] In *Night and Fog*, Resnais explores how the dead may impinge on the living. He does not give words to the dead in his film but he makes use of their images, of images of once and future death which exceed the frame, which touch us mimetically in a visceral apprehension of the ghostly presence of film images as tactile, as embodied. Davis, through Levinas, finds in commerce with the dead 'an opening onto what cannot reply'.[30] This seems to recall the very image from *Aeneid VI* where Aeneas seeks to grasp what he cannot hold.

I want to turn to the passages from *Totality and Infinity* where Levinas writes about the caress. His theorization of this mode of contact exists in the context of thoughts about love and the approach to the other. He writes: 'To love is to fear for another, to come to the assistance of his frailty';[31] he continues: 'The *way* of the tender consists in an extreme fragility, a vulnerability.'[32] He lays emphasis on the way the caress transcends the sensory or the sensate, arguing:

> The caress consists in seizing upon nothing, in soliciting what ceaselessly escapes its form toward a future never future enough, in soliciting what slips away as though it *were not yet*. It *searches*, it forages. It is not an intentionality of disclosure but of search.[33]

Levinas adds: 'what the caress seeks is not situated in a perspective and in the light of the graspable.'[34] Can this offer insight into the haptic, affective and perhaps ethical moves that Resnais's film might be making? The exposure of the other's fragility, her vulnerability, her naked flesh, might warn us to approach with caution, to seek but not to seize, to refuse *dévoilement* but to engage in *recherche*, the anxious questioning of art that Mondzain proposes.

In *Precarious Life*, Judith Butler explores the possible outcomes of grief and vulnerability. The context she writes about – the United States after 9/11 – is very different from the one I am exploring here. Yet I am curious about the implications of her work for the questions I am raising about flesh and exposure. Butler writes:

> That we can be injured, that others can be injured, that we are subject to death at the whim of another, are all reasons for both fear and grief. What is less certain, however, is whether the experiences of vulnerability and loss have to lead straightaway to military violence and retribution. There are other passages. If we are interested in arresting cycles of violence to produce less violent outcomes, it is no doubt important to ask what, politically, might be made of grief besides a cry for war.[35]

Bodily vulnerability and injury are essential to Butler's argument: 'The body implies mortality, vulnerability, agency: the skin and the flesh expose us to the gaze of others, but also to touch, and to violence.'[36] She goes on to suggest: 'We must attend to it [this vulnerability], even abide by it, as we begin to think about what politics might be implied by staying with the thought of corporeal vulnerability itself.'[37]

For Butler, attending to the vulnerability of the other, acknowledging the other as damageable and the self as also vulnerable to this damage, is or should be a part of human inter-relation and an ethical approach to the other:

> We're undone by each other. And if we're not, we're missing something. This seems so clearly the case with grief, but it can be so only because it was already the case with desire. One does not always stay intact. One may want to, or manage to for a while, but despite one's best efforts one is undone, in the face of the other, by the touch, by the scent, by the feel, by the prospect of the touch, by the memory of the feel.[38]

Butler questions whether there is something to be gained from 'tarrying with grief, from remaining exposed to its unbearability'.[39] This is something I think that Resnais too is questioning in his exposure of images in *Night and Fog*. I am still uneasy about whether we should expose or circulate these images of departed loved ones. After such damage, reparation, screening, restitution of undamaged memories – a work of protection – seems urgent. Yet in the quick of Resnais's images, in their nauseous passage before my eyes, I am reminded of why reparation and protection are so urgent. I am opened up to what I cannot ever touch or hold. I am made anxious about the act of looking, its violence, and its desire. I am led to imagine a longing for connection, a wish to touch, and to be held in return. Through its re-editing of found footage, its delirious formal patterning, *Night and Fog* finds an aesthetic of incremental horror which locates the body as site of common human vulnerability. It finds a cinematic form to gesture towards the longing to touch and hold which is forever denied the film viewer, and, so much more grievously, those in commerce with the dead.

Sylvie Lindeperg describes *Night and Fog* as 'this fragile, anxious and lyrical film'.[40] For me, the film's political purchase comes from its reminder of the dead as once sentient and now untouchable; the gaze it invites is one which respects this fragility and hesitance. In its exposures to human vulnerability, the film may yet open us to more prescient and ethical modes of love and grief.

Notes

1. Marie-José Mondzain, 'La Shoah comme question de cinéma', *Le Cinéma et la Shoah: Un art à l'épreuve de la tragédie du 20e siècle*, ed. Jean-Michel Frodon (Paris: Cahiers du Cinéma, 2007), pp. 29–36. See English version 'The Shoah as a Question of Cinema', in *Cinema and the Shoah: An Art Confronts the Tragedy of the Twentieth Century*, trans. Anna Harrison and Tom Mes (New York: SUNY Press, 2010).
2. See Emma Wilson, 'Material Remains: *Nuit et Brouillard*', *October* 112 (Spring 2005), pp. 89–110 and Emma Wilson, *Alain Resnais* (Manchester: Manchester University Press, 2006).
3. Laura Mulvey, 'Compilation Film as "Deferred Action": Vincent Monnikendam's *Mother Dao, the Turtle-Like*', *Projected Shadows: Psychoanalytic Reflections on the Representation of Loss in European Cinema*, ed. Andrea Sabbadini (London and New York: Routledge, 2007), pp. 109–18, p. 109.
4. Mulvey, 'Compilation Film as "Deferred Action"', p. 116.
5. Griselda Pollock, *Encounters in the Virtual Feminist Museum: Time, Space and the Archive* (London and New York: Routledge, 2007), p. 194.
6. Max Silverman, 'Horror and the Everyday in Post-Holocaust France: *Nuit et brouillard* and concentrationary art', *French Cultural Studies* 17 (2006), pp. 5–18, p. 7.
7. Wilson, 'Material Remains', pp. 97–98.
8. Wilson, 'Material Remains', pp. 101–2.
9. Wilson, 'Material Remains', p. 102.
10. Sylvie Lindeperg, *'Nuit et brouillard': un film dans l'histoire* (Paris: Odile Jacob, 2007), p. 241. ['[L]e film d'Alain Resnais assura la fonction symbolique de révélateur de la mort des parents et de déclencheur d'un travail de deuil']. Translations from the French are my own unless otherwise stated.
11. Wilson, 'Material Remains', p. 104.
12. Jacques Derrida and Bernard Stiegler, *Echographies of Télévision: Filmed Interviews*, trans. Jennifer Bajorek (Cambridge: Polity Press, 2002), p. 115. Jacques Derrida and Bernard Stiegler, *Echographies de la television: Entretiens filmés* (Paris: Galilée – INA, 1996), p. 129. ['[C]e dont on est privé, justement, aussi bien dans la spectralité que dans le regard porté vers les images, le cinéma, la télévision, c'est bien la sensibilité tactile. Le désir de toucher, l'effet ou l'affect tactile, se voit alors appelé avec violence par la frustration même.']
13. Pollock, *Encounters in the Virtual Feminist Museum*, p. 184.

14. Virgil, *Aeneid* 6, trans. John Dryden accessed at http://classics.mit.edu/Virgil/aeneid.6.vi.html (6 January 2009).

15. Mondzain: 'La Shoah comme question de cinéma', p. 149. ['La voix off ne nous parle que des bourreaux même si les images montrent surtout les victimes. Cette voix ne désigne donc pas ce qui est montré, au contraire, elle désigne ce qu'on ne voit pas.']

16. Mondzain: 'La Shoah comme question de cinéma', p. 149. ['Les images d'archives ne sont doc pas convoquées pour "montrer" tout ce qui a été, mais pour que s'établisse un décalage avec, précisément, ce qui est dit du bourreau.']

17. Marianne Hirsch, *Family Frames: Photography, Narrative, and Postmemory* (Cambridge, MA: Harvard University Press, 1997), p. 256.

18. Hirsch, *Family Frames*, p. 267.

19. Charlotte Delbo, *Auschwitz and After*, trans. Rosette C. Lamont (New Haven, CT and London: Yale University Press, 1995), p. 12. Charlotte Delbo, *Aucun de nous reviendra. Auschwitz et après I* (Paris: Minuit, 1970), p. 23. ['Ma mère/c'était des mains un visage/Ils ont mis nos mères nues devant nous/Ici les mères ne sont plus mères à leurs enfants.']

20. Hirsch, *Family Frames*, p. 20.

21. Julia Kristeva, *Powers of Horror: An Essay on Abjection*, trans. Leon S. Roudiez (New York: Columbia University Press, 1982), p. 3. Julia Kristeva, *Pouvoirs de l'horreur: Essai sur l'abjection* (Paris: Seuil [Points], 1980), p. 11. ['Si l'ordure signifie l'autre côté de la limite, où je ne suis pas et qui me permet d'être, le cadavre, le plus écoeurant des déchets, est une limite qui a tout envahi.']

22. Jean Cayrol, 'De la mort à la vie', *Nuit et brouillard* (Paris: Fayard, 1997), pp. 45–114, p. 51. ['un art né directement d'une telle convulsion humaine'].

23. Cayrol: 'De la mort à la vie', p. 54. ['qui n'ont pas honte d'enjamber les cadavres ou la pourriture.']

24. Lindeperg, *Nuit et brouillard*, p. 243. ['Michel de Certeau disait que faire de l'histoire, c'est aller visiter les morts pour qu'à l'issue de cet "étrange dialogue", ils retournent moins tristes dans leurs tombeaux.']

25. Colin Davis, *Haunted Subjects: Deconstruction, Psychoanalysis and the Return of the Dead* (Basingstoke and New York: Palgrave Macmillan, 2007), p. 64.

26. Davis, *Haunted Subjects*, p. 111.

27. Davis, *Haunted Subjects*, p. 112.

28. Davis, *Haunted Subjects*, p. 114.

29. Davis, *Haunted Subjects*, p. 116.

30. Davis, *Haunted Subjects*, p. 117.

31. Emmanuel Levinas, *Totality and Infinity: An Essay on Exteriority*, trans. Alphonso Lingis (Pittsburgh: Duquesne University Press, 1969), p. 256. Emmanuel Levinas, *Totalité et infini: Essai sur l'extériorité* (The Hague: Martinus Nijhoff [Livre de poche], 1971), p. 286. ['Aimer, c'est craindre pour autrui, porter secours à sa faiblesse.']

32. Levinas, *Totality and Infinity*, p. 256. Levinas, *Totalité et infini*, p. 286. ['La *manière* du tendre, consiste en une fragilité extrême, en une vulnérabilité.']

33. Levinas, *Totality and Infinity*, pp. 257–8. Levinas, *Totalité et infini*, p. 288. ['La caresse consiste à ne se saisir de rien, à solliciter ce qui s'échappe sans cesse de sa forme vers un avenir – jamais assez avenir – à solliciter ce qui se dérobe comme s'il *n'était pas encore*. Elle *cherche*, elle fouille. Ce n'est pas une intentionnalité de dévoilement, mais de recherche.']

34. Levinas, *Totality and Infinity*, p. 258. Levinas, *Totalité et infini*, pp. 288–9. ['ce que recherche la caresse ne se situe pas dans une perspective et dans une lumière du saisissable.']

35. Judith Butler, *Precarious Life: The Powers of Mourning and Violence* (London and New York: Verso, 2004), p. xii.

36. Butler, *Precarious Life*, p. 26.

37. Butler, *Precarious Life*, p. 29.

38. Butler, *Precarious Life*, p. 24.

39. Butler, *Precarious Life*, p. 30.

40. Lindeperg, *Nuit et brouillard*, p. 139. ['ce film fragile, inquiet et lyrique.']

CHAPTER 5

Night and Fog and the
Concentrationary Gaze

LIBBY SAXTON

Alain Resnais's *Night and Fog* has frequently been seen as an exemplary template for ethical representation and the solicitation of moral responses through cinema. For Jacques Rivette and Serge Daney, Resnais's aesthetic strategies provide a corrective to an immoral reframing in Gillo Pontecorvo's *Kapo* (1960).[1] Other critics have argued that *Night and Fog* stages an ethical encounter for the viewer by refusing to offer any omniscient or totalizing perspective on the Nazi camps. Such approaches have deflected consideration away from the historical and political import of the drama of looking played out within the images themselves. This chapter attempts to nuance the view of *Night and Fog* as a monumental ethical injunction or lesson in virtuous viewing, by examining the concrete acts of looking embedded within it and asking how they position us in relation to the contagion of violence that Jean Cayrol calls 'the concentrationary plague'.[2]

Although Resnais has sometimes been criticized for prioritizing the aesthetic over the political, a concern with the politics of spectatorship runs through his documentaries and early feature films. *Guernica* (1950) explores viewers' reactions to Picasso's vision of civilian deaths during the Spanish civil war, while *Les Statues meurent aussi* (*Statues Also Die*, 1953) expresses suspicion of the 'colonial gaze' directed by European viewers at African art objects. Cross-cultural viewing relations are also addressed in *Hiroshima mon amour* (1959), where, as in *Guernica*, the question of what it means to witness atrocity becomes freighted with political implication. More explicitly political in its agenda, *Night and Fog* explores how human and mechanical gazes have been harnessed to serve totalitarian power. Through its extensive use of Nazi photographs and footage, some of which feature observation devices or onlooking guards, the film builds up a portrait of what might be termed the 'concentrationary gaze', a scopic regime that sustains the concentrationary system and is revealed to be multiform and mutable. One of the ways in which the film opens up a critical perspective on this regime is by juxtaposing Nazi visual records with images created by others – including camera-operators embedded with the Allied armies, a member of the Auschwitz *Sonderkommando* who secretly photographed the cremation of bodies (Plate 38), and belated witnesses such as Resnais. Just as Resnais's camerawork is defined by mobility, so the film's incessant shifts between competing points of view work to destabilize any too-fixed spectatorial positions, disrupting the straightforwardly objectifying relation often associated with Nazi images of the ghettos and camps and suggesting a more complicated and fluctuating distribution of power.[3] In line with Cayrol's metaphorical reference to a plague, the violence of the concentrationary gaze is shown to be contagious, liable to infect ostensibly innocent or neutral images and vantage points. I argue that attention to the multiple, oscillating and sometimes apparently contradictory viewing positions constructed by *Night and Fog* can help us to understand what, for Resnais and Cayrol, a properly vigilant response to the camps entailed.

Surveillance and complicit onlooking

From the outset of *Night and Fog*, the camp is established as a theatre of surveillance. In the second shot, the camera tracks backwards to reveal barbed wire and a watchtower at the perimeter of Auschwitz-Birkenau (Plate 6). The third shot features a line of observation posts, which stretches into the distance as far as the eye can see, providing a first indication of the scale of the site (Plate 7). While the towers are now deserted and decaying, these images forewarn us of the film's concern with the surveying and witnessing, as much as the experiencing, of suffering and atrocity. Moreover, these initial shots establish a connection between the observation tower and the film camera: both are optical devices commanding views over the camps. The correlation hinted at here reminds us of the integral role played by photography and film in the Nazi project. By alluding, albeit indirectly, to the perpetrators' exploitation of these technologies, the opening sequence simultaneously acknowledges cinema's historical implication in totalitarian violence and announces the film's intention to critique this history using cinematic means. These early images also anticipate the succession of photographs of watchtowers at concentration camps such as Struthof and Vught (shots 20–24) which appear in the first series of black-and-white images. Shifting between eclectic temporal and geographical coordinates, the monochrome stills visualize a transnational architecture of surveillance. Cayrol's commentary, revised by Chris Marker, transforms the towers from optical machines into objects of aesthetic judgement: 'alpine style, garage style, Japanese style, no style'.[4] Central to Resnais's film, then, will be the relation between technologies of vision, concentrationary violence, and beauty.

The association between onlooking and potential violence is reinforced in other ways in this initial set of historical images. While few images of German civilians outside the camps appear in the film, a brief excerpt from a German newsreel features enthusiastic spectators at a Nazi rally (shot 11). Unlike *Le Chagrin et la pitié* (*The Sorrow and the Pity*; Marcel Ophuls, 1969), *Shoah* (Claude Lanzmann, 1985) and other later films, *Night and Fog* does not explicitly investigate the extent of the knowledge or guilt of civilian populations in the countries where camps were located. Nevertheless, the fragment of newsreel footage emblematizes the film's wider interest in collusive spectating, a concern which prefigures later debates about the phenomenon of the Holocaust 'bystander'.

The thus far anonymous, abstract, disembodied regime of observation assumes a human face and form in the subsequent images of round-ups and deportations. This sequence begins with a now familiar photograph of women and children under arrest in Warsaw (shot 35).[5] While our attention is initially drawn to the young boy standing, arms raised, in the foreground, a closer look (solicited by the duration of the shot) reveals that it makes an object of the gaze itself – specifically the triangular exchange of looks between the civilian woman on the left, the Nazi soldier on the right and the photographer. This is the first of a number of Nazi-era photographs in the film which feature soldiers or guards as onlookers on the periphery of scenes of degradation and brutality, rendering visible the surveillant gaze evoked by the earlier images of watchtowers. Four shots later we encounter another permutation of this scenario, an image of inspection made famous by the identity of the viewer on the sidelines. The political controversy spawned by the photograph of Pithiviers (Plate 11), a French-administered internment camp for foreign-born Jews in the Loiret region, is well known. The official censorship commission ordered Resnais to excise the image, which, according to Jean-Marc Dreyfus, was construed as a denunciation of French collaboration in the Holocaust.[6] Resnais opted instead to superimpose a beam across the *gendarme's képi* (distinctive peaked cap), thereby concealing his nationality. In the current context, it is revealing that the only image in the film which concerned the commission captured a gaze associated with power, and that Resnais opted to preserve a trace of this look, when it might have been easier to enlarge and crop the photograph. As Emma Wilson points out, like the iconic Warsaw photograph, this image seems 'self-consciously posed and pictorial'.[7] The ledge across the bottom of the shot and the upper body of the *gendarme* in the foreground form a second, internal frame for the distant figures of Jewish prisoners. The well-balanced composition of the Warsaw and Pithiviers photographs arouses uncertainty about the extent to which they were staged, thereby drawing attention to the act of photographing itself, and, in the latter case, to the location of the photographer, close to the *gendarme*, probably in a watchtower, indicating at least some degree of complicity with those in power.

Eleven minutes into the film, during a section detailing prisoners' daily routines in the camps, the voice-over mentions the invigilatory role performed by the SS: 'The SS watches, oversees, gathers, inspects and frisks them before they return to the camp.'[8] The black-and-white photographs shown here have a direct illustrative relation to the accompanying commentary, which alerts us to visual details we might otherwise overlook. At first glance, the photograph in shot 115 appears to show two prisoners welding unsupervised in a factory, but Cayrol's remarks draw attention to the profile of an SS guard just visible in the top left corner of the frame, presiding over the action from above. Anticipating Cayrol's later comment that the deportee did not want to be seen – 'Call no attention to oneself. Make no sign to the gods'[9] – the labourers' lowered gazes evoke the self-regulating mechanism of control which Michel Foucault finds modelled by the Panopticon.[10] As in the Warsaw and Pithiviers photographs, the composition of this image brings off-screen space into play; the partial exclusion of the guard's body from the frame heightens our awareness of the invisible presence of the photographer and his/her shot's collusion with the concentration camp regime.

By associating photography and cinema with the surveillant concentrationary gaze, the colour and black-and-white images discussed thus far encourage viewers to reflect on the integrity of the viewing positions offered to them by the film. Both the link between Resnais's camera and the watchtowers and the photographs of attentive guards remind us that mediated – just as much as unmediated – looking is always already implicated in structures of power, calling into question any conception of film spectatorship as neutral bystanding. The photographs of Warsaw, Pithiviers and the camp factory suggest a politicized economy of looking in which the deportee is framed as the object of the SS gaze, where the subject-object relation is replicated at the level of the photographic apparatus. Each of these pictures was taken by photographers with affiliations to the Nazis. Yet, as we shall see, Resnais's handling and contextualization of such images and Cayrol's commentary work to disturb such fixed subject and object positions, hinting at more complex and fluid configurations of power. The next section looks briefly at wider debates about Nazi visual records and spectatorial positioning, before exploring the political effects of Resnais's juxtaposition of the perpetrators' perspectives with a series of alternative points of view.

Optical point of view and political positioning

The dehumanizing, altericidal gaze inscribed within Nazi photographic and filmic records has been the subject of extensive discussion. Such images are often assumed to place viewers in a rigid, unitary relation to their subjects. Joshua Hirsch summarizes many critics' misgivings when he observes that Nazi footage 'positions the spectator as a victimizer, potentially eliciting a voyeuristic or sadistic response'.[11] Hirsch proposes this as a possible motivation for Lanzmann's exclusion of historical images from *Shoah*. Lanzmann's controversial comment that he would destroy any footage he found of a working gas chamber has also been attributed to concerns about the pernicious effects of witnessing events from the Nazis' point of view.[12] Jean-Jacques Delfour offers the following commentary on Lanzmann's remark:

> Lanzmann would destroy the film shot by the Nazis because it *contains and legitimizes* the Nazi position; to watch it would necessarily mean inhabiting that spectatorial position, exterior to the victims, thus adhering *filmically, perceptually*, to the Nazi position itself, and then fixing its image in memory. Indeed, it would be like seeing the victims through the side of an aquarium, that is, at a distance which reduces the killing to a *piece of information*. ... [The] spyhole is a technical tool producing information which, in this case, *neutralizes* the factual and human import of what is happening on the other side and *banalizes* the voyeuristic, irresponsible psychic position of the person observing through this scopic device.[13]

I would argue, however, that Delfour's argument about hypothetical footage overlooks the mobility and inconsistencies of viewers' responses to actual films. Firstly, Delfour posits a fixed correlation between the viewer and the Nazi officer operating the camera. This paradigm recalls the one-dimensional models of viewing relations influentially proposed by apparatus theorists such as Jean-Louis Baudry, Christian Metz and Laura Mulvey in relation to classical narrative film. Yet, as Linda Williams explains, 'whereas 1970s and 1980s film theory tended to posit ... a *unitary* way of seeing, contemporary discussions of spectatorship emphasize the plurality and paradoxes of many different, historically distinct viewing positions.'[14] The contention that Nazi films and photographs legitimize a unitary voyeuristic-sadistic perspective disregards the fact that our identifications are, as Judith Butler has pointed out, not fixed but plural, fluid and unstable.[15] Secondly, Delfour's reasoning conflates optical perspectives – the spatial positions from which we view – with figurative ones – our affective and ethico-political identifications. As Nick Browne has demonstrated in his analysis of 'specular texts', films in which 'the significant relations have to do with seeing' and whose 'complexity and coherence can be considered as a matter of "point of view"', discussions of spectatorial identification must take account of discrepancies between literal and figurative perspectives.[16] While Browne's examples are taken from a fictional narrative (John Ford's *Stagecoach* (1939)), his argument also has implications for documentary, and acquires particular significance in relation to 'found footage' compilations such as those created for Resnais's film.

Night and Fog might be viewed as a 'specular text', insofar as the positions from which we survey the concentrationary universe emerge in the film as a locus of political inquiry. Resnais's selection, arrangement and treatment of images work to deconstruct the notion of a homogeneous Nazi gaze which traps us within a fixed, objectifying perspective. This he achieves not only by highlighting the diversity of Nazi visual records and their original functions, but also, in certain cases, by manipulating our perception of them.[17] A number of the Nazi-period stills, such as the identity photograph seen in shot 74, are reframed by Resnais, whose interventions in the static pictorial space alter the ideological signifiers embedded in the originals, recalling his work with painting in *Guernica* and sculpture in *Les Statues meurent aussi*. Moreover, our relation to the Nazi-era images is further unsettled by the intersecting perspectives presented in the black-and-white segments of the film.

The determining effects of optical point of view are called into question by Resnais's juxtaposition of Nazi photographs with monochrome images from different historical periods. The lengthy section of the film devoted to the functioning of the concentration camps alternates between images created while they were in operation and others produced by the Allies at their liberation. Certain images from this latter period are used anachronistically to evoke the prisoners' everyday lives under the Nazi regime. As Sylvie Lindeperg observes, some of the historical images were apparently selected for what they *symbolized* rather than what they actually *documented*.[18] There is also evidence to suggest that Resnais and his historical consultants, Olga Wormser and Henri Michel, may have erroneously attributed certain Allied images to the Nazis. What interests me in the current context, however, is how the conflicting points of view embedded in the montage and potential uncertainty over the authorship of individual images affect the political positioning of the viewer, whether or not such conflict and uncertainty were consciously cultivated by Resnais.

At certain moments, the voice-over does not simply withhold information about the origins of the visuals, but actively obfuscates this issue. The photograph shown in shot 125, for example, was taken at Wöbbelin, a subcamp of Neuengamme in Germany, by a photographer with the American army. According to the shooting script published in Richard Raskin's 1987 book on the film, it depicts deportees who have collapsed due to lack of food.[19] The accompanying commentary describes a slightly different scenario: 'Many are too weak to defend their ration against blows and thieves. They wait for the mud and snow to take them.'[20] A photograph of liberated prisoners waiting for assistance is thereby transformed into an image of approaching death snapped by a Nazi photographer. To complicate matters, some of the black-and-white images were filmed by Resnais's cinematographers Ghislain Cloquet and Sacha Vierny during their visits to the camps in 1955. Such footage was used to supplement the historical images made available to Resnais, along with excerpts from Wanda Jakubowska's feature film *The Last Stage* (1948), introducing a third and fourth point of view into the monochrome segments of the film. Despite the distinctive *mise-en-scène* and texture of Cloquet's, Vierny's and Jakubowska's shots, they blend into the mass of monochrome visuals, exacerbating the difficulty of determining origins and point of view and further destabilizing the position of the viewer.

At first glance, no such uncertainty over perspective pertains to the newly-shot colour footage of Auschwitz, Birkenau and Majdanek. Resnais's tracking shots contrast with Lanzmann's unsteady handheld shots of the crematoria in Auschwitz and Birkenau in *Shoah*, which assume a referential relation to the accompanying testimony of Filip Müller, a survivor of the Auschwitz *Sonderkommando*. The gliding, questing camera in *Night and Fog* suggests an impersonal, disembodied, mechanical perspective rather than an attempt to imitate the point of view of the deportees. Yet, as suggested above, the camera's gaze accrues ambivalent connotations through association with Nazi surveillance and documentation devices, connotations which disrupt any straightforward identification with Resnais's roaming camera-eye. This ambiguity is heightened at subsequent junctures where the film plays with our expectations about perspective. Shots 140–42, for example, draw attention to the filmmaker's perennial dilemma: where to position the camera. Two black-and-white images show the town of Lublin and a chateau seen through barbed wire demarcating camp perimeters (Plates 23 and 24). Both echo the opening sequence of the film in their juxtaposition of quotidian normality and horror. The commentary places us in the position of a prisoner pondering the incomprehensible proximity of these two worlds: 'the real world ... could appear in the distance – or not so distant'.[21] Cayrol's words conceptualize this relationship in terms of reality and illusion; the 'real world' appears to the deportee as 'an image', further compelling the identification between deportee and film viewer. The film then cuts to a colour shot in which the camera pans leisurely over Birkenau from a fixed position in a watchtower, while the voice-over describes soldiers surveying the camp and shooting prisoners out of boredom (Plate 25).

Physically the colour shot replicates the point of view of the restless, murderous soldiers; momentarily, we find ourselves looking at the camp down the barrel of a gun. In this sense it functions as a counter-shot to the black-and-white images, which implicitly adopt the point of view of the camp inmates. Via the juxtaposition of two opposed angles of view, this series of shots and the accompanying commentary expose the symbolic violence of the soldiers' panoramic perspective. Yet, at the same time, the sequence troubles clear-cut distinctions between innocent and culpable vantage points by foregrounding what Susan Sontag, writing more generally about war and photography, calls 'the irrepressible identification of the camera and the gun'.[22]

Through its disruptive transitions between discrepant perspectives, then, *Night and Fog* confirms that the physical position from which we see structures and defines our responses to a lesser degree and in more complex ways than critics like Delfour assume. The perspectival shifts and, in the case of the black-and-white footage, the strategic withholding of attributions at times disturb the distinctions between the points of view of victims, perpetrators and other witnesses, without denying their specificity. The political potential of this function of the montage lies in its capacity to implicate us in the drama of looking staged by the film, by refusing to allow us to contemplate the concentrationary gaze from a safe distance or neutral or stable position. The final section of this chapter turns to the specific yet no less mobile or composite perspectives offered by the film on the extermination sites.

Birkenau and beyond

One of the charges repeatedly levelled against *Night and Fog* is that it downplays the distinctions between the concentration camps and those conceived exclusively for the purpose of killing, where four-fifths of the Jews deported from France were murdered.[23] While almost no images have survived from Chelmno, Belzec, Sobibor and Treblinka, due to the Nazi ban on photographing and filming events related to the Jewish genocide, there are two known sets of photographs of Auschwitz-Birkenau from the Nazi period, and one from each appears in *Night and Fog*. The first comes from the so-called 'Auschwitz Album', a series of pictures taken by SS photographers, whereas the second was taken secretly by deportees, and occupies a singular position in the film's critical investigation of the concentrationary gaze.

This photograph (Plate 38) belongs to a set of four taken secretly in August 1944 by a Greek Jew called Alex (whose surname remains unknown), assisted by other members of his *Sonderkommando*, in the vicinity of Crematorium Five at Auschwitz-Birkenau. These images have been at the centre of recent debates in France about the vexed issue of the representability of the Holocaust and the identity of the privileged or paradigmatic witness.[24]

The photographer's vantage point has been a pivotal issue in these discussions. Two of the images show the cremation of corpses in pits. The angle from which they were taken and the dark doorframe visible in the originals suggest that the photographer may have been hiding inside the gas chamber, making them a rare document of the end of the 'production line' of death. The shooting script for *Night and Fog* indicates that Resnais was aware that the photograph he selected was taken clandestinely by a *Sonderkommando* member, even if, as Lindeperg notes, he could not have recognized its particular significance at the time of making the film.[25] The photograph appears three shots after the colour images of what we are informed is a gas chamber at Majdanek, in the midst of harrowing excerpts from French and Soviet newsreels showing burnt, disfigured and decomposing bodies discovered as armies entered the camps. Nevertheless, shot 240 (Plate 38) stands out in this sequence as the only still shot and the only image which has a straightforward mimetic relation to the voice-over narration – 'When the crematoria are insufficient, pyres are constructed' – since it captured the process of incineration as it took place, rather than its aftermath.[26] However, in another act of intervention, Resnais enlarges and crops the original photograph, excising the doorframe and, with it, the visible index of the photographer's position in the gas chamber, the secrecy in which he was working and the physical risk to which he was exposing himself. While the aim of this reframing may have been to make the image more coherent, easier for the viewer to comprehend, in removing a clue to the photographer's identity, it uncomfortably recalls the enforced masking of the *gendarme*'s *képi*. On one hand, then, as a rare document of the *Sonderkommando*'s work immediately after a gassing, the photograph exposes a blindspot in the concentrationary gaze, while, as a clandestine shot, it registers the power and reach of Nazi surveillance. On the other, Resnais's editing of the image compounds the doubts and suspicions cultivated by the film about the role played by physical point of view in shaping processes of spectatorial identification and sense-making.

Eleven years after Alex hid with a camera in the gas chamber, Resnais returned to Birkenau and filmed what was left of one of the crematoria. In the final two shots of *Night and Fog*, the camera tracks alongside and then apparently inside the ruins of this structure (Plates 42 and 43). Despite the film's hesitant negotiation of the boundaries between the concentration and extermination camps, the fact that it begins and ends at Birkenau, and that the camera finally comes to rest, more precisely, on the threshold of a collapsed crematorium, suggests a recognition of the specificity of this location within the topography of the concentrationary universe. Reflecting on the significance of the four *Sonderkommando* photographs, Clément

Chéroux likens the gas chambers to 'chambres noires', photographic darkrooms, an ambivalent simile which transforms the murder zones from fields of invisibility into sites of witnessing.[27] Face to face with the crematorium in the concluding shots of *Night and Fog*, Cayrol proposes an alternative scopic image: the 'observatoire', which translates both as 'observatory' (in an astronomical context) and 'observation post' (in a military context; the term used elsewhere in the commentary is 'mirador'). 'Who among us keeps watch from this strange watchtower [*observatoire*] to warn of the arrival of new executioners? Are their faces really different from our own?' he asks.[28] Here Cayrol's words and Resnais's visuals produce a composite image which invites us to imagine ourselves in two ostensibly incompatible positions at once. While the camera places us at ground level at the epicentre of the genocide, the third person plural pronoun 'nous' [we] positions us with Cayrol in one of the watchtowers, as his commentary explicitly questions what differentiates us from the perpetrators, intensifying our sense of disorientation. Max Silverman clarifies Cayrol's point: 'what is really troubling here is not that opposites are now indistinguishable, that we are all Nazis or that we are all victims (positions that would imply a reckless disregard of history), but that they both overlap and maintain their specificity at one and the same time.'[29] This unsettling of the distinctions between ostensibly conflicting positions charges the film's interrogation of the concentrationary gaze with political significance, orienting it towards the present and the future. Through its exploration of perspectival multiplicity and mobility, *Night and Fog* fosters an awareness that the violence of this gaze is not hermetically sealed within the Nazi-era images but infiltrates other scopic regimes and framing mechanisms, as intimated by the connections established in the course of the film between the camera, the watchtower and the gun. Cayrol's ambiguous reference to 'cet étrange observatoire' in the closing seconds of the film complexifies and nuances his appeal for perpetual vigilance, by summoning the spectre of the concentrationary gaze one final time and reminding us that it can haunt even the most apparently humane perspectives and guileless images.

Notes

I am grateful to the editors of this book for their invaluable comments on an earlier draft of this essay. Some of the material in this essay first appeared in a different form in Libby Saxton, *Haunted Images: Film, Ethics, Testimony and the Holocaust* (London: Wallflower, 2008).

1. See Jacques Rivette, 'De l'abjection', *Cahiers du cinéma* 120 (1961), pp. 54–5 and Serge Daney, 'Le Travelling de *Kapo*', *Trafic* 4 (1992), pp. 5–19. See also Chapter 11.
2. '[L]a peste concentrationnaire'.
3. For discussion of the tendency of Nazi footage to objectify Jews, see, for example,

Lucy Dawidowicz, 'Visualizing the Warsaw Ghetto: Nazi Images of Jews Refiltered by the BBC', *Shoah: A Review of Holocaust Studies and Commemorations* 1/1 (1978), pp. 5–6, 17–18.

4. '[S]tyle alpin, style garage, style japonais, sans style.'

5. This photograph is the subject of Richard Raskin's book *A Child at Gunpoint: A Case Study in the Life of a Photo* (Aarhus: Aarhus University Press, 2004).

6. Jean-Marc Dreyfus, 'Censorship and Approval: The Reception of *Night and Fog*', in *Uncovering the Holocaust: The International Reception of Night and Fog*, ed. Ewout van der Knaap (London and New York: Wallflower, 2006), pp. 35–45, p. 38. A detailed account of 'l'affaire du képi' appears in Sylvie Lindeperg, Nuit et Brouillard: *un film dans l'histoire* (Paris: Odile Jacob, 2007), pp. 143–56.

7. Emma Wilson, 'Material Remains: *Nuit et Brouillard*', *October* 112/1 (2005), pp. 89–110, p. 97.

8. 'Et le SS les guette, les surveille, les fait rassembler, les inspecte et les fouille avant le retour au camp.' Translation by Libby Saxton.

9. 'Ne pas se faire remarquer, ne pas faire signe aux dieux.' Translation by Libby Saxton.

10. See Michel Foucault, *Surveiller et punir* (Paris: Gallimard, 1975).

11. Joshua Hirsch, *Afterimage: Film, Trauma, and the Holocaust* (Philadelphia: Temple University Press, 2004), p. 72.

12. 'I used to say that if there had been – by sheer obscenity or miracle – a film actually shot in the past of three thousand people dying together in a gas chamber, first of all, I think that no one human being would have been able to look at this. Anyhow, I would never have included this in [*Shoah*]. I would have preferred to destroy it. It is not visible. You cannot look at this.' Claude Lanzmann in 'Seminar with Claude Lanzmann, 11 April 1990', ed. David Rodowick, *Yale French Studies* 79 (1991), pp. 82–99, p. 99.

13. 'Lanzmann détruirait cette bande filmée par les nazis parce qu'elle *contient et légitime* la position du nazi; la regarder impliquerait nécessairement d'habiter cette position de spectateur, extérieur aux victimes, donc d'adhérer *filmiquement, perceptivement*, à la position nazie elle-même, puis d'en fixer l'image dans la mémoire. En effet, les victimes y seraient vues comme à travers une vitre d'aquarium, c'est-à-dire à une distance telle que la mise à mort n'est rien d'autre qu'une *information* … [Le] hublot est donc un outil technique producteur d'information qui, dans ce cas, *neutralise* la portée événementielle et humaine de ce qui se passé de l'autre côté et qui *banalise* la position psychique de voyeurisme et d'irresponsabilité propre à celui qui regarde par ce dispositif scopique.' Jean-Jacques Delfour, 'La Pellicule maudite: sur la figuration du réel de la Shoah', *L'Arche* 508 (2000), pp. 14–17, pp. 14–15.

14. Linda Williams (ed.), *Viewing Positions: Ways of Seeing Film* (New Brunswick, NJ: Rutgers University Press, 1995), pp. 3–4.

15. See, for example, Judith Butler, *Gender Trouble: Feminism and the Subversion of Identity* (New York and London: Routledge, 1990).

16. Nick Browne, 'The Spectator-in-the-Text: The Rhetoric of *Stagecoach*' [1975–76], in *Movies and Methods*, Vol. 2, ed. Bill Nichols (Los Angeles, CA: University of California Press, 1985), pp. 458–75, p. 460.

17. For discussion of the functions of photographs taken in the concentration camps, see Ilsen About, 'La Photographie au service du système concentrationnaire national-socialiste (1933–1945)', in *Mémoire des camps: photographies des camps de concentration et d'extermination nazies (1933–1999)*, ed. Clément Chéroux

(Paris: Marval, 2001), pp. 29–53 and Janina Struk, *Photographing the Holocaust: Interpretations of the Evidence* (London: I. B. Tauris, 2004), pp. 99–123.

18. Lindeperg, Nuit et Brouillard*: un film dans l'histoire*, p. 105.

19. Richard Raskin, Nuit et Brouillard *by Alain Resnais: On the Making, Reception and Functions of a Major Documentary Film* (Aarhus: Aarhus University Press, 1987), p. 94.

20. 'Beaucoup, trop faibles, ne peuvent défendre leur ration contre les coups et les voleurs. Ils attendent que la boue, la neige les prennent.'

21. '[L]e monde véritable ... peut bien apparaître au loin – pas si loin'.

22. Susan Sontag, *Regarding the Pain of Others* [2003] (London: Penguin, 2004), p. 60.

23. See, for example, Annette Wieviorka, *Déportation et génocide: entre la mémoire et l'oubli* (Paris, Plon, 1992), p. 223.

24. Key interventions in these debates included Georges Didi-Huberman, *Images malgré tout* (Paris: Minuit, 2003), Gérard Wajcman, 'De la croyance photographique', *Temps modernes* 613 (2001), pp. 47–83 and Elisabeth Pagnoux, 'Reporter photographe à Auschwitz', *Temps modernes* 613 (2001), pp. 84–108.

25. Raskin, Nuit et Brouillard *by Alain Resnais*, p. 119; Lindeperg, Nuit et Brouillard*: un film dans l'histoire*, p. 113.

26. 'Quand les crématoires sont insuffisants, on dresse des bûchers.'

27. Clément Chéroux, 'Les Chambres noires ou l'image absente?', in *Mémoire des camps*, ed. Chéroux, pp. 213–17.

28. 'Qui de nous veille de cet étrange observatoire pour nous avertir de la venue des nouveaux bourreaux? Ont-ils vraiment un autre visage que le nôtre?'

29. Max Silverman, 'Horror and the Everyday in Post-Holocaust France: *Nuit et Brouillard* and Concentrationary Art', *French Cultural Studies* 17/1 (2006), pp. 5–18, p. 14.

CHAPTER 6

Auschwitz as Allegory in *Night and Fog*

DEBARATI SANYAL

Night and Fog closes with a disquieting admonition: the narrative voice declares that we who have watched these images of atrocity fail to see the ongoing reality of concentrationary terror as it unfolds in different times and places, just as we fail to hear the endless cry of human suffering:

> Those of us who feign to take hope again as the image fades, as though there were a cure for the concentrationary plague. Those of us who feign to believe that all this happened only once, at a certain time and in a certain place, and those who do not look around us, and who do not hear the cry to the end of time.[1]

The film's final gesture breaches the limits of historical documentary and opens up an allegorical reading of its testimony. In so doing, it also positions the spectator as a blind and deaf witness – if not accomplice – to contemporary iterations of the Nazi terror. The intersection of allegory and complicity upon which the film closes, indeed through which it *refuses* closure, might well explain the enduring force of its critique across historical horizons and geopolitical sites. In what follows, this chapter will probe *Night and Fog*'s role in constructing an allegorical topography of the concentrationary experience. More specifically, I will propose that the dialectical force of allegory, along with the film's visual and verbal positioning of the audience as a potentially complicitous witness, open *Night and Fog* out to alternative historical projects, specifically in a colonial and postcolonial context. As examples of such projects, I will also be putting *Night and Fog* into dialogue with subsequent allegorizations of the concentrationary experience. At the same time, I will take up the troubling ethical questions that such allegoresis raises even as it mobilizes political action at various historical junctures.

An aesthetics of complicity

As several critics have noted, *Night and Fog* pulls its spectators into the perceptual field of Nazism.[2] From its opening sequence, the filmic perspective seamlessly connects norm to extreme and puts into circulation different positions, creating resonances between here and there, as well as then and now, and perhaps most uncomfortably, between victims, perpetrators and viewers. Text and montage coerce us to enter into history through multiple dislocations, to step into a zone of contaminating identifications. As the camera pans across Auschwitz's deserted landscape, the narrator reminds us that this ground was once marked by the 'shuffling of the detainees' ('le piétinement des concentrationnaires'). Today, however, there remains 'no footstep save our own' ('plus aucun pas que le nôtre'). The next sequence is footage from German newsreels and Leni Riefenstahl's *Triumph of the Will* that show Nazi soldiers marching in 1933 as the war machine gears up ('1933, la machine se met en marche'). The shuffling of now-vanished detainees is figurally chained to our own visual footsteps as viewers who follow the camera as it paces through the camp's remains and abruptly yields to the German military's goosestep. The step becomes a rhetorical figure enmeshing the detainees, viewers, Resnais's camera and Nazism itself into a perceptual web that invites identification, not with the experience of victims or of executioners in any stable way, but with a *circulation* of perspectives. At points, the documentary's perspective aligns itself with the perpetrator's gaze itself. In one sequence, the camera pans across the remnants of Birkenau's empty bunkbeds with the deliberate sweep of a surveillance camera, as the narrator describes the brusque nocturnal incursions of the SS into the barracks (shots 91–95). In a later sequence, the camera enlists the viewer's complicitous gaze with extermination itself (shots 235–237). A forward tracking shot guides us into Majdanek's gas chambers and we follow the victims' journey to their death. In a lateral pan, however, our perspective is shuttled from the gas chamber door to an SS observation post and then to another shut door, while the voice-over dispassionately utters 'One would close the doors. One would observe' ('On fermait les portes. On observait'). The viewer included in the address is indeed compelled to observe the now empty gas chamber from the perspective of the SS.

The perspectival shifts of *Night and Fog* periodically position the spectator as a collaborator or accomplice to the Nazi gaze. In doing so, the film deliberately stages the cinematic medium's capacity for transference and complicity with the violence that it documents. This formal self-reflection is especially acute in sequences portraying Nazism's aestheticization of terror. The unification of Germany through the exclusion of its undesirables is conveyed by a musical metaphor: 'We need a nation without a false note' ('Il faut une nation sans fausse note'). The concentration camps that implement this murderous metaphor are inspired by various architectural designs; even the crematorium acquires the picturesque quality of postcards ('un petit air carte postale'). We are constantly reminded of the spectacularization of suffering in the concentrationary universe. From the theatricality of the deportee's entry into an expressionist nocturnal setting to the orchestras that accompanied a day of harrowing labour or even an execution, the film opens a meditation on what Primo Levi powerfully describes as the 'voice of the *Lager*, the expression of its geometric madness'.[3] The geometric madness of Nazi terror is also evoked by Jean Cayrol, who recalls of his days in Mauthausen 'the impressive and invariable formalism of morning call … the bloody and public rites of execution'.[4] Over and over, *Night and Fog* reminds us of the production of aesthetic form within the crucible of pain, humiliation and annihilation.

This reflection on the aesthetic forms of concentrationary terror inevitably implicates the documentary's representation of suffering. The film deliberately points to the violence of its own formalizing procedures and their complicity with the practices of Nazi terror. In keeping with its investment in complicity as a vehicle of critique, however, Resnais and Cayrol's attunement to the potential violence of their own formalism is, paradoxically, what enables a historical and material critique of the Nazi regime. Their self-conscious formalism stages continuities between the concentrationary system and the processes of its historical and artistic representation in their converging violence upon the bodies that circulate within these economies. Formalism opens a passage, or complicity, between horror and the everyday by showing the proximities between Nazi extermination and the phantasmagoria of capitalist production.

Some early edits of *Night and Fog* express a more direct historical critique of the camps' economy of production in relation to the process of extermination. In the *tapuscrit* housed at the Institut mémoire de l'édition contemporaine, Nazism's ideology and technology of productive extermination are explicitly invoked and racialized: 'The final solution to the Jewish problem decided in 42. Inferior races must work for us: Jews, Poles, gypsies, Russians must be annihilated, but productively so: annihilation by work is the most productive.' A handwritten marginal note by Resnais reads: 'the two aspects of the system: economic/extermination' ('les deux aspects du système: économique/extermination').[5] What remains in the final version on Himmler's 1942 visit to Auschwitz is the terse: 'one must annihilate, but productively' ('Il faut anéantir, mais productivement'), followed by a sequence on the process of mass extermination and the recuperation of the victims' property and remains. As many have noted, the racial specificity of the Final Solution is almost evacuated in Cayrol's rewriting of the script, a point to which I will return. The final version also mutes the materialist critique of productivity and extermination. The historical complicity between the camps' deadly economy and the logic of capitalist productivity is nevertheless retained in the text's poetic registers. Consider for example the grim symmetry of 'Not enough coal for the crematoria, not enough bread for the men' ('Le charbon manque pour les crématoires. Le pain manque pour les hommes'), an ironic analogy that inserts the starving detainees and the crematoria into which they will be fed into a continuous cycle of consumption. Throughout the documentary, the camps' role in the wartime military-industrial economy is underscored, and Nazism's ideology of productive annihilation is both expressly and rhetorically linked to capitalist modernity. The sequence on extermination lingers on the industrialization of death and the attempt to reap a posthumous profit from the victims by recycling their remains. Such technologies of bodily expropriation, extermination and recuperation are portrayed not as atavistic hiccups of barbarism in civilization (as they were at the Nuremberg trials and specifically in relation to the use of human remains) but as continuous with western modernity's instrumental logic of productivity.[6]

The sequence that portrays the attempt to recycle human remains is the most chilling literalization of Himmler's logic of 'productive annihilation'. It is here that the film's form and montage most forcefully convey the four vectors of complicity I have traced thus far: the historical proximity between Nazi atrocity and an ongoing capitalist modernity, the spectator's coercion into a sensory collaboration with the perpetrators' gaze, the aestheticization of suffering and annihilation in the camps' 'geometric madness', and the cinematic image's collusion with this aestheticism. Sequence XXIIa (Shots 246–268) begins with the narrator's declaration that everything is recuperated. Piles of glasses, combs, shaving brushes and shoes are followed by masses of hair turned into cloth, charred bodies whose ashes will fertilize cabbage fields, decapitated corpses that will be turned into soap, and finally a pile of skin that yields to an enigmatic display of images. Human bodies have become commodities in a mad capitalist phantasmagoria where profit is literally reaped from the dead as their remains are recycled into fertilizer, cloth, soap and artifacts. Yet Resnais's camera visually returns these commodified remains back to nature. We see oceans of hair, fields of bone, torsos aligned like logs amidst logs, with severed heads displayed in a bucket. The camera stages a *nature morte*, in a shocking literalization of the expression, one that poignantly conveys the brute materiality of these remains and yet also gestures to the disquieting possibility of their aestheticization.

If there is a moment in *Night and Fog* that stages a crisis of representation, it would perhaps be the series of shots that concludes the sequence on the recuperation of human remains. The text recedes before the images as the narrative voice falters, 'With the corpses ... but we can say nothing more,' and yet resumes, 'with the corpses, they want to make soap' ('on veut fabriquer du savon') only to trail off in an ellipsis, 'As for the skin ...' The narrative voice falls silent as the camera slowly pans over a pile of human skin, followed by a swift panoramic shot of images displayed on an outdoor table, eerily fluttering in the breeze. Although the viewer is prepared by the shots that precede this display, the images on the table are initially confusing in the absence of explanatory text. Are they drawings on paper? Plans of how the victims' skin will be used for lampshades and other artifacts? Is it actual skin turned into some sort of canvas for art? Upon re-viewing the sequence, it becomes clear that these images are sections of tattooed human skin, stripped from the victims and displayed as artifacts. This is footage from Buchenwald which Resnais would have seen in the documentary *Les Camps de la mort* produced by *Actualités françaises* in 1945; the patches of tattooed skin were exhibited as evidence of Nazi atrocity at the Nuremberg trials.[7]

The excision of tattoos from the dead culminates a corporeal expropriation that begins at the camp's very gates, where 'under the pretext of hygiene ... nudity delivers an already humiliated human being to the camps,' and as the numerical tattoos of Nazism's delirious accounting system or 'comptabilité délirante' are imprinted upon this nudity. The tattoos exhibited at Buchenwald were images once chosen or imagined and imprinted by the detainees' own agency upon the intimacy of their body, as markers of their personal history. Their surgical removal and subsequent display is the most shocking visual illustration of Nazism's instrumentalization of bodies both living and dead. The body's private materiality is brutally dematerialized into artifact or art, in a logic that Resnais shows as continuous with the concentrationary logic of productive reification.

Yet, as we watch the exhibition of these human traces from Buchenwald, what unfolds before our eyes is a series of decontextualized images that initially we cannot help but consume *as* images (this seems particularly true of the final tattoo of a woman's face looking at the camera). As viewers who may not instantly grasp the historical context and evidentiary status of these images, we are forced into a bewildered consumption of what Brett Kaplan has called 'unwanted beauty' in the context of Holocaust imagery.[8] The images of flayed skin visually attest to a violence that remains unspoken by the text, perhaps because it is indeed unspeakable in the normative sense of the word. Yet I want to pause on this ellipsis and draw attention to what the accompanying images convey, for they speak volumes, although their rare treatment in critical commentary on the film is perhaps due to an understandable reticence about transference in critical discourse, a resistance to complicity with the sadism that produced these images in the first place.

Nevertheless, the silence that accompanies the exhibition of Buchenwald's tattoos compels the viewer to carefully scrutinize these traces and decipher their provenance, context and meaning, so that we may 'Try to look. Just try and see', as Charlotte Delbo challenges her reader to do in some of the most unbearable scenes of *Auschwitz et Après*: 'Essayez de regarder. Essayez pour voir'.[9] Try to look. Just try and see, but also try to look so that you may see, if you can see, let's see if you can see. Yet how are we asked to look and see Resnais's exhibit of the Buchenwald tattoos, to fathom their significance and the ethical stakes of their silent display?

On the one hand, the entire sequence on attempts to recycle human bodies could perhaps be approached through Jean Cayrol's aesthetic of the remnant, of the poet as a *chiffonier* or ragpicker conducting a Lazarean resurrection of those who have perished through their discarded possessions and remains: 'to give life again, so that a shoe lost in a garbage can may be part of our legacy. The concentrationary experience had taught me to leave nothing aside. Man lives on in his remains'.[10] Yet the legacy of Buchenwald's *aestheticized* human remains is a precarious one to grasp within the logic of a testimonial project solely devoted to the resurrection of the victims, precisely because of the extraordinary sadism that has yielded these images, and the inadvertent aesthetic consumption they invite.

Emma Wilson's reflection on material remains in *Night and Fog* powerfully captures the vertigo that such a visual sequence induces in its 'unknowing and undoing of the viewer' by the 'visceral shudder of indeterminacy'.[11] Her reading of the nailmarks left by the victims of extermination on the ceiling of Majdanek's gas chamber illustrates the obtrusively tactile, traumatic and literal imprint of particular images and their intractable resistance to assimilation. Yet while this account of the nailmarks' singular testimonial force is both compelling and persuasive within the frame of *Night and Fog*, it is nevertheless striking to find the visual echo of these nailmarks a few years later in Resnais's *Hiroshima mon amour*, when a young girl devastated by the loss of her German lover and buried alive in her family's basement cellar can only find relief by digging her nails into its walls and sucking her lacerated fingers. The nailmarks in Resnais's later film are also a tactile image of trauma, albeit of a different scope altogether.[12] Yet their appearance in a damp cellar of Nevers, France, cannot but remind us that these are quotations of an imprint whose dreadfully literal origins lie in Majdenek's gas chamber. At the very least, the figural migration of such traces in Resnais's own corpus suggests that the testimonial legacy of *Night and Fog* is far from stably anchored in the memory of those who perished in the Nazi camps. The material trace of these victims undergoes an aestheticizing historical displacement and becomes a trope that circulates across distinct histories, sites and subject positions.

To remark on this is not to fault Resnais for his figural recycling of historical traces. As I will suggest, this formalizing violence and its evacuation of materiality is at the core of the film's allegorical practice. Indeed, it is precisely this kind of figural violence that, in its betrayal of testimonial specificity, opens up a politics of memory. My point is that, as perhaps is the case in the nailmarks' intriguing reappearance in *Hiroshima mon amour*, the silent travelling shot of Buchenwald's tattoo display suggests once again the complicity of the filmic medium with the very atrocity that it documents. This performance of cinematic complicity is entirely consistent with Resnais's reflection on the violence of representation. From the 'botany of death' performed in the colonial displays of African artifacts in *Les Statues meurent aussi* to the museum's framing of nuclear disaster as spectacle in *Hiroshima mon amour*, Resnais's formalizing reflection constantly reminds us that the petrification and circulation of suffering bodies is the treacherous cost of representation.

In *Night and Fog*, the mutilation of the human body and the dispossession of its most private inscriptions compel a consideration of the complicit violence of documentary representation and its transformation of real bodies into reified images. The display of Buchenwald's tattoos are a *mise-en-abyme* of Resnais's own montage, which cuts up, reassembles and displays images of the camps' victims as art. Resnais was still aware of the transferential violence of his representational practice 30 years later when he reported that 'In the cutting room ... I had the strange impression of manipulating documents of corpses, or what is even worse, of living people – when they're dead it's less terrible than when they're alive – and of trying to conduct research on form.'[13] This reflection on the violence of montage, the cutting or *découpage* and reassembly of images of bodies that are ripped out of context, shorn of their specificity and recycled in the documentary, conveys Resnais's recognition of the dangers of transference, of replicating past violence in the representation of this past.[14] His feeling of contamination and shame at various stages of the film's making, for instance as he manipulated still and moving images to create visual drama ('I was a bit ashamed during the *montage*') also reminds us that the documentary risks turning the suffering of victims into a spectacle of circulating commodities.[15] In their perilous capacity for beauty, such images recall Theodor Adorno's cautionary words on the betrayal of the image in the artistic testimony of lived violence:

> [B]y turning suffering into images, despite all their hard implacability, they wound our shame before the victims. For these are used to create something, works of art, that are thrown to the consumption of a world ... that destroyed them. The so-called artistic representation of sheer physical pain ... contains, however remotely, the power to elicit enjoyment

out of it. The moral of this art, not to forget for a single instant, slithers into the abyss of its opposite.[16]

Resnais's attunement to the complicitous violence of his formalism refuses what Geoffrey Hartman has termed the realistic purism that we typically associate with documentary form, one defended as the most appropriate medium for Holocaust representation along with the chronicle by theorists such as Berel Lang.[17] Instead, Resnais gives us a volatile, anxious testimony alert to the ambiguities and double-binds facing representations of genocide. Just as the film reflects on its complicity and betrayal, it also forces us, as viewers, to reckon with our own complicity. Not only as consumers of such images, perhaps engaged in our own forms of distancing or catharsis, but most importantly for the film's political thrust, as blind witnesses, if not accomplices, to an ongoing genocidal catastrophe that constitutes post-Auschwitz modernity. This turn to historical complicity finds its fullest allegorical expression at the close of the film, as the narrator admonishes viewers about their own unwitting complicity with the violence of History. A close reading of the film's concluding passage through a sustained consideration of allegory lets us discern more clearly the ethical, memorial and political stakes of the film's often criticized formalism and universalization of the Holocaust.

Allegory, ruins and history

'Allegory views existence, as it does art, under the sign of fragmentation and ruin.'[18]

Night and Fog concludes with the following lines:

As I speak to you, the cold water of marshes and ruins fill the hollows of the charnel houses, water that is as cold and opaque as our bad memory.

War has sunk into slumber, one eye still open. Grass has faithfully returned to the Appel-platz around the blocks.

An abandoned village, still full of menace.

The crematorium is obsolete. Nazi ruses are out of fashion.

Nine million dead haunt this landscape.

Who among us stands guard from this strange observatory to warn us of the coming of new executioners? Are their faces really different from our own?

Somewhere, amongst us, there remain lucky kapos, recuperated leaders, unknown denouncers. There are those of us who sincerely look at these ruins as if the old concentrationary monster lay dead under its debris, those of us who feign to take hope again as the image fades, as though there were a cure for the concentrationary plague, those of us who feign to believe that all this happened only once, at a certain time and in a certain place, and those who do not look around us, and who do not hear the cry to the end of time.[19]

At the moment of the film's testimony, when the narrator addresses the spectators viewing the ruins of Birkenau's crematoria, Auschwitz is far from an established *lieu de mémoire*. It is a precariously receding image, susceptible to dissolution by the ebb of memory and the flow of time. The figural operations of the passage perform an unexpected naturalization of history, one that takes place through the spatialization of time, or the merging of history into setting. In this landscape of ruin and desolation, nature – like postwar collective memory – bears the mark of historical time and has been contaminated by genocide, yet it still returns to claim its terrain. 'The peculiar grass that covered over the traces of the deportees' footsteps now faithfully shows up to morning call on the Appel-Platz, taking the place of those who were counted there under unbearable conditions each dawn.'[20] The bodies have vanished, and it is the landscape that is endowed with a disquieting kind of survival. Like the muddy streams that seep through the terrain of Auschwitz and reflect the bogs of collective memory, the passage itself erodes the dams of temporal, spatial and memorial representation, revealing the precarious threshold between history and nature, memory and forgetting, here and there, then and now, and us and them.

Significantly, the film ends on the material traces of the apparatus used for extermination rather than on the victims' remains. The final images of abandoned ruins reclaimed by nature returns us to our earlier consideration of the film's materialist critique. We view the remains of capitalist modernity's most violent phantasmagoria: the industrial production of death itself. 'The crematorium is obsolete, Nazi ruses are out of fashion,' the narrative voice assures us. Yet the discarded fetishes of genocide nevertheless remind us that the forces once animating these ruins were no passing fashion, for the endless suffering of concentrationary experience continues even as we fail to heed its cries. At the documentary's close, Auschwitz emerges as an unstable temporalized space, one precariously poised between the 'now' of address, the apparent obsolescence of Nazi extermination, and the timeless suffering of victims. Auschwitz becomes a spatialized time as well. Once a site of internment and extermination, its ruins become a hieroglyph for history as infinite catastrophe.

Night and Fog concludes on a series of dislocations that bring the concentrationary legacy to bear on multiplying horizons, provoking a tension between its documentary project and its allegorical relevance for other times and places. As we have seen, the visual and rhetorical strategies of the film deliberately destabilize a number of key distinctions: the categories of time and space are blurred such that the site and limit-event of Auschwitz becomes a figure for the violence of history itself, a synecdoche for a trans-historical phenomenon that Albert Camus called *le fait concentrationnaire* and that is also allegorized as a concentrationary monster and plague: epic and pathological figures that endow historical processes with the cyclical inevitability of myth or natural disease.

The allegorical dimension of *Night and Fog* as a film not only about the Nazi camps but as a cautionary parable about the concentrationary peril is precisely what constitutes its ever-actual political force. But for now I wish to pause on some of the tensions produced by this unexpected passage from the testimonial specificity of documentary to the more shadowy realm of allegory, a passage where Walter Benjamin's reflections on allegory's form and politics may prove illuminating.

Benjamin's reflections on allegory convey a topography of this figure that makes a striking commentary on the conclusion of *Night and Fog*:

> The allegorical physiognomy of nature-history … is present in reality in the form of the ruin. In the ruin history has physically merged into the setting. And in this guise history does not assume the form of the process of eternal life so much as that of irresistible decay … Allegories are in the realm of thought what ruins are in the realm of things.[21]

In this analogy between ruins and allegory, between material productions and processes of representation, Benjamin underlines the converging instrumental violence of these practices upon the bodies and things that inhabit their respective economies. Both the commodity object and the object of allegorical representation are hollowed out ciphers that are unmoored from their context and injected with meaning, yet that meaning itself is arbitrary and infinitely substitutable. As Benjamin later describes it, and in terms that resonate with Jean Cayrol's testimonial project, the allegorist is an avatar of the *chiffonier*:

> Through the disorderly fund which knowledge places at his disposal, the allegorist rummages here and there for a particular piece, holds it next to some other piece, and tests to see if they fit together – that meaning with this image, or this image with that meaning. The result can never be known beforehand for there is no natural mediation between the two … At no point is it written in the stars that the allegorist's profundity will lead it to one meaning rather than another. And though it may have once acquired such a meaning, this can always be withdrawn in favour of a different meaning.[22]

The unmooring of image and object described by Benjamin is precisely what reinvests allegory with shifting and renewable meaning through time, a pertinent if disquieting commentary on the end of *Night and Fog*, where one might assume that the allegorical objects are the Nazi genocide's nine million ghosts whose memory is now pressed in service of other bodies, times and places.

Benjamin's remarks on allegory recall us to the formal complicities that can vex representations of Nazi concentrationary production: the extraction of labour, life and value from bodies both living and dead. As *Night and Fog's* reflection on complicity suggests, the documentary's production of an allegorical landscape is contaminated by the historical processes that constitute the site-event of Auschwitz. Of particular relevance to the gradual dematerialization of bodies in Resnais's film is Benjamin's remark that allegory opens onto a desolate terrain in which 'death digs most deeply into the jagged line of demarcation between physical nature and its significance'.[23] Cayrol and Resnais's film both denounces and rehearses this 'jagged line of demarcation' or forceful sundering of the victims' physical being and the meanings that are invested in them. From the fragile material traces of the victims' passage through the gas chamber, to the exhibition of their private bodily inscriptions in the Buchenwald display, to their immaterial resurrection as nine million ghosts in an unpeopled landscape and their diffraction into the resonance of history's universal cry of suffering, the arc of *Night and Fog* performs the spectralization that for Benjamin constituted the contradictory force of allegory in its destructive fervour and its redemptive thrust.

As Gordon Teskey has argued, 'Allegory oscillates between a project of reference and a project of capture.'[24] Its inscription of matter into form cannot be exempt from the incorporative and irrealizing violence of capture. Also pertinent is Paul de Man's formulation of the distinction between symbol and allegory. Whereas the symbol's premise is the continuity between material perception and figuration, allegory exposes the temporal gap and arbitrariness of this link: 'the allegorical form appears purely mechanical, an abstraction whose original meaning is even more devoid of substance than its "phantom proxy", the allegorical representative.'[25] This formulation takes on unexpected material weight when we consider that the nine million ghosts that haunt Auschwitz's landscape in *Night and Fog* themselves become allegorical representatives or 'phantom proxies' of other bodies and histories; they risk vanishing under the abstraction of history as an eternal recurrence of the same catastrophe.

Allegory's ghosting effect on its objects, its spectral temporality of eternal recurrence, along with its naturalization of history were some of Benjamin's reservations about and fascinations with its Baroque practice. As committed as he was to the rescue of material objects, Benjamin (like Cayrol and Resnais) was acutely aware of allegory's treacherous tendency to reinvest dead matter with shifting and renewable meanings: 'these allegories fill out and deny the void in which they are represented … the intention does not faithfully rest in the contemplation of the bones but faithlessly leaps forward to the idea of resurrection.'[26] One might recall *Night and Fog*'s final gesture, which distracts us – albeit knowingly – from the contemplation of Auschwitz's bones and ghosts to the idea of their resurrection in alternative concentrationary histories.

Despite both its status as documentary and its formal modernism, *Night and Fog* provides an unexpected illustration of Benjamin's theory of allegory and its melancholy vision of history as the eternal return of the same in the new and the new in the same. The film's concluding imagery imprints history's decaying physiognomy upon nature, thus spatializing and naturalizing history itself while mirroring the same contamination in the spectators' collective memory. The rhetoric of ruins, cyclical pestilence and contagion inaugurates a temporality of repetition that blurs the site specificity of Auschwitz and its history, placing it on the verge of a concentrationary mythology with its ghosts, plagues and monsters. Auschwitz emerges as a synecdoche and an allegorical emblem for a concentrationary catastrophe whose antecedents are as ancient as the plague but that paradoxically defines the new time, space and psychic structure of post-Holocaust capitalist modernity.

Yet here I want to rescue the figure of allegory from its overwhelming association with this melancholy politics of 'petrified unrest' by turning to its destructive pole of critique.[27] As a rhetorical figure, allegory harbours a force of political relevance and historical contestation that is evident from its Baroque expressions through Baudelaire and beyond. Like irony, allegory is a structure of both violence and counterviolence; its destructive impulse retains the very state that it both contains and contests. For Benjamin, this doubleness animates allegory's dialectical force of progression and regression. Allegory shatters the organic appearance of mythic history to expose the contingency, fragmentation and ruin behind its official veil. In its disclosure of death as 'the jagged line of demarcation between physical nature and its significance', allegory makes visible the costs of its own production. As Teskey puts it, the greatest allegorical poets 'do not simply transform life into meaning. They exacerbate the antipathy between the living and the significant by exposing the violence entailed in transforming one to the other.'[28] This exposure is made possible by allegory's structural complicity with what it represents or contests, its capacity to mirror dynamically and critically the violence of history. Allegory's *complicity* with the instrumentalizing economies from which it draws its equivalences, its exposure and retention of violence, are what give this rhetorical figure its critical force and historical duration.

As we have seen, allegory's specular complicity with the violence of history is repeatedly performed in *Night and Fog* in its gestures to transferences and continuities between the film's aesthetic operations and Nazi technologies of production, destruction and representation. Paradoxically, it is through the figure of allegory, its contradictory structure and dialectical force of regression and progression, that the film splinters the petrification and forgetting of monumental history, opening Auschwitz out to other proximate histories connected to the Third Reich in ideology, technology, practices and even personnel. The following section will pursue the film's legacy as a counterblow to what Georges Perec, in his own brilliant allegorization of history, called '*l'Histoire avec sa grande hache*' (simultaneously History with a capital H and History with its great axe).[29] I will initially address the reception of *Night and Fog* as an allegory of Algeria, to then trace the documentary's splintering effects on the *cloisonnement des mémoires* or memorial walls that remain embedded in French post-war history and historiography, but also in discourses on the Holocaust's unrepresentable singularity.

The politics of concentrationary memory

At its release, both Resnais and Cayrol expressed anxiety that *Night and Fog* would be misconstrued as a purely testimonial monument to the dead, that its commemoration of history's darkest chapter would close the book on a concentrationary reality which remained all too current in post-war France. As we have seen, their visual and textual rhetoric cautions against the ossification of memorial projects that would turn the ruins of the past into a monument that organizes forgetting.[30] The film's simultaneous performance of and resistance to this kind of memorial petrification is evident in its self-conscious montage and editing. Resnais's use of heterogeneous archives, including Nazi footage, is an embrace of the film's own contaminated status as a transient artefact, ruin, or commodity that can and will be subject to allegorical violence in its citation and recycling into alternative histories and political projects.

In his protest against the film's removal from Cannes, Jean Cayrol expressed this anti-monumental and desacralizing intention in an evocative metaphor: 'The canvas of the screen is not Veronica's shroud. This is a film that burned the gaze …', referring here to Saint Veronica's cloth bearing the imprint of Christ's face.[31] For Cayrol, the filmic screen was neither a blank page receiving the imprint of history, nor a cultic object of commemoration. It was like a fire that burned the eyes with its contaminating force, one whose embers would continue to spark and light up future representations of historical violence, and not only of the Holocaust. We could not be further from the critical orthodoxy of the Holocaust as a 'crisis of representation', a proposition that is both epistemological and ethical in its simultaneous interdiction of the comparative nature of human understanding *and* of figural representation. As we shall see, the spreading fires of *Night and Fog* and its mobilization towards alternative histories challenge the 'ring of fire' that Claude Lanzmann will later seek to draw around the Holocaust: 'The Holocaust is above all unique in that it erects a ring of fire around itself, a borderline that cannot be crossed because there is a certain ultimate degree of horror that cannot be transmitted.'[32]

The allegorical registers of *Night and Fog* are what forged this passage into the actuality of the 'scandale raciste' [racist scandal] decried by Cayrol at its release.[33] The poet clarified the film's rhetoric of complicity by suggesting that there was more than one history at stake in this documentary about the Nazi camps: 'It told a story that didn't only engage the Nazis, sweet Germany ('la douce Allemagne'), but also our country, for we had no right to modestly avert our gaze before a drama that had contaminated us all.'[34] Cayrol alludes of course to France's collaboration with deportation, a fact erased by the famous censorship of the French *képi* at the Pithiviers camp, but he also gestures to the unnamed war with Algeria. The allegorical cartography of *Night and Fog* brought home the proliferation of concentrationary reality, from 'la douce Allemagne' to the 'doux humus quotidien' or sweet quotidian soil of *douce France* itself.[35] The film's meditation on contagion and complicity sought to show the historical proximities and ideological circulations that tied Nazi Germany to France, not only in relation to its occupied collaborationist past but its occupationist present as the military entered into the most violent phase of the Algerian war, extending a concentrationary network that, as historian Sylvie Thénault reminds us, had been in place in France since the Spanish Civil War and reached into the shadowlands of its colonial territories.[36]

When Charles Krantz asked Resnais about the ultimate point of *Night and Fog* in 1985, the director provocatively responded that 'The whole point was Algeria.' Disquieted by Resnais's allegorical use of the Holocaust as a screen memory for Algeria, Krantz concluded that 'even the noblest of creations may begin with ulterior motives that may remain secret long afterward.'[37] This critique of allegory's universalization echoes a number of other indictments since of the documentary's failure to signal the Jewish specificity of the Nazi extermination, and of its collaboration with the erasure of Holocaust memory in post-war France.[38] Yet the notion that Algeria serves as an ulterior motive for *Night and Fog* inscribes allegory and the historical memory it conveys within a finite and hierarchical economy of petrified equivalences. It suggests that making one history visible happens at the cost of rendering another one invisible, as if there were an inevitable tension between a testimonial relationship to the past and the attempt to reanimate this past in service of current and invisible strains of the plague. Such a view of allegory and of historical memory itself fails to account for what Michael Rothberg has importantly defined as 'multidirectional memory', a vision of collective remembrance that accounts for its capacity to grasp historical similarity and difference across geopolitical sites and resists what Rothberg terms as the 'zero-sum logic' of competitive memory and its fixed hierarchies of suffering.[39]

The challenge that *Night and Fog* continues to pose to viewers is how to reanimate the contestatory potential of its testimony to the Nazi camps across historical horizons, how to recover the ongoing force of its critique of complicity while also resisting a kind of poetics of criticism, in which its rhetorical figures (of cries, plagues and monsters) are cut off from their circumstances and diminished in their political as well as commemorative relevance. Allegory's operations are ambivalent and dialectical; while its regressive pole can indeed petrify history into a zone of universalizing equivalence, its dynamic force of critique also makes it a vehicle for actualizing a differential memory across historical horizons. As we shall see, it was the allegorical register of *Night and Fog* that, in its betrayal of this historical specificity of the Judaeocide, enabled the film to invoke the repressed events of Algeria. The film's transhistorical figures for complicity may have compromised the testimonial specificity of the film as a documentary about the Holocaust, yet this compromise is precisely what enabled an engagement with other histories of racialized violence.

Allegory's betrayal of specificity, including the specificity of the Holocaust, opened the film out to the political horizon of its day and constructed a figural iconography of the concentrationary experience that forged and mobilized its emblematic imagery to ends both testimonial with regard to the Nazi past and politically engaged with regard to Algeria. The visual language of the film brought into relief a concentrationary reality that was all-too-proximate and yet repressed as massive government censorship over the Algerian war went into effect. By suggesting the historical analogies between the Nazi regime and the French Republic, between Fascism and colonialism, the film performed an important *décloisonnement des mémoires* or bringing down of memorial walls that was grasped even before the time of its release.

Indeed, even before its battles with censorship, the documentary's incendiary potential to connect the Nazi past to France's present was grasped by military and censorship apparatus. When Resnais was refused a photograph by the *Service Cinématographique des Armées* (SCA), it was presumably because of his anti-colonialist convictions (his *Les Statues meurent aussi* was censored until 1963). For the director, the SCA's refusal signalled the military's complicity with the double repression of Vichy collaboration and Algerian pacification: 'I felt that there was already a solidarity between armies, whether these were French, English (or German, even) that made them unwilling to *talk about all this* ('parler de tout ça', my italics).'[40] To talk about all this would entail superimposing two histories of occupation and deportation, inscribing the Algerian 'events' within a logic of complicity that France was at pains to disavow. As Benjamin Stora explains, 'To take a lucid look at the Algerian war's unfolding is to risk thinking of Vichy. This will be a good reason to *not talk about* ('ne pas parler') either period.'[41] By projecting France into the mirror of Auschwitz, *Night and Fog* gave an allegorical face to the war without a name.

Resnais later makes the Algerian context for the film quite clear: 'we were right in the midst of the Algerian war ... and there were already zones in the centre of France with regroupment camps ... we made the film ... with the idea that, in a way, it was all starting to happen again in France.'[42] The opening shots of fields suddenly sectioned and reframed by barbed wires and watchtowers visually brought home this apparently alien concentrationary reality, one that was not established in France until 1957, when the discretionary special powers were extended to the metropole and camps such as Larzac or Rivesaltes interned over 14,000 Algerians suspected of harbouring ties with the Front de Libération National (FLN). But in Algeria, a network of underground repression camps was already well in place, and as early as 1955, entire sectors of the rural population had been displaced into regroupment camps in an effort to isolate insurgents. Their numbers would soar to over a million by 1959. Michel Rocard's report, published in the pages of *Le Monde* that year, describes the dire consequences of this policy. The displacement, regroupment and internment of these Algerians stripped them of their means of subsistence, kept them malnourished, in terrible sanitary conditions and with insufficient medical care, causing appalling rates of child mortality (an estimated 500 deaths per day) in what Tassadit Yacine has denounced as 'a genocide that does not speak its name'.[43]

Resnais and Cayrol were thus pioneers in the disclosure of a concentrationary topography that was reaching into the French homeland itself. They joined ranks with Robert Antelme, David Rousset, Marguerite Duras, Dionys Mascolo (and later Jean-Paul Sartre, Aimé Césaire and Jean Amrouche) in one of the earliest intellectual mobilizations against the Algerian war and the only unified post-war anti-colonial movement, the short-lived *Comité contre la poursuite de la guerre en Afrique*. In the autumn of 1955, several months after the Philippeville massacre (in which the FLN killed 123 French settlers, leading to French military reprisals that claimed an estimated 15,000 Algerian lives) and as *Night and Fog* was in production, Resnais signed the *Comité*'s letter to Jacques Soustelle, then governor-general of Algeria. Published in *Combat,* the letter denounced the establishment of a concentrationary universe in Algeria precisely by superimposing histories that France did not want to see implicated, and in terms that would haunt the decade. Several years before the explosion of the debate around torture on the French public scene, the committee's letter to Soustelle drew its rhetorical force from its repeated analogies between Nazism and colonialism, Gestapo techniques and French pacification, concluding that a systematic concentrationary regime was already operating at all levels of the French bureaucracy, police and administration in Algeria, implementing an order of terror that mirrored that of the Third Reich.[44]

Throughout the Algerian war, the legacy of the occupation, collaboration and deportation provided a template and a justification for resisting French military policy and its practices of internment and torture. *Night and Fog* was a crucible for shaping this resistance, for its concluding imagery was charged with a recognizable force in the war's aftermath. The concentration camp as an incurable disease or a world with no exit, the victim turned executioner, the unheard cry of unseen suffering, the enemy whose face is one's own, the culpable blindness or deafness of bystanders, these are all tropes that circulate both in Resnais's documentary and throughout a number of films, plays and novels of the period. Such figures brought into relief the proximities between the wartime experience and colonial history, addressing the disquieting irony of a nation previously occupied and victimized by Nazi Germany, yet guilty of internment, torture and summary executions in the service of an ongoing occupation less than a decade later. These figures of reversal and complicity opened a passage in post-war cultural production between France and Algeria, Fascism and colonialism, liberation and decolonization, thus serving as a powerful call to political resistance.

A key figure for these analogies is that of the concentrationary plague, or 'peste concentrationnaire' that has yet to be eradicated. There are many iterations of this figure, but perhaps none more striking than *The Plague* by Albert Camus, an author whom Cayrol had hailed as one of the first historians and explorers of Lazarean, concentrationary art and whose cautionary words in the French press were crucial to building an awareness of the Algerian conflict during the making of *Night and Fog*.[45] It is therefore fitting that the documentary would end its investigation of the camps with a gesture to Camus's allegory of the fascist peril as a plague. By resignifying this plague into a concentrationary condition that could infect any state at any time, Cayrol was faithful to Camus's final call for ceaseless vigilance against a disease that would inevitably reawaken and send its rats to die in a happy city. Yet there is a fascinating paradox in the plague's allegorical circulation between these works. Whereas the allusion to the concentrationary plague is precisely what opened *Night and Fog* up to the censored events of Algeria, Camus's allegory of occupation, although set in Algeria, self-consciously erases the native population out of its frame and with it, the colonial plague that was analogous to Fascism (an analogy embodied by the demonstrators massacred after the Liberation at Sétif, who bore banners saying 'Down with Fascism and colonialism'). The circulation of this figure between the two works illuminated distinct histories and generated competing political readings. The plague's appearance in Resnais's documentary on the Nazi camps reactivated a history of colonial violence that was provocatively erased in Camus's own allegory of the Nazi occupation. The parallel between fascism and colonialism, an apparent blindspot in Camus's novel (although the matter is far more complex) becomes 'the whole point' of Resnais's film.[46]

Yet Albert Camus was one of the first to articulate the ironic proximities between Nazi Germany and the post-war French republic; his writings on

Algeria in the press of the day opened a dialogue between these two repressed histories of occupation and racialized violence. As early as 1947, in an article significantly titled 'Contagion', he denounced France's contamination by the plague of Hitlerism in its colonial 'pacification' of Algeria and Madagascar: 'we are doing what we reproached the Germans of doing.'[47] In the immediate aftermath of the Second World War, Camus predicted that the exorcism of Nazi poison from the nation's body was far from over; in the columns of *L'Express* a decade later, he sought to make audible the 'solitary cries of those slaughtered in that strange land lost in a fog of blood'.[48] In the wake of the Philippeville massacre, Camus reminded the public that the cries of French and Arab Algerians alike had been falling on deaf ears since Sétif, and demanded that France examine its historical conscience: 'Who shut its ears to the cries of Arab wretchedness? Who but France has waited with disgusting good conscience for Algeria to bleed before finally noticing its existence?'[49] There is an unmistakable resonance between Camus's indictment and the documentary's final words on the murky waters of a faulty collective memory that is deaf to the endless cry of suffering. *Night and Fog* and its figures for complicity such as the concentrationary plague, the victim turned executioner, the endless cry and the culpably blind or deaf bystander, was thus engaged in a dialogue with Camus and others in an attempt to make the Algerian crisis both visible and audible to the French public.

One compelling illustration of *Night and Fog*'s power to convert a reflection on complicity into an act of resistance within the horizon of its immediate reception is that of Aline Charby, interviewed by Martin Evans in his investigation of how the memory of the Second World War fuelled opposition to the Algerian war. The daughter of Catholic settlers in Algeria, Charby moved to Paris in the early 1950s and viewed the documentary as it opened in theatres. She describes its impact upon her as a traumatic shock that forever fractured and reconfigured her identity, historical consciousness and political commitments:

> I was shattered [...] At that moment it brought home to me what Nazism amounted to ... it was truly a horrifying shock. And rightly or wrongly, I made the link between those around me who'd supported Marshal Pétain and those who'd aided Hitler and the Nazis ... It shouldn't be thought that all Nazis were very wicked, utterly vile and hateful people. Your neighbor or your brother might be one; that's what I thought to myself ... and I've never changed my mind on that matter.[50]

The documentary's images and its meditation on complicity awakened Charby to a constellation of links, specifically those between *pied noirs* who supported the Vichy régime (including her immediate family), French collaborators and Nazi perpetrators. The representation of Nazi atrocity alerted her to a series of complicitous links between perpetrators, accomplices and various kinds of enablers and bystanders, including neighbours and brothers whose faces were no different from her own ('Who among us stands guard from this strange observatory to warn us of the coming of new executioners? Are their faces really different from our own?'). The transnational deployment of these links, from Algeria to France to Germany, indicates the productive force of allegorical displacement in its invitation to link ('rightly or wrongly' as Charby puts it) different sites of historical violence by pointing out their ideological kinship and physiognomical resemblances. Instead of paralysing Charby into identification with either the perpetrators or the victims, the complicities woven by *Night and Fog* galvanized her into joining the clandestine Jeanson network, which among other things provided arms to the Front de Libération National. For Charby, the film's final interpellation translated the values of the French Resistance into the anti-colonial struggle, and in this she was like many other dissenters for whom the wartime legacy made support of French Algeria and the military tactics that this entailed unthinkable. At the time of its reception, then, the documentary's register of complicity, its allegorical overlay of multiple legacies of violence proved a catalyst for political action in an altogether different context from the one represented.

In one of the earliest representations of the Nazi genocide, then, the petrification of Auschwitz into modernity's emblematic landscape was at the same time fractured into a differential site of memory and political mobilization. While the film's gesturing toward the violence of French colonialism in Algeria was readily grasped by certain audiences, such a reading also met with resistance. Perhaps the most astonishing illustration of an attempt to recontain the film's allegorical relevance for the anti-colonial struggle is by one of its founders, Henri Michel, secretary general of the *Comité d'histoire de la Deuxième Guerre mondiale* which commissioned *Night and Fog*, and with Olga Wormser, co-editor of its central historical source, *Tragédie de la déportation*. In 1965, as Michel and Wormser sought to integrate *Night and Fog* into school curricula, Michel worried about the links that could be made between the history of Nazi deportation and the Algerian crisis, presumably the wrong ones this time since he qualifies them as 'tendentious and inopportune'.[51] In an educational plan submitted the same year to the Ministry for Cooperation (formerly the Colonial Ministry), Michel sought to rehabilitate French colonialism in light of the anti-fascist struggle by proposing an educational programme for France's ex-colonies in Africa and Madagascar that would show *Night and Fog* in tandem with a documentary by François Villiers on wartime colonial troops, *Ils étaient tous des volontaires* (*They Were All Voluntary Conscripts*). This double bill was intended by Michel to remind the former colonies of their voluntary

Figure 6.1 Still from *Camp de Thiaroye* (Ousmane Sembene and Thierno Faty Sow, 1988), presented by the Société Nouvelle de Promotion Cinématographique, Dakar. ENAPROC and SATPEC (Tunisia)

Figure 6.2 Still from *Camp de Thiaroye* (Ousmane Sembene and Thierno Faty Sow, 1988), presented by the Société Nouvelle de Promotion Cinématographique, Dakar. ENAPROC and SATPEC (Tunisia)

enlistment against Nazism so that they would 'measure the peril from which people of colour have escaped, in order to allow them, by comparison, to judge French colonization more equitably'.[52] It was through a comparison, or rather, a contrast between Nazi Germany and France that Michel sought to mitigate and relativize, if not rehabilitate, French colonialism and its colonial regime of racialized violence.

As a response to this attempted recontainment of *Night and Fog's* allegorical legacy, I now turn to *Camp de Thiaroye* by Senegalese director Sembene Ousmane, a film that 20 years later provides the colonial countermemory to the history that Henri Michel sought to mobilize for the education of France's ex-colonies. *Camp de Thiaroye* (1988) not only juxtaposes the concentrationary horrors of Nazism with the violence of French colonialism, but it also uses footage from *Night and Fog* in order to pursue the very analogy that Michel sought to forestall and repress. Sembene probes the overlapping violence of the Nazi and colonial regimes of concentrationary violence precisely through the example of the *tirailleurs sénégalais* or colonial conscripts in the war, who, as he suggested in his earlier film *Emitaï* and presumably in sharp contrast to Villiers's documentary, were far from being 'all voluntary conscripts'.[53] The reappearance of Resnais's film in Sembene's work proves a compelling illustration of how the allegorical force of *Night and Fog* continues to splinter the memorial walls that separate histories of racialized violence.

In a crucial scene that visually stages the continuities between the Nazi and French concentrationary terror, a serviceman who was interned in Buchenwald comes upon the barbed wires of the transit camp. The serviceman is significantly named Pays (country or nation) and becomes a complex allegory for the traumas of post-war colonial identity. Pays lost his mind and ability to speak during the war and carries an SS helmet with him at all times as an insignia of power and perhaps as a protective talisman. Despite his apparent madness, Pays is the only one to *see* the continuities between Buchenwald and Thiaroye. As he runs his fingers along the barbed wires and convulsively grips their knots (and indeed these knots visualize the entwinement of concentrationary histories that he is the only one to 'grasp'), Pays' friend Corporal Diarra takes his hand off the wire and gently rubs some native soil onto it, reassuring him that Buchenwald is over and that Pays is safely back on African land: 'plus Buchenwald, fini, ici terre Afriki, terre sauve' (Fig. 6.1). Unconvinced, Pays dons his SS helmet and coat, and guards the barbed wire fence from some conscripts who want to hang their clothes out to dry, pointing to the watchtowers with inarticulate cries. Pays's profile then dissolves into that of a German guard holding binoculars in a camp tower, in a curiously mediated flashback to Buchenwald that passes through his own gaze and that of the SS guard (Fig. 6.2). We hear the rattle of machine guns followed by three shots of dead bodies. The first two stills are of dead detainees who hang from the camps' electrified wires, either shot dead or having committed suicide, and the third still shows two bodies lying on the ground next to a barbed wire fence (Plates 26–28).

This traumatic flashback is composed of a sequence of three stills from Resnais's *Night and Fog* (shots 143–145). It is a scene in which the Nazi camps erupt in Lazarean fashion within the barbed wires of an African landscape.[54] Pays's hallucination signals a *dépaysement* or dislocation that is at once psychic, spatial and temporal. The Nazi genocide is lodged in his psyche and this intermemorial splinter attests to his historical entanglement with the Holocaust. The resurrection of this imagery belies his companion's faith that the concentrationary terror is over and that they are on safe, native land, for it visually brings home the murderous continuities between two regimes of violence and foreshadows the conscripts' massacre. Pays' surreal recollection of Mauthausen and Buchenwald in Senegal is far from a subjective and private trauma; indeed it marks the emergence of historical consciousness as Walter Benjamin conceived it: 'To articulate the past historically does not mean recognizing it "the way it really was." It means to seize hold of a memory as it flashes up at a moment of danger.'[55]

The dislocation of Holocaust imagery from Germany to Senegal by way of French imperialism allegorically conveys a psychic trauma with concrete historical roots. As Pays stands inarticulate on a land that eludes his grasp, caught in a time of extermination that seems to have no end, we understand that the condition of imperial assimilation is the subject's willingness to die over and over again — as bare and unqualified life — for a nation or *pays* to which he will never belong.[56] At the end of the film, as he stands guard at the watchtower and sees the colonial tanks roll in, Pays visually embodies the final warning of *Night and Fog*: 'Who among us stands guard from this strange observatory to warn us of the coming of new executioners?' Pays recalls Elie Wiesel's prophetic figure Moshe the Beadle, who witnesses extermination and yet fails to persuade the Jews of Sighet to flee. Like the mad prophet of *Night*, Pays tries to warn the celebrating troops but fails to avert their massacre. He cries out unintelligibly and brandishes his SS helmet as a metonym for the surrounding French tanks, but is dismissed for seeing Nazis everywhere.

In an intriguing twist on *Night and Fog*, which concludes by asking whether the new executioners' faces differ from our own, Sembene Ousmane's *Camp de Thiaroye* does not show us the faces of those inside the gleaming French tanks that anonymously spit fire at the soldiers in flight. Yet historically, these faces were no different from the faces of those killed, since the massacre was implemented by loyal colonial troops. This elision is no doubt due to Sembene's investment in maintaining the polarity between victims and executioners, colonizer and colonized. But such polarities are complicated by the very figure of Pays, who is at once witness, victim and embodiment of the kind of complicity I have sought to trace in its various post-war articulations. He is a *tirailleur* and as such, a structural agent of colonial power as well as a supposed example of the assimilated imperial subject. Yet on his own native soil and abroad, he is a phantom whose mind and body are destroyed by overlaying regimes of racialized violence. The historical circumstances of camp Thiaroye's massacre, one implemented by colonial troops following French military orders, remind us that imperial regimes deploy a grey zone binding executioners and victims to implement their territorial reach both into the spaces and psyches of their subjects.

When *Camp de Thiaroye* first opened in Dakar, the French ambassador marched out of the theatre. Sembene then defended his film in the following terms:

> The history of the world involves everyone, all races. We are going to highlight our participation in history (*extraire de l'histoire notre participation*) but it will also be your history ... You don't create a history to take revenge but in order to be rooted in your history and culture. That is why we made the film for the whole world, not for any one race. So that you could see that blacks participated in the war and we are not yet done with our history, which is your history as well.[57]

This articulation of history as a continuous and open process of retrospection and projection, memory and futurity, differentiation but also convergence, points to a temporality that has been recently elaborated by Achille Mbembe as 'emergent' or 'entangled' time: 'this time is not a series but an *interlocking* of presents, pasts, and futures that retain their depths of other pasts, presents, and futures, each age bearing, altering, and maintaining the previous ones.'[58] This emergent time is also the dialectical time of allegory, which in its destructive retention of the past, its complicity or folding together of distinct experiences, continues to both particularize and bind histories in asymmetrical and differential relations of reciprocity, in *noeuds de mémoire* or knots of memory, and to thereby animate ongoing engagements.

Coda: from *Night and Fog* to Guantanamo Bay

Jean Cayrol's post-war reflections on the escalating reach of the concentrationary phenomenon into territories that are both geopolitical and psychological remain strikingly resonant: 'Concentrationary influence, solicitude, continues to grow not only in its uninterrupted materializations (one imagines new maps in which the kingdoms of Murder will be marked for the next "explorers" of these desolate lands) but also in the European and even global psyche.' 'With horror,

I think of the refinements that could be brought to the next concentration camps and their even more singular forms, where even the gift of suffering, the ultimate withdrawal of their nights, may be denied to human beings.'[59] The concentrationary cartography that Cayrol drew in the aftermath of the Second World War is uncannily prescient of new technologies of internment and torture developed under the Bush administration's war on terror and its creation of an indefinite state of exception that found one of its most obvious territorial locations in the US detention camp of Guantanamo Bay.

This chapter has sought to trace the memorial force of *Night and Fog*'s legacy through a consideration of its allegorical status and reception. In that

Figure 6.3 Still from *The Road to Guantanamo* (Michael Winterbottom and Mat Whitecross, 2006)

spirit, and mindful of both the ethical perils and political force of allegory itself, I conclude with a brief consideration of two very different images of detainment. The first, from *Night and Fog*, is the photograph of a detainee who has either committed suicide or been shot, and whose hands still cling to the barbed wires of Mauthausen (Plate 26). As we have seen, it is one of the photographs that appears in the traumatic flashback of *Camp de Thiaroye*. The second is a still from the docudrama *The Road to Guantanamo* (2006) by Michael Winterbottom and Matt Whitecross and portrays a detainee kneeling before a barbed wire fence in Guantanamo (Fig. 6.3). I turn to these two images not to analogize and conflate their irreducibly distinct historical context and generic status (the photograph of a victim of the Nazi camps and the figure of a prisoner in a fictionalized documentary on the costs of the war on terror) but to suggest that their visual continuities and differences convey shifts in the deployment of what Jean Cayrol described as 'concentrationary solicitude'. The still from *The Road to Guantanamo* represents a mock-up of Guantanamo Bay and uses the visual iconography of the Nazi camps (one that *Night and Fog* centrally established) to stage what is distinctive in the technology and administration of sovereign power over the bodies it detains. The panoptical surveillance of the concentrationary system is visually conveyed by the contrast between the prostrate prisoner wearing earphones and an eye-mask and the panoramic gaze of the camera-wielding guard in the watchtower. Fully hooded and clad in orange jumpsuits, covered in sensory deprivation equipment, the detainees dropped by their plane transports into Guantanamo present a sharp visual contrast to the humiliated nudity of those who entered the gates of the Nazi camps in *Night and Fog*. The apparatus worn by Guantanamo's prisoners are visual markers of the disquieting 'solicitude' of touchless torture, the engineering of new techniques such as sensory and sleep deprivation, hyperstimulation or individualized phobia programmes. Sleep deprivation and its inducement of hallucinations and psychosis illustrate Cayrol's chilling prediction that new concentrationary forms will deny detainees 'the ultimate withdrawal of their nights'. While the apparatus of touchless torture may be new, there is a historical continuity in its development. From the psychological warfare developed by the French military by way of Indochina during the Algerian war to Guantanamo Bay's behavioural scientific laboratory, technologies of power have expanded their terrain of inscription from the body and the visible marks of violence that it bears to the entire psychosomatic organism.

A final particularity of recent concentrationary deployments that seems visually conveyed by the image of Guantanamo's kneeling prisoner in relation to the photograph of the victim of the Nazi camp is the denial of the right to die. The figure of the kneeling detainee isolated and immobilized at a short distance from a fence he's been ordered not to touch conveys the growing reach of sovereign power.[60] Suicide constitutes the detainee's right to the ultimate 'retranchement' or withdrawal by death at one's own hand; it is a last sliver of agency in the face of unbearable physical and moral anguish. While I do not suggest that this right was in any way granted by the Nazi concentrationary regime, I am recalling the many testimonies and visual images of detainees committing suicide by touching the camps' electrified wires. *The Road to Guantanamo* came out in the wake of several suicides, leading to greater preventative measures to ensure that these detainees stay alive, if not to confess their complicity with terror – that most slippery of metonymies – at least to show the world that the enemy has been located, made visible and embodied.

'The ruses of Nazism are out of fashion' *Night and Fog* assures us, while reminding us that the concentrationary deployment of imperial power takes on new faces and engineers new ruses as it reaches into uncharted territories, including the psychic intimacy of the subject. We may be poised to see the ruins of Guantanamo Bay, but we would also do well to heed Cayrol and Resnais's ever-actual injunction, and watch keenly from the multiplied observatories of our global information network for the coming of new executioners whose faces may be no different from our own.

Notes

My thanks to the participants of the French Culture Workshop at Stanford University (2007), to the Concentrationary Memories seminar on *Nuit et Brouillard* at the University of Leeds (2008), and to Sona Arutunyan.

1. '*Nous qui feignons de croire que tout cela est d'un seul temps et d'un seul pays, et qui ne pensons pas à regarder autour de nous et qui n'entendons pas qu'on crie sans fin*: Jean Cayrol, *Nuit et Brouillard*, Dossier DVD Arte Vidéo and Argos Films (2003). All further citations of the screenplay refer to this edition; future reference to materials in the dossier will list the author, followed by Dossier DVD. All translations of the dossier are mine.

2. See, for example, Leo Bersani and Ulysse Dutoit, *Arts of Impoverishment: Beckett, Rothko, Resnais* (Cambridge, MA: Harvard University Press, 1993), pp. 181–8; Jay Cantor, 'Death and the Image', *TriQuarterly* 79 (1990), pp. 173–98; Andrew Hebard, 'Disruptive Histories: Toward a Radical Politics of Remembrance in Alain Resnais's *Night and Fog*', *New German Critique* 71 (1997), pp. 87–113.

3. Primo Levi, *Survival in Auschwitz: The Nazi Assault on Humanity*, trans. Peter Woolf (New York: Collier, 1961), p. 45.

4. Jean Cayrol, *Oeuvre Lazaréenne* (Paris: Seuil, 2000), p. 774. For an important discussion of Cayrol's Lazarean aesthetic as an anti-fascist politics of representation that constitutes a neglected alternative to dominant postwar discourses on the Holocaust, see Max Silverman, 'Horror and the Everyday in Post-Holocaust France: *Nuit et Brouillard* and Concentrationary Art', *French Cultural Studies* 17/1 (2006), pp. 5–16.

5. *Nuit et brouillard*, Tapuscrit, Institut Mémoire de l'Edition Contemporaine: Fond Cayrol, A1.1.5. On the status of the Final Solution in earlier versions and its subsequent attenuation in Cayrol's text, see Sylvie Lindeperg's invaluable study of the film and its legacy. Sylvie Lindeperg, *Nuit et brouillard: Un Film dans l'Histoire* (Paris: Odile Jacob, 2006), pp. 76–80, p. 10.

6. As Lawrence Douglas explains, at the Nuremberg trials, artifacts such as the shrunken head or the flayed skin of Buchenwald represented Nazi crimes as atavistic aberrations in civilization, as 'hiccups of barbarism' within occidental modernity. Lawrence Douglas, 'The Shrunken Head of Buchenwald: Icons of Atrocity at Nuremberg', in Barbie Zelizer (ed.), *Visual Culture and the Holocaust* (New Brunswick, NJ: Rutgers University Press, 2000), pp. 275–99. The opposition between Nazism's regressive barbarism and the disciplining practices of modernity has been contested, notably by Zygmunt Bauman in *Modernity and the Holocaust* (Ithaca, NY: Cornell University Press, 2001).

7. On the source of this sequence, see Sylvie Lindeperg, *Nuit et brouillard*, p. 105. In stark contrast with Resnais's use of this footage, the montage documentary *Les Camps de la mort* deliberately frames Buchenwald's display of tattoos. A wide angle frame shows the table's contents followed by a left to right and then right to left tracking shot over the human remains, as the narrator explains, 'The factory churned. The SS had fun. The camp commander's wife liked original tattoos (*aimait les tatouages originaux*). Woe to those who bore one. They were instantly shot and their flayed and tanned skin served to make a new lampshade.' *Les Camps de la mort*, *Actualités françaises*, 10 June 1945. Accessed at http://www.ina.fr/archivespourtous/index.php?vue=notice&id_notice=AFE00000275.

8. Brett Ashley Kaplan, *Unwanted Beauty: Aesthetic Pleasure in Holocaust Representation* (Urbana, IL: University of Illinois Press, 2007).

9. Charlotte Delbo, *Aucun de nous ne reviendra* (Paris: Editions Minuit, 1970), p. 84. On Delbo's injunction to the reader of testimony, see Ross Chambers, *Untimely Interventions: Aids Writing, Testimony and the Rhetoric of Haunting* (Ann Arbor, MI: University of Michigan Press, 2004), pp. 209–31.

10. Cayrol, *Il était une fois Jean Cayrol* (Paris: Seuil, 1982), p. 110.

11. Emma Wilson, 'Material Remains: *Night and Fog*', October 112 (2005), p. 102.

12. The scenes in the cellar evoke the invisible victims of the war and the untold costs of life under Occupation, while offering a striking image for the burial of collaboration in national memory. In a paper entitled 'Traces of History' at the 20th–21st Century French and Francophone Studies Colloquium held in Tallahassee, Florida (April 2004), Rosemarie Scullion presented a compelling reading of the nailmarks' iteration as a figure in Resnais, Duras and Perec in the context of postwar France's erasure of the Jewish specificity of the Holocaust. Also see Leah Hewitt, who notes the repetition of the scratches on the wall as a sign of the Holocaust's haunting absence in *Hiroshima mon amour* and of the reverberation of two collective cataclysms. *Remembering the Occupation in French Film: National Politics in Postwar Europe* (Palgrave Macmillan, 2008), p. 43.

13. Alain Resnais, *Nuit et brouillard* Dossier DVD, p. 27.

14. On transference, historiography and the Holocaust, see Dominick LaCapra, *Writing History, Writing Trauma* (Baltimore, MD: Johns Hopkins University Press, 2000).

15. Richard Raskin, Nuit et brouillard *by Alain Resnais: The Making, Reception and Functions of a Major Documentary Film* (Aarhus University Press, 1987), p. 58.

16. Theodor Adorno, 'Commitment', in *The Essential Frankfurt School Reader*, ed. Andrew Arato and Eike Gebhardt (New York: Continuum, 1992), p. 312.

17. Geoffrey H. Hartman, *The Longest Shadow: In the Aftermath of the Holocaust* (Bloomington, IN: Indiana University Press, 1996), p. 112; Berel Lang, 'The Representation of Limits' in *Probing the Limits of Representation: Nazism and the 'Final Solution'*, ed. Saul Friedlander (Cambridge, MA: Harvard University Press, 1992), pp. 300–17.

18. Walter Benjamin, *The Arcades Project*, ed. Rolf Tiedemann, trans. Howard Eiland and Kevin McLaughlin (Cambridge, MA: Harvard University Press, 1999), p. 330.

19. (Au moment où je vous parle, l'eau froide des marais et des ruines remplit le creux des charniers, une eau froide et opaque comme notre mauvaise mémoire. La guerre s'est assoupie, un oeil toujours ouvert. L'herbe fidèle est revenue sur les Appel-platz autour des blocks. Un village abandonné, encore plein de menaces. Le crématoire est hors d'usage. Les ruses nazies sont démodées. Neuf millions de morts hantent ce paysage. Qui de nous veille de cet étrange observatoire pour nous avertir de la venue des nouveaux bourreaux? Ont-ils vraiment un autre visage que le nôtre?
Quelque part, parmi nous, il reste des kapos chanceux, des chefs récupérés. Des dénonciateurs inconnus.
Il y a nous qui regardons sincèrement ces ruines comme si le vieux monstre concentrationnaire était mort sous les décombres, qui feignons de reprendre espoir devant cette image qui s'éloigne, comme si on guérissait de la peste concentrationnaire, nous qui feignons de croire que tout cela est d'un seul temps et d'un seul pays, et qui ne pensons pas à regarder autour de nous et qui n'entendons pas qu'on crie sans fin.)

20. 'Une drôle d'herbe a poussé et recouvert la terre usée par le piétinement des concentrationnaires'; 'L'herbe fidèle est revenue sur les Appel-Platz autour des blocks.' Cayrol, Dossier DVD.

21. Walter Benjamin, *The Origin of German Tragic Drama* [1963], trans. John Osborne (London: NLB, 1977), pp. 177–8.

22. Benjamin, *Arcades Project*, pp. 368–9. The imagery of Birkenau's ruins is reminiscent of the discarded commodity fetishes of nineteenth-century urban modernity catalogued in the *Arcades Projects*, suggesting extermination to be the most literal incarnation of the capitalist phantasmagoria.

23. Benjamin, *Origin of German Tragic Drama*, p. 166.

24. Gordon Teskey, *Allegory and Violence* (Ithaca, NY: Cornell University Press, 1996), p. 8.

25. Paul de Man, 'The Rhetoric of Temporality', in *Blindness and Insight: Essays in the Rhetoric of Contemporary Criticism* (Minneapolis, MN: University of Minnesota Press, 1971), p. 206.

26. Benjamin, *Origin of German Tragic Drama*, p. 233.

27. 'In Blanqui's view of the world, petrified unrest becomes the status of the cosmos itself. The course of the world appears, accordingly, as one great allegory' (Benjamin, *Arcades Project*, p. 329). For a compelling examination of allegory as a figure for the disruptive force of history in Benjamin's thought, see Beatrice Hanssen, *Walter Benjamin's Other History: Of Stones, Animals, Human Beings, and Angels* (Berkeley: University of California Press, 1998).

28. Teskey, *Allegory and Violence*, p. 24.

29. Georges Perec, *W ou le Souvenir d'Enfance* (Paris: Denoël, 1975), p. 13.

30. I refer to Henry Rousso's definition of memory as 'une organisation de l'oubli' in *Le Syndrome de Vichy, de 1944 à nos jours* (Paris: Seuil, 1987), p. 12. Resnais expressed

this anxiety in the following terms: 'j'avais d'autant plus de raisons d'être anxieux avec le côté "monument aux morts" et "tout le monde d'accord sur ce passé affreux qui ne pouvait pas recommencer." Bon, moi je sentais que *ça* pouvait recommencer, justement.' Dossier DVD, p. 23.

31. Cayrol, Dossier DVD, p. 18.

32. Claude Lanzmann, 'Why Spielberg Has Distorted the Truth', *Guardian Weekly*, 3 April 1994, p. 14.

33. Cayrol, Dossier DVD, p. 9.

34. Cited in Raskin, *Nuit et brouillard*, p. 19.

35. 'Nous avons voulu décrire cette prolifération concentrationnaire ou lazaréenne sur le doux humus quotidien' ('We sought to describe this concentrationary or lazarean proliferation on sweet quotidian terrain'). Cayrol, *Oeuvres Lazaréennes*, p. 764.

36. Sylvie Thénault, 'Interner en République: le cas de la France en guerre d'Algérie', *Amnis* 3 (2003), pp. 213–28. Thénault shows that while torture was seen as a gangrene infecting the republican state's army, various methods of internment were established by laws and ordinances within the Republic's institutions.

37. Charles Krantz, 'Resnais's *Night and Fog*: A Historical and Cultural Analysis', in Sanford Pinsker and Jack Fischel (eds), *Literature, the Arts, and the Holocaust* (Greenwood, FL: Penkevill Publishing, 1987), pp. 112–13. This important essay, one of the first to trace the Algerian context for Resnais's documentary, gives a persuasive critique of *Night and Fog* for its universalization of complicity and subsequent blurring of historical responsibility. I have sympathy for Krantz's critique, which signals history's reification into a zone of ethical undecidability. But my readings seek to focus on the contestatory valences of complicity and its call to historical responsibility both in the immediate reception of the film and its subsequent appropriations by other political struggles.

38. This absence has even led some to accuse Resnais of complicity with the very extermination that he documents. Robert Michael goes so far as to say that the silence over Jewish victims of the genocide is an unintentional enactment of Himmler's order that 'in public ... we will never speak of the ... annihilation of the Jewish people' (cited in *Nuit et Brouillard*, p. 159). Without justifying what remains a troubling lack, it is important to remember some historical factors that account for it, among which are the legacy of French Republican universalism and its resistance to isolating Jewish identity, the Resistancialist legacy that foregrounded the figure of the political deportee, a tendency to cast the Second World War as one against Fascism more generally, and the temporally belated emergence of the Holocaust itself as a category, one to which the Eichmann trial of 1961 was crucial. On this last point, see Annette Wieviorka, *L'Ere du témoin* (Paris: Plon, 1998).

39. Michael Rothberg, *Multidirectional Memory: Remembering the Holocaust in the Age of Decolonization* (Palo Alto, CA: Stanford University Press, 2009).

40. Resnais, Dossier DVD, p. 24. On the censorship imposed by the SCA as a response to Resnais's reputation as an anti-colonial film maker, see Christian Delage and Chris Darke, '*Nuit et Brouillard*: A Turning Point in the History and Memory of the Holocaust', in Toby Haggith, Joanna Newman, David Cesarani (eds), *The Holocaust and the Moving Image: Representations in Film and Television since 1933* (London: Wallflower, 2005), p. 130 and Sylvie Lindeperg, *Night and Fog*, p. 60.

41. Benjamin Stora, *La Gangrène et l'oubli: la mémoire de la guerre d'Algérie* (Paris: La Découverte, 1998), p. 112. For an analysis of Vichy as a screen memory for

Night and Fog
Film Stills

All images are taken from *Night and Fog*
(Alain Resnais, Argos Films, 1955).
They are identified with plate numbers.

Full details for each plate are provided in the
List of Illustrations on page vii.

1

2 3

6 7

10 11

4

5

8

9

12

13

16

17

20

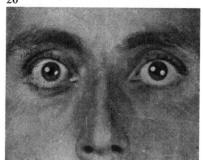

21

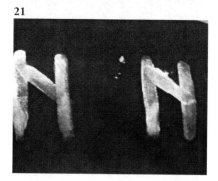

23

24

27

28

29

30

32

33

36

37

40

41

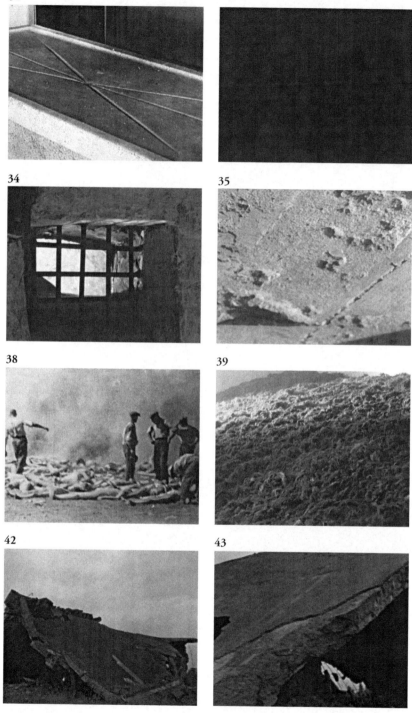

the Algerian war, see Anne Donadey, ' "Une Certaine idée de la France": The Algeria Syndrome and Struggles over "French" Identity', in Steven Ungar and Tom Conley (eds), *Identity Papers: Contested Nationhood in Twentieth-Century France* (Minneapolis, MN: University of Minnesota Press, 1996), pp. 215–33.

42. Resnais, Dossier DVD, p. 23. In 1948, three years after the Sétif massacre, Jean Cayrol participated in a Franco-Algerian cultural encounter at Sidi-Madani, Algeria (which also included Albert Camus and Francis Ponge) and met young Algerian nationalist writers such as Mohammed Dib and Kateb Yacine. The painful irony of a massacre resulting from the Algerian bid for independence just as France was celebrating its own liberation from Germany would not have been lost on Cayrol, and his partipation in this encounter strengthens the pertinence of the Algerian frame for *Night and Fog.*

43. See Michel Rocard, *Rapport sur les camps de regroupement et autres textes sur la guerre d'Algérie* (Paris: Mille et une nuits, 2003) pp. 13, 17, 126; Tassadit Yacine, *Le Monde diplomatique* (Actualités, Février 2004), p. 29. The CICRC (Commission internationale contre le régime concentrationnaire) had published a report on the Algerian camps as early as 15 May 1957 in *Le Monde*. David Rousset, who had been deported to Buchenwald and famously denounced the Soviet gulag was then Vice-President of the Commission. On this point, see Thénault, 'Interner en République', p. 3. By 1959, Algeria had 936 Centres, and according to Pierre Bourdieu's study, 2,157,000 Algerians were interned by the following year (1960), that is to say about a quarter of the population (Rocard, *Rapport*, p. 17.) In his study of France's concentration camps during the Algerian war, sociologist Michel Cornaton argues that in spite of their differences 'we must have the courage to recognize that the margin between the Nazi concentration camps and some of the *centre provisoires* seemed infinitesmal.' *Les Camps de regroupement de la guerre d'Algérie* (Paris: Harmattan, 1998), p. 81 (my translation).

44. The letter declares that this concentrationary order of terror is by 1955 a systemic reality in Algeria:

'1. Il existe des camps de concentration en Algérie pour des civils non-delinquants.
2. La torture policière, un moment suspendu ou freiné, a repris en Algerie.
3. Des civils et des militaires se sont rendus coupables d'assassinats collectifs des populations civiles en Algérie. Nous pouvons *également* affirmer qu'il s'agit non de phénomènes isolés mais d'actes systémiques.'

Comité d'Action contre la poursuite de la guerre en Afrique, Lettre à Jacques Soustelle, IMEC, p. 3.For a history of the *Comité d'Action*, see James D. LeSueur, *Uncivil War: Intellectuals and Identity Politics During the Decolonization of Algeria* (Lincoln, NE: University of Nebraska Press, 2005), pp. 32–61.

45. Cayrol, *Oeuvre Lazaréenne*, p. 805.

46. I would argue that the native Algerians' erasure in *The Plague* is a deliberate, ironic denunciation of censorship on Algeria in the contemporary French press. It is significant that the 'unheard and endless cry' on which the documentary concludes reappears as the leitmotif of Camus' novel *La Chute* (1956).

47. Albert Camus, *Essais*, eds. Roger Quillot and Louis Faucon (Paris: Gallimard, 1965), p. 512. Camus is also denouncing the torture of leaders of the *Mouvement démocratique de Révolution Malgache* after an insurrection on 29 March 1947.

48. Camus, *Essais*, p. 969.

49. Camus, *Essais*, p. 974.

182 | *Debarati Sanyal*

50. Martin Evans, *The Memory of Resistance: French Opposition to the Algerian War, 1954–1962* (Oxford: Berg, 1997), p. 58.
51. Cited in Lindeperg, *Nuit et brouillard*, p. 226.
52. Lindeperg, *Nuit et brouillard*, p. 227.
53. In *Emitaï*, the French commander declares to the troops that have been forcibly conscripted in the war that they are all volunteers ('Vous *êtes* tous des engagés volontaires').On the forced conscription of *tirailleurs* into the colonial army and the representation of this figure in Sembene's work, see David Murphy, 'Fighting for the Homeland? The Second World War in the Films of Ousmane Sembene', *L'Esprit Créateur* 47/1 (2007) pp. 56–67.
54. For an important discussion of photography and post-memory, see Marianne Hirsch, 'Surviving Images: Holocaust Photographs and the Work of Postmemory', *The Yale Journal of Criticism* 14/1 (2001), pp. 5–37. Hirsch examines the iconic status of particular images in cultural post-memory that serve both as screens and points of entry into historical trauma. Hirsch's remarks on the ambiguities of the photographic gaze and the viewer's subsequent implication are of particular pertinence to this sequence of *Camp de Thiaroye* and its shifting perspective, from Pays's gaze to the watchtower's guard to the binocular-wielding SS officer presumably observing the shooting or suicide of the camp detainees.
55. Walter Benjamin, *Illuminations*, ed. Hannah Arendt, trans. Harry Zohn (London: Pimlico, 1991), p. 247.
56. On 'bare life', see Giorgio Agamben, *Homo Sacer. Sovereign Power and Bare Life*, trans. Daniel Heller-Roazen (Stanford, CA: Stanford University Press, 1998).
57. Samba Gadjigo, Ralph H. Falukingham, Thomas Cassirer and Reinhard Sander (eds), *Ousmane Sembene: Dialogues with Critics and Writers* (Amherst, MA: University of Massachusetts Press, 1993), pp. 83–4.
58. Achille Mbembe, *On the Postcolony* (Berkeley, CA: University of California Press, 2001), p. 16.
59. Cayrol, *Oeuvre Lazaréenne*, pp. 801, 776.
60. In *The Road to Guanatnamo*, the prisoner is dragged off to his position near the barbed wire fence as guards shout 'don't let him look,' 'get off the fence,' 'stay off the fence.'

CHAPTER 7

Night and Fog and Posttraumatic Cinema

JOSHUA HIRSCH

When I speak about *Night and Fog*, I speak as the child of a Jewish Holocaust survivor. I state this not to claim a special privilege, but rather to acknowledge my position and thus the limitations of my work. In 1944, at the age of 16, my father was deported with his family from Hungary to Auschwitz. When he was liberated at Buchenwald in 1945, only one cousin remained from his extended family. No photograph remains to show that my grandparents, my uncle, and all the rest had ever existed. Their images existed only in my father's decaying memory. In fact, it was a struggle for him just to call up an image of his mother's face, and even then, it was often the image of a photograph of her that he carried through the selection line at Auschwitz, and that a guard finally knocked from his hand.

Night and Fog, which I was shown at my synagogue as a child, functioned as a substitute for these absent images. The image from that film of a bulldozer pushing a pile of emaciated bodies into a mass grave became the most vivid icon with which I visualized the Holocaust. I pictured the corpses and thought, 'Jews, what we are.' Preparing a paper on *Night and Fog* for a graduate seminar, I watched the film again on videotape. When the bulldozer scene appeared, I watched it over and over, trying to repress my feelings of horror in order to record the details. In my memory of seeing the film as a child, the bulldozer was a weapon driven by a Nazi. Viewing the film again, I realized the scene was shot after the liberation, and the bulldozer was probably driven by an Allied soldier. In any case, the driver never appears in frame.

My book – *Afterimage: Film, Trauma, and the Holocaust* – began not with a theory or argument about what might be called – but uncomfortably – 'Holocaust films', but with a series of encounters with individual films that seemed to articulate in one way or another a paradox that felt familiar to me: the paradox of trying to visualize and narrate a trauma that could not be captured in an image; of trying to remember an absence; of trying to represent the unrepresentable. I suppose the process of trying to understand these films is, among other things, my attempt to work through a set of childhood experiences that might be profitably condensed as that first viewing of *Night and Fog*. As I struggled to conceptualize these films as a discourse, I explored various concepts of memory and modernism before arriving – with the help of works by Cathy Caruth and others – at the concept of trauma. Coincidentally or not, I came to see *Night and Fog* as a film that profoundly changed not only me, but also – and 20 years earlier – the cultural representation of history itself.

In the book, I argued that *Night and Fog* originated a new discourse of historical trauma, and I then traced that discourse as it was disseminated and transformed in a series of paradigmatic Holocaust films – the documentary *Shoah* (Lanzmann, 1985), the fiction film *The Pawnbroker* (Sidney Lumet, 1964), and a series of early, autobiographical films by the Hungarian Jewish Holocaust survivor István Szabó. The book did not completely segregate the representation of the Holocaust from other types of representations, however. Representation is, in practice, a fluid, continually cross-pollinating phenomenon. Thus, discussions of Holocaust films in the book led to and from discussions of other posttraumatic films that influenced and were influenced by them, including *Chronicle of a Summer* (Jean Rouch and Edgar Morin, 1960) and several other films directed by Alain Resnais (*Guernica* (1950); *Hiroshima, mon amour* (1959); *Muriel* ... (1963)). In fact, in Szabó's films Holocaust memories are but one strand in a fabric of traumatic Hungarian and Jewish memories. This attention to cultural cross-pollination led to a major shift in emphasis in the final chapter of the book – a case study of a film not about the Holocaust, but rather the internment of Japanese Americans in the United States during the Second World War: Rea Tajiri's *History and Memory: For Akiko and Takashige* (1992).

In this chapter I will: review my concept of posttraumatic cinema; review, by way of contrast, an earlier Holocaust documentary, *Nuremberg* (as opposed to *Mein Kampf*, which I discussed in the book); review *Night and Fog* as the most important origin of posttraumatic cinema; and 'flash forward' to a much later example of posttraumatic cinema representing a different historical trauma – not *History and Memory* this time, but *Sankofa*, a film about African-American slavery – examining similarities to and differences from *Night and Fog*.

Posttraumatic discourse in film

In a society that has suffered a massive blow, there arises (unless it is repressed, but perhaps even then) a discourse of trauma. The significance of this discourse transcends the literal referencing of any particular experience of trauma or vicarious trauma – of surviving genocide, witnessing it, or seeing images of it – and lies, rather, in the staking out, in the languages of various media, of a space common to all these experiences. One may be traumatized by an encounter with the Holocaust, one may be unable to assimilate a memory or an image of mass death, but the discourse of trauma – as one encounters it in conversation, in reading, in film – gives one a language with which to begin to represent the failure of representation that one has experienced.

When photographic evidence of genocide first appears, it may need relatively little narrative support in order to cause vicarious trauma. It would be enough for the image to be presented by a reputable source (newspaper, magazine, newsreel), to be identified in historical context ('this is a liberated concentration camp'), and to be authenticated ('this is an actual photo taken by Allied photographers'). The cinematic relaying of trauma occurred on a massive scale in 1945 when military film crews accompanied Allied troops liberating the camps. This initial phase does not last long, however. Public interest wanes; collective numbing sets in; the images leave the broad public sphere and become a speciality interest.

In the second phase, however, when the images themselves no longer traumatize, the text – or film in this case – must, in a sense, work harder. It must overcome defensive numbing. Documentary images must be submitted to a narrative discourse whose purpose is, if not to literally traumatize the spectator, at least to invoke a posttraumatic historical consciousness – a kind of textual compromise between the senselessness of the initial traumatic encounter and the sense-making apparatus of a fully integrated historical narrative, similar to Dominick LaCapra's notion of 'muted trauma'.[1] The resulting cinema, exemplified by *Night and Fog*, formally repeats the shock of the original encounters with atrocity – both the original eyewitnessing of the atrocities themselves, and the subsequent cinematic encounter with the images of atrocity.

As trauma is less a particular experiential content than a *form* of experience, so the discourse of trauma in this second phase is defined less by a particular image content than by the attempt to discover a form for presenting that content that mimics some aspects of Posttraumatic Stress Disorder (PTSD) itself – the attempt to formally reproduce for the spectator an experience of suddenly seeing the unthinkable. And insofar as what is historically thinkable is partly constituted by the conventions of the historical film genre, the instigation of a cinematic discourse of trauma becomes a question of upsetting the spectator's expectations not only of history in general, but also of the historical film in particular.

Trauma and narration: realism and modernism

The conventional form of the historical film at the time of the Second World War can be described most broadly as realist. The realist historical film, in both its documentary and fictional variants, consisted of an array of formal and rhetorical techniques by which a film could claim to make the past masterable by making it visible. The fictional variant, a sub-genre of the classical realist film discussed extensively by film theorists during the 1970s, can be traced back to films like *The Birth of a Nation* (D.W. Griffith, 1915). The documentary variant coalesced in a more piecemeal fashion, and arguably, it was the Second World War itself that provided the impetus for its coalescence in films like the US government's *Why We Fight* series (1943–45).

In discussing the narration of trauma in film, I will borrow the method of analysing literary narration that Gerard Genette elaborated in his book *Narrative Discourse.*[2] Adapting this model to the historical documentary, I propose that *tense* regulates the relations among the temporality of the film text, the temporality of the events recounted by the film, and the temporality of the filmic evidence (for example, concentration camp footage); *mood* regulates the point of view of the film on the images and events represented; and *voice* regulates the film's self-consciousness of its own act of narration.

In the realist historical film, tense works to provide the spectator with a sense of mastery over time, a sense of power to travel back in time to see the past, or to make the past visible to the present on command, usually in the form of a linear chronology. Realism assumes the omniscient point of view of one who is outside history epistemologically, emotionally and morally – one who is free to enter into history through the image and assume a variety of embedded points of view, to vicariously see and feel history, on the condition of being free to return again unscathed to that exterior position from which one can know and judge the past without being personally implicated in it. And realism presents the past unselfconsciously, drawing attention to the events and interpretations presented, and away from the film's own act of presentation.

Realist narration – mastery over time and point of view, and unselfconscious voice – renders a highly 'secondarized' representation of the past, one that is masterable in the way that the French psychiatrist Pierre Janet argued in 1889 that normal, 'narrative memories', as opposed to posttraumatic (then called hysterical) ones, are masterable.[3] In the 'tense' of narrative memory, one can call up an image of the past at will, make it present to consciousness, and insert it into the proper chronology. Narrative memory is characterized by flexibility of point of view. One's point of view on the memory changes depending on the conditions pertaining to a specific instance of remembering. One can become like an outsider, narrating one's own memory as if in the third person. And narrative memory is relatively unselfconscious. The recall process is largely automatic, and does not call attention to itself.[4]

In posttraumatic memory, as opposed to narrative memory, linear chronology collapses. Time becomes fragmented and uncontrollable. The past becomes either too remote or too immediate. It remains inaccessibly in the past (amnesia), or presents itself uninvited, seizing consciousness (hypermnesia).[5] Posttraumatic memory maintains the fixed and inflexible point of view of the witness to past events. Whereas normal memories change over time as the rememberer and the conditions of remembering change, traumatic memories often remain as literal recordings of past traumatic perceptions. Insofar as posttraumatic narration is a kind of failure of narration – a collapse of mastery over time and point of view – it too tends towards a self-conscious voice, toward a consideration of its own failure to master the past.

During the late nineteenth and early twentieth centuries, a form of literary narration did in fact arise that adopted disorienting time shifts, extreme subjectivity in point of view, and narrative self-consciousness. We call it modernism, and Walter Benjamin argued that it originated as a response to the traumas of urbanization and industrialization that characterized modern capitalism.[6] Subsequently, modernism arose in the cinema following, not surprisingly, the First World War. One can find instances of posttraumatic narration in this early modernist cinema, for example in *Menilmontant* (Dimitri Kirsenoff, 1925) and *La Maternelle* (Jean Benoît-Lévy and Marie Epstein, 1932). However, it wasn't until *Night and Fog* that a coherent discourse of historical trauma appeared in cinema. In fact, *Night and Fog* constitutes a key link between the genre of Holocaust films, the development of film modernism, and the appearance of posttraumatic cinema.

Of course, not all films about the Holocaust and other historical catastrophes attempt to invoke a posttraumatic historical consciousness. There are a variety of reasons to produce a Holocaust film – pedagogical, ideological, economic, etc. – many of which are inconsistent with the project of invoking trauma. Some films present images with traumatic potential only to formally counteract that potential by retaining a conventional form of historical narrative. Eric Santner has called this textual strategy 'narrative fetishism', which he describes as 'consciously or unconsciously designed to expunge the traces of the trauma or loss that called that narrative into being in the first place'.[7] The discourse of trauma, on the other hand, works towards a form of narration that can speak from the collective space of traumatic historical experience. It is, as Cathy Caruth has written, 'a voice that cries out from the wound'.[8]

Nuremberg and the conventional Holocaust documentary

In a 1986 interview, Alain Resnais said of *Night and Fog*,

> Then there was another problem, which was the form of the film: how to
> treat such a subject? Myself, I was completely overwhelmed (I always am,
> in any case). And I said to myself: there have already been many films on
> the concentration camps. Everyone has said this is very good but it doesn't
> seem to have had a very striking effect on people. Then since I am a
> formalist, perhaps I must ignore my qualms and attempt in the film,
> despite its subject, a formal experiment.[9]

The attempt by Resnais and his collaborators to experiment with the form of
historical documentary cinema in order to produce a more striking (*'frappant'*)
effect – what I am calling a posttraumatic effect – must be contextualized in relation
to the conventions of historical documentary at the time, those 'very good' but, by
1955, no longer striking concentration camp films to which Resnais refers.

A significant example was *Nuremberg*, produced in 1946 for the United
States Office of Military Government in Germany by famed documentarian
Pare Lorentz, and directed by Stuart Schulberg. It was produced for
distribution in Germany in order to illustrate to the German people the legal
and moral crimes of the Nazi leadership. After being screened in Germany in
1948, and then, according to some sources, on US television in 1949, it was
suppressed by the US government for decades, partly out of deference to
Germany as a US ally against the Soviet Union.[10] Whereas I have previously
stated that *Night and Fog* was the first documentary I had been able to identify
that contained flashbacks, I have since discovered that *Nuremberg* actually
employed this technique prior to *Night and Fog*. This does not lessen the
importance of *Night and Fog* as an origin of posttraumatic cinema, however.
Indeed, the striking difference between the uses of the flashback in the two
films makes the originality of *Night and Fog* all the more apparent.

Nuremberg is structured around alternations between footage of the
International Military Tribunal at Nuremberg (1945–46) and historical
footage that functions as evidence of the guilt of the Nazi defendants. A brief
culminating segment narrates the extermination of Jews. The segment begins
with footage of the French prosecutor speaking, while a dubbed voice
performs his argument about the Nazis' plans for exterminating the Jews of
Europe. We then see Rudolf Höss testifying, while hearing a different dubbed
voice performing Höss' testimony describing the extermination process at
Auschwitz. As Höss describes the selection line, we see footage of a column of
concentration camp prisoners walking along barbed wire. This pattern
continues with Höss describing the selection of children for extermination,

prisoners being sent to the 'showers', gassing, and the extraction of gold fillings from the bodies. Each of these descriptions is illustrated by historical footage. The segment concludes with the narrator (presumably not the French prosecutor this time) quoting from admissions of Nazi criminality by defendants Robert Ley and Hans Frank, while we see footage of emaciated corpses being buried in a mass grave. Finally, we see the French prosecutor again, while the narrator says, 'The prosecution rests'.

While *Nuremberg* departs from the conventional linear chronological structure of the historical documentary of the time, its flashbacks evoke no less a sense of mastery over the past. Didactically framed by the forensic discourse of the film, they present the audience with clearly motivated and labelled visual evidence of the crimes elucidated in the commentary. That this chronology will lead to a guilty verdict is a foregone conclusion in three senses: the ideological sense in which the victor's prosecution of the defeated always leads to a guilty verdict, the rhetorical sense in which the audience is encouraged to trust in the rightness of the prosecution, and the historical sense in which the outcome of the trial was past and known at the time the film was distributed. Of course, this forensic discourse, backed by and speaking for the reassuring authority of the victorious Allied governments, maintains a thoroughly impersonal point of view, since to admit a subjective point of view would be to undermine the entire forensic project of the film.

Once each flashback begins, it retains the seamless illusion of a historical narrative unfolding in the present tense that characterizes the conventional historical documentary – not the literal or indexical present tense that characterizes all photography, but a figurative present tense specific to the classical realist film. In the way it combines commentary with a variety of pieces of historical footage, *Nuremberg* smoothes over and covers up a tremendous gap in the photographic record of the Holocaust: the absolute lack of a photographic image of the gassing of millions of people. This gap – the missing image of what Himmler would not allow anyone to film, and what therefore disappeared forever with the victims – this gap, rather than being preserved as a gap, or amnesia, in the image track of the film, is covered over by a post-liberation shot of emaciated prisoners lying on the floor, one of them slowly lying down. By placing this shot over Höss' description of the gassing of prisoners, the film creates the impression that we are actually witnessing the gassing itself. This technique is repeated in virtually every shot in the segment, with post-liberation footage cleverly arranged and combined with commentary in order to create the illusion of a seamless visual narrative. Thus, in *Nuremberg*, there are no rhetorical limits placed on the spectator's ability to witness the Holocaust as a self-explanatory scenario, no temporal gaps or blockages of perspective. The spectator is positioned as having visually accompanied the victims to their extermination, miraculously emerging from the gas chamber to continue watching even as the victims' gold fillings are removed.

The voice of the film is relatively unself conscious, within the limits of documentary (which is inherently more self-conscious than the classical fiction film). *Nuremberg* directs the spectator's attention toward the criminal evidence and the guilt of the Nazis, and away from the epistemological, moral or psychological problematics of this act.

Nuremberg employed the narrative techniques of the conventional documentary to extend and strengthen the spectator's temporal and perspectival mastery over the memory of an historical catastrophe. The traumas of concentration camps and genocide were thus contained and assimilated into the master narrative of the Allied victory.

Night and Fog

The attempt by Resnais and his collaborators to experiment with historical documentary form in order to produce a more striking effect – what I am calling a posttraumatic effect – is most significant in terms of the film's representation of time. As such, *Night and Fog* draws from a variety of modernist traditions in literature and cinema that have in common the rejection of classical linear temporal structures in favour of hyper-subjective and fragmented inscriptions of time.[11]

This temporal subjectivity becomes apparent from the first moment of the film: a static, colour shot of a field, which then proceeds to crane slowly and smoothly down, revealing a barbed wire fence in the foreground, and finally comes to rest gazing out from inside the fence at Auschwitz. This gesture is repeated in the second and third shots. In the second, the camera tracks backward to reveal the fence (Plate 3). In the third, the track is lateral (Plates 5 and 6). The accompanying commentary is as follows: 'Even a peaceful landscape; even a meadow in harvest, with crows circling overhead and grass fires; even a road where cars and peasants and couples pass; even a resort village with a steeple and county fair can lead to a concentration camp.'[12]

In these three opening shots, the relation between the present and the past is characterized by the image track as one of entrapment. In whichever direction one travels – downward, backward, laterally – one is pulled from an apparently harmless present, as if by an irresistible gravitational force, into the black hole of some terrible memory, embodied in the mute but threatening *mise-en-scène* of the past – the wire – that one encounters wherever one turns. This gravitational relationship between the field and the wire can be seen as a metaphor for posttraumatic memory, in which the present is indeed a field of anxiety and hyper-vigilance, in which one fears that any encountered object may trigger a terrifying memory of events from which time provides no escape (Plate 8).

The flashback that follows this first colour segment – the transition from a colour shot tracking alongside the Auschwitz fence in 1955 to a black-and-white shot taken from *Triumph of the Will* showing German soldiers marching in formation at the Nuremberg Nazi Party Congress in 1934 – is presented formally as a shock (Plate 10). Almost every conceivable formal element of the two joined shots undergoes a violent reversal at the edit point. Colour turns to black and white; clean footage to aged; an eye-level camera position to one on the ground; a moving shot to a stationary one, and simultaneously a stationary *mise-en-scène* (fence) to a moving one (marching soldiers); from slow, smooth movement (tracking) to fast, jagged movement (soldiers); from the incantory voice-over of the first segment to the staccato '1933'; from a drum roll that is soft, slow, sustained, low-pitched and hollow-timbred to one that is loud, fast, brief, high-pitched, and using a snare. Thus, the film's movement from the present to the past is not characterized by the ease of mastery, but by the shock of trauma; one is jolted into the past, or, alternately, the past intrudes violently on the present.

The one element of the two joined shots that does not undergo a violent reversal is, of course, the graphic match between the fence and the soldiers, in which the soldiers uncannily repeat the prior shot's pattern of vertical lines receding at an angle into the distance. This complex match – in which the left-to-right camera movement past the fence is transposed into the right-to-left movement of the soldiers past a static camera – does not contradict the discourse of trauma I have described, however. In fact, it can be interpreted as a metaphor for the triggering of posttraumatic flashbacks by associative memory, evoking the notion of the witness for whom any number of images or sounds in the present might trigger an associated traumatic memory. While Resnais was not the first to use the graphic match as a representation of associative memory, he continued to develop it in *Hiroshima, mon amour* (1959), with a graphic match between the living hand of a Japanese lover in the present and the dying hand of a German lover in the past. (*The Pawnbroker*, released in 1965, turned this technique into a trope that repeats throughout the film.)

Whereas the flashbacks in *Nuremberg* are framed as evidence within a clearly identified forensic discourse, the flashbacks in *Night and Fog* have no such clearly identified framing. As opposed to the reassuringly obvious context of the courtroom, the colour segments that frame Resnais's flashbacks seem to hover in a kind of timeless no man's land of anxiety. It is in this lack of a clearly identifiable framing for the flashbacks that a space arises for a discourse of posttraumatic memory to enter in.

In its use of crosscutting to establish a set of relations between the present and the past, *Night and Fog* could be said to apply Eisenstein's montage theory to the representation of posttraumatic historical consciousness. Eisenstein, one of the first great film modernists, rejected the view (later theorized by Bazin and

Kracauer) of the shot as a window onto reality, in favour of a different kind of realism. For Eisenstein, reality inhered not in the ontology of the photographic image but in the structural relations between images.[13] Similarly, in *Night and Fog* Resnais rejects both the notion of the archival image as a window onto history and the notion of the image of the present as a window onto memory. He constructs a cinematic theory of historical consciousness from the montage relations between the image of the present and the image of the past.

Like this montage historical consciousness, posttraumatic memory is characterized by relations of intrusiveness and remoteness, of vision and blindness, of remembering and forgetting. PTSD is characterized by a symptomological dialectic of hypermnesia and amnesia; memories are not mastered, but rather are experienced as involuntary, hallucinatory repetitions, or, alternatively, are blocked. Accordingly, the black-and-white segments of *Night and Fog* are like hypermnesic or hallucinatory episodes; we see too much. The image of the past repeats with a shocking literality, intruding on the present. The image track takes the lead, the commentary at times registering its own inability to make sense of the images, as when a series of shots of brutalized corpses discovered in the liberated camps is accompanied by the words, 'There is nothing left to say'. The images continue in silence; the spectator must watch helplessly.

With the return of colour footage, the image of the past is blocked by the image of the present; we do not see enough. With the failure of visual memory, the commentary must take the lead, attempting to describe what no image exists to show, or simply pointing out the failure.

This sense of the remoteness of the past also becomes apparent in comparing the temporal framing of historical footage in *Night and Fog* and *Nuremberg*. In *Nuremberg*, as I have described it, the actual lack of footage of gassing is disavowed when post-liberation shots of a gas chamber and of emaciated prisoners lying on the floor are cleverly stitched together into a putative illustration of the commentary's description of gassing before the liberation. A post-liberation shot of a gas chamber appears in *Night and Fog* as well. But the present tense of this shot – a colour shot moving slowly and smoothly through the chamber – is literal. It accompanies the words, 'The only sign – but you have to know – are [sic] the fingernail scrapings on the ceiling. Even the concrete was scratched up.'[14] In this case, no attempt is made to substitute the gas chamber shot for the missing image of the gassing itself. *Night and Fog* thus suggests that the spectator understand the image of gassing precisely as missing, something that can only be confronted through the image of its ruins.

Whereas point of view in the black-and-white segments of *Night and Fog* resembles that of *Nuremberg* in its externality, the colour segments introduce a different, more implicated point of view – one that is both more internal and less confident. The extended duration and ceaseless motion of the colour

Auschwitz footage, indicative of modernism, eschews an objective historiographic or forensic gaze into the camps in favour of one that is more characteristic of the troubled gaze of the traumatized witness. Indeed, the point of view of the colour segments may be thought of as conflating Cayrol's own point of view as a survivor returning to the scene of his victimization (Auschwitz substituting for Mauthausen), and Resnais's point of view as interlocutor – the outsider who attends to the survivor's memories not as prosecutor or historian but as a witness to trauma, whose sympathy with the other places him in danger of vicarious traumatization, and whose decision to relay the witnessing experience keeps the trauma moving.

The sense of entrapment suggested by the opening three shots continues after the camera assumes a position firmly imprisoned in the world of the camp, where no suturing edit provides an escape from the camera's melancholy, walking stare at the remnants of atrocity. The deeper affective knowledge of the camps implied in the witness's position, however, does not result in a more confident epistemological stance. The commentary repeatedly asserts the failure of the film to capture the past:

> The reality of these camps, despised by those who built them, and unfathomable to those who endured them, what hope do we have of truly capturing this reality. The wooden barracks where people slept three to a bed, the burrows where they hid and ate in furtive fear, and where sleep itself presented a threat – no description, no image can reveal their true dimension: endless, uninterrupted fear.[15]

There are two types of self-consciousness in *Night and Fog*: formal and historical. By formal self-consciousness, I mean the film's efforts to draw attention to its own form. There is a degree of self-consciousness implicit in the film's rigorous experiments with documentary form, such as the crosscutting between monochrome and colour footage, or the highly controlled, extended tracking shots. These devices draw attention to themselves by virtue of their excessiveness, their rigour and their deviation from documentary convention. The commentary, on the other hand, becomes explicitly self-referential at times during the colour segments. 'The blood has dried, the tongues have fallen silent. The only visitor to the blocks now is the camera … No footstep is heard but our own.'[16] By historical self-consciousness, on the other hand, I mean the film's interrogation of itself as a representation of history. The problem of historical representation is even implicit in its title, which, unlike *Nuremberg*, fails to make a clear historical reference, naming instead the very crisis of historical representation engendered by the Holocaust – the night and fog that intervenes between us and a history of annihilation.

At times, the film's historical self-consciousness takes the form of a questioning of the truth-value of artefacts. Whereas, in *Nuremberg*, onscreen artefacts are presented unselfconsciously as evidence of historical truths, *Night and Fog* problematizes the artefacts it surveys in the colour segments: 'The reality of these camps ... what hope do we have of truly capturing this reality. The wooden barracks where people slept three to a bed ... No description, no image can reveal their true dimension.'[17]

Through consideration of its own form, its own limitations, its own failures, *Night and Fog* draws attention not just to the past but to the traumatic effects of the past on us – its deformation of historical memory – and the necessity of working through those effects. *Night and Fog* does employ some of the realist narrative conventions of the diachronic historical documentary to present direct images of atrocity. Anecdotal evidence suggests that the film transmitted a significant shock to a percentage of the children who saw it in school. At the same time, the film attempts to do something different: to respond at the level of narrative form to the problem of collective defence against the traumatic potential of the images. *Night and Fog*, in other words, employs realism to traumatize the spectator, but then goes further: it stages a modernist break from realism in order to model a posttraumatic historical consciousness.

Flashforward: *Sankofa* (Haile Gerima, 1993)

The link between *Night and Fog* on the one hand and, on the other hand, later Western modernist films representing the Holocaust in a posttraumatic vein – like *Shoah*, *The Pawnbroker*, and the early, autobiographical films of István Szabó – is relatively obvious. The link between *Night and Fog* and *Sankofa* (1993, dir. Haile Gerima), an African-US-European co-production dealing with trans-Atlantic slavery, may be less obvious. Exploring this link, and others like it, is one purpose of the concept of cross-cultural posttraumatic cinemas. How have other filmmakers, working in other cultures, used film to represent the memories of other historical traumas? What have these filmmakers inherited from *Night and Fog* and the posttraumatic cinema of the Holocaust, and what have they given in return? What relationships between different posttraumatic film cultures might we record or encourage?

Sankofa presents the story of a group of slaves on a plantation in the American South, focusing on the transformation of a house slave, Shola, from a state of subservience to a state of resistance, and culminating in her participation in a slave uprising. This story, however, is embedded within a frame story taking place in the present, and it is on this frame structure that I will be focusing here.

The film begins with an incantation containing these excerpts:

Spirit of the dead, rise up

Lingering spirit of the dead, rise up and possess your vessel

You raped, slave bred, castrated, burned, tarred and feathered, roasted, chopped, lobotomized, bound and gagged

You waiting Africans, step out and tell your story.

The first scene takes place in the present at a former slave castle in Ghana, where Africans were imprisoned before being shipped across the Atlantic. Mona, an African-American model, is shooting a sexy photo spread at the castle, when she is confronted by a drummer named Sankofa who serves as spiritual guardian of the castle. He holds out a staff topped by a wooden bird, a symbol of the Ashanti concept of Sankofa – meaning, literally, 'go back and take' – and he tells her, 'Go back to your past.'[18] Later she follows a tour group into the castle. Lingering behind the group, she finds herself alone in a dungeon-like room. The lights go out, and when they come back on, she is surrounded by chained slaves. In a panic, she tries to run out of the castle, but is stopped by soldiers in archaic uniforms. They drag her back to the slaves inside, strip her, and brand her.

The next scene takes place in Louisiana. We see the face of 'Mona', while we hear her voice identify herself as the house slave Shola. No further references to Mona or the present day occur until the end of the film, when, after Shola joins a slave uprising, she is transported back to the room in the castle. In the final scene, she stumbles naked from the castle door, apparently traumatized, and is joyfully welcomed by an older African woman. Wrapped in African dress and now serene, she joins a group of Black people, apparently representing the African diaspora, sitting on the ground, surrounding the drumming guardian.

On the surface, *Night and Fog* and *Sankofa* might seem to have little in common. One is in the tradition of European modernism, restrained and anxious; the other is in the tradition of post-colonial cinema, didactic and enraged. And yet, the relationship between the present and the past in the two films has some striking commonalities. Both start in the present, at a site of historical trauma, now – as both films point out – problematically transformed into a tourist attraction (fig. 7.1). (Is it a coincidence that both films, too, begin with a drum beat?) In both, the camera lingers over the ruined bricks that once imprisoned the victims, while a voice points out that their blood once flowed here, thus pointing out a disturbing conflict between what we see in the present and what we know about the past. Finally, both sites trigger the appearance of traumatic historical memories, as if the memories were, as in Bergson, Proust and Cayrol, somehow contained within the physical presence of the ruins.

Figure 7.1   Still from *Sankofa* (Haile Gerima, 1993). (Courtesy Sankofa Films)

Figure 7.2   Still from *Sankofa* (Haile Gerima, 1993). (Courtesy Sankofa Films)

If you must be here, be aware. Blood has been spilled here.

Figure 7.3   Still from *Sankofa* (Haile Gerima, 1993). (Courtesy Sankofa Films)

Like *Hiroshima, mon amour* and *The Pawnbroker*, *Sankofa* provides an onscreen character to experience the return of traumatic memory, whereas *Night and Fog* lacks any such onscreen figure, leaving only the audience to bear witness to the return of memory. Where we might posit in *Night and Fog* the role of the invisible interlocutor who relays Cayrol's memories to the audience, *Sankofa* gives us the figure of Sankofa himself as the one whose function is to keep the trauma moving (Fig. 7.2).

In both films, the return of memory is shocking, disorienting, involuntary and re-traumatizing. The uncanny cut from the Auschwitz fence to the marching German soldiers becomes Mona's – and insofar as the audience identifies with Mona, our own – uncanny slippage from a present peopled with vacationing tourists to a past peopled with chained prisoners (Fig. 7.3). As the audience is pulled back into the past, we too become symbolically imprisoned in a world in which the victims are stripped, branded and dehumanized.

Even one of the most striking contrasts between the films suggests a point of contact. Whereas the relationship between the present and the past in *Night and Fog* is defined most explicitly by a discourse of existentialism (the discourse of trauma operating, for me, as an implicit or symptomatic discourse), this relationship in *Sankofa* is defined most explicitly by a spiritual discourse. Mona's encounter with the past is experienced as a haunting by the ghosts of dead slaves. As scholars like Avery Gordon have pointed out, however, there has been a rich history of contact between the mythic discourse of haunting and the psychoanalytic discourses of trauma, mourning and the unconscious.[19] Even *Night and Fog* contains the phrase, 'Nine million dead haunt this landscape.'

Films like *Sankofa* exist in a cross-cultural, dialogic relationship with the posttraumatic cinema of the Holocaust. This relationship demonstrates something that Cathy Caruth proposes in her book, *Unclaimed Experience*: 'the way in which one's own trauma is tied up with the trauma of another, the way in which trauma may lead, therefore, to the encounter with another, through the very possibility and surprise of listening to another's wound.'[20]

Notes

1. Dominick LaCapra, 'Lanzmann's *Shoah*: "here there is no why"', *Critical Inquiry* 23/2 (1997), p. 267.

2. Gerard Genette, *Narrative Discourse: An Essay in Method*, trans. Jane E. Lewin (Ithaca. NY: Cornell University Press, 1980), pp. 26–32.

3. I am adapting the term *secondarized* loosely from Freud's concept of 'secondary revision', defined by Laplanche and Pontalis as the '[R]earrangement of a dream so as to present it in the form of a relatively consistent and comprehensible scenario'. See Jean Laplanche and J. B. Pontalis, *The Language of Psycho-analysis*, trans. Donald Nicholson-Smith (New York: W. W. Norton, 1973), p. 412.

4. Bessel van der Kolk and Onno van der Hart, 'The Intrusive Past: the Flexibility of Memory and the Engraving of Trauma', in Cathy Caruth (ed.), *Trauma: Explorations in Memory* (Baltimore, MD: Johns Hopkins University Press, 1995), pp. 159–64.

5. Hypermnesia: 'unusually exact or vivid memory'; *The American Heritage Dictionary of the English Language* s.v. 'hypermnesia'.

6. Walter Benjamin, 'On some Motifs in Baudelaire', *Illuminations*, ed. Hannah Arendt, trans. Harry Zohn (New York: Harcourt, Brace, & World, 1968), pp. 157–202.

7. Eric Santner, 'History beyond the Pleasure Principle: some Thoughts on the Representation of Trauma', in Saul Friedlander (ed.), *Probing the Limits of Representation: Nazism and the 'Final Solution'* (Cambridge, MA: Harvard University Press, 1992), p. 144.

8. Cathy Caruth, *Unclaimed Experience: Trauma, Narrative, and History* (Baltimore, MD: Johns Hopkins University Press, 1996), p. 2. LaCapra also articulates this view, without, however, fully endorsing it: '[One] may insist that any attentive secondary witness to, or acceptable account of, traumatic experiences must in some significant way be marked by trauma or allow trauma to register in its own procedures' (LaCapra, 'Lanzmann's *Shoah*', p. 244).

9. Richard Raskin, 'Interview with Alain Resnais', (Paris 18 February 1986), *Nuit et Brouillard by Alain Resnais: On the Making, Reception and Functions of a Major Documentary Film, Including a New Interview with Alain Resnais and the Original Shooting Script*, Foreword by Sascha Vierny (Aarhus: Aarhus University Press, 1987), p. 52. (My translation).

10. Philip Kennicott, 'Art of Justice: The Filmmakers at Nuremberg', *Washington Post*, 29 November 2005, http://www.washingtonpost.com/wp-dyn/2005/11/28/AR2005112802026. html (accessed 8 February 2009).

11. Literary influences on Resnais's experiments with tense were writings by Marcel Proust, and the French New Novels of Marguerite Duras, Alain Robbe-Grillet and Jean Cayrol. Among fiction films, he was influenced by Delluc's *Le Silence* (1921), Carné's *Le Jour se lève* (1939), Welles's *Citizen Kane* (1941) and Cocteau's *Orpheus* (1950).

12. All English translations are from the revised subtitles that appear in the Criterion Collection release of 2003. The original French commentary is as follows. 'Même un paysage tranquille. Même une prairie avec des vols de corbeaux, des moissons et des feux d'herbe. Même une route où passent des voitures, des paysans, des couples. Même un village pour vacances avec une foire et un clocher peuvent conduire tout simplement à un camp de concentration.'

13. Sergei Eisenstein, 'A Dialectic Approach to Film Form', *Film Form*, ed. and trans. Jay Leyda (New York: Harcourt Brace Jovanovich, 1949), pp. 45–63; Andre Bazin, 'The Ontology of the Photographic Image', *What Is Cinema?*, ed. and trans. Hugh Gray (Berkeley, CA: University of California Press, 1967), pp. 9–16; and Siegfried Kracauer, *Theory of Film* (New York: Oxford University Press, 1960).

14. 'Le seul signe, mais il faut le savoir, c'est ce plafond labouré par les ongles. Même le béton se déchirait.'

15. 'Cette réalité des camps, méprisée par ceux qui la fabriquent, insaisissable pour ceux qui la subissent, c'est bien en vain qu'à notre tour nous essayons d'en découvrir les restes. Ces blocks en bois, ces châlits, où l'on dormait à trois, ces terriers ou l'on se cachait, où l'on mangeait à la sauvette, où le sommeil même était une menace, aucune description, aucune image ne peuvent leur rendre leur vraie dimension, celle d'une peur ininterrompue.'

16. 'Le sang a caillé, les bouches se sont tues, les blocks ne sont plus visités que par une caméra ... Plus aucun pas, que le notre.'

17. 'Cette réalité des camps ... C'est bien en vain qu'à notre tour nous essayons d'en découvrir les restes. Ces blocks en bois, ces châlits, où l'on dormait à trois ... Aucune description, aucune image ne peuvent leur rendre leur vraie dimension.'

18. Kwadwo Asafo-Agyei Okrah, 'Sankofa: Cultural Heritage Conservation and Sustainable African Development', *The African Symposium: An Online Journal of the African Educational Research Network* 8/2 (2008), p. 26.

19. Avery Gordon, *Ghostly Matters: Haunting and the Sociological Imagination* (Minneapolis, MN: University of Minnesota Press, 1996).

20. Caruth, *Unclaimed Experience*, p. 8.

CHAPTER 8

Fearful Imagination:
Night and Fog and Concentrationary Memory

MAX SILVERMAN

Fearful imagination

In an essay entitled 'The Concentration Camps' published in 1948, Hannah Arendt criticizes the way in which the stock responses to those returning from the camps simply assimilate their stories to psychological and other normalizing narratives of understanding:

> There is a great temptation to explain away the intrinsically incredible by means of liberal rationalizations. In each one of us, there lurks such a liberal, wheedling us with the voice of common sense. We attempt to understand elements in present or recollected experience that simply surpass our powers of understanding. We attempt to classify as criminal a thing which, as we all feel, no such category was ever intended to cover. What meaning has the concept of murder when we are confronted with the mass production of corpses?[1]

Arendt likens this process to the resurrection of Lazarus. To all intents and purposes a man has returned to the human world with 'personality or character unchanged'. However, 'the reduction of a man to a bundle of reactions separates him as radically as mental disease from everything within him that is personality or character.'[2] Lazarus is the living dead, not a man as we know him. No psychological rationalization is sufficient to describe him and no reportage (like that of the Allied films of the opening of the camps) can fully represent the horror of where he has been,[3] just as the word 'murder' fails miserably to comprehend 'the mass production of corpses'. Arendt's response to the way in which the absolute novelty of 'totalitarian rule' (of which 'the concentration camps are the most consequential institution'[4]) poses a fundamental challenge to our habitual modes of understanding is to propose the approach of 'fearful anticipation' founded on a 'fearful imagination'.[5] 'Fearful imagination' must be as far removed from 'normal' imagination as the concentration camp is from our known world: the 'mad unreality' of the camps 'can be described only in images drawn from a life after death, that is, a life removed from earthly purposes'.[6] In the rest of her essay, Arendt employs her 'fearful imagination' to define how a life can be 'removed from earthly purposes' to produce, ultimately, 'living corpses'. The process comprises, first, the murder of the juridical person in man, then the moral person, and, finally, his individuality, uniqueness and spontaneity 'to establish the superfluity of man'.[7] What remains might resemble a man outwardly but, inwardly, he has been stripped of everything that we know to be constitutive of the human. How, then, to capture the uncanny idea that what seems familiar on the surface in fact resembles nothing that we already know?[8]

Jean Cayrol's 'concentrationary art', and the film *Night and Fog* for which Cayrol wrote the spoken text, both constitute a remarkable response to Arendt's challenge to portray the 'mad unreality' of the camps 'in images drawn from a life after death'. Like Arendt, Cayrol, in his critical writings, also uses the figure of Lazarus as the symbol of the new art:[9] an art which will show human life shocked out of its familiar contours through revealing the 'invisible thread' ('fil invisible') that ties it to the presence of death, humanity haunted by its inhuman double, the known always subject to its deformation into the grotesque.[10] Lazarean art will, therefore, be founded on a 'doubling' (and troubling) effect ('this doubling of the Lazarean being')[11] to cast us into a state of the 'in-between', 'into a sensation of floating, a state of mental and rootless wandering'. Cayrol states '(t)he Lazarean hero is never there where he finds himself [...] because he has lived in a world which is situated nowhere and whose frontiers are not marked out since these are the frontiers of death. He permanently mistrusts the place at which he has just arrived.'[12] Cayrol's Lazarean art is one in which time and place are haunted by an elsewhere, and life is permanently haunted by death.[13]

In this chapter I will propose that Cayrol's discussion of Lazarean 'doubling' is central to what Griselda Pollock and I have termed 'concentrationary memory'. I will suggest that the concentrationary art of *Night and Fog*, which transforms 'the image of man' into the living corpse, institutes a notion of memory as the haunting (and hence disturbance) of the present, a site of the in-between, of doublings and overlappings, of an uncanny superimposition of the visible and the invisible. Like the Lazarean hero, detached from his entrapment within the humanistic version of Man and split across space and time, memory in the wake of the camps is not psychological memory (that is, centred within the 'known' psychology of the individual) but de-individualized, de-temporalized and de-spatialized. Concentrationary memory is never there where it finds itself, both here and elsewhere, the present disfigured, tainted permanently by the presence of death and oblivion. *Night and Fog* transforms the Lazarean 'in-between' into a politicized aesthetic which will radically open up the becalmed aftermath of the war to the persistence of horror.

Fearful vision

The opening shots of *Night and Fog* announce the aesthetic and political vision of 'concentrationary art' (Plates 2–5). As the camera pans down to show that the first image of sky and land is being filmed through (from behind) the barbed wire of the camp, and as the next tracking shot from left to right similarly disturbs the clear vision of the countryside beyond by filming through the same fencing close up, we are presented with a world that can no longer be apprehended in a pure and uninterrupted fashion (could it ever or was this not always just western utopian hubris?). Now, in the wake of the camps, the world can only be seen through the prism of camp barbed wire. The filmmakers (like us?), who have come from the world outside to look into the camp of horror, present a look from the inside of the camp looking out. A multiple splitting and doubling takes place as the barbed wire acts as an ambivalent conduit for a new vision: the vision from the present looking in at the past is doubled by the vision from the past looking back at the present, outside and inside the camp are no longer mutually exclusive, and filming itself is composed of a vision split by the barbed wire. The panning and tracking shots on a vertical and horizontal axis, which will subsequently guide us through the camp, are thus, from the very beginning, incorporated into a new scopic regime of the 'in-between' of the post-concentrationary universe. This is a fearful vision of doublings, hauntings and contaminations in which the filmic representations of people, objects, places and times are forever shadowed by their ghosts from elsewhere. The text which accompanies the tracking shot across the ruins of Birkenau in shot 5 (Plate 9) – 'the only visitor to the blocks is a camera', grass has covered the former 'tread of the inmates' so that now there are 'no steps other than our own'[14] – makes explicit the link between material traces in the present and superimposed layers (invisible but present) of different times, spaces and looks to construct a sort of palimpsest or Benjaminian 'double ground'.[15] Emma Wilson observes how the tension between 'material remains' and elsewhere is a constant feature of Resnais's films:

Resnais seeks to know or understand a relation between the unimaginable (the invisible, the unsayable) and the very matter that remains – the material remains, the relics and traces of past experience. His films work at that difficult junction between events that cannot be known, seen, or felt (in their occurrence or in retrospect) and the matter, the images and objects, which seem conversely to offer material proof and evidence.[16]

The disturbance of time, space and vision effected in this way in the opening sequences means that when the cut occurs to the first black-and-white 'flashback' to the past (although, as I argue below, 'flashback' is not the right word to describe the temporal confusion here), it is not only steps which are made to carry an ambivalent charge (the steps of the Nazi jackboots in shot 6 echoing the steps of the film-crew and those of the inmates mentioned in the previous shot). The horizontal movement of the Nazi camera to record the process of the machine 'starting up' also seems to mimic the tracking shots of the opening of the film to establish a troubling complicity between the look in the present of filming the disused camp and the sweeping embrace of Leni Riefenstahl's camera filming the crowd cheering Hitler in those images taken from her 1935 film *Triumph of the Will*.[17] Furthermore, the remnants of the 'machine' (the ruins of Auschwitz-Birkenau that we see in the present) and its initial stirrings ('the machine gets under way') are also drawn together to unsettle beginnings and endings and challenge the way in which the teleological reading of History becomes intelligible.[18] Does the present (the opening) trigger the past or vice-versa? Does the filming of bearing witness to the concentrationary universe trigger the filming of its construction and celebration, or vice-versa? Is our look in the present so different from the look that recorded the celebration of the dictator in the past?[19] To accommodate this blurring of 'different' temporal sequences, Gilles Deleuze quite rightly eschews all talk of 'flashback' in the cinema of Resnais (grounded as it is in a chronological notion of time). What we have instead are overlapping and superimposed 'layers' or 'sheets' of time, not a teleology which allows us to talk of 'past' and 'present' as separate categories or the present as the major organizing principle of time:

> *Night and Fog* could even be thought of as the sum of all the ways of escaping from the flashback, and the false piety of the recollection-image [...] In Resnais' case, however, this inadequacy of the flashback does not stop his work as a whole being based on the coexistence of sheets of past, the present no longer even intervening as centre of evocation.[20]

This temporal dislocation matches visual and spatial dislocation: centred visual and spatial fields (the distinctions between objective and subjective points of view and between here and there, inside and outside, respectively) are disrupted by a similar 'coexistence of sheets' which denies the specificity and singularity of each. The haunting quality of the Lazarean derives from the repetitions and similarities that cut across demarcated temporal, spatial and scopic regimes.

Hence, the following shots which develop the theme of the 'machine' of the concentrationary universe (the drawing up of plans for the construction of the camps, the styles employed in their design, the round-up and transportation in cattle-trucks of those who will populate this universe and eventually perish there) continue to trace multiple connections between the world of the camp and 'everyday life'. The film draws a patchwork of interconnecting and overlapping lines, like the rail-tracks which draw diverse European locations and people to their concentrationary destination. The cut back to the tracks leading up to Birkenau in the present (Plate 18) once again juxtaposes and overlays past and present (especially through the draining of the colour filming of the present to resemble the black and white of the past) and, similarly, overlays our present vision of the camp with that of the past through the shared connections between camera and rail-track.[21]

When we return once again to Birkenau in the present (Shot 91), the inter-penetration of different regimes of time, space and vision already created means that the 'known' surfaces over which the camera glides are now rendered strange and unknowable (because haunted by an elsewhere), or rather 'uncanny' in the Freudian sense of being both familiar and strange at the same time:

> this reality of the camps [...] unattainable for those who endure it and beyond the grasp of we who, in turn, seek to convey its meaning. These wooden barracks, these bedsteads on which three would lie, these holes in which they hid and where they ate illicitly and in fear, where sleep itself was a threat – no description, no image can render their true dimension: that of interminable fear.[22]

A fearful vision is, precisely, one of permanent anxiety and 'interminable fear'. Stripped of its habitual apparatus for perceiving and making sense, a fearful vision knows that the familiar appearance of objects is like a husk or stage-set hiding unimaginable horror (like Lazarus whose external appearance tells us nothing of the living corpse that he has become):

> Of this brick dormitory, this threatened sleep, we can but show you the shell, the surface. Here is the décor: these buildings which could be stables, barns or workshops, impoverished land turned into wasteland, an autumn

sky now indifferent. These are all we have left to imagine this night of piercing cries, of checking for lice, of chattering teeth.[23]

The 'doubling' regime of the Lazarean transforms all 'known' objects into deceptive surfaces and sites of fear: familiar activities like drinking soup and going to the lavatory are life or death events; words hide the truth rather than reveal it, as in the Nazi slogans '"CLEANLINESS IS HEALTH" – "WORK IS FREEDOM" – "TO EVERYONE HIS DUE" – "ONE LOUSE MEANS DEATH"' (Plate 22);[24] for the deportee 'the real world, that of peaceful countryside and of former times' is an illusory image;[25] and hospital is a torture chamber ('at a glance, you could have imagined that you were in front of a real clinic'). Fearful vision is not fooled by this deception. It asks 'there is a décor, but behind?';[26] it knows that the SS's 'life-like town with hospital, red-light district, residential area and even – yes – a prison' is a sham;[27] it is sceptical of the ways in which what we take to be the real are, in fact, screens and images ('A crematorium could be the opportunity for a postcard. Later – today –, tourists can take pictures of themselves there');[28] it knows that death lurks behind the most banal of objects ('Nothing distinguished the gas chamber from an ordinary block');[29] and it is aware of Man's capacity, now that 'everything is possible',[30] to turn fellow humans into everyday objects (fabric, fertilizer, soap …). The everyday has become a façade hiding the most unimaginable of crimes.[31]

Resnais's technique of disturbing demarcated regimes of sense produces an anxious apprehension of the real throughout.[32] By destabilizing the familiar, Resnais refuses to allow meaning to congeal into a fixed image (like the postcard) and opens up the surface to the superimposed layering of history. Hence, when the atrocity images are shown (especially shots 272–292), the lifeless corpses should not simply be seen as objects or 'figuren', as was the intention of Nazi dehumanization, or be allowed to disappear without trace, as was the intention of the policy of *Nacht und Nebel*, but are themselves returned to the land of the living through their palimpsestic relationship with other times and spaces (Plate 40).[33] Resnais's fearful imagination disturbs the discrete nature of life and death (and indeed all binary opposites): it breathes life into the dead and shows life haunted by death; it overlays the familiar with the concentrationary but also reminds us that the corpse was a living being; it reawakens us to the ever-present threat of disappearing without trace into the night and fog, and reverses the very policy which attempted to put this into effect by making the traces speak.

Resnais's fearful vision is a new way of seeing in the light of the camps. 'An interminable fear' requires keeping an eye open to survey the permanently open eye of the dormant (but certainly not extinct) concentrationary universe ('war dozes, one eye always open').[34] The concentrationary eye (or 'I') is split, doubled, in part formed (contaminated) by the concentrationary itself (looking out from inside the camp), in part aware of the machine that dehumanized the world and able to read the surface as a trace or sign (looking in from outside the camp): 'They closed the doors. They watched. The only sign – but you must know how to recognize it –, is the ceiling scored by nails. Even the concrete was torn' (Plate 35).[35] The key to the self-consciousness of this vision is in the words 'but you must know how to recognize it' ('il faut le savoir'). Like Walter Benjamin's 'lisibilité de l'image', discussed by Georges Didi-Huberman in his chapter in this volume, this part of the vision at least allows the possibility of reading the flat surface of the image in terms of multi-layered history.

The final shots of the film (Plates 42–43) leave us in that in-between state conjured up at the beginning: between the known world and the world of horror ('an abandoned village still bristling with danger', 'nine million dead haunt this landscape', the remains of the crematorium set against the white sky above); between the perpetrator, the victim and the bystander ('who amongst us watches over this strange observatory to warn us of the coming of the new executioners? Do they really have a different face from our own? Somewhere amongst us there remain duplicitous kapos, re-assimilated leaders, unknown informers'); between the spatio-temporal context of Auschwitz-Birkenau during the war and other times and places ('we who fool us ourselves into believing that all that happened in one country and who do not think to look around us, and who fail to hear the endless cry'); between the unconscious immersion in the concentrationary and the conscious awareness of its eternal presence. 'Our bad memory', which assumes that 'the old concentrationary monster has died beneath the ruins [...] as if one can be cured of the concentrationary plague' must be jolted into recognition of humanity's new state of concentrationary contamination, and replaced by concentrationary memory.[36]

Concentrationary memory

Alain Resnais famously stated that he preferred to talk of his work in terms of imagination rather than memory.[37] As is evident from his early films, both of these terms are jolted out of their familiar definitions to create something far more fluid, for memory and imagination are not mutually exclusive categories. *Night and Fog* reworks memory so that it is no longer what we thought it was. Detached from its framing within an individualist, humanist and teleological context, memory is incorporated into a Lazarean regime of doubling, splitting and overlapping to propose a radical transformation of our ways of seeing in the light of the concentrationary experience. In this sense, Resnais's treatment of memory and imagination seems to correspond closely to Arendt's plea for a 'fearful imagination' by which perception is forever shocked out of its familiar apprehension of the real, the present is haunted by the past, the self is haunted by its own otherness and the visible is haunted by the elsewhere. We can call this 'concentrationary memory' – rather than 'traumatic memory' – because this haunting is the indelible (invisible but ever-present) trace of the concentrationary universe, and brings with it the political charge of permanent surveillance of its ruses.

I have already invoked the idea of the palimpsest as a metaphor for the type of process underpinning concentrationary memory: the mechanism by which the intelligibility of one layer of 'text' is confused (or disturbed) due to the appearance (invisible but present) of another layer (or other layers) so that the whole becomes a superimposition of interconnected traces.[38] The analysis in the previous section attempted to show how memory as palimpsest works in the film. Here I would like to suggest that palimpsestic, concentrationary memory is not only an aesthetic device but also becomes the model for a politics of representation. The merging and re(e)merging of traces[39] gives us a way of understanding the concentrationary not as belonging to any one time or place, nor as a universal phenomenon, but as occupying a new space and time in-between the two, composed of overlapping or superimposed sheets of time (or, to use the Lazarean metaphor, a time always haunted by its own elsewhere). Employing Bergson's concept of 'souvenir pur', a form of a-temporal memory as opposed to the 'image-souvenir' which maintains the distinction between past and present, Deleuze compares Resnais's treatment of memory with dream-work in a way that also evokes a palimpsestic concept of time:

> In a dream, there is no longer one recollection-image which embodies one particular point of a given sheet; there are a number of images which are embodied within each other, each referring to a different point of the sheet. Perhaps, when we read a book, watch a show, or look at a painting, and especially when we are ourselves the author, an analogous process can be triggered: we constitute a sheet of transformation which invents a kind of transverse continuity or communication between several sheets, and weaves a network of non-localizable relations between them. In this way we extract non-chronological time.[40]

In this new space, repetitions and similarities across time disturb the singularity of the event by splitting it between its presence in the here and now and its dispersal across time and space. Andrew Hebard is right to suggest in his reprinted article in this volume that the uncanny in *Night and Fog* 'forces a reconsideration of the possibility that an event can be contained within a "certain" time or place. To question this possibility is also to question the temporality of the event, a temporality no longer contained by a historical telos.'[41] Sylvie Lindeperg suggests something similar when, referring to the last line of the spoken text, she states '(t)his endless cry, substituting for the incantatory "never again" of monuments to the dead, captures the floating definition of victims and executioners.'[42] Time and space out of joint – both of one place and multiple places, of one time and multiple times – means that palimpsestic concentrationary memory draws the present (no matter how banal) into the realm of history and politics by revealing its complicitous concentrationary shadow.

The indeterminate nature of concentrationary memory not only merges present and past, here and elsewhere, the particular and the universal, but also unsettles the boundaries between the individual and the collective and between public and private. As we float between the pronouns 'on', 'ils', 'nous' and 'je' in the film (caught up in what Lindeperg has called 'a slippage of meaning'),[43] and as vision fragments across different regimes of point of view, each fixed demarcation of identity is decentred through its confusion with the others, and individual psychology and collective memory are revealed as categories (like life and death, the human and the inhuman, etc.), ill-equipped to meet the challenge of the non-binary, post-concentrationary world. Deleuze once again highlights the way in which this memory confuses a conventional psychological understanding: 'Throughout Resnais' work we plunge into a memory which overflows the condition of psychology, memory for two, memory for several, memory-world, memory-ages of the world.'[44] This floating concept of memory is central to the political and ethical charge starkly articulated at the end of the film through the question 'who is responsible?' ('qui est responsable?'). A palimpsestic, Lazarean aesthetic has disturbed the dichotomy between individual and collective guilt and blurred the boundaries between victim, perpetrator and witness to such an extent that this now becomes an unanswerable question in conventional 'psychological' terms.

Resnais's palimpsestic memory is thus a radical post-concentrationary aesthetic which incorporates a new (non-humanist and resolutely anti-psychological) post-concentrationary politics and ethics. Cayrol's spoken text and Resnais's montage invoke multiple connections, continuities and ruptures that convert the physical traces in the present into the new field of a non-teleological history. This (fundamentally modernist) practice transforms Auschwitz-Birkenau in the present of filming into a site of superimposed inscriptions of other places and times to suggest that the present is always contaminated by other scenes and that questions of responsibility for unimaginable crimes against humanity haunt seemingly innocent everyday life. Seen in this light, concentrationary memory provides a model of cultural memory which resembles Walter Benjamin's notion of the 'constellation' in which the moment is forever in dialectical tension with History (in Benjamin's

memorable formulation 'dialectics at a standstill', which captures the
paradoxical relationship between movement and stasis explored in the film).[45]
Concentrationary memory does not simply bring back the memory of one
specific event (in fact, it counters the very idea of the singularity of the event);
instead it puts each event into contact with a complex history. Concentrationary
memory is, therefore, not Holocaust memory, which specifies the event as the
genocide of the Jews. By its very definition (or rather its refusal of any
conventional definition), concentrationary memory escapes any such ethnocultural or religious particularization. The criticisms that have been made of
Night and Fog for its silence on the genocide of the Jews (which are, I believe,
inaccurate in any case)[46] are not only based on an anachronistic reading of the
film (that is, reading the film through the contemporary lens of the Holocaust
paradigm, as we suggest in the introduction to this volume), but also ignore
the principles of doubling and haunting of Lazarean art underpinning the
film's aesthetic and political purpose. Concentrationary memory denies
specificity by showing us how the particular is always haunted by its absent
other ('the Lazarean hero is never there where he finds himself'). In this way
(and as the final sequence of the film so powerfully demonstrates), we are all
contaminated by the concentrationary gaze and the concentrationary plague
but can be, simultaneously, shocked into a recognition of (and hence challenge
to) the hidden complicity and continuities that post-war modernization has
repressed. Mixing and splitting, rather than historical verisimilitude, are both
aesthetic and political strategies: they interrupt the self-presence of the present
by making visible its hidden elsewhere, they create the connections between
times and places which disturb the innocence of 'a peaceful countryside' ('un
paysage tranquille'), they make the unimaginable part of our normalized
reality, and they give us the means to read a buried history.[47]

Concentrationary memory presents a model of cultural memory as a
mongrel process: it politicizes the aesthetic strategies of modernism to capture
the strangeness, ambivalences and historical interconnections of a post-
concentrationary reality. It belongs to that post-war moment of refusal of the
objectification of human relations and the normalization of reality that
inspired David Rousset and Hannah Arendt and Aimé Césaire and Frantz
Fanon, all of whom naturally saw the overlaps between different sites of
racialized violence and dehumanization, especially between western capitalism
and extermination and between fascism and imperialism, within Europe and
outside its frontiers.[48] My reading of the aesthetic and political practice of
concentrationary memory is, therefore, with a view to reinscribing its radical
message into the field of cultural memory at a time when this has often
become dominated by monolinear histories of ethnocultural difference.
Reading *Night and Fog* as an allegory of the Algerian war (see, for example,
Debarati Sanyal's essay in this volume), and thereby recognizing the overlaps

and interconnections between the concentrationary universe and colonialism, is not simply one way of understanding the film; it is a required reading because of the formal structures of complicity that the film establishes. Concentrationary memory is itself a blueprint for what Michael Rothberg has more recently termed 'multidirectional memory' in his fascinating study of memory in a transnational age.[49] Seeing *Night and Fog* as the first (or the first major) Holocaust film, therefore, blurs its innovatory treatment of time, space, memory and imagination. Relocating it within Cayrol's concept of the Lazarean and concentrationary art, and Arendt's plea for a fearful imagination in the wake of the camps, allows us, on the contrary, to recognize its multidirectional character and its radical political aesthetic.

In words that echo the last spoken words of the film, Cayrol suggests that, in the realm of the Lazarean, 'the mouth will always be open, not for the word but for the cry.'[50] *Night and Fog* overlays the here and now of the known world with the endless cry of suffering to produce a disturbing vision of the human condition in the wake of the camps. This is truly a 'fearful imagination' composed, in Arendt's words once again, of 'images drawn from a life after death'.

Notes

1. Hannah Arendt, 'The Concentration Camps', *Partisan Review* XV (1948), p. 745.
2. Arendt, 'The Concentration Camps', p. 746.
3. Arendt, 'The Concentration Camps', p. 750.
4. Arendt, 'The Concentration Camps', p. 746.
5. Arendt, 'The Concentration Camps', pp. 744 and 746.
6. Arendt, 'The Concentration Camps', p. 749.
7. Arendt, 'The Concentration Camps', p. 762.
8. One of the major areas of interest of Arendt's subsequent monumental work, *The Origins of Totalitarianism*, is precisely the tension in the text (largely unresolved) between, on the one hand, the continuities between anti-Semitism, imperialism and totalitarianism (as apparently announced in the title itself) and, on the other, the rupture between totalitarianism and preceding forms of dehumanization. For an excellent discussion of this tension, see Michael Rothberg, *Multidirectional Memory: Remembering the Holocaust in the Age of Decolonization* (Stanford, CA: Stanford University Press, 2009), Chapter 2.
9. See Jean Cayrol, *Lazare parmi nous* (Paris: Seuil, 1950).
10. Jean Cayrol, 'De la vie à la mort', in *Nuit et brouillard* (Paris: Fayard, 1997), pp. 45–114, p. 67. (First published as 'D'un romanesque concentrationnaire', *Esprit*, no. 9 (September 1949) and reprinted as 'Pour un romanesque lazaréen', in *Lazare parmi nous*, pp. 67–106.) All translations from the French, here and elsewhere, are my own, except where otherwise stated.
11. 'ce dédoublement de l'être lazaréen', Cayrol, 'De la vie à la mort', p. 67.
12. 'dans une sensation de flottement, d'état de vagabondage mental et sans racines', *Lazare parmi nous*, p. 27; 'Le héros lazaréen n'est jamais là où il se trouve [...] car il

a vécu dans un monde qui ne se trouvait nulle part et dont les frontières ne sont pas marquées puisque ce sont celles de la mort. Il se méfie toujours de l'endroit où il vient d'arriver,' Cayrol, 'De la vie à la mort', pp. 106–7.

13. The use of the figure of Lazarus in a post-concentrationary definition of art recasts humanism by the spectral haunting of the sovereign and autonomous individual. In his book on the return of the dead, Colin Davis observes that '(t)he entry on superstition in the *Encyclopédie* (1751–1772) lists ' "spectres, dreams and visions" as the tools of fear and imagination', Colin Davis, *Haunted Subjects: Deconstruction, Psychoanalysis and the Return of the Dead* (Basingstoke: Palgrave Macmillan, 2007), p. 6.

14. 'les blocks ne sont plus visités que par une caméra'; 'le piétinement des concentrationnaires'; '(p)lus aucun pas que le nôtre', Jean Cayrol, Nuit et brouillard *(commentaire)*, in *Nuit et brouillard*, pp. 17–43, p. 18. Shot numbers refer to the reassembled shooting script reproduced in Richard Raskin, Nuit et brouillard *by Alain Resnais: On the Making, Reception and Functions of a Major Documentary Film* (Aarhus: Aarhus University Press, 1987).

15. Walter Benjamin, *The Arcades Project* (Cambridge, MA: Belknap Press of Harvard University Press, 1999), p. 416.

16. Emma Wilson, 'Material Remains: *Night and Fog*', *October* 112 (Spring 2005), p. 93. For a discussion of the opening images in terms of the Cayrolian 'in-between', see Sylvie Lindeperg, Nuit et brouillard: *un film dans l'histoire* (Paris, Odile Jacob, 2006), pp. 87–90.

17. For overlaps between Resnais's filming and Nazi footage, see André-Pierre Colombat, *The Holocaust in French Film* (Metuchen, NJ: Scarecrow Press, 1993), pp. 130–1. Susan Sontag cites Ernst Jünger's observation in 1930 that 'the camera and the gun, "shooting" a subject and shooting a human being [...] are congruent activities', Susan Sontag, *Regarding the Pain of Others* (London: Penguin, 2003), p. 60. Resnais's montage reveals the inevitable contamination of 'shooting' a film in the present and objectifying and dehumanizing the other in the past.

18. 'la machine se met en marche,' *Nuit et brouillard (commentaire)*, p. 18. It is interesting to compare the disturbance of beginnings and endings here with the opening of Charlotte Delbo's *Aucun de nous ne reviendra (Auschwitz et après 1)* (Paris: Editions Minuit, 1970). For an excellent analysis of the problematization of arrivals and departures in Delbo's *Auschwitz et après* trilogy, see Michael Rothberg, *Traumatic Realism: The Demands of Holocaust Representation* (Minneapolis, MN: University of Minnesota Press, 2000), pp. 141–5.

19. See Leo Bersani and Ulysse Dutoit, *Arts of Impoverishment: Beckett, Rothko, Resnais* (Cambridge, MA: Harvard University Press, 1993).

20. '*Nuit et brouillard* peut même être considéré comme la somme de toutes les manières d'échapper au flash-back, et à la fausse piété de l'image-souvenir [...] Dans le cas de Resnais, cette insuffisance du flash-back n'empêche pourtant pas que toute son oeuvre soit fondée sur la coexistence des nappes de passé, le présent n'intervenant même plus comme centre d'évocation.' Gilles Deleuze, *Cinéma 2: L'Image-Temps* (Paris: Minuit, 1985), p. 160; *Cinema 2: The Time-Image*, trans. Hugh Tomlinson and Robert Galeta (London: Athlone Press, 1989), p. 122.

21. For a detailed account of how Resnais subverts the simplistic dichotomy between colour (present) and black-and-white (past), see Lindeperg, Nuit et brouillard: *un film dans l'histoire*, p. 8 and the chapters by Hebard and Lindeperg in this volume.

22. 'Cette réalité des camps, [...] insaisissable pour ceux qui la subissent, c'est bien en vain qu'à notre tour nous essayons d'en découvrir les restes. Ces blocks en bois, ces chalits où l'on dormait à trois, ces terriers où l'on se cachait, où l'on mangeait à la sauvette, où le sommeil même était une menace, aucune description, aucune image ne peuvent leur rendre leur vraie dimension: celle d'une peur ininterrompue,' *Nuit et brouillard (commentaire)*, p. 23.

23. 'De ce dortoir de briques, de ces sommeils menacés, nous ne pouvons que vous montrer l'écorce, la couleur. Voilà le décor: ces bâtiments qui pourraient être écuries, granges, ateliers, un terrain pauvre devenu terrain vague, un ciel d'automne devenu indifférent: voilà tout ce qui nous reste pour imaginer cette nuit coupée d'appels, de contrôle de poux, nuit qui claque des dents,' *Nuit et brouillard (commentaire)*, p. 24.

24. 'LA PROPRETÉ C'EST LA SANTÉ'; 'LE TRAVAIL C'EST LA LIBERTÉ'; 'CHACUN SON DÛ'; 'UN POU C'EST LA MORT', *Nuit et brouillard (commentaire)*, p. 28.

25. 'le monde véritable, celui des paysages calmes, celui du temps d'avant', *Nuit et brouillard (commentaire)*, p. 29.

26. '[p]our un peu, on se serait cru devant une vraie clinique'; 'il y a un décor, mais derrière?', *Nuit et brouillard (commentaire)*, p. 33.

27. 'cité vraisemblable avec hôpital, quartier réservé, quartier résidentiel, et même – oui – une prison', *Nuit et brouillard (commentaire)*, p. 36.

28. 'Un crématoire, cela pouvait prendre à l'occasion un petit air de carte postale. Plus tard – aujourd'hui –, des touristes s'y font photographier,' *Nuit et brouillard (commentaire)*, p. 37.

29. 'Rien ne distinguait la chambre à gaz d'un block ordinaire', *Nuit et brouillard (commentaire)*, p. 38.

30. Hannah Arendt, *The Origins of Totalitarianism*, [1951] (London: Allen and Unwin, 1967), p. 459.

31. *Nuit et brouillard (commentaire)*, p. 39. I have written about the anxious relationship between horror and the everyday in 'Horror and the Everyday in Post-Holocaust France: *Nuit et brouillard* and Concentrationary Art', *French Cultural Studies* 17/1 (2006), pp. 5–18. Cayrol draws out the tension between horror and the everyday that one finds in Arendt's work from her very early post-war writings through to *Eichmann in Jerusalem: A Report on the Banality of Evil*.

32. For the purpose of my present argument, I am limiting the discussion of techniques of defamiliarization to certain key aspects. However, one could equally talk of the disjunction between image, music and spoken text, the constant tension between the still and moving image, the uncertain relationship between filmic addressor and addressee, and others.

33. Our perception of the archive images of atrocity in *Night and Fog* (and especially the Sonderkommando image of the smouldering bodies of victims recently gassed) has, more recently, been caught up in the debates about the ethics of representation and the use of the archive. However, the dichotomy 'representation versus anti-representation', in which *Night and Fog* is placed on the side of representation because of its use of archive material and Claude Lanzmann's *Shoah* on the side of anti-representation because of its refusal to use the archive, is, I would suggest, itself a misrepresentation of Resnais's use of archive footage and photographs in the film. These photographs are themselves broken images rather than a direct representation of horror giving us unmediated access to the real. They are, like the split vision

announced at the beginning of the film and the traces in the present gesturing to an elsewhere, part of the Lazarean regime by which clarity of vision has been replaced by 'haunted images'. In her excellent book on film, ethics and the Holocaust, Libby Saxton acknowledges this treatment of the archive in *Night and Fog* (and gives a brilliant critique of the false oppositions established in the heated polemical debates in France in recent years about the representation of atrocity): '(I)n *Nuit et brouillard* the archive images too, in their turn, become haunted, the emaciated, traumatized survivors and the mounds of corpses evoking, but not supplanting, the missing bodies of those who were murdered in the gas chamber, incinerated in the crematoria or recycled in the various appalling ways mentioned,' *Haunted Images: Film, Ethics, Testimony and the Holocaust* (London and New York: Wallflower Press, 2008), p. 90.

34. 'la guerre s'est assoupie, un oeil toujours ouvert,' *Nuit et brouillard (commentaire)*, p. 42.

35. 'On fermait les portes. On observait. Le seul signe – mais il faut le savoir –, c'est ce plafond labouré par les ongles. Même le béton se déchirait,' *Nuit et brouillard (commentaire)*, p. 38.

36. 'un village abandonné encore plein de menaces'; 'neuf millions de morts hantent ce paysage', *Nuit et brouillard (commentaire)*, p. 42; 'qui de nous veille dans cet étrange observatoire pour nous avertir de la venue de nouveaux bourreaux? Ont-ils vraiment un autre visage que le nôtre? Quelque part, parmi nous, il est des kapos chanceux, des chefs récupérés, des dénonciateurs inconnus,' *Nuit et brouillard (commentaire)*, pp. 42–3; 'nous qui feignons de croire que tout cela est d'un seul pays, et qui ne pensons pas à regarder autour de nous, et qui n'entendons pas qu'on crie sans fin,' *Nuit et brouillard (commentaire)*, p. 43; 'notre mauvaise mémoire', *Nuit et brouillard (commentaire)*, p. 41; 'le vieux monstre concentrationnaire était mort sous les décombres [...] comme si on guérissait de la peste concentrationnaire,' *Nuit et brouillard (commentaire)*, p. 43.

37. 'I've always refused the word "memory" a propos my work. I'd use the word "imagination"', cited in James Monaco, *Alain Resnais* (New York: Oxford University Press, 1979), p. 11.

38. Thomas Elsaesser has developed this point to show that it is precisely the idea of memory as palimpsest that informs Freud's understanding of the mechanism of the unconscious. Elsaesser highlights the way in which Freud likens the psyche to a mystic writing-pad (or *Wunderblock*, recalling the palimpsest) which, in Freud's own terms in 'A Note upon the "mystic writing-pad"' (1925), 'combines an '"ever-ready receptive surface" with the "permanent traces of the notes that have been made upon it"', Thomas Elsaesser, 'Freud as Media Theorist: Mystic Writing-pads and the Matter of Memory', *Screen* 50/1 (2009), p. 2. Antoine de Baecque has used the term 'concentrationary palimpsest' to refer to the way in which images from the camps form a sort of unconscious bedrock to the whole of modern cinema (see Saxton, *Haunted Images*, p. 4).

39. Elsaesser, 'Freud as Media Theorist', p. 5.

40. 'Dans un rêve, il n'y plus une image-souvenir qui incarne un point particulier de telle nappe, il y a des images qui s'incarnent l'une dans l'autre, chacune renvoyant à un point de nappe différente. Il se peut que, quand nous lisons un livre, regardons un spectacle ou un tableau, et à plus forte raison quand nous sommes nous-mêmes auteur, un processus analogue se déclenche: nous constituons une nappe de transformation qui invente une sorte de continuité ou de communication

transversales entre plusieurs nappes, et tisse entre elles un ensemble de relations non-localisables. Nous dégageons ainsi le temps non-chronologique,' Deleuze, *Cinema 2: L'Image-Temps*, pp. 161–2 ; *Cinema 2: The Time-Image*, p. 123.

41. Andrew Hebard, 'Disruptive Histories: Toward a Radical Politics of Remembrance in Alain Resnais's *Night and Fog*', *New German Critique* 71 (Spring–Summer, 1997), pp. 87–113, p. 101. See also this volume, Chapter 9.

42. 'Ce cri sans fin, substitué à l'incantatoire « plus jamais ça » des monuments aux morts, donne son sens à la définition flottante des victimes et des bourreaux', Lindeperg, *'Nuit et brouillard'*, p. 128.

43. 'un glissement sémantique', Lindeperg, Nuit et brouillard: p. 123. This suggests that testimony (like vision and memory) is also de-psychologized and de-individualized to be a witnessing of the 'in-between'.

44. 'D'un bout à l'autre de l'oeuvre de Resnais on s'enfonce dans une mémoire qui déborde les conditions de la psychologie, mémoire à deux, mémoire à plusieurs, mémoire-monde, mémoire-âges du monde', Deleuze, *Cinema 2: L'Image-Temps*, p. 155 ; *Cinema 2: The Time-Image*, p. 119. Jean-Pierre Salgas talks of the construction in the film of an 'a-temporal present' 30 years before Claude Lanzmann's *Shoah*, Jean-Pierre Salgas, 'Shoah, ou la disparition', in Denis Hollier (ed.), *De la littérature française* (Paris : Bordas, 1993), pp. 1005–13, p. 1007.

45. Walter Benjamin, *The Arcades Project*, p. 462.

46. See, for example, Robert Michael, 'Night and Fog', *Cineaste* 13/4 (1984), pp. 36–7. Although it is true that the word 'juif' is only mentioned once in the film ('Stern, a Jewish student from Amsterdam', 'Stern, étudiant juif d'Amsterdam', *Nuit et brouillard (commentaire)*, p. 19), the Jewish presence is clearly implicit in 'Schmulski, a merchant from Krakow' ('Schmulski, marchand de Cracovie'), 'rounded up in Warsaw [...] rounded up in the Vel' d'Hiv' ('(r)aflés de Varsovie [...] raflés du Vel' d'Hiv', *Nuit et brouillard (commentaire)*, pp. 19 and 20, respectively) and the images of deportees with yellow stars. Sylvie Lindeperg explains that 'the marginal but very real place given in the screenplay to the account of the genocide of the Jews' and 'the research done in Poland [which] considerably reinforced the presence in the film of shots and photos referring to the extermination of the Jews of Europe' were heavily excised in Cayrol's own commentary (Lindeperg, Nuit et brouillard: pp. 6–7). See also Lindeperg's chapter in this volume.

47. Resnais's use of montage is a crucial part of this political aesthetic. This is not to say that the painstaking effort involved in re-historicizing Resnais's promiscuous collage of places and times is not of the utmost importance (for example, distinguishing between those images relating to the concentration camps and those of the extermination camps, or recognizing that the young girl framed in the doorway of the cattle-truck (shot number 61) was not a Jew but, a Romany). However, we should recognize that montage serves the purpose of overlaying 'different' sites to arrive at a more Benjaminian concept of history.

48. See my 'Interconnected Histories: Holocaust and Empire in the Cultural Imaginary', *French Studies* 62/4 (2008), pp. 417–28.

49 Rothberg, *Multidirectional Memory*.

50 'la bouche sera toujours ouverte, non pour la parole mais pour le cri,' Cayrol, 'De la vie à la mort', p. 84.

CHAPTER 9

Disruptive Histories:
Toward a Radical Politics of Remembrance in Alain Resnais's *Night and Fog*

ANDREW HEBARD

A scandal occurred at the Cannes Film Festival in 1956.[1] A short film produced a long series of problems that reverberated in the European press for the next two years. The film was Alain Resnais's *Night and Fog* (1955), a 32-minute documentary on the Holocaust. Banned from the festival because of German protests, the film made public a whole process of historical repression. The initial complaint pressed by the German foreign office claimed that the film would incite anti-German hatred. A combination of these protests, Cold War anxiety, and the French government's own reservations about archival material in the film (showing French policemen helping with the deportation of prisoners) all helped to get the film removed from the festival. In a weak attempt to assert a moral economy of retribution, the festival organizers also threw out a German film as a token of appeasement.

While the German foreign office did anticipate the reaction of other European nations to their protests, truly unexpected was the reaction within Germany. *Night and Fog* became a site of contention for a wide range of issues. Within months it was being shown at film festivals and film clubs in the major German cities. Willy Brandt, then the president of the Berlin House of Commons, came out with a statement explicitly supporting the film.[2] Likewise Paul Bausch, the chairman of the Federal Bureau for the Press, Film, and Radio, released a statement proposing that the government should support free screenings of the film to all civil servants.[3] A flurry of articles and editorials appearing in the German newspapers put the film directly into the public light. What began initially as an international scandal became a site for a prolonged consideration and discussion of the Nazi past within Germany.

What was the source of this scandal? Was it the attempt to bring a representation of the Holocaust into a public (and international) forum? Was it the film's propensity to collapse and contaminate the difference between past and present that Adenauer's post-war policy called for? Certainly the historical moment in which the film was initially received had much to do with the heightened public discourse that followed the film's suppression. I would, however, also like to suggest that the film itself, particularly its mode of representation, was also responsible for what followed. The scandal resulted not so much from the images themselves, but rather from the use of the images mediated through montage and commentary. Resnais's use of archival material juxtaposed with present-day footage worked to defamiliarize the archive and to complicate a facile distinction between past and present.

This distinction between the past and the present has become one of the primary focuses of work concerning the Holocaust. The Holocaust poses a profound problem to a traditional mode of historical scholarship, which assumes a distance of the past imposed by the idealized objectivity of the historian. Such a fiction of critical distance produces further fictions of closure in relation to historical knowledge. Because of the traumatic nature of the Holocaust, however, because the events were so violent and unfathomable that they continue to confound attempts to understand them let alone represent them, the Holocaust has come to challenge such closure and has left many of the writers on the Holocaust paradoxically struggling with both a need to articulate something, and the difficulties as well as the inadequacies of any articulation. Jean-François Lyotard theorizes this dilemma when he places the Holocaust within the logic of the *différend*, that is in 'the unstable state and instant of language wherein something which must be able to be put into phrases cannot yet be.'[4] Lyotard points to precisely what representations of the Holocaust must negotiate: the aporias framed between necessity and impossibility. The subsequent outcome of these problems is that the closure of traditional historiography is criticized or, at the very least, problematized. History must submit to what Saul Friedlaender labels as 'the imperative of rendering as truthful an account as documents and testimonials will allow, without giving in to the temptation of closure', for 'closure in this case would represent an obvious avoidance of what remains indeterminate, elusive, and opaque.'[5]

Many recent writings, particularly in light of the dwindling generation of Holocaust survivors, have concerned themselves with what I will call 'a politics of remembrance', that is, the difficulty of representing the Holocaust in a way that is both sensitive to the problems of representation, and yet also works specifically as a critique of and a warning against the forms and aesthetics of fascism and mechanized violence. This work has often questioned and shifted the grounds of critical history. In order to negotiate the tension between critical history and memory, much of this discussion has turned to the language of psychoanalysis, because its terminology – trauma, mourning, acting out and working through – is intricately invested in issues of remembrance and history.[6]

Much recent scholarship has aligned itself specifically with the need to 'mourn' or 'work through' the past. While it would be possible to trace these theories through the works of many critics, perhaps the two most comprehensive statements of the implications of such a view on remembrance can be found in the works of Dominick LaCapra and Eric Santner.[7] *Night and Fog* suggests both a critique of and an alternative to these theories of mourning and working through, both in terms of its formal construction and in terms of the history of its reception. Before moving on to an examination of the film and its reception, it is important to situate the work of LaCapra and Santner with respect to the larger critical tradition of Holocaust representation and historiography which they react against.

One can glean a sense of what has become the contested ground of Holocaust memory by situating it within the two extremes LaCapra presents as the limits of current theoretical discourse on the Holocaust. Keeping in mind the traumatic nature of the Holocaust and the problems that trauma poses for memory, LaCapra claims that writings on the Holocaust have often restricted themselves to two polarized extremes for responding to a traumatic history.

> One response involves denial or repression, for example, in a redemptive, fetishistic narrative that excludes or marginalizes trauma through a teleological story that projectively presents values and wishes as viably realized in the facts, typically through a progressive, developmental process.[8]

The other extreme is a response that tends:

> intentionally or unintentionally to aggravate trauma in a largely symptomatic fashion. This may be done through a construction of all history (or at least all modem history) as trauma and an insistence that there is no alternative to symptomatic acting-out and the repetition compulsion other than an imaginary, illusory hope for totalization, full closure, and redemptive meaning.[9]

Santner establishes an analogous opposition, staking out two poles: 'narrative fetishism', which is based on a narcissistic denial of trauma, and the other pole, the 'most extreme alternative to narcissism: the instabilities of schizophrenia'.[10] The schizophrenic alternative for Santner is one that implies the dissolution of 'political' identity along with the inability to distinguish between victim and perpetrator, and, similar to the 'history as trauma' model, an inability to historicize the Holocaust.

Both of these critics are reacting to two divergent tendencies in writings about the Holocaust. The first is the 'narrative fetishism' of historical revisionists like Ernst Nolte, Michael Stürmer and Andreas Hillgruber, who have attempted to rewrite the history of the Holocaust by subordinating it to narratives of German victimage at the hands of Bolshevik expansion on the Eastern front. Such narratives try to both relativize the inhumanity of the Holocaust and to displace responsibility away from German nationalism. Both LaCapra and Santner justifiably criticize such a historiography for its attempt at false closure, one that shortcircuits the need to struggle with the immense burden that such a past necessarily entails. Such a closure, through its teleological fixing of historical meaning, also adopts a 'conventional identification' that dangerously echoes the specularization of national identity seen in the 1930s and 1940s. Santner writes that, a 'conventional identity' signifies in this context a self-structure still rooted in a specular relation to the particular norms, roles, 'contents' of a specific social formation such as family, *Volk*, or nation.[11]

The other tendency that they are reacting against – all history as trauma or all historical agents as schizophrenic – can be found both in the extremes of trauma theory and in some versions of poststructuralism (both LaCapra and Santner produce extensive critiques of the work of Paul de Man). Their criticism is directed at the way that these theories flatten out the actual complexity of the historical field which becomes transformed into a symptomatic acting out of past traumas (in the case of trauma theory) or into 'purely linguistic complication' (in the case of de Man). Although LaCapra and Santner are at times too hasty in their critiques of poststructural thought (there is no consideration of Foucault's work on historiography in either book), certainly their discomfort with a theoretical totalization of historiography seems appropriate.

LaCapra's alternative is one that 'would engage a process of mourning that would attempt, however self-questioning and haltingly, to specify its haunting objects and (even if only symbolically) to give them a "proper" burial.'[12] Santner's alternative is one that similarly calls for a mourning through a 'homeopathic' cure which would consist of 'the dosing out of a certain negative – a thanatotic – element as a strategy of mastering a real and traumatic loss.'[13] Both theorists rely upon a psychoanalytic therapeutic praxis that attempts to grapple with the traumatic element of the past without either narcissistically denying it (by fetishizing narrative historical meaning) or giving in to it. Santner and LaCapra propose a psychoanalytic process of transference as a model for a politically responsible historiography of the Holocaust. Such a move avoids the closure of traditional historical scholarship

218 | *Andrew Hebard*

because a transference model admits to the impossibility of ever working through all traumatic affect. It also avoids the endless repetition of aggravated trauma because it is fundamentally a process of psychic healing that bears upon the symptomatic excesses of traumatic memory.

While I do not take issue with LaCapra's and Santner's critical accounts of recent Holocaust scholarship, I do take issue with their proposed alternative. Their alternative falls short for three important reasons. First, despite their criticism of narrative closure, mourning and working through, as they have formulated it, become reinscribed within a psychoanalytic narrative. Second, this psychoanalytic model becomes a kind of procedural ethics that all too predictably mediates the role of memory, effectively flattening out its historical complexity and remaining blind to the multiple ways that memory interacts with culture, power and historical tradition in non-psychoanalytic ways. Lastly, LaCapra's and Santner's notions of mourning and working through inevitably rely upon a version of identity politics that is not all that fundamentally different from the one they set out to critique. As an alternative, I would like to delineate the contours of a politics of remembrance that functions through the anxiety of the uncanny. Such an anxiety, as I will formulate it, is not completely submerged in a psychoanalytic discourse, engages with a multiplicity of historically contingent fields, and does not fall back upon a link between identity and agency. From my reading of *Night and Fog*, I would like to consider an anxious politics that does not work against the ambivalence of traumatic aporia, but works within it. Such a politics functions along different axes from those of mourning and working through. Working through as it has been articulated in current critical discourse is really a working upon and working over memory. It takes the traumatic ambivalences of memory as the object of its procedural operation. Anxiety, as I wish to formulate it, is working 'through' ambivalence in a more literal sense, for it inhabits the very agonies of ambivalence and posits no exteriority as the location from which to launch a 'politics'. Implicit to my argument will be the call to substantially rethink the way that psychoanalysis has been used to talk about the Holocaust.

First, I would like to provide a brief formal reading of *Night and Fog*, followed by the implications of this in terms of the uncanny, anxiety and ambivalence. Then I will continue with my consideration of LaCapra and Santner's work while fleshing out my own proposed alternative and its implications for agency and ethics. Finally I would like to situate this discussion with respect to the reception of the film in Germany.

*   *   *

In criticism on documentaries about the Holocaust, it has almost become a truism that Claude Lanzmann's *Shoah* (1985) has, since its release, often been the work against which all others are compared. The film's innovation lies in its exclusive reliance on filmed testimony rather than documentary or fictive reconstruction. It contains no archival footage and is concerned with the problematics of witnessing rather than with the problematics of historical documentation. Without criticizing *Shoah's* achievements, I would like to suggest that the foregrounding of this film has often been at the expense of the critical recognition of other documentaries engaging the problematics of the Holocaust. Shoshana Felman, for example, in her book on testimony, not only implicitly discounts other films in light of *Shoah's* 'power', one 'that no previous film on the subject could attain', but subsequently implies that part of this power is due to the film's refusal to use archival footage. 'The film [*Shoah*] is not simply, nor is it primarily, a historical document on the Holocaust. That is why, in contrast to its cinematic predecessors on the subject, it refuses systematically to use any historical, archival footage.'[14] Felman's comment is particularly telling in that it equates archival material with the creation of a 'document' and carries with it the insinuation that the use of archival materials entails a certain amount of historical closure.

Night and Fog, in which archival material plays an essential part, is certainly one of the casualties of Felman's sentiment, and whether or not one believes that her statements represent the general attitude of current criticism, a glance at recent scholarship certainly provides evidence of the relative neglect of Resnais's film. Such neglect is unfortunate, for *Night and Fog,* far from creating a straightforward historical document of the Holocaust, fundamentally confounds notions of past, present, history and memory.

Night and Fog begins with an unsettling of the spectator's view. The first shot of the film is framed upon a colourful field. 'An ordinary landscape', the narrator says as the camera cranes down to reveal a barbed wire fence. Much of the first sequence follows this pattern. 'An ordinary road' is shown, at first directly, and then through the wires of a fence. The voice-over informs us that 'this is the way to a concentration camp.' The estrangement of the seemingly familiar carefully constructed in the film's first few shots becomes the primary structural motif of the film. This motif does not remain confined to the use of camera movement in the space of the abandoned concentration camp, but also relies on the use of archival images and the juxtaposition of past and present. These juxtapositions could be read as an attempt to produce a distance between past and present. A closer look at the film, however, reveals that it sets out these oppositions only to undermine them, to fundamentally confuse our ideas about past and present to such an extent that, by the end of the film, the commentator is able to ask while referring to the SS, 'Are our faces so different from theirs?' At a formal level the establishment and then subsequent breakdown of the opposition between past and present, between archival material and Resnais's own footage, can be separated into three areas of contamination: colour, movement and sound. In addition to these three formal aspects, there is also what I will call the 'moral contamination' of the camera.

The most immediately obvious difference between present footage and past archive is the opposition between colour and black-and-white. Resnais intentionally heightens this contrast by using Eastmancolour instead of Agfacolour. Ghislain Cloquet, the director of photography for the film, is quoted as saying, 'Resnais wanted a bright colour. He sought to modify through colour the way people habitually look at things.'[15] The colour/black-and-white opposition would seem to be the most difficult to break down simply because the contrast at the beginning of the film is so stark. Leo Bersani and Ulysse Dutoit write,

> But there are moments in the film when we can't be sure of whether we are being given a sequence from the archives or whether Resnais has filmicly reconstructed moments from the past ... scenes filmed in a sepia-like 'compromise' between colour and black and white, and whose photographic texture is closer to that of the present-day scene than to that of the documents.[16]

This observation points to an important aspect of the film's montage, but in a way that is perhaps a bit too strained. I agree that there is a crossover between colour and black-and-white, but believe that it moves in precisely the opposite direction, that it is not so much the archive which becomes infected by colour, but rather the colour footage that is shown to have the potential to fade into black-and-white. This view is suggested by the night scene about eight minutes into the film. The expressive movement of the camera and the apparent emptiness of the buildings clearly indicate that the shot is filmed in the present, but the night-time lighting explicitly removes colour from the shot. A fading of colours also occurs as the camera penetrates the interiors of the camp. Perhaps the most deliberate use of this draining of colour comes in the two sequential shots that track along rows of bunks. The first shot, though in a relatively dark room, manages to reveal the textures and colours of the wooden bunks. The following shot looks at a different row of bunks from a similar angle and matches the previous shot's forward tracking movement. However, in the second shot, the bunks are made of concrete, and the shot consists primarily of monochromatic shades rather than colours.

Another formal opposition between archival material and Resnais's footage lies in his use of camera movement. The colour footage is taken with a camera that not only pivots and tilts, but also tracks relentlessly through the spaces of the abandoned camp. Much of the archival material, on the other hand, appears in the form of black-and-white, still photographs. The archival film footage is, with very few exceptions, shot by a stationary camera, a camera that occasionally pivots and tilts, but never moves. This oscillation between fixed and moving points of view initially structures a formal difference between past and present.

Similar to its use of colour, the film initially establishes a dichotomy, only to subject it to a crossover where once again formal aspects of archival material infect the camera of the present. The camera's movement, though reasonably steady throughout the film, often pauses on objects, like the ovens, or a corner in the gas chamber. The film even ends with a stationary shot, and similar to the way that the archival photographs interrupt the camera's movement through the camp, the camera itself begins to pause and take what could be considered snapshots of the abandoned camp. This technique of pausing is formally linked to the archival photographs in that the camera often pauses right before a cut to a photograph.

Another aspect of camera movement that both establishes a contrast and then performs its contamination is the particular direction of the movement. The scenes in which Resnais's camera pans, tracks, cranes or combines all three movements are set up in such a way that stationary objects within the frame seem to move from right to left. Despite jumps to different locations in the abandoned camp, the continuity of camera movement ensures that space is generally well established and readable. The viewer is relatively clear about the images she/he looks at. The archival footage, on the other hand, often depicts a general confusion of movement, particularly with respect to the deportees. A high angle shot of the crowd in the large room about five minutes into the film is just one example. In contrast to the present-day footage where stationary objects move from right to left in a kind of procession as the camera pans or tracks to the right, the movement of prisoners within the stationary frame of the archival shot is marked by a chaotic motion of both dispersion and assembly. In another sequence, the one in which prisoners are being loaded onto the train, the editing of archival footage actually serves to disorient the audience's sense of space. Officers are filmed from different directions, and there is a general confusion in the way the deportees move through the frame. In the case of some of the grainier photographs, the poor quality of the images can even confuse our sense of what an object is.

Again, the crossover or contamination of previously established oppositions is from the archive into the present. The most notable breakdown of the film's binary structure occurs in the scene in the gas chamber. The first shot begins with a track and pan to the left, a movement which the next shot repeats. These are the only non-archival shots in the whole film where the camera pans or tracks to the left, causing the stationary objects within the frame to move from the left to the right. This movement is linked to a loss of orientation in the next shot when the camera, prompted by the voiceover statement, 'The only sign – you have to know it – is this ceiling dug into by fingernails. Even the concrete was torn,' tilts up and pans across the ceiling, completely disorientating the viewer until the camera finally comes to rest in a corner at the opposite end of the room.

One should also note the differences between the film's first and last shots. The first shots challenge our notion of what we are seeing in the sense that they question whether the 'ordinary landscape' and the 'ordinary road' are at all ordinary. What is not questioned is whether we are looking at a field or a road. Similar to some of the film's (more difficult to decipher) still images, the last shot leaves the very nature of what we are looking at in question. The camera moves across what is presumably a ruined building, but the movements are so intricate, and the space so ambiguous that the viewer gets no sense of the layout of the building. The shot combines a panning, tilting and tracking movement, often all at once. The shot even ends with a stationary camera and a predominance of grays, blacks and whites, drawing distinctly upon the formal qualities of the archive and imposing them on the present-day footage.

The sound track is another area of formalistic contamination of the separation between past and present. Hanns Eisler's score, which runs throughout the whole soundtrack, initially reinforces the contrast between past and present. The film's first use of archival material is set off by a harsh change in the music from a melodious, softer tune to the abrupt use of pizzicato. The soundtrack initially heightens the difference between present-day footage and archival material with abrupt changes in tempo, tone and instrumentation. As the film progresses, the soundtrack's differentiating role becomes contaminated as musical continuity occasionally spans the jumps between archival material and Resnais's footage. Abrupt changes in the musical score also begin to occur in the middle of shots, unprompted by any editing.

The final area of crossover that I will consider is what I shall call the 'moral corruption' of the camera. It is important to remember that most of the archival images used by Resnais were taken by Nazi photographers and used explicitly for propaganda or for the purpose of documenting and cataloguing the process of extermination. The meandering camera that wanders through the camp in the first sequence of the film is immediately juxtaposed to the marching Nazi soldiers in the next sequence, a sequence taken directly from Leni Riefenstahl's well-known propaganda film, *Triumph of the Will* (1934). Surveillance is also a motif throughout the film, and much of the archival material shows German soldiers controlling the deportees through their gaze. The narrator even says, 'He [the deportee] belonged to only this self-contained universe, hemmed in by observation posts where the behaviour of the camp was watched, and soldiers spied on the deportees, killing them on occasion, having nothing better to do.' The Nazi gaze contaminates Resnais's present-day footage in quite deliberate ways. At the same moment that the commentary mentions these observation posts and the gaze of the guards, the camera pans across the camp from one of these very same observation posts. A similar moment occurs in the second of the two pans along the row of bunks that I discussed earlier. The narrator warns of the 'sudden appearance of the SS, zealous in their check-ups and inspections.' As this line is spoken, the camera effectively 'patrols' along the bunks, and then for no apparent reason, pans to the right and 'inspects' an object tucked away in a corner. It is notable that this bunk shot is the one where the more archival qualities of black-and-white infect the colour footage. Similar to the archive which consists largely of Nazi photographs and films, the gaze of Resnais's camera becomes the gaze of the Nazi.

*   *   *

Before exploring how the dominant stylistic of juxtapositions and their subsequent contaminations function within the framework of the uncanny, it is important to briefly state how they do not work within the film. They do not facilitate a historical narrative. The commentary in the film is primarily descriptive and non-narrative. The dates and historical events tend to interrupt rather than facilitate the film's relentless portrayal of concentration camp existence. The voice-over narration is shown to be both unreliable and inadequate. For example, as Ilan Avisar observes, 'The narrator refers to those "who are too weak to defend their ration against thieves" but the image reveals a moving glimpse of two prisoners sharing the same bowl of soup.'[17] There are also moments when the narration breaks off, seemingly unable to find appropriate words, and yet the camera continues to show. In the shots where the film portrays the Nazis' use of human bodies for making soap and cloth, the narrator is unable to complete the sentence, 'As for the skin ...'; it is the image that completes what language cannot by showing drawings upon canvasses of dried skin. Narrative explanation is problematized rather than fortified by the film's images.

The film also does not use its rhetoric of juxtaposing past and present footage as a form of progressive, dialectical montage. In contradistinction to Eisensteinian montage, the juxtaposition of images is a corrupted and non-dialectical one. It collapses differences, but not in the service of a new understanding of what we see. The commentary relentlessly reminds us of the film's inability to represent and describe the Holocaust as it was experienced – 'no description, no shot can restore their true dimension. ... It is useless to describe what went on in these cells.' One should also note that the slippage between past and present does not occur in the form of a progression through the film, but rather occurs as an interruption. The general use of camera movement, space and colour are still dealt with in the same way throughout the film, even toward the end. The formal aspects of the archival material serve to interrupt, rather than take over the techniques of the empty camp footage.

The establishing and then subsequent collapsing of difference in this film effects a sense of return, a return that is uncanny. This film is undeniably unsettling. The 'tranquil landscape' with which the film begins is one that, by the end, is 'haunted by the ghosts of nine million'. The past, both in its formal cinematic qualities and in its historical and symbolic weight, infects our view of the present. Such a return resembles the return in Freud's concept of the uncanny.

Freud's essay 'The Uncanny' is full of complexities and contradictions. Rather than use it to produce a psychoanalytic reading of the film, a project that I find problematic to begin with, I would like to extract two concepts from Freud's essay and then translate them to elucidate the cultural politics of this film. These concepts are the return of the repressed, or rather the return of repression, and its symptomatic manifestation through anxiety which I will analyse for its temporal implications.

The uncanny in Freud's essay is an experience invoked through a return. It is the return of the once familiar, estranged through repression. In this sense it is both a doubling, a repetition with a difference (estrangement), and a return, the return of the repressed. So what is it that returns distorted through repression in *Night and Fog*? The simplest explanation would be to say that it is the past that returns, that it is the past that is repressed. I believe, however, that this is not the case. To claim that the repressed past returns is to assume a certain distance between past and present that, as I have shown, the film works to undermine. Many readings of Freud's essay merely focus on the return of the repressed past event. But when Freud writes of the uncanny as 'something which ought to have been kept concealed but which has nevertheless come to light', his essay points to more than merely the notion of return. It points to the breakdown of repression as well.[18]

Repression is quite clearly what is at issue in *Night and Fog*. The narrator ends with the lines,

> Are their faces any different from ours? ... There are those of us who sincerely look upon the ruins today, as if the concentration camp monsters were dead and buried beneath them. Those who pretend to take hope again as the image fades, as though there were a cure for the plague of these camps. Those of us who pretend to believe that all this happened only once, at a certain time and in a certain place, and those who refuse to see, who do not hear the cry to the end of time.

These concluding lines explicitly deny the pastness of the past. In essence, what is repressed, and what this film tries to bring about as a return, is not merely the past, but the existence of the past within the present. Furthermore, these lines are centrally concerned with the process of repression. What is repressed and then returns by the end of the film is the process of repression itself. It is repression that, once transparent (familiar), suddenly becomes opaque (defamiliarized). The film initially employs naturalized metaphors of forgetting: 'Faithful as ever, the grass flourishes on the muster ground.' In contradistinction, the verb 'pretend' [feigner] in the commentary at the end of the film points to an active, rather than passive, practice of forgetting and blurs a facile distinction between the repression and the suppression of memory. The blurring of the past/present opposition along with the moral corruption of the camera implicates the viewer in this act of repression/ suppression by collapsing any position of exteriority from which the viewer might judge the events from afar. The film's formal techniques of alternating differentiation and contamination reveal the line between the past and the present to be an ambivalent one, a line haunted and accused by the narrator's questions – 'Who is responsible? Are their faces any different from ours?'.

The existence of a culturally repressed past within the present is not one where they coexist within the same temporality, but rather where the past interrupts and unsettles the present, challenging ideas of both closure and progress. A dialectical relation between the past and present is undercut by the uncanny's relation to the disjunctive temporality of traumatic repetition. Freud writes that 'whatever reminds us of this inner repetition-compulsion is perceived as uncanny.'[19] The landscape at the end of the film (the collapsed building) is literally one of ruin, one ripped through by holes. The present returns in the film's last shot, but it is not just the violence of the past that makes it uncanny, it is that there are '[t]hose of us who pretend to believe that all this happened only once, at a certain time and in a certain place', that repression returns defamiliarized. The disjunctive and non-progressive disintegration of formalistic differentiation between the archive and the colour footage, a disintegration that evokes the uncanny through its laying bare of the process of repression, forces a reconsideration of the possibility that an event can be contained within a 'certain' time or place. To question this possibility is also to question the temporality of the event, a temporality no longer contained by a historical *telos*.

The temporal ambivalence that accompanies this breakdown of repression has its symptomatic manifestation in the trope of anxiety. The uncanny creates a feeling of anxiety. The destabilizing anxiety of the uncanny, however, should not be considered to be identical to a traumatic neurosis. Although it is intricately bound to the idea of trauma, anxiety is not caught up in the endless and unproductive 'acting out' of traumatic repetition. Freud claims that the uncanny is a class of anxiety that comes from the repetition of repressed events. In this sense a remembrance through the uncanny never banishes, or even works through the traumatic, but rather originates from it

226 | *Andrew Hebard*

without having to endlessly act it out. It is a symptomatic expression of a traumatic repetition without itself being one in its pure sense. As I have already shown through the analysis of *Night and Fog*, the uncanny also does not erase the trauma through 'narrative fetishism', but is instead always evoking trauma's shadow to unsettle any sense of closure. Furthermore, the temporality of such an anxiety is split, for anxiety is 'on the one hand an expectation of a trauma, and on the other a repetition of it in a mitigated form.'[20] This unsettling and paradoxical temporality posed between expectation and repetition works against the homogeneous time of historical narrative and is one aspect of the political potential of the uncanny.

Earlier, I posed the problem of Holocaust representation as the negotiation of historical trauma and its ambivalent aporias. Mourning is a negotiation *of* traumatic ambivalence. With anxiety, however, we are given this ambivalence *as* a form of negotiation. If anxiety is 'on the one hand an expectation of a trauma, and on the other a repetition of it in a mitigated form', then anxiety as such paradoxically tries to make sense of a trauma (history as paradox and disaster) and repeats its senselessness.[21] Psychoanalysis, as a therapeutic practice, presents a theory for the negotiation *of* traumatic memory. To assume the position of anxiety is not to assume this position of psychoanalysis.

*   *   *

This brings me to my first critique of mourning and working through as a cultural politics: its particular use of psychoanalysis. The move that LaCapra and Santner make by turning towards mourning and working through as a historiographic procedure of transference has great merit in its rigorous critique of historical narratives. The psychoanalytic 'cure' that it works toward is never a form of closure that works through all traumatic affect. Working through is not a process of turning the 'unreason' of trauma into the 'reason' of narrative. It is the establishment of 'a self that feels entitled to play with its boundaries (rather than denying them or reifying them).'[22] It is a process of coming to terms with a 'subject position [that] is at best a partial, problematic identity.'[23]

Despite these potentially radical innovations, I would question these tropes of mourning and working through in terms of their relation to a psychoanalytic discourse, for it seems that they import a psychoanalytic narrative, one that begins with repression and ends with cure. Memory might open up a field of play, but similar to a playground bully, psychoanalysis sets the rules of the game. This leads to two substantial problems: the problem of translating terms from a psychoanalytic discourse into a historical one and the need to historicize psychoanalysis and analyse its own intersections with power.

In a consideration of psychoanalysis Michel de Certeau posits: 'When a theoretical view is extended beyond the field within which it was elaborated, where it remains subject to a system of verification, does it not . . . cross the line between scientific "theories" and scientific "ideologies"? That is frequently the case.'[24] The problems of providing psychoanalytic 'readings' of culture or history are well known. To use psychoanalytic concepts in other discourses without a process of translation is at best ideological. LaCapra and Santner are certainly aware of these problems. LaCapra in particular considers this issue extensively in his writings. He proposes a 'dialogue' between the fields of history and psychoanalysis, giving neither one a dominant position. This dialogue, as it unfolds in LaCapra's text, implies a prior autonomy to each field. Working through necessitates this approach, for it needs the psychoanalytic discourse to remain intact so as to justify transference as a 'good' procedural ethics. It is precisely this preservation of psychoanalytic discourse that I find questionable. Translation between disciplines is not merely a matter of finding analogues in a different vocabulary. Every act of translation is also an act of re-enunciation and therefore changes the function of the terms it translates. Homi Bhabha, drawing upon Walter Benjamin, writes:

> [The] disjunctive play of symbol and sign makes interdisciplinarity an instance of the borderline moment of translation that Walter Benjamin describes as the 'foreignness of languages.' The 'foreignness of languages' is the nucleus of the untranslatable that goes beyond the transferal of subject matter between cultural texts or practices. The transfer of meaning can never be total between systems of meaning, or within them.[25]

It is precisely the narrative coherence of psychoanalytic procedure that must get lost in the process of its translation.

The anxiety of the uncanny as I have tried to formulate it is a fragment of a psychoanalytic discourse. I have not tried to situate its politics in a procedural ethics of psychoanalysis. Rather than reify the discourse of psychoanalysis, I have attempted through an act of translation to employ psychoanalytic terms as useful analytic tropes, tropes that remain fragments of a larger psychoanalytic discourse and that assume new enunciative meanings as they cross disciplinary boundaries. By concentrating on the temporal aspects of anxiety, I have tried to deploy anxiety as such a fragment. Psychoanalysis and anxiety are deeply involved in the problems and paradoxes of temporality. Concentrating, however, on this fragmentary aspect of anxiety implies a departure from a psychoanalytic economy which is far more interested in the normalization and control of anxiety than in the temporal specifics of its paradoxical construction. One of the greatest strengths of psychoanalysis has been its ability to accept paradox and unreason within a field of reason; but rather than instrumentalize this paradox towards therapeutic logic, I would like to examine anxiety displaced from its psychoanalytic narrative and translated into the specificity of a historical field.

My reading of *Night and Fog* has attempted to work within this paradigm, and rather than trying to produce psychoanalytic knowledge or meaning out of the temporal ambivalence that the film produces, I have tried to use the trope of uncanny anxiety to open up questions rather than provide resolutions. This is why my later consideration of the historical reception of the film is so crucial to my analysis, for it is in the discourse surrounding the film that one sees how anxiety was re-enunciated in other discourses in ways that cannot be reduced to psychoanalytic interpretations of memory.

This brings us to the problem of the relation between history and psychoanalysis. Although LaCapra gestures towards the Frankfurt School to point out the need to think critical historiography and psychoanalysis together, he omits a consideration of works like 'Psychology and Sociology' in which Adorno cites the way that psychoanalysis claims a false exteriority to the immanence of the social field. This critique is in some ways similar to the one that Foucault levels in *History of Sexuality*, where he analyses the way that psychoanalysis creates categories of desire so as to regulate them, pointing to an immanent relation between power and psychoanalytic knowledge. Deleuze and Guattari, in *Anti-Oedipus*, take this one step further when they link psychoanalysis's Oedipalization of desire to capitalism and fascism.[26]

While it would be ridiculous to link theories of working through to fascism, it is worth noting a similarity between the Oedipalization of desire and the mourning of traumatic ambivalence. Deleuze and Guattari note that the radical innovation of psychoanalysis is the way that it decoded flows of desire, divorcing desire from cognitive rationality. What they question is the way that psychoanalysis 'reaxiomitizes' these decoded flows into a psychoanalytic practice of 'normalization' and Oedipalization. Such an organization leads to the differentiation between neurosis, psychosis, and a third option of 'normal' Oedipalization through proper socialization or psychoanalytic cure. Similarly, LaCapra and Santner introduce the radical ambivalence of traumatic memory only to 'reaxiomatize' it in terms of psychoanalytic procedure. In other words, they introduce the element of radical ambivalence but with the condition that it is dealt with either through narcissistic denial (narrative fetishism), aggravated trauma (acting out) or a process of working through. Psychoanalysis is reified in these writings as the filter through which all memory gets processed. Such an approach overlooks the fact that memory and culture interact in ways that require a reconsideration of the terms as they are re-enunciated (translated) in different cultural contexts.

At its worst such a 'psychoanalyticization' of memory leads to theories like ones that claim that the Holocaust was repressed and absent from public discourse until the 1970s, a view that the reception of *Night and Fog* shows to be a gross oversimplification. Even at their best these theories are inevitably led to overlook an examination of memory like the one that Michael Geyer provided in his recent essay, 'The Politics of Memory in Contemporary Germany.'[27] His account productively analyses many of the ways that memory, or rather 'a culture of memory', emerged in both elite and mass-mediated discourses. His analysis, though informed by psychoanalytic interpretations, does not fall back upon a psychoanalytic reading of memory. It is instead interested in the intersections between memory, generational conflict and cultural power. My brief look at the reception of *Night and Fog* will suggest similar intersections.

Again, I do not want to link theories of mourning to fascist discourse the way that a certain reading of Deleuze and Guattari might. It is, however, at least important to question the stakes of this reaxiomatization of traumatic ambivalence. One stake is an identity politics, which brings me to my third critique of LaCapra and Santner. Both of them, despite their avowed criticism of 'conventional identity', eventually fall back upon an identity politics. LaCapra wants a theory of 'subject positions' and 'partial identifications'. He then goes on to tell us that 'the notion of a subject position is a beginning, not an endpoint, in analysis and argument,' effectively only changing the 'position' of the subject, but fixing it in the same *telos*.[28] This positionality of the subject exists as the prior condition for the negotiation of traumatic ambivalence rather than emerging with it. Santner similarly wants a subject that can play with its boundaries, but in his writing the subject that plays exists prior to that play. These are complications rather than radical revisions of the notion of subjectivity and are perhaps reasons why neither of these writers engaged with the historiographical theory of Michel Foucault, who posits a subject that emerges immanently along with a field of power. In other words, a more radical revision of enlightenment subjectivity is one that sees these 'subject positions' emerging at, not prior to, the enunciative moment of negotiation.

Of course, my critique has no force if it can be reduced to the trend that both LaCapra and Santner criticize in postmodern theory, a trend that has only play and no politics. As I will show, however, anxiety as I have formulated it contains both a critical agency and ethical implications. Mourning, as LaCapra and Santner have suggested, is a partial working through, one that makes a qualified gesture towards a cure even while acknowledging the impossibility and undesirability of such an end. It makes a gesture similar to the one made by Gayatri Spivak when she speaks of 'strategic essentialism' or calls herself a 'deconstructive Marxist', a gesture similar to the kind of cultural politics that has been the focus of many discussions within both American and British academia.[29] These seemingly paradoxical phrases acknowledge a need for politics to operate in essentialist terms, while, at the same time, acknowledging that this essentialism is merely strategic and must simultaneously be dismantled in its contingency.

But is this the only possible option for a politics that avoids the endless repetition of trauma and the over-reductive essentialism of narrative fetishism?

Mourning requires an object (implying specular distance between the object and negotiating subject, a subject ultimately in its 'conventional' sense). It sees a history that cannot possibly have closure, but then goes on to base its politics in the question, 'What of this can we possess?'. This politics of remembrance is one that creates its notion of constructive agency through the act of closing off and operating upon traumatic ambivalence from a procedural ground exterior to it. A politics of the uncanny asks a fundamentally different question. It asks what aspects of history can and do possess us? How can history unsettle us in the way that *Night and Fog* does, corrupting and making uncanny our present forms of representation and repression? How can one remember in such a way that the traumas of the past disrupt our present moment, dispelling and dismantling the fantasies of wholeness that allow for mechanized violence and oppression, that give the '*Volk*' the fantasy of a utopian destiny? How can memory place us in the position of ambivalence, a position that demands negotiation but does not set the rules for it?

The uncanny gives a traumatic past a radical potential. It is similar to the view of historical materialism that Walter Benjamin sets out in his essay, 'Theses on the Philosophy of History' when he writes of a 'present as the "time of the now" [*Jetztzeit*] which is shot through with chips of Messianic time.'[30] It differs in that it makes no claims upon a redemptive moment; offers no 'gate through which the Messiah might enter.'[31] Santner also draws upon Benjamin's work, but the 'stranded objects' of the past only disrupt in distinctly psychoanalytic ways.

The uncanny is not a politics of negation. It is one of ambivalence, and rather than negate certitude, the uncanny problematizes it and destabilizes it. The link between the open ambivalence of anxiety with its paradoxical temporality and the construction of political agency has more recently been explored by Homi Bhabha in his work on the temporality of agency. Similar to my claims about anxiety, Bhabha places the emergence of agency in a time lag between the *telos* of the pedagogical (anxiety as expectation) and the interruptive repetition of the performative (anxiety as traumatic repetition).[32]

At stake here is not just the issue of agency, but also the issue of responsibility, a term that was an essential part of the discourse surrounding *Night and Fog*. To merely negotiate a paradox the way that mourning and working through do is to remain in a position exterior to paradox. Psychoanalysis provides an outside to ambivalence from which it is interpreted at a distance. Conversely, to negotiate through paradox demands a proximity to its historical crisis and calls for a reconsideration of responsibility. Responsibility in a moment of proximity is not one of pure reciprocity or recognition. It is neither the sublation of a Hegelian dialectic, nor simply politics as a form of negation. Being within the paradoxical negotiations of anxiety denies the stability of distance needed for a politics of negation or identification. Anxiety is forever the deferral of identification. It is what prevents us from providing a substantive account of political action. The words of Maurice Blanchot provide a helpful index of the implications of such a position.

> But now [in the moment of disaster or crisis] responsibility – my responsibility for the other, for everyone, without reciprocity – is displaced. No longer does it belong to consciousness ... Responsibility, which separates me from myself (from the 'me' that is mastery and power, from the free and speaking subject) and reveals the other in place of me [we are you], requires that I answer for absence, for passivity. It requires, that is to say, that I answer for the impossibility of being responsible.[33]

History in Blanchot's work unfortunately becomes an endless post-structural disaster of traumatic repetition. We are left with an aporia, not a politics, and it is for this reason that we must question his sense of passivity. Setting these important considerations aside, however, Blanchot's work interestingly points the way to a politics that calls for a new form of responsibility through (not of) the paradoxes of anxiety. This responsibility does not entail, 'in a prosaic, bourgeois manner – a mature, lucid, contentious man, who acts with circumspection, who takes into account all elements of a given situation, calculates and decides.'[34] Blanchot's displaced responsibility is one that requires the viewer to be responsible for the paradox of historical crisis and violent oppression through the paradox of responsibility. It is the openness of an ellipsis, the indeterminacy of an ending, the responsibility not for the means and ends of a traditional historiography nor for a psychoanalytic procedure with its own narrative of memory, but for 'a deferred death: disaster'.[35] The notion of responsibility that I am forwarding is not one where ethical judgement becomes impossible, but rather one where judgement is never finished. Such a judgement, placed in the temporal ambivalence of anxiety, is not a discrete event, and does not occur once and for all.

I would suggest that negotiation is not the agency of a pre-existent subject; it is an enunciative practice. Negotiation through ambivalence creates the subject of negotiation in and at the moment of negotiation. One of Foucault's innovations was to point out that the subject of enunciation does not exist prior to enunciation. This is not to deny, however, a process of differentiation, one that would necessarily distinguish between victim and perpetrator. The subject of enunciation is one that constantly reconstitutes the lines of differentiation, doing so in a field that includes personal memories, cultural morals and political power. Such a model demands the differentiation of victim and perpetrator, but never posits such a differentiation as a prior given, nor as a future fact. To set such differentiation as either prior given or future fact is to no longer negotiate it, to place it somewhere where it can no longer uncannily emerge to haunt us again.

*   *   *

I began this chapter with the historical account of this film's reception because of what I see as the need to translate psychoanalytic terminology into the contingencies of historical contextualization. This points to some of the limits of the model that I have tried to set out through the analysis of this film, limits that are contingent upon both the cinematic apparatus and the historical moment of reception. The emergence of the uncanny is not an inevitable phenomenon in the representation of a traumatic history. Trauma can be 'forgotten' through fetishization or through a variety of cultural mechanisms that have no easy psychoanalytic analogue. Within *Night and Fog*, there is distinct wariness of such closure, and as I pointed out earlier, the 'naturalism' of forgetting, 'Faithful as ever, the grass flourishes on the muster ground,' is replaced by the uncanny disclosure of repression.

The film's evocation of the uncanny functions as a construction. Such a construction, particularly a cinematic construction, must be questioned for its possible ideological distortions. Jean-Louis Baudry asks the question, 'Does the technical nature of optical instruments, directly attached to scientific practice, serve to conceal not only their use in ideological products but also the ideological effects which they may themselves provoke?'[36] We see the potential implications of this in the way that the Nazi camera catalogues the process of extermination, attempting to reduce it to the application of scientific procedure. Resnais puts pressure on such a use of the camera through what was earlier referred to as the moral corruption of the camera, and the film is hyper-aware of the camera and its potential uses. The camera is referred to directly in the first sequence – 'Only the camera goes the round of the blocks' – and one should again note that the first sequence of archival footage is taken from *The Triumph of the Will*. Such references point out and explicitly caution that many of the archival materials used were originally filmed and manipulated by Nazi photographers. My point is simply that for the uncanny to function, its construction must confront the resistances and counter-uses of the specific medium it operates within.

The same specificity is true with respect to the historical moment in which such a representation is received. The restaging of the traumatic event in the process of working through is always in the service of a procedural movement to reduce negative affect. The shift to anxiety is one that I believe is attendant to the openness of enunciation, and one that accounts for the contingencies of the time, place and process of remembrance and representation. The functioning of the uncanny in this film is as contingent upon its place and time of articulation as it is upon the formal construction and editing of the images. The historic centrality of the visual image in the case of Holocaust representations plays a key role in the film's effect. With the many years of official silence about the Holocaust immediately following the war, it was the visual images that said what words could not. Avisar writes, 'Historical photos have been key instruments in transmitting, spreading, and impressing the events of World War II. Since many of the Nazi atrocities were literally unbelievable, the photographic image has become an indispensable evidence of this awful past.'[37] Anton Kaes also notes the distinct ability of film to 'translate the fears and feelings, hopes and delusions and suffering of the victims, all unrecorded and undocumented, into pre-verbal images and thereby trigger memories, associations, and emotions that precede the kind of rational reasoning and logical-linear discourse needed in historiographical writing.'[38] The use of the visual archive was particularly effective at the time of the film's release, because, in light of the relative verbal and written silence, the visual archive was certain to evoke a whole network of pre-verbal imaginings and anxieties about the Holocaust.

Perhaps even more important to the way that the anxiety of the uncanny emerges historically through this film is the relation of the archival material to the war crimes trials. I am not merely referring to the footage of the trials in the film, but also to the way that these trials used archival material as a form of evidence. The status of the visual archive as a form of evidence in the war crimes trials was one that stressed the indexical quality of the medium. As evidence, the visual archive allows one to definitively state 'that all this happened only once, at a certain time and in a certain place,' a view that *Night and Fog*, however, works explicitly against. In figuring archival material as evidence there is the dangerous potential that the archive will stand in for memory as a form of complacent closure, the closure of merely stating 'this happened' without negotiating its implications. The ability of *Night and Fog* to create the scandal that it did was due in a large part to its unsettling of this particular relation between a visual archive and evidence, a relation that must be seen as historically contingent.[39]

Such a claim might seem unfounded, but one only needs to look at the rhetoric of the public debates to substantiate the link that I am making between the uncanny of this film and the status of evidence. What emerged from the scandal at Cannes was a reconsideration of German culpability, not in terms of who did what or what was done, but in terms of thinking more unsettling distinctions between guilt and responsibility. In a sense, *Night and Fog* caused the German public briefly to restage the war crimes trials, not in a courtroom and not in terms of individual culpability (Who did what? What was done?), but in the press, and in terms of national responsibility. This restaging, however, was not in the service of a working through of trauma, but

234 | *Andrew Hebard*

was displaced into a variety of other historical discourses, interacting with a whole range of contentious cultural sites.

Although the rhetoric surrounding the film raised some global questions concerning Germany's position in a newly divided Europe, it concentrated primarily on the issues of guilt [*Schuld*] and responsibility [*Verantwortlichkeit*]. Most of the defences of the film at one point claim that the film is not about blaming the German people, but more about an ethical imperative to confront the past. Willy Brandt is quoted as saying:

> This film does not accuse our people, and I am happy that the horrible questions which it poses do not have to be treated any more as a question of guilt. Nevertheless, there is a new generation coming of age which must know that the therapy of forgetting is not sufficient by itself to come to terms with the past.[40]

The issue of guilt did not drop out, however, for in a sense the public discourse surrounding the film foregrounded it. Interestingly, the critical reception of the film focussed the issue of guilt upon individuals, while the notion of responsibility was figured as a present that generations need for collective, national remembrance. One sees this not just in statements such as, 'There is no collective guilt, but there is the membership of the individual to his people,'[41] but also in the official translation of the film's voice-over. The 'I am not responsible' ['Je ne suis pas responsable'] of the defendants in the scene of the war crimes trials is translated as 'I am not guilty' ['*Ich bin nicht schuld*'] in the German version, allocating the issue of guilt to the past actions of individuals while placing responsibility at the heart of the film's more general message about the need to remember. Although such a move in the public rhetoric is problematic at many levels, I would argue that it also had some distinctly positive effects. At a moment in German history when the public was beginning to negotiate its re-emergence as a nation state along with the anxieties about nationalism that such an emergence would bring, the uncanniness of *Night and Fog*'s represented past became a site for the articulation of generational conflicts and for confronting an ageing ruling class left largely intact after the war. By restaging issues from the war crimes trials, the film became a site of open ambivalence that necessitated a wide range of negotiations – negotiations that did not necessarily confine themselves to the predictable narrative of working through a traumatic past, but rather opened sites for political agency to emerge unpredictably in ways that were not necessarily directed towards the management of the memories from which they sprang.

The reception of *Night and Fog* in Germany exemplifies the ways memories emerge and interact – often in ways that resist or complexify the psychoanalytic paradigm. Even if one were to maintain that the discourse surrounding the film combines all three of the options prescribed by LaCapra and Santner, a close examination of the newspaper articles reveal the multiple (and unexpected) ways the film navigated a field of cultural power, bringing to light generational conflicts and ethical questions of responsibility that were not 'worked through' by the public. In other words, memory opened up a space for negotiation that often had very little to do with the working through, denial, or aggravation of trauma. A politics of anxiety opens up a field of ambivalence in which traumatic ambivalence is not the issue. Instead it is through such ambivalence that other issues come to demand negotiation.

Our current historical situation is, of course, somewhat changed. We are now located in an era when Holocaust remembrance is performed primarily through the media of testimony (*Shoah*, the Yale Video Archives, etc.) or narrative (*Schindler's List*, *Sophie's Choice*, etc.). This is not to say that *Night and Fog* is no longer effective. The montage and juxtaposition of past and present still create a sense of unease. The film also unsettles in new ways. The marked absence of any discussion about the European Jews and the project of genocide, set against a multitude of people in the archival footage wearing Jewish stars, not only reveals the extent of historical repression in the 1950s along with the continual presence of anti-Semitism both then and now, but also perhaps reminds one of the most recent attempts to deny genocide through many of the revisionist histories that have been written over the last ten years. By rendering uncanny the process of repression, this film still confronts and unsettles our current modes of forgetting. With new forms of Holocaust remembrance and representation emerging, with the commercial success of *Schindler's List* (Spielberg, 1993) and the attention afforded to the United States Holocaust Memorial Museum in Washington, a new textuality and contextuality of the familiar is emerging. This is not to deny that the images of the archive are often in excess of the attempt to contain them at any given historical moment, which is just one reason why *Night and Fog* should be afforded another look. Nevertheless, the use of the uncanny in representation must also find new ways of reading against the grain, new ways of unsettling and haunting.

Notes

1. Eds: This article first appeared in *New German Critique* 71 (Spring–Summer, 1997), 87–113. Its significant argument about uncanniness and anxiety remains extremely pertinent to the current discussions that have emerged in the last decade. For the historical study of the critical analysis of the film, we felt it important to include this article in this collection of newer studies.

2. Willy Brandt, 'Mut zur Wahrheit,' *Der Abend*, 14 November 1956.

3. 'Nacht und Nebel Synchronisiert', *Frankfurter Abendpost*, 12 July 1956.

4. Jean-François Lyotard, 'The Différend, the Referent, and the Proper Name', *Diacritics* 14/3 (Fall, 1984), p. 7.

5. Saul Friedlaender, 'Trauma, Memory, and Transference', in Geoffrey H. Hartman (ed.), *Holocaust Remembrance: The Shapes of Memory* (Oxford: Blackwell, 1994), p. 261.

6. The use of psychoanalysis in the current debate is evident in many of the writings that have come out about the Holocaust in the past decade. A few noteworthy examples are the writings of Cathy Caruth, Shoshana Felman, Saul Friedlander, Geoffrey H. Hartman, Dominick LaCapra, Dori Laub and Eric L. Santner.

7. Dominick LaCapra, *Representing the Holocaust: History, Theory, Trauma* (Ithaca, NY: Cornell University Press, 1994); Eric L. Santner, *Stranded Objects: Mourning, Memory and Film in Postwar Germany* (Ithaca, NY: Cornell University Press, 1990). 'Mourning' and 'working through' also emerge as analytical terms for the consideration of other traumatic histories. Mae Henderson's essay 'Toni Morrison's *Beloved*: Re-membering the Body as Historical Text', which provides an analysis of African-American history in Toni Morrison's *Beloved* and Douglas Crimp's work on the cultural politics of the AIDS epidemic in his essay 'Mourning and Militancy' are just two examples. See Mae Henderson, 'Toni Morrison's *Beloved*: Re-membering the Body as Historical Text', in Hortense Spillers and Marjorie Pryse (eds), *Comparative Identities: Race, Sex and Nationality in the Modern Text* (New York: Routledge, 1991); Douglas Crimp, 'Mourning and Militancy', in Russel Ferguson, Martha Gever, Trinh T. Minha and Cornell West (eds), *Out There: Marginalization and Contemporary Cultures* (Cambridge, MA: MIT Press, 1990).

8. Dominick LaCapra, *Representing the Holocaust*, p. 192.

9. Dominick LaCapra, *Representing the Holocaust*, p. 193.

10. Eric L. Santner, *Stranded Objects*, p. 29.

11. Eric L. Santner, *Stranded Objects*, p. 50.

12. Dominick LaCapra, *Representing the Holocaust*, p. 193.

13. Eric L. Santner, *Stranded Objects*, p. 20.

14. Shoshana Felman, 'The Return of the Voice: Claude Lanzmann's *Shoah*', in Shoshana Felman and Dori Laub (eds), *Testimony: Crises of Witnessing in Literature, Psychoanalysis and History* (New York: Routledge, 1992), p. 205.

15. Roy Armes, *The Cinema of Alain Resnais* (New York: A.S. Barnes, 1968), p. 50.

16. Leo Bersani and Ulysse Dutoit, *Arts of Impoverishment: Beckett, Rothko and Resnais* (Cambridge, MA: Harvard University Press, 1993), p. 183.

17. Ilan Avisar, *Screening the Holocaust: Cinema's Images of the Unimaginable* (Bloomington, IN: Indiana University Press, 1988), p. 9.

18. Sigmund Freud, 'The Uncanny', *Standard Edition of the Complete Psychological Works of Sigmund Freud*, ed. and trans. James Strachey, Vol. 17 (London: Hogarth Press, 1962), p. 394. Author's emphasis.

19. Sigmund Freud, 'The Uncanny', p. 391.

20. Sigmund Freud, *Inhibitions, Symptoms and Anxiety*, ed. James Strachey, trans. Alix Strachey (New York: W.N. Norton, 1959), p. 102.

21. Sigmund Freud, *Inhibitions, Symptoms and Anxiety*, p. 102.

22. Eric L. Santner, *Stranded Objects*, p. 162.

23. Dominick LaCapra, *Representing the Holocaust*, p. 12.

24. Michel de Certeau, *Heterologies: Discourse on the Other*, trans. Brian Massumi (Minneapolis, MN: University of Minnesota Press, 1986), p. 7.

25. Homi K. Bhabha, *The Location of Culture* (New York: Routledge, 1994), p. 163.

26. Gilles Deleuze and Félix Guattari, *Anti-Oedipus: Capitalism and Schizophrenia*, trans. Robert Hurley, Mark Seem and Helen R. Lane (Minneapolis, MN: University of Minnesota Press, 1983).

27. Michael Geyer, 'The Politics of Memory in Contemporary Germany', in Joan Copjec (ed.), *Radical Evil* (New York: Verso, 1996), pp. 169–200.

28. Dominick LaCapra, *Representing the Holocaust*, p. 13.

29. Gayatri Chakravorty Spivak, *The Post-colonial Critic: Interviews, Strategies, Dialogs*, ed. Sara Harasym (New York: Routledge, 1990).

30. Walter Benjamin, 'Theses on the Philosophy of History', in Hannah Arendt (ed.), *Illuminations*, trans. Harry Zohn (New York: Schocken Books, 1968), p. 263.

31. Walter Benjamin, 'Theses on the Philosophy of History', p. 263.

32. Homi K. Bhabha, 'Dissemination: Time, Narrative and the Margins of the Modern Nation' and 'The Postcolonial and the Postmodern: The Question of Agency', *The Location of Culture*, pp. 139–70 and pp. 171–97.

33. Maurice Blanchot, *The Writing of Disaster*, trans. Ann Smock (Lincoln, NE: University of Nebraska Press, 1986), p. 25.

34. Maurice Blanchot, *The Writing of Disaster*, p. 25.

35. Maurice Blanchot, *The Writing of Disaster*, p. 146.

36. Jean-Louis Baudry, 'Ideological Effects of the Basic Cinematographic Apparatus', in Philip Rosen (ed.), *Narrative, Apparatus, Ideology* (New York: Columbia University Press, 1986), pp. 286–7.

37. Ilan Avisar, *Screening the Holocaust*, p. 4.

38. Anton Kaes, 'Holocaust and the End of History: Postmodern Historiography in Cinema', in Saul Friedlaender (ed.), *Probing the Limits of Representation: Nazism and the Final Solution* (Cambridge, MA: Harvard University Press), p. 208.

39. One need only look at the Rodney King trial to see just how historically contingent this relation is.

40. Willy Brandt, 'Mut zur Wahrheit'.

41. *Stuttgarter Zeitung*, 3 July 1956.

Cinema as a Slaughterbench of History: *Night and Fog*

John Mowitt

Preface 2010

Some films, such as what are now referred to as 'blockbusters', bear or solicit repeated viewing because they are marketed that way. One returns to them – even repeatedly – because the prospect of not being part of their 'market share', their 'draw' is, if not intolerable, then certainly unacceptable. Oddly, it is as if we refuse, in relation to such films, to abandon the very sociality whose destruction they both herald and, at the same time, defer.

Other films, such as Resnais's *Night and Fog*, bear or solicit repeated viewing because repeated viewing forms their very subject matter. It is not that they are simply enigmatic or overflowing with what Benjamin might have called 'cult' value. Not at all. These are films, and they are unusual without being exactly rare, that stage, even on a first viewing, the problem, the socio-historical event of repetition. *Night and Fog* is nothing if not such a film. It speaks to us of repetition, of seeing seeing and listening to listening, from within the very event avowed by many to be the very essence of the unrepeatable. Never again. Again.

What follows exhibits this very structure, this very rhythm. It is a two-part study that joins an early analysis of *Night and Fog* to a re-visitation, a showing, of both the film and its analysis. As such it seeks to do justice to, to take responsibility for, something at work within the film that might otherwise have simply escaped attention. That is, the fact that what lies concentrated, coiled up, within the film is the incitement to screen that which is and remains resolutely off-screen. Not the Holocaust, but our cinematic intimacy with it.

1987

A splinter in your eye is the best magnifying glass.
Theodor W. Adorno[1]

I

Hegel remarks somewhere near the beginning of his introduction to *The Philosophy of History* that reflection on history leads one to see it as 'the slaughter-bench at which the happiness of peoples, the wisdom of states, and the virtues of individuals have been victimized.'[2] Though not explicitly thematized, Hegel does indicate that this experience of history belongs to the epoch in which the *principium individuationis* has asserted itself with a vengeance in the subjectivity of the middle class. It was up to Marx to link the tragedy of irreversible historical loss to the farce of middle-class consciousness in which history appeared as the product of isolated, 'thing-like' strivings. The irony of *The Philosophy of History* having been written during the century of middle-class self-assertion was stripped of its humorous aspect in the wake of fascism. Deplorably, a more brutal rejection of the false sublation of the tension between individuals and the historical process is once again becoming imaginable. Those, however, who seek or have sought to root the genealogy of fascism in the texts of Hegel do not always recognize, and, therefore, seek to justify, the equation their efforts draw between history and its representation – whether philosophical or popular. If it makes any sense at all to hold the texts of Hegel responsible for fascism it is because the historical process has, during the epoch of the middle class, caused to blossom a distinctive mode of self-representation and reproduction. This distinctive mode includes as one of its most powerful machines the cinematic apparatus which Walter Benjamin had the foresight to recognize as 'an orchid [*blaue Blum*] in the land of technology'.[3]

For Benjamin, cinema acquired this marvellous status as the result of the dialectical development defining its very character. On the one hand, cinema embodied reality's adjustment to the masses. It was not only the first mode of cultural production through which the masses could appear to themselves; cinema was also a technical embodiment of the political demand that reality register in its appearance the standpoint of the masses. On the other hand, cinema functioned to adjust the masses to what Benjamin in his book on Baudelaire called the 'shock' of industrialized reality. Cinema provided at the level of cultural reception, a corollary to industrialized production where technology 'subjected the human sensorium to a complex kind of training'.[4] This meant that if historical reality was so violated by equipment that an image of unmediated reality was possible only through the supplementary technical operation of editing, then the reality in question was fundamentally constituted by the subject/object dyad. Cinema was an adjustment to an adjustment that precipitated the decay of aura. Its uncanny blossom took root there.

Benjamin was not his own best reader. In his responses to Adorno he acts as though his essay is less dialectical than I have suggested it is.[5] At the moment that mechanical reproduction breaks up auratic art and accelerates the proletarianization of culture, it enables aura to enter historical consciousness for the first time as that which has just been lost. Whatever prematurely utopian conclusions the text could be accused of drawing are tempered by Benjamin's compulsive return to the question of fascism's relation to art. It is clear by the end of the essay that the cinematic apparatus, as an embodiment of mechanical reproducibility, is instrumental to both the aestheticization of politics and the politicizing of art. Before we heave a sigh of relief and draw the obvious conclusion, namely that Benjamin recognized that socialism would not develop simply as a result of a cultural transformation, I think we should pursue at least one of the implications of Benjamin's insight a bit further. This will take us back to my title and forward to the analytic thesis I want to explore in relation to *Night and Fog*.

At the end of the concluding footnote in the essay, Benjamin writes the following:

> Mass movements are usually discerned more clearly by a camera than by the naked eye. A bird's eye view best captures gatherings of hundreds of thousands. And even though such a view may be as accessible to the human eye as it is to the camera. The image received by the eye cannot be enlarged the way a negative is enlarged. This means that mass movements, including war, constitute a form of human behaviour which particularly favours mechanical equipment.[6]

I am particularly interested in the last sentence whose force will be best gauged if we situate it explicitly in the context I have been developing.

The dissemination of monumental history and the authority of the original upon which it was based was achieved through the violence of mechanical reproduction. The result of this breakup is that reality, and especially the historical record of reality as a decisive dimension of culture, is put at the disposal of the masses who have been adjusted to its fragmentary character. In aesthetic terms, cinema immediately outflanks the debates about its status as an art form by deconstructing – for better or for worse – the *episteme* inside of which the terms of the debate are rooted. Politically, cinema is more contradictory, because it seems, unavoidably, to fuse the possibility of proletarianizing social reality and the violent dissemination of the very historical process that brought cinema into being. The decay of aura is not restricted to the aesthetic dimension because by definition this decay involves the transformation of this dimension as such. Cinema irrevocably politicizes culture once the aesthetic must resort to electro-shock in order to survive.

The much anticipated moment of world historical consciousness on the part of the proletariat apparently coincides with a substitution of cinema for those 'arts of memory' which had previously served to gather the events of history; a substitution that constituted a definitive tear in the already frayed historical fabric. Moreover, this substitution confirmed the discursivity of history that now poses as the very reality of history itself. This substitution may have been the first and last media event – perhaps this is because it is still taking place. What is decisive here, is not whether this development implies that the masses can no longer act upon or within 'real' history. Instead, Benjamin, in a manner that is wholly consistent with the view articulated in his fifteenth thesis on history, is arguing that the cinematic apparatus is itself a manifestation of the concrete proletarianization of historical reality. The dialectic, which Benjamin was frequently accused of betraying, operates here to fuse this position with what is at stake in the Hegelian metaphor of the slaughterbench.

Instead of being fashionably late, as is the philosopher's habit, Hegel was embarassingly early. History becomes a slaughterbench only after the slaughterbench has become an editing table where the mechanical orchid winds down its petals. Individuals are made victims of the production of history when the technological violation of reality that makes cinema at once possible and responsible for the production of an image of unmediated reality has displaced them. The collective agency of the masses that is expressed in this displacement remains a terrifying murmur as long as the equipment world remains in invisible hands. As Foucault once cautioned, it is perhaps impossible to represent cinematically the subjectivity of the masses and yet, if Benjamin is right, cinema cannot help but do this. The masses may only 'appear' in the working apparatus and the absences it creates.[7] Is this not the implication of Benjamin's reference to Baudelaire's '*Le Squelette laboureur*', where Benjamin recognizes the secret presence of the crowd in the mechanically reproduced engravings of skeletons?[8]

Let us return to the long neglected citation from Benjamin's remarkable essay. Its final sentence ('This means that mass movements, including war, constitute a form of human behaviour which particularly favours mechanical equipment'), which otherwise simply punctuates the argument bearing on the representational side of reality's adjustment to the masses, can be reversed and read as a disturbing dialectical diagnosis. In other words, because wars, for example, so favour mechanical equipment (and here Benjamin is simply being a Marxist historian), is it not conceivable that mechanical equipment, particularly those machines which embody the capacity to make history on a mass scale, could help precipitate those conditions under which they would be brought to perform that task with which they share such a special affinity: representing a mass movement. In the footnote from which the citation was extracted Benjamin mentions newsreels as specific examples; I see no reason to restrict the implications of this reading to this application of the cinematic apparatus. Even if we temper these implications by remarking that cinematic technology is only a single apparatus in an ensemble capable of contributing to the precipitation of an international conflict, the historical weight on cinema remains heavy. This is perhaps nowhere more pressing than in the genre of film referred to today as 'direct cinema', where Benjamin's observations about the cinematic violation of historical reality have become axiomatic.[9]

In 1955, Heidegger was asked to address publicly the topic, 'Art in the Technological Age'. He delivered a lecture entitled, 'The Question Concerning Technology' which developed themes first presented in two papers read six years earlier. A brief discussion of Heidegger's position will help to sharpen the cutting edge of Benjamin's analysis and clarify the problematic I am developing here.

Towards the end of the 1949 lecture entitled, 'The Turning', Heidegger argued that under the rule of radio and film we were becoming people whose senses of hearing and seeing were perishing. In the context established by 'The Question Concerning Technology', this observation places film on the side of technology in the opposition between 'Enframing' and *poiesis*. This opposition, though predictable in a certain way, is used by Heidegger to undermine the prevalent instrumental view of technology. Enframing, as the coming into presence of technology, indicates how it is that, '(e)verywhere everything is ordered to stand by, to be immediately at hand, indeed to stand there just so it may be on call for further ordering.'[10] Once reality presents itself in this way, human beings themselves are set upon by the frame of technology so that they grasp themselves as a 'standing-reserve', that is, as mere instrumental potential. The danger here for Heidegger is that enframing forces the mode of presencing characteristic of *poiesis* into oblivion and in the process forgets this very fact. History is reduced to what is chronicled by those empowered to administer oblivion as the stuff of which memories are made. Film, as the agency of a growing blindness, finds its philosophical footing in the oblivion of oblivion that defines the essence of technology for Heidegger. Human beings are the instruments who have been made to recognize in technology only its instrumental character. As such, we are the standing reserve awaiting further ordering.

If, at this point, we recall that a discussion of the Proustian categories of memory frames Benjamin's analysis of Baudelaire, we can see that Heidegger's preoccupations are crucial to the analysis of the decay of aura. Voluntary memory, exemplified in the fragmented, journalistic presentation of facts, is for Benjamin, a presentation of the past that contains no trace of it. He anticipates Heidegger almost explicitly when he writes, '(t)he perpetual readiness of volitional, discursive memory, encouraged by the technique of mechanical reproduction, reduces the scope for the play of the imagination.'[11] What separates Heidegger and Benjamin here are really only two things: first, the slight shift in emphasis from a sense to a faculty and second, the unnerving dialectical tenacity of Benjamin who sees the future garden in the compost of aura. In spite of these differences, both Heidegger and Benjamin oblige us to approach cinema with at least one eye fixed on its forgotten technical character; that dimension of the apparatus that quietly prepares us to await with anticipation the spectacle of our own annihilation.

The problem I have been tracing here becomes particularly acute in the instance where a film seeks to compile evidence that will indict a particular historical development; evidence that includes the cinematic recording of history itself. To explore the strategies open to cinema once faced with this problem, I want to turn our attention to the short film made by Alain Resnais in 1955: *Night and Fog*. Specifically, I want to indicate how this film, both at the level of cinematic statement and at the level of cinematic enunciation, is able to question simultaneously the ideological character of the so-called pro-filmic event and the ideology of cinematic representation itself. To accomplish this, the film must literally retrace its steps as it advances. As a consequence, it is very difficult to see (in) *Night and Fog*. Resnais's film raises the stakes of documentary cinema, making it rather difficult for those who naively trust in the radical authority of the document as such, to remain in the game of cultural politics. Detailing this in relation to *Night and Fog* will obviously have a direct bearing on the broader concerns articulated under the heading of cinema and ideology.

II

In turning to the film proper, it should be understood that my reading is organized by three preliminary questions. First, what is at stake in having titled the film itself, *Night and Fog*? Second, is there any sense in which cinema itself, despite the grammatical problem, serves as a response to the question posed at the close of the film – 'But, then, who is responsible?'. Third, how is cinema's relation to the historical production of the past enunciated by the film? Obviously these questions are neither independent nor exhaustive.

Despite the fact that this film involved the collaborative efforts of Resnais, Hanns Eisler, Jean Cayrol and Chris Marker – all figures who have been instrumental in the articulation of a cultural problematic that currently orients much theoretical activity – *Night and Fog* has not received much sustained critical attention.[12] The exceptional treatments of it are, nonetheless, provocative. In reading William F. Van Wert's 'Point/Counterpoint in *Hiroshima mon amour*', I was struck by the following sentence: 'And, whereas the piercing mobile camera of *Night and Fog* functioned primarily to enter into the unpeopled past, the mobile camera in *Hiroshima*, in dealing with the past of Nevers, surrounds it with lateral pans, reserving the forward tracking

244 | *John Mowitt*

shots for entry into the asphalt and neon of rebuilt Hiroshima.'[13] Whether Van Wert is right about the typological claim he is making is not as interesting to me as his characterization of the camera movement in *Night and Fog* as 'piercing'. Presumably because he is really concerned about *Hiroshima mon amour*, Van Wert does not bother to ponder the curious relation between a camera piercing into an unpeopled past and a film indictment of the fascist technologies designed to relieve the past of an obscene number of people. Guattari's claim notwithstanding ('Everybody wants to be a fascist'), this cortical feature of the film is not explicable in terms of Resnais's unconscious fascist tendencies.[14] The relation between the depicted horrors and the act of filming is far too systematically elaborated to be simply unconscious. Consider the following sequence.

Following a pattern I will later detail, the film confronts us with a cut that joins a long, left to right, tracking shot of what the narration refers to as a 'surgical block', to a close-up, black-and-white photograph of a Nazi doctor. He is looking off frame to the left. The next cut is to newsreel or documentary footage of what the narration identifies as a 'disquieting nurse'. She is cropped at the waist and is also looking off frame to the left. The subsequent cut is to more black-and-white photography and documentary footage. We enter a room full of surgical equipment, approaching an operating table in a medium shot that bisects the room obliquely, front to back. The narration asks, 'Here is the decor, but what is behind it? Useless operations, amputations, experimental mutilations.' Beneath the narration another cut occurs placing us above the table top, still bisecting the room from front to rear but now from right to left (Plate 30).

What unsettles one about the deep grooves we see inscribed on the table top is not just the fact that they are designed to channel the blood of innocent victims, but that these grooves serve as the directional models for the very shots that have brought them to our attention (Plate 31). Fortuitous, perhaps. But what about the narration? 'Decor' is as denotatively rich in English as it is in French. Clearly, it is used ironically in the film to mark the medical equipment as a façade behind which sadistic violence is perpetrated. But the irony does not stop here. This sequence fits into a syntagmatic code of erasure that characterizes the film.[15] 'Decor' also refers to the cinematic *mise-en-scène* as such. The narration, therefore, also addresses the façade of the photographs and documentary footage that has been compiled as the 'scenery' of *Night and Fog*. What is behind this decor? Little that is tremendously different from what was behind the medical equipment – cutting or, in keeping with the letter of the narration, 'experimental mutilations'. The film quite literally places itself under erasure here and it is not, therefore, surprising that this brief tour of the operating room concludes with a centred image of the slaughterbench traversed by the characteristic lines of erasure. The frame is graphically cancelled.[16]

Before generalizing from this brief sequence, let us attempt to situate it within a larger filmic pattern. Most commentators on *Night and Fog* succeed in drawing our attention to its methodical alternation of the past and the present. Clearly this is important to the film both thematically and strategically. Thematically, because it immediately raises the question of the present's responsibility for the past as that which could facilitate its repetition. Strategically, because it supports the film's essential reflexivity. It is, however, also important to stress that the film's alternation between the past and the present unavoidably poses the question of editing as the means by which the relation between the past and the present is technically mediated. Certainly any film that raises the issue of the present's relation to its past will, to some extent, thematize its own procedures. What is distinctive about *Night and Fog* is that it succeeds in joining a painful reflection about an atrocious past to an unsettling reflection on the place of the very technical apparatus of memory in the production of that horror. The cinematic ability (shared, of course, with other modes of narrative production) to reorganize the flow of time is held responsible for reducing the historical record to a narrative plot. At the same time, this ability, or at least its technical preconditions, is turned back against themselves in order to condemn any merely well-intentioned attempt to represent cinematically the 'truth' of the Holocaust. In doing this, *Night and Fog* clarifies for the present the scope of the political task at hand.

To fasten these remarks to the film and answer, however provisionally, the questions I have raised regarding it, I will restrict myself to an analysis of its first three segments which include one complete circuit of alternation between the past and the present.

After the title (to which we will return) and the credits (that document the film's relation to the historical record) which are enveloped in Eisler's stringy and brooding score, we are shown an extreme long shot of a field and sky in deep focus. Almost immediately the camera begins to move vertically downward. This crane shot situates us inside a barbed wire enclosure and through a combination of a slight left to right pan and a tracking shot we are transported into the ruins of a concentration camp. The disembodied narration (itself a significant detail) is telling us, 'Even a tranquil landscape, an ordinary field traversed by crows, with harvests and grass fires. Even an ordinary road, where cars, peasants and lovers pass. Even an ordinary village for vacationers with a market and a steeple, can lead to a concentration camp.'[17] Everything referred to in the narration is shown in the image. This surplus of discourse underscores the duplexity of the narrative statements that pivot on the verb 'lead'. From the outset Resnais formulates a political thesis: fascism is a monstrous extension of the dynamics of crisis-ridden capitalism. That which we experience as ordinary or common, harbours terror. On the other hand, and at the same time, the syntagm of the opening configuration of narration and image is itself addressed by the narration. Literally, the shots of fields and roads lead to, that is to say, are succeeded by, shots of a concentration camp. Therefore, with equal immediacy the political thesis of the film is completed: this film is structured so as to lead to a concentration camp, but beyond that the cinematic apparatus itself may lead under certain conditions to the camps. These conditions are presented in the film through the logic that threads together photography, tourism, state surveillance and colonized leisure in late capitalism. Significantly, these issues are underscored at the moment where the film's present is edited with its past. The camera continues tracking left to right on a path perpendicular to the barbed wire fences causing the wires themselves to serve paradoxically as the *lignes de fuite* of Renaissance perspective (Plate 9).

The narration continues. 'The blood has dried, the tongues are silent. The blocks are visited only by a camera. Weeds have grown where prisoners used to walk. The wires are no longer alive. No footstep is heard but our own.' Abruptly, we cut to black-and-white footage that we recognize as apparently documentary material. It depicts storm troopers goosestepping shot from a very low angle to accentuate the compositional rhythm of the marching legs (Plate 10). A subtitle positions us, '1933'. The narration states, 'The machine gets under way.' What has happened?

It would appear that we have stepped into the past. But have we? First, there is the ambiguity established by the narration's relation to the image. The line, 'no footstep is heard but our own,' lies twice. We never hear the film crew's footsteps and the only footsteps we see – but do not hear (a staccato roll on a snare drum serves as the aural metaphor) – are those of the Nazi soldiers. The noisy unheard footsteps belong therefore to both film crew and soldiers. How could we step into the past if we were already there, though unheard? Moreover, through the ingenious graphic match between the receding fences and the marching soldiers we are momentarily unable to decide whether much has changed in having passed into the past.

Second, there is the problem of deciding what past 'we' have stepped into. Seconds after the initial cut to black-and-white footage which we assume to be documentary, we discover that in fact it is an extended citation of Leni Riefenstahl's *Triumph of the Will* (1935). This raises several problems, not the least of which is the notoriously complex issue of the relation of *Triumph of the Will* to the historical event of the Nazi Party Congress at Nuremberg.[18] Can one document (in the strict sense) a political event staged for a camera crew? To have selected this material to inaugurate the encounter with the past is terribly important. Not only does this selection problematize the notion of 'the' past, but it does so precisely by raising the question of the cinematic production of historical events. As a consequence, the film makes it difficult to decide not just whether we have stepped or not, but whether we have stepped into 'the' past at all. Clearly, this is volatile material for a film which otherwise appears designed to throw light on our relation to the past of fascism. Once again, the filmic enunciation seems to be erasing itself in the very moment of its unwinding. Nonetheless, by turning briefly to the cut that transports us back to the present from the past we can detect how this erasure functions to advance, in fact, the film's analysis and critique.

After making our way through the citation of *Triumph of the Will*, rhythmically intercut still photography and 'genuine' documentary footage, we encounter a fairly long documentary sequence in which deportees are being loaded into cattle trucks under the surveillance of Nazi soldiers and guard dogs. This sequence is only one among many during which one is inclined to ask, 'Why was this filmed?'. Of course, the difficulty of answering this question rebounds back onto *Night and Fog* itself, which struggles to take responsibility for re-posing the problem. For the most part, the deportation sequence, perhaps unconsciously, obeys the cinematic principles of continuity editing (Plates 12–14).

The train is consistently shot so that its intended destination corresponds with the vanishing point of the frame. The code for arriving at the train is established as entering the frame from the left and moving across it to the right. The departure of the train will follow the same path. Everything about this hideous scene is running smoothly until the train actually departs. We should not forget that, as in the opening shots of the film, we are on our way to the camps. It is precisely this match up that signals to us that the film is preparing to confront us with a now familiar problem.

The first several shots of the train's departure have it moving left to right as anticipated (Plate 15). But then a series of reversals occur (Plate 16). The next two shots have the train moving from right to left as though suddenly it had reversed its direction. There is a subsequent shot in which the train is once again moving left to right. And then, once the train arrives at nightfall, its motion is again reversed (Plate 17). Significantly, this is when, for the first time since the title, the phrase 'night and fog' is introduced in the narration. It occurs as a description of the conditions of the deportees' arrival at the camps. Immediately following the shot of the train's arrival we cut to the brightly coloured present where the narrator continues: 'Today, along the same tracks, it is a day with sun. We travel slowly along them, looking for what? For a trace of the corpses that fell out of the cars when the doors were opened? Or the footprints of those first arrivals?' The image here is a medium, high angle shot of the weed-choked tracks (Plate 18). The frame is mobile moving left to right, the shot is, in fact, a tracking shot that ends by panning upward to reveal the ruins of the camp.

Briefly allow me to draw out the decisive details of this sequence and to draw some general conclusions. Just as one steps into the past, one apparently rides into the present. Or do we? On our way to the camps we have turned around several times. Are the camps to the left or to the right? According to the spatial system established in the documentary footage, we actually *arrive* at the camp through the tracking shot in the present, which, in explicit contrast to the documentary shot, occurs during the daytime with the sun out. But what then was the purpose of the documentary footage that otherwise seemed clearly to situate the arrival in the past? Or did it? The shot of the arrival was at night in the fog. The narrator anchored this part of the image for us. As such, the entire theme of 'arrival' is plunged in night and fog. This includes not only the question of arriving at the camp, but the question of arriving in the present from the past. Did we make it or are we now actually on the tracks that lead to the present. There is little hope of containing the effects of this development. The film itself, appearing under the cover of *Night and Fog*, enters this dizzying historical spiral. Moreover, once we recognize that the cinematic apparatus is itself implicated in the tracking shot bridging the past and the present, the camps and our photographic memories, we can both identify this moment of the film as another instance of its erasure and clarify the political stakes of this procedure.

In a rather systematic fashion, *Night and Fog* implicates cinema in the horror it has compiled. The two transitions I have analysed are not isolated. Significantly, the conditions of night and fog are announced at the very moment where the past is edited to the present. The film is named after this uncanny transition. Why?

The second and last time the title appears in the diegesis, it opens a sequence delineating the humiliating and sinister classificatory system used by the Nazis to position and survey the deportees. Those who fall outside (specifically in what was decreed to be the 'occupied territories') the categories marked by the various coloured triangles, end up in the nebular class of those otherwise lacking classification, *'Nacht und Nebel'*. The close-up in which we see the N/N inscription on the prisoner's jacket exhibits a *mise en scène* that bears an uncanny resemblance to the title credits that open the film (Plates 1 and 21).

The film is at once victim and instrument of victimization. Precisely because *Night and Fog* has unsettled this relation in the context of an equally unsettling examination of the relation between cinema and history, the fact that it is itself unclassifiable stands forth as a cunning condemnation of the cinematic documentation of history. All cinematic attempts to negate the possibility of a second Holocaust are challenged to enunciate and thereby break their complicity.

Benjamin's analysis of cinema clarifies the circumstances under which cinema can be recognized as the slaughterbench of history by connecting cinema's adjustment of the subject/object dyad, the instrumentalization of memory that breaks up the aura of tradition and the representation of the masses who are, through the breakup of tradition, deprived of the means to register themselves in the symbolic order. This is why aura, above all, must be lived as an historical loss. *Night and Fog* bears the imprint of these developments. Cinema's part in the enframing that leads us to treat ourselves as a standing reserve waiting to be ordered is, however, turned against the apparatus itself by this film. Resnais refuses to represent the subjectivity of the masses. Like Baudelaire he signals their presence in the traces left by their annihilation before the camera. We are shown gaping latrines, bunks, eyeglasses, ovens, photographs and documentaries – everything marking an absence that mechanical reproduction has caused to appear. Perhaps only by marking the means by which this absence has been marked can the slaughterbench be recognized for what is has become, namely, the most pressing forgotten political problem of our time. *Night and Fog* does not tell us to abandon cinema, but it does enable us to experience the necessity of pursuing into its darkest chambers those aspects of cinema that give us every right to.

Night and Fog wants to raise the political question of responsibility. Yet, like Oedipus, it discovers that as the investigation proceeds its own historical traces are part of the trail it is following. Though this discovery could have led to two versions of a rather classical blindness – paralysing self-flagellation or righteous self-deception – it leads to neither. Instead of putting its eyes out, *Night and Fog* places itself in the range of its narrator's question by ruining the immediacy of historical vision. By attempting to show cinematically how the cinematic apparatus mediates our relation to the history of the present, Resnais erases the reality effect of cinema while allowing us to see beneath the erasure, the machinic character of historical reality in the age of late capitalism and its modes of cultural reproduction. Perhaps only by placing its own technical character on trial while engaged in a necessary historical reflection can a film of the Holocaust show us what we should no longer have to see. *Night and Fog* is what it says it is. It restricts our visibility not because it has anything to hide, but because we have forgotten that it cannot show us the truth. Unfortunately, we need, perhaps as much now as ever before, more films that are difficult if not impossible to see.

Après la lettre

In March 2008 I was invited to present – or as I countered, 'show' – the preceding essay at the 'Concentrationary Memories' seminar convened at the University of Leeds. Aware that almost a quarter of a century had passed since its conception, it seemed appropriate to reconstruct the context of the text; not in order to fasten the text – and this of all texts (given its argument) – to the past, but in being clearer about the distance travelled, to put pressure on those aspects of the text that would allow it to speak more immediately to the seminar it inspired.

The piece was originally presented as a conference paper at the annual meeting of the Midwest Modern Language Association. It emerged from a course I was offering on the topic of 'cinema and ideology', and was written expressly in the context of the national debate regarding the Brady Bill (a handgun control bill finally passed by the US Congress in 1993, but rescinded in 1998). Public debate regarding the bill, a debate whose terms then and now have largely been set by lobbyists for the National Rifle Association, had reached a now familiar impasse: guns do not kill people, people do, or, if guns are outlawed, only outlaws will have guns. Uncomfortable with the alternative – simply aligning with law enforcement's demand that it have a monopoly on guns – I set out to speculate in a different direction. Without succumbing to the dubious wisdom to be found in Erik Barnouw's sentence, 'Papyrus begat bureaucracy,' it seemed worth considering not only that guns in fact kill people, but perhaps they even incite collaboration in their use.[19] In effect, guns provoke people to kill people. Recent high profile cases in the US suggest that even the police – those professionally trained in the use of firearms – not only abuse them (firing many more bullets into 'suspects' than necessary), but are legally indemnified for doing so.

For reasons that seem over-determined if mysterious, the gun control debate of the 1980s was triggered by the Reagan assassination attempt in 1981. If the Freudian concept of 'over-determination' is relevant here it is because the assassination was multiply cinematic. Not only was Reagan a former film star (his last film was Don Siegel's *The Killers* from 1964 in which he plays a brutal mob boss), but the assassin 'wanna-be', John Hinckley, was acting to impress another film star, Jodie Foster. He had fallen in love with her upon compulsive re-screenings of Martin Scorsese's *Taxi Driver* (1976). This was a film about, among other things, the attempted assassination of a candidate for public office in which Foster played a child prostitute, named, so as to ensure that no one missed the film's reflexive optic, Iris. Story of the eye indeed.

The force of the cinema here, as crystallized in the collapse of viewfinder and gun scope, brought vividly to mind the line from Susan Sontag's 1977 book, *On Photography*, that I had assigned to my class: 'Like guns and cars, cameras are fantasy machines whose use is addictive.'[20] Indeed, it was from a fortuitous encounter between this essay, and the introduction to Hegel's *Philosophy of History* that the title of my own was derived.

Such speculations formed the analytical hunch that informed my thinking about *Night and Fog*. Perhaps one way to make sense of some of the reflexive risks it seemed to be taking was in terms of a meditation on the force, perhaps even addictive force, of the cinema. Of course, the 1980s and 1985 in particular was when Claude Lanzmann's exhausting film *Shoah* made its debut, rejoining the debate over the historical reality of the Holocaust recently reanimated in France by the shouting match between Robert Faurisson and Jean-François Lyotard. Not long after I finished my essay, Lanzmann screened *Shoah* in Minneapolis. I had the good fortune, I think, to participate in a roundtable discussion with him, and try out a version of my argument about *Night and Fog*. After first objecting to the perceived suggestion that his work was not original, he put his difference of opinion on the table. What bothered him was the ethically ambiguous way in which I read the film so as to clarify how 'the cinema' might be its answer to the question posed towards the film's end: but then who is responsible? As Max Silverman has observed in his thought-provoking study of Jean Cayrol's contribution to Resnais's film, this is a profoundly unsettling suggestion; for it rebounds directly upon the very medium of the statement's enunciation.[21] For Lanzmann, *Shoah* was concerned with ethical ambiguity and self-deception, but from a secure distance, and this despite the fact, as I insisted, that his film seemed every bit as concerned with trains and tracking shots as Resnais's. Needless to say, I stuck to my guns.

My epigraph was an afterthought, but one that elegantly condensed the logic of my analysis. It derives from the section of Adorno's *Minima Moralia* (published only four years before Resnais's film) called, in inadvertent homage to Meerepol and Holiday's masterpiece, 'Strange Fruit', 'Dwarf Fruit'.[22] It served as a condensation by proposing that one sees more about seeing in rendering sight obstructed, even painful. Oddly, this section serves a similar strategic purpose for Adorno. Written while in exile and working with Horkheimer on *Dialectic of Enlightenment*, the aphorisms gathered under this heading are snapshots of the damaged life that figures in the volume's subtitle ('Reflections from Damaged Life'), condensed perhaps in the zinger? 'In psycho-analysis nothing is true except the exaggerations.'[23] If truth be told, were I in a position to have used a clip from the film as my epigraph it might well have been the following.

This brief ghoulish pan through a gas chamber opens with the longstanding cinematic motif of the screen as a window. The window is barred (Plate 34). Perversely, it reminds those familiar with it of the painting, Moritz von Schwind's 'The Prisoner's Dream', that serves as the frontispiece to volume 15 of the *Standard Edition of the Complete Works of Sigmund Freud*. The camera dollies and pans away as if cornered (Plates 35 and 36). The narration in this brief sequence reminds us – 'the only sign, but one would have to know it' – that we cannot see the most disturbing visual evidence of extermination without the supplement of knowledge. In Lacanian terms one might say that here gaze encroaches upon, even splinters, vision.

The sequence closes on a geometric *trompe l'oeil*, a corner that both regresses and egresses while tracing the perspective lines of the viewfinder. For the spectator the question of spatial orientation – is one in the corner or outside the block – becomes acute. As with Adorno's splinter, seeing the question of seeing as posed by that most in need of being seen, the Holocaust.

However deftly either the aphorism or the film sequence can be said to capture the logic of the analysis, the aphorism's accent on perception only indirectly (see footnote 11) posed the theme of the seminar, 'Concentrationary Memories'. Elaborated at somewhat greater length is the important distinction made by Benjamin (drawing on Proust) between voluntary and involuntary memory. If the former is, in effect, an archive of erasure, could we not argue that Resnais's implication of the cinema in the atrocity whose imminent erasure only hastens its eternal recurrence, is already both a critique of historiography and a subtle meditation on the politics of memory? It may even be a statement about 'concentrationary memory'.

How so? 'Concentrationary', in English, is an inelegant word. As such it warns that a certain philosophical unpleasantness, perhaps even the unpleasantness of philosophy itself in the era of deliverables, is near. In fact, it aspires to a certain ontological generality, a condition of existing that, like Heidegger's *Angst*, is pervasive, not unsurpassable as Lukács would have it, but pervasive. Reading David Rousset's *L'Univers concentrationnaire* one finds a concerted effort to think the general state of affairs that survives the camp as its perverse afterglow, one that expresses itself, if in an unabashedly masculinist register as 'castrated brains' (a figure that has its warrant in a brief segment depicting survivors from Resnais's film).[24] In short, intellectual sterility as the upgraded and abridged form of the social contract. One finds a similar notion in Cayrol where, as I note above (note 12), the concentrationary is written as the *Lazarean*. Both Cayrol and Rousset are concerned with the motif sounded in the final moments of the film where spectators are warned against believing that the monster is dead, that the past is past. This is not just a plea for heightened vigilance, a repudiation of false confidence. More profoundly, it is recognition that something that has survived the camps, for Adorno, the world in which lyric poetry was unseemly if not impossible, has taken hold. In terms of a reflection on concentrationary memory, this concern, as crystallized in Resnais's motif of the undead monster, obliges us to think carefully about the relation between memories (as mental content) and memory (as mental faculty) and whether it has succumbed to the concentrationary. Put interrogatively: does the solemn oath, 'never forget', already express the oblivion to which the faculty of memory has succumbed in treating mental contents as the objects of forgetting? Is this the most insidious form of the concentrationary?

With Cayrol things become even more perplexing. To invoke Max Silverman a final time, it seems urgent to extend some of his insights concerning the important roles that Cayrol and Roland Barthes played in each other's careers, by reading the following passage from one of the latter's several early essays on Cayrol, 'Erasure'. There is here much more at stake than the *chosisme* that earlier caught my eye.

> We know where this work comes from: from the concentration camps. The proof of which is that *Lazarus Among Us (Lazare parmi nous)*, a work that effects the first junction between the experience of the camps and literary reflection, contains in germ, with great exactitude, all of Cayrol's subsequent work. 'For a Lazarean Literature,' [an essay in LAU] is a programme still being carried out today in a nearly literal fashion: the best commentary on *Muriel* is *Lazarus Among Us*. What must be suggested, if not explained, is how such a work, whose germ lies in a dated history, is nonetheless fully a literature of today. The first reason for this may be that the Concentrational is not dead; there occur in the world odd concentrative impulses, insidious, deformed, familiar, cut off from their historical model but spread in the fashion of a style; Cayrol's novels are the very passage from the concentrative event to a concentrative daily life.'[25]

On earlier pages of this essay, Barthes has emphasized precisely those aspects of Cayrol's writing – the neutrality of narrative voice, the absence of the author, the obsessive but impassioned race of words and things, and so on – that he later understands as textuality. If there is even a grain of truth in the contention that the Theory of the Text arose at the invaginated border between literature and philosophy, then Barthes's point about Cayrol's novel serving as the relay between literature and post-war daily life might clearly be thought to imply not only that his project is 'concentrational' (to preserve his wording), but that the entirety of so-called French new criticism – from early Barthes to late Derrida – its style, is concentrational. While this certainly helps us to understand the proto-deconstructive gesturing to be found in *Night and Fog*, to put it with brutal concision, the politics of complicity, it also challenges us to think carefully about our own relation to such a concentrationary. The question is not first and foremost the merely cynical one – is the framing of concentrationary memory itself concentrationary? – but rather what might be the intellectual cost of our not being able to decide whether it is or it is not? Castration is far too divisive a word, but the matter is important. What incapacity is it that drives us to think in the style that we do?

Although 'Cinema as a Slaughterbench of History' notes elements of the soundtrack (for example, the aural metaphor of steps and drums), no sustained effort is made to weave Eisler's score into the texture of Resnais's meditation on cinematic complicity in the Holocaust. Precisely because, in light of the foregoing, this may be construed as an avatar of the concentrationary, more deserves to be said. Although the authorship of *Composing for the Films* has long been a contentious matter, one can say with reasonable certainty that 'Melody is what one always misses' is an aphorism penned by Eisler.[26] In English it contains an important semantic instability, one that links through 'misses', longing (and in that general sense, memory) and failure. Thus, melody is what one misses most about a composition when it is no longer being performed, but melody is also what, even while the composition in question is being performed, is what fails to take place, to be there. It is already the piece missing from the piece. Certainly one way to stabilize this instability is to regard melody as what in a composition streaks ahead, so to speak, to the moment in which it will be missed. It is the future anterior, what will have been missed. If Eisler's aphorism is brought to bear on his score for *Night and Fog*, however, another less obvious way to approach the two 'misses' stakes its claim upon our attention. Consider here the passage on music that Cayrol cites from Chaplet's *Light in the Darkness*, a passage adduced to demonstrate the very proposition advanced in Barthes's reading of Cayrol.

> Maurice proposed that I attend a rehearsal of his quartet. I followed him through a block that had always seemed mysterious to me (the scene takes place at Buchenwald [authorial interpolation]). Some rare privileges were extended those admitted there. It was here that the pathologists worked. They dissected cadavers and edited reports on diseases (*maladies*). The musicians set up in this museum where the pared decapitated heads of detainees, rotten lungs, intestines, hearts, and viscera would soak in jars. On the shelves figures shrunken in the manner used by the Jivaro were lined up. ... I sat near to hear a quartet by Haydn. Close to me half a face bathed in alcohol. The eye was open. It stared at me. It was impossible to escape. The gaze came from the beyond, inexpressive and glassy, but alive. I changed seats preferring to this heady witness, the lobes of a brain where narrow bloody channels flowed. Haydn spread his grace over this sinister collection. Maurice listened to sublime passages. Aroused, leaning on their mats, heads forward, the invalids seemed to be exiting a tomb. Mute, fascinated, they were under the spell of a miraculous apparition. They did not know that Mozart was being performed for them. They were told, but the name had little importance: it was music; it worked on them, it transfigured them ... a dazzling spectacle passed before their eyes, a form of paradise, a luminous whiteness that provoked their tears. Resuscitated in their rags, marvellously consoled, and when the incantation was finished they would thank Maurice, their missionary.[27]

Cayrol locates the concentrationary in the juxtaposition of the barbaric and the sublime. It finds its reiteration in the film when the narration, in tracking the 'surprises' to be found in the camps lists both zoos and orchestras among them. Indeed, in one scene the narrator observes that an orchestra is playing a '*marche d'opérette*' as prisoners trundle off to their toil (pointedly *not* work). But there is a discrepancy, and it is an important one. Eisler is neither Haydn nor Mozart. In this film, there is no sublime, only the barbaric. Literally. There is, in fact, what Rifaterre might call the musical 'hypogram', the generative kernel of the piece that, to my ears, derives from the melodic motif that organizes Bartók's 'Allegro Barbaro'. C G# F (for the sake of example). Consider, for example, what is being played by the oboe in the sequence of shots documenting the end of the day of toil. This melodic material appears at about 12 minutes into the recorded score, and repeats at 15 minutes, again on the oboe, but this time performed under two gruesome photographs of dead prisoners entangled on the barbed wire that has frustrated their escape. Originally introduced on the piano (perhaps in homage to the fact that it was composed for solo piano), but in strident, fortissimo chords, this material winds its way through the score drifting back and forth between winds and strings, and stated sometimes in inverted form. What separates it most sharply from the Bartók melody is the second part of the phrase: in Bartók the shifting, almost menacing G# F G# F, G# F G# F, and in Eisler the more tentative C C G# F. Here then the melody is missing not for reasons already given, but because it is the nature of the hypogram, as with the figure of god the watchmaker, to disappear, to go into hiding once the process it controls is triggered. It is missing in the sense that the repressed is missing from the dream in which it takes shape and gives form. This is not really about the anxiety of influence or some compromise of originality, but rather in this case, the status of an Hungarian ethnomusicologist in the context of what Adorno and Eisler would call 'advanced or authentic music'. Spelled half in German — *Volk* music — the vexed matter becomes easier to get one's head around. Perhaps this is how we should make sense of Adorno's obvious ambivalence toward Bartók where, for example in 'On the Social Situation of Music', he tries, by periodizing the corpus, to wedge the Hungarian between the adored Schönberg and the despised Stravinsky.

The discrepancy between a Haydn and an Eisler generates others. These, like Lichtenberg figures, branch through the entire film. Among them, the absence of synchronization between images and sounds that generates the wood-windy lyricism of forced deportation, but also the utter muteness of the past, is nowhere more emphatic then when, in citing/dubbing Streicher's speech in *Triumph of the Will* he speaks French and he says something completely other than what he is recorded as having said at the podium. In fact, his recorded (actually, re-recorded, obviously someone really wanted this in there) line, 'The nation that does not value its racial purity will perish,' is the only explicitly racist statement in the entire film. Given that the *Nacht und Nebel Erlass* cancelled national sovereignty and with it *habeas corpus* in the occupied territories, it may have seemed more urgent to invoke the theme of national unison.

Put differently, if it makes sense to ask after the concentrationary character of the visual style of Resnais's film, then it makes no less sense to pose this question not only to the score and soundtrack of the film, but to the style that results from their interplay with the image track. At the risk of ending on an unstable note, if *Night and Fog* still reaches us, this is not chiefly due to the stunning character of its achievement, but to the difficulty of the questions it reminds us we have yet to come to terms with.

Notes

1. Theodor W. Adorno, *Minima Moralia: Reflections from Damaged Life*, trans. E.F.N. Jephcott (London: Verso, 1978), p. 50.
2. Georg Wilhelm Friedrich Hegel, *The Philosophy of History*, trans. J. Sibree (New York: Dover, 1956), p. 21.
3. Walter Benjamin, *Illuminations*, ed. Hannah Arendt, trans. Harry Zohn (New York: Schocken, 1969), p. 233.
4. Walter Benjamin, *Illuminations*, p. 132.
5. Ronald Taylor (ed.) *Aesthetics and Politics* (London: New Left Books, 1977), pp. 134–41.
6. Walter Benjamin, 'The Work of Art in the Age of Mechanical Reproduction', *Illuminations*, p. 251.
7. Michel Foucault, 'Film and Popular Memory', trans. M. Jordin, *Radical Philosophy* 11 (1975), p. 26.
8. Walter Benjamin, *Illuminations*, p. 123.
9. Jean-Louis Comolli, Untitled contribution to Christopher Williams, *Realism in Cinema* (London: Routledge Kegan Paul, 1980), pp. 226–7.
10. Martin Heidegger, *The Question Concerning Technology and Other Essays*, trans. W. Lovitt (New York: Harper Colophon Books, 1977), p. 17.
11. Walter Benjamin, 'The Work of Art', p. 146.
12. Jean Cayrol, a frequent contributor to the early *Tel Quel*, had developed what he called a 'Lazarean' or 'concentrationary' literature in the wake of his experience in the camps during the Second World War. In his discussion of Cayrol, Maurice Nadeau (in *Le roman français depuis la guerre*) claims that he never wrote an account of his 'life' in the camp. I wonder if the script of *Night and Fog* could not be read as exactly that when we consider that Lazarean literature is a precursor to *chosisme* where human experience is entirely mediated by things. Who would speak in a Lazarean confession? The script contains what we can now recognize as an 'enframing' effect. On Cayrol's impact on Resnais's film, see Max Silverman, 'Horror and the Everyday in post-Holocaust France: *Nuit et brouillard* and Concentrationary Art', *French Cultural Studies* 17/1 (2006) pp. 5–18.

13. William F. Van Wert, 'Point/Counterpoint in *Hiroshima mon amour*', *Wide Angle* 2/2 (1978), p. 32.

14. Félix Guattari, 'Everybody Wants to be a Fascist', *Semiotexte* II, 3:86 (1977), reprinted in Félix Guattari, *Chaosophy Collected Essays and Interviews*, ed. Sylvère Lotringer (Cambridge, MA: MIT Press, 1995).

15. I wonder if it might not also be possible to see here an attempt by Resnais to implicate the critical discourse on cinema as well as cinematic practice in his critique. In 1951 Andre Bazin had written a lengthy exploration of cinematic specificity titled 'Cinéma et théâtre', the second part of which contained a segment called 'l'envers du decor'. In this segment Bazin differentiates theatrical and cinematic decor by marking the fact that the latter is, in principle, limitless. Cinematic decor reaches into every corner of reality. Strictly speaking, there is no 'behind' to cinematic decor. Resnais's echoing of this problem simultaneously confirms and cancels Bazin's argument by suggesting that criticism itself is one of the means by which cinema enframes the real.

16. Concerning the concept of erasure, see Jacques Derrida, *Of Grammatology*, trans. G. Spivak (Baltimore, MD: Johns Hopkins University Press, 1976), xiv–xviii and p. 60 in particular. The dynamic character of this 'concept' requires that Resnais's 'piercing' camera be understood, if its critical edge is retained, as an 'apotropaic' stylus. For an elaboration of this term, see Jacques Derrida, *Spurs: Nietzsche's Styles*, trans. B. Harlow (Chicago, IL: University of Chicago Press, 1979).

17. All citations from *Night and Fog* are taken from the English screenplay published in Robert Hughes (ed.), *Film: Book Two – Films of War and Peace* (New York: Grove Press, 1962), pp. 234–55. Translations have been modified to conform to Cayrol's screenplay, 'Nuit et brouillard', published in *L'Avant scène du cinéma* 1 (1961), pp. 51–54.

18. Susan Sontag, 'Fascinating Fascism', in *Under the Sign of Saturn* (New York: Vintage Books, 1980), pp. 78–83.

19. Erik Barnouw, *A Tower In Babel: A History of Broadcasting in the United States, Vol. 1* (New York: Oxford University Press, 1966), p. 3.

20. Susan Sontag, *On Photography* (New York: Delta, 1978), p. 14.

21. Max Silverman, 'Holocaust and the Everyday in Post-Holocaust France', *French Cultural Studies* 17/1 (2006), pp. 5–18.

22 Theodor W. Adorno, 'Dwarf Fruit', in *Minima Moralia: Reflections from Damaged Life*, trans. E. Jephcott (London: New Left Books, 1974).

23. Theodor W. Adorno, 'Dwarf Fruit', p. 49.

24. David Rousset, *L'Univers concentrationnaire* (Paris: Le Pavois, 1946) translated into English as *The Other Kingdom* (New York: Cornell Press, 1947) in the United States and as *A World Apart* (1951) in the United Kingdom.

25. Roland Barthes, *The Rustle of Language*, trans. R. Howard (New York: Hill and Wang, 1986), p. 187 and Roland Barthes, *Oeuvres Complètes, Vol. 2*, ed. Eric Marty (Paris: du Seuil, 2002), p. 599, translation modified.

26. Hanns Eisler, *A Rebel in Music*, trans. Marjorie Meyer (New York: International Publishers, 1978), p. 24.

27. Jean Cayrol, *Lazare parmi nous* (Paris: du Seuil, 1950), pp. 81–82.

CHAPTER 11

Death in the Image:
The Responsibility of Aesthetics in *Night and Fog* (1955) and *Kapò* (1959)

GRISELDA POLLOCK

I

In his essay against commitment – *engagement* – in art written in 1962, Theodor Adorno addressed the problem of aesthetics and suffering: 'I have no wish to soften the saying that to write lyric poetry after Auschwitz is barbaric: it expresses *in negative form* the impulse which inspires committed literature.'[1] This debate between Sartre and Adorno about politics and aesthetics, between existentialist commitment and disenchanted Marxism, between political intentionality and self-consciously artistic formalism may seem remote to us today. None the less, it introduces the key question I aim to propose in this chapter: responsibility in the image towards the atrociously dead that we may have to encounter in works of art or film that take upon themselves the burden of remembering atrocity.

It was, paradoxically, Sartre himself whom Adorno quoted to pose the question if, after such atrocious violence and violation of humanity as when 'men beat people until their bones break in their bodies', art has any right to exist at all.[2] Does the excessive quality of such a reality knock out the conditions for metaphysics, for art as imaginative fiction? None the less, Adorno asserts: 'the abundance of real suffering tolerates no forgetting.'[3] Is representation – doomed as barbaric – to be understood as being distinct from the required but still aesthetic act of remembering? Disqualified by overwhelming reality, art cannot meet that reality for it is by definition not-reality. It is metaphysical. Yet art now faces a demand to create and sustain memory. Thus, while the reality of certain historical events in their catastrophic extremity of both human violence towards vulnerable others and human suffering extinguishes the very grounds for art as the imagining and transfiguring of suffering and violence, at the same time, Adorno suggests, 'it is now virtually in art alone that suffering can still find its own voice, consolation, without being *immediately* betrayed by it' (my emphasis).[4]

Betrayed art may – must – ultimately be. How can it not be once this has indeed happened in the real? What, however, is the brief moment of possibility of genuine encounter between art and the real that it must invoke for us, for those who must become the affected and also thinking subjects of the event's posterity? Here Adorno has smuggled in a distinction between the aesthetic, encoded in lyric poetry indulging in the individual's intensified sensibility and romantic subjectivity, and the formal radicalism of avant-garde, modernist aesthetics that might, in their *formal* violations of the lyric impulse and the illusory consciousness it sustains, allow to art, but only *momentarily*, a 'terrifying power' – that is, a power to *terrorize* us.

Detailing the brave case of composer Arnold Schönberg's recitative, *The Survivor of Warsaw* (1947), Adorno regretfully notes that even this avant-garde musical stylization that attests to the final hours of the resistance in the Warsaw Ghetto betrays itself ultimately by the final affirmation of its Chorus singing *Schema! Israel* as the survivors die. This moment of elevation betrays the work's witnessing, offering to the listeners redemption of the suffering through inescapably attributing meaning to it – human dignity and faith survives despite all inflicted upon it.

Thus Adorno warns against the terrible possibility of the emergence of genocide as a theme, or worse, a genre, in a literature or an art, that appears to be politically committed, or even morally motivated by the need to remember. Such a development integrates the horror into regularizing cultural forms, despite the political intent of the artist, making it 'easier to play along with the culture which gave birth to murder.'[5] For one thing, the tendency is to affirm that even in horrific circumstances, humanity still flourishes and thus to console the culture that despite all its beastliness, humanity will or can survive. It is here that cultural practice fails to register in its own body and flesh, as it were, the terrible wounding to the flesh of human bodies and, in effect, to humanity itself, effected by the novel political event of systematic industrial, state-sponsored genocidal murder. Indirectly indicting Sartrean existentialism, which proposes a common human condition suspended above the general existential nothingness, and which disables the necessary distinction between executioners and victims, Adorno proceeds to examine the practices of Franz Kafka, who preceded and Samuel Beckett who succeeded 'what everyone knows and no one will admit'. Adorno declares that Beckett's works:

...deal with a highly concrete historical reality: *the abdication of the subject*. Beckett's *Ecce Homo* is what human beings have become. As though with eyes drained of tears, they stare silently out of his sentences. The spell they cast, which also binds them, is lifted by being reflected in them. However, the minimal promise of happiness they contain, which refuses to be traded for comfort, cannot be had for a less price than total dislocation, to the point of wordlessness.[6]

Then, linking Beckett's plays with Kafka's prose, Adorno asserts that they

arouse a fear which existentialism merely talks about. By dismantling appearance, they explode from *within the art* which committed proclamation subjugates from without, and hence only in appearance. The inescapability of their work *compels* a change of attitude which committed works merely demand (my emphasis).[7]

Adorno substitutes affect for representation – talking about. Fear takes hold to displace Aristotelian mimetic representation and its vicarious catharsis. Affect is generated from within the artwork of the calculated, avant-garde formalization of the real of barbarism. Thus a formally strategic dislocation of the humanist and humanizing aspirations of bourgeois culture, seeing itself mirrored in lyric poetics, does not so much produce a representation, a mediated translation of feeling or history. It is itself an event that the spectator must now witness and, through being subjected to the affective work, be compelled into a change of attitude, a transformation that is at once subjective and cognitive. In Beckett plays, that is, actors are not allowed to interpret the character; directors have no freedom to reframe the text because Beckett crafted every dimension to inhibit such interpretative 'play'. Audiences cease to be spectators; they are forced to endure what is present/presented, becoming obligated witnesses to an event – non-event – that happens in its relentless temporal duration before their eyes and disenchanted minds.

From Adorno's 'after Auschwitz' indictment of 'Commitment', published in 1962, I want to derive a larger theoretical and political context within which to place the debate about aesthetics and historical catastrophe: about the distinction between the contradictory potential of self-critically aesthetic (not merely aestheticizing) forms and practices for either creating resistance or offering consolation. The aesthetic *after Auschwitz* is the Beckettian paradox of a destroyed art that inflicts its own violence, *formally*, an art that may thus incite resistance to that which – unrepresented – produces this violence, through an encounter created by means of artistic practice. Resistance resists the endemic, embedded, seeping allure of fascism – the culture that gave rise to murder being shared between fascism and those who appeared to oppose it, but, in effect, failed to stop it. Resistance also resists the desire for the consolation of art, a consolation that distracts us from the necessity of constant vigilance against totalitarianism and its menace that is an ever-present possibility. Totalitarianism may be understood here as the extreme instance of all that is not progressive and democratizing, in any sense, in modern, industrial capitalist social formations, precisely at their more anguished and confused mismatching of ideology and necessity. In what follows I am going to use Adorno's argument to approach *Night and Fog* obliquely through a film that has been presented as its counter-face, a fictional recreation of the concentration camp experience, in order to ask if Resnais's filmic strategies do indeed escape the problems for which *Kapò*, my counter-example, has been condemned by those who elevate *Night and Fog*.

II

A *close-up* of a woman's face: an actress, Emmanuelle Riva acts for the camera with well-trained micro-movements of her striking and affecting features (Fig. 11.1).

The close-up is one of the definitive elements of the cinematic. It is a paradox involving enlargement (in French *gros plan*) and proximity (close-up). Mary-Ann Doane has tracked the centrality of the close-up across major bodies of film theory, including that of Gilles Deleuze for whom the close-up, be it of people or things is always not only a face, but is *faciality* itself. 'As for the face itself, we will not say that the close-up deals with it or subjects it to some kind of treatment: there is no close-up of the face, the face is itself the close-up, the close-up is by itself face and both are affect, affection image.'[8] Doane also

Figure 11.1 Still from *Kapò* (Gilles Pontecorvo, 1958). Close up: Terese (Emmanuelle Riva)

commends the dissonant point of view expressed by Sergei Eisenstein who saw the close-up shot as an enlargement rather than as a zoomed-in-on detail; thus Eisenstein proposes a politics of the close-up. Doane writes: 'As opposed to the American cinema's use of close-up to suggest proximity, intimacy, knowledge of interiority, Eisenstein argues for a disproportion that transforms the image into a sign, an epistemological tool, undermining identification and hence empowering the spectator as analyst of, rather than vessel for, meaning.'[9] Doane furthermore notes that while the viewer often remembers the close-up extracted from and stilling the narrative, suspending time and collapsing space, the production of meaning by means of the close-up generally occurs only because of the shot sequencing within which the close-up functions semantically through alternations, rhymes and differences.[10]

Figure 11.2   Still from *Kapò* (Gilles Pontecorvo, 1958). Electrification on the wires

Figure 11.3   Still from *Kapò* (Gilles Pontecorvo, 1958). Close up of Terese, dead

Drawing on all three arguments, I want to discuss the sequence initiated by the close-up of a woman's face. Let me describe it. We see, close-up, a woman whose brows are furrowed. Her gaze is uncertain with eyes unfocussed and a little downcast. Her mouth hovers ever so slightly open. These are the dramatic signs that connote inner anguish; the unfocussed gaze and opened mouth signal indetermination, and thus indicate imminent decision. Thus in the next shot, the woman suddenly turns away from the camera and begins to run into the opening cinematic space that the camera's pull backwards opens up. Another woman, with dark hair and black jacket, moves across the camera's vision. On her arm an armband with the letters KAPO. She shouts to the running woman to halt. The woman, seen now from the front, dressed in baggy, striped prisoner's garb with a number above a dark, inverted triangle, runs across the open space between two barracks, crossing a line of other women prisoners being marched by another black-jacketed KAPO. We hear an order repeatedly screamed: *Stop!* Dramatic music assists the running prisoner to her destination. There is then a cut and the camera now awaits the running prisoner's arrival; the camera is positioned on the outside of an electrified barbed wire fence that defines the periphery of the camp. We see clearly the ceramic bulbs that carry the deadly charge. Screaming, the woman runs at the fence and, as she grasps it with both hands, she and the screen are engulfed in brilliant illumination, signifying visually the electrocution she has sought (Fig. 11.2). A cut follows to a second close-up, of her now-passive face behind a single line of barbed wire, immobile against the flowing movement of disturbed prisoners who form a thronging background for her deadly stillness (Fig. 11.3).

Then, situated at a short distance from the hanging body, again outside the fence, the camera begins a tracking shot that moves in at 45 degrees and slightly curves around to rest, not quite frontally, framing the woman, her face now obscured by a double-strand of roughly intertwined barbed wire. Both arms are now raised high above her head, her hands no longer gripping the deadly wires but gracefully, almost balletically, posed against the sky in a modernized, crucifixion pose (Fig. 11.4).

There are continuity issues here about the single wire versus the double wires behind which the woman is positioned after death and about the relation of hands to head and the action of the hands, which, after electrocution, would remain gripped to the deadly wire. It is, however, the planned and choreographed tracking shot leading to a second close-up that has become the focus of a major debate about the morality of cinematic representations of death and the politics of the cinematic image in the context of the concentrationary as memory.

In *Cahiers du cinéma*, 1961, the auteurist critic and director Jacques Rivette (b.1928) wrote a short piece titled 'De l'Abjection/On Abjection' that

Figure 11.4a Still from *Kapò* (Gilles Pontecorvo, 1958). The tracking shot begins

Figure 11.4b Still from *Kapò* (Gilles Pontecorvo, 1958). The tracking shot closes in

sets the film, *Kapò* by Gillo Pontecorvo (1959), from which this scene has been extracted, against Resnais's *Night and Fog* (1955) through the lens of the then urgent 'politique des auteurs': translated as the authorship debate, it loses the vivid sense of a politics of representation.[11]

The tracking shot which follows the scene described above when a starved and punished inmate, Terese, played by Emmanuelle Riva, kills herself against the electrified fence is the moment, for Rivette, of a total and contemptible abjection that damns Pontecorvo's film and the filmmaker – although, in the film's story and its telling, there is so much to disown or to despair over. Rivette condemns *Kapò* through a reading of the aesthetic and political immorality of a single tracking shot that has become an exemplary demonstration for auteurist criticism. 'La politique des auteurs' refuses the distinction between form and content and seeks instead to identify the moral compass of a film as a whole. It refuses to treat the film as the expressive unity created out of a single creative mind. The author is not the originating consciousness; rather across a film text's many codes and processes, the film registers a distinctive attitude that may then be named with an author name. The author is the effect not the origin. Auteurism, however, holds the auteur *responsible* for the tone, nuance and point of view that penetrate every aspect of the film, from choice of shot to *mise-en-scène*, from dialogue to acting style. Resisting incipient structuralism and semiotics, which disenchants by focussing only on the inherent hence impersonal textuality of film as language, and without succumbing to romanticist individualism, Rivette, in a manner not unrelated to Adorno's debate with Sartrean *engagement*, takes the filmmaker to task for the effects of a formal, filmmaking decision that contaminates the 'morality' of the entire film.

In his brief review, Rivette argues that tackling a subject such as the concentration camps – the topic of *Kapò* – demands that the director ask 'certain preliminary questions'. Due to incoherence, inanity or cowardice, Pontecorvo, representing the logical culmination of a certain Italian formalism, did not do so. Without this self-critical anxiety before this subject matter, the film falls into its own anti-politics, despite the 'commitment' exhibited by the director in choosing the subject, writing a screenplay and directing one of the earliest fictionalized representations of the concentrationary universe.

The first question Rivette demands that Pontecorvo should have considered is the problem posed by cinematic realism in relation to the 'real' of what its conventions of realism would reconstruct. Making a film about the concentrationary will place the horrific reality of the event in the hands of 'realistic' reconstruction, with actors re-enacting on constructed sets. It would inevitably produce the simulation of violence and of death which the spectators would consume knowing it to be an image of a death that is not real, however realistically the film attempts to deliver it scenographically and dramatically. Given the egregious nature of the event to be reconstructed cinematically, even the most attentive verisimilitude is doomed, according to Rivette, to remain *unachieved*. Instead, the transposed event will be exposed to the spectator's voyeurism and worse, the possibility of pornography.

For cinema to sell its pleasures to buying customers, whatever is shown must, by definition, be tolerable to the viewer. As a result of inevitable modifications of the event's horror to accommodate the tolerability of being shown/seen, the viewer may derive from the fact that the cinema has made the scene bearable, if not moving, and at times aesthetically or even erotically pleasurable, that, perhaps, the event thus represented, might also have been just about tolerable, even survivable for the human being. Narrative cinema, moreover, demands a closure and an exit strategy for the viewer. If stunned silence is often the response to watching Resnais's *Night and Fog,* it is, in part, because that film provides no closure. Its final scenes deal with the trial of perpetrators and it ends under confusing and menacing ruins beneath which, the voice-over suggests, lurk the germs of a continuing concentrationary pestilence. Narrative cinema ends when we can accept who will not make it and who must survive as the viewer's surrogate, confirming continuity even while cathartically sacrificing someone whose loss or destruction the audience has been led to tolerate.

Rivette argues that accommodating the concentrationary to the necessities of cinematic realism in commercially determined narrative cinema produces an inevitably anodyne version of the horror that may adjust its viewers, piecemeal, to violence, making them increasingly accustomed to horror:

> At the same time, everyone unknowingly becomes accustomed to the horror which little by little is accepted by morality, and will quickly become part of the mental landscape of modern man. Who, the next time, will be able to be surprised or irritated at that which will in effect have ceased to be *shocking?*[12]

Against Pontecorvo's 'thoughtless', inadequately considered use of the conventions of fictional cinema's modes of representational realism to reconstruct the concentrationary universe, Rivette poses Resnais's *Night and Fog:*

> It's here that one understands that the force of *Night and Fog* came less from [its use of] records than from montage...

Thus Rivette defends Resnais's choices in the formal organization – the art not the content – and his manner of showing.

> ...from the art with which the brute *real* facts were (alas!) offered to our gaze, in a restless movement that is precisely that of a lucid consciousness, somewhat impersonal, that is unable to accept or understand or admit this phenomenon. One could see more monstrous records elsewhere than those retained by Resnais: but what isn't man able to accustom himself to? Yet you cannot accustom yourself to *Night and Fog;* the point is that the filmmaker judges that which he shows and is judged by the way in which he shows it.

Thoughtfulness on the part of the auteur induces thought at the level of the spectator. The restless movement of the camera and the pacing of the montage signal the lucid consciousness on the part of the filmmaker in having considered a mode appropriate to the seeing and showing of its selection of the material traces of the event. It is at this point in the argument that Rivette targets as the quintessential moment of abjection in Pontecorvo's film *Kapò* the tracking shot or rather a dolly in to tilt up, to linger and to freeze-frame the body of a woman who has thrown herself to die on the electrified wire with which I opened this section. This is the moment from which as a still – differently posed yet again – the scene has been used on the cover of the DVD release of the film. It functions there as the unconscious confirmation of the scene as iconic of the entire film, but for a very different reason from Rivette's highly critical objections. Far from focussing on the pacifying conflation of femininity and death, which I shall discuss later, that assists in making horror bearable, Rivette expresses and demands of others profound contempt for the filmmaker, Pontecorvo. Why? Because he decided to make a tracking shot that repeated and thus prolonged, while soliciting and nourishing, the viewer's scopic if not sadistic mastery of the image of the beautiful dead woman, pathetically reposed for the photographic frame and aestheticized as a modern crucifixion, endowing the unprecedently novel political reality of the concentrationary universe which is the film's ostensible topic with pre-existing, Christianized tropes of pathos on the one hand, and feminized, aestheticized death on the other.

In the documentary photographs that show Resnais and his crew at work at Auschwitz-Birkenau setting up the opening shots of *Night and Fog* (see cover image), we can see that the making of the opening tilts and pans involves considerable preparation as the tracks have to be laid for the camera to be dollied or the crane has to be elevated for the tilt.[13] Thus Pontecorvo's tracking shot cannot be arbitrary. It had to be planned, accepted and confirmed in the shooting script, rehearsed, constructed, costed, paid for in time and extra labour.

From Rivette's auteurist point of view, it is the attitude, tone or nuance adopted by the director to what he decides to film and how he does so that, at the same moment, decides or declares his attitude to the world and everything. The choice of shot, the aesthetic decision is at the same time an ethico-political reflex and index. The problem resides, therefore, firmly at the level of production that is identical with the strategic conceptualization of the film as a series of shots that require careful preparation in order to be cinematographically realized. Refusing to separate form from content, production process from result and effect, Rivette places the defining element for judgement in the *thoughtfulness* (again I purposively invoke Arendt's condemnation of the banality of evil as lying in *thoughtlessness*) of choices made with regard to the attitude towards the topic because this attitude will also predetermine the attitude that the spectator will be invited to share.

There are things that should not be addressed except in the throes of fear and trembling; death is one of them, without a doubt; and how, at the moment of filming something so mysterious, could one not feel like an impostor? It would be better in any case to ask oneself the question, and to include the interrogation, in some way, in what is being filmed; but doubt is surely what Pontecorvo and his ilk most lack.[14]

For Rivette, cinema is primarily about *showing;* it offers something to be seen and hence simultaneously proposes a position from which the world is disclosed to a *viewing* consciousness; it generates a cognitive response initiated by the visual encounter with a world. Hence cinema implicates an ethics that penetrates every aspect including its technological, formal and aesthetic procedures. This does not imply transparency; rather Rivette is trying to specify what makes the image *qua* image visible to us as a procedure that represents decision, thought, attitude, rather than as mere essence seen in the mirror of the camera. For instance, in a very similar vein, philosopher and cinéphile Jacques Rancière argues that film shows us images that 'refer to nothing else: they are the performance.' Of Bresson's films, Rancière writes:

The images of *Au Hasard Balthasar* are not primarily manifestations of the properties of a certain technical medium, but operations: relations between wholes and parts, between visibility and a power of signification and affect associated with it; between expectations and what happens to meet them.[15]

Rancière seeks to define imageness as the dialectic of visibility and signification: 'Cinematic images are primarily operations, relations between the sayable and the visible, ways of playing with the before and after, cause and effect.'[16]

I do not know if the post-Marxist philosopher Rancière shares any terrain theoretically with new wave director and auteurist critic, Jacques Rivette. They both seem to belong to a French tradition that wishes to specify the *image* in its complex relations between disclosure and analysis, mediated by aesthetic operations, but also bound to a relation to some other, social and historical materiality, that may be made known through an image, and through an image that is not an image *of* that world, but an image created *for* the knowledge of, and response to, the meaning-infused, political world on which the art form reflects *cinematically*.

For Rivette, Resnais is the counter-director and *Night and Fog* the counter-example to Pontecorvo's thoughtless and abject film, *Kapò*. In what follows, I shall subject Rivette's claims on behalf of Resnais's *Night and Fog* to closer examination across the field established by Adorno's critique of politically committed art *after Auschwitz* and Rivette's admonishments about the politics of the shot. Does the distinction between Pontecorvo and Resnais rest on

Rivette's analysis of the shot? What happens if we find Resnais also manipulating images through cutting and extracting them from context, repositioning the spectator in relation to his modifications of a found image? I shall also set a reading of the ways in which Resnais's film shows death in the image (in distinction from Emma Wilson's subtle paper in this volume on the film's fashioning of an encounter with the dead) in a philosophical framework offered by the convergence between Primo Levi and Hannah Arendt as to wherein lies the novel core of the concentrationary. This will raise other kinds of questions of Resnais's own thoughtlessness with regard to his pre-established troping of death, the aesthetic and the feminine in ways which echo what occurs in Pontecorvo's key scenes of death. Having tested out both these lines of argument, I hope to return to the question of Resnais's status as a filmmaker in the Adornian mode of critical formalism.

III

If the making of a film about concentration camps requires preliminary questioning, let me start with some fundamental ones about what an image of that world might concern in relation to two facets already put into play: the face as the site of humanness and alterity and the concentrationary universe as a place of a non-human dying.

On 10 January 1946, Italian chemist and survivor of Auschwitz-Monowitz Primo Levi signed and dated a poem titled: *Shemà*. This means *Listen! Shemà* is in the vocative, a command addressed to another. You – **listen**! Levi is quoting/repeating the opening line of the central and only Jewish declaration of monotheistic faith that is traditionally repeated twice a day on retiring and on rising. Levi's command to *Hear!* is, however, not aimed at fellow-believers. Written by an atheist, secular and politically-active Jewish-Italian scientist, this poetic invocation to pay attention calls to the radically other who never experienced what the writer has survived in that other universe, from which physically he returned but from which psychologically he can never fully return:

> **You** *who live secure*
> *in **your** warm house*
> *who return in the evening to find hot food and friendly faces* (my emphasis).

These are ordinary things. Being thus specified, the reader senses that such conditions of home and hearth are not, however, universally enjoyed. Those fortunate souls who do enjoy them are asked to

> *Consider if this is a man …*

In the history of the world, how could such a question be posed? By whom? The very phrasing insinuates further anxiety that what might be considered beyond question – a man/human being – and taken as given, could, in fact, be suspended such that a 'this' might exist whose humanness is at once unquestionable and disqualified. The question is not: Is this a man or a god? Is this a man or a beast? Is this a man or a devil? 'This' [*Questo*] is not about clear boundaries. It touches on an internal dissolution combined with an external destruction which means that those who live in warm houses with daily food and regular human warmth must confront a fellow being not merely deprived of such comforts, but profoundly compromised in the very human identity he shares with those who do live in warm houses.[17]

The poem proceeds to define the other to be considered in equally precise and simple prose:

> *who labours in the mud/ who knows no peace/ who fights for a crust of bread/ who dies at a yes or a no.*

Relentless work, desperate hunger and arbitrary death define the existence of the concentrationee deprived of time, rest and sufficiency. There follows a repeat: '*Consider if this is a woman*': the poem notes a different list of afflictions of women concentrationees, introducing gender into its potential universalism of human life: '*without hair or name*' and with '*womb cold as a frog in winter*'. Labour, violence, hunger and radical uncertainty are matched by anonymity, erasure of personal identity, desire and the deadness to the future.

At this point, verbal violence erupts in the poem. After a parody of the religious invocations to remember typical of the biblical paragraphs of the *Shema*, the poet uses the injunction 'consider' for a third time: '*Consider that this has been.*' What appeared at first as a philosophical enquiry into the question posed by a certain scenario 'if this is a man' and 'if this is a woman', the demand to consider is now directed at historical fact. *This has been.* The use of this particular tense denies 'this' enclosure in the past. That 'it' has been opens up possibility. But no more thinking. The poet takes over the power of the ancient commandments by demanding eternal faithfulness to what has been: '*Engrave these words on your hearts, repeat them to your children.*' Like the jealous Deuteronomic God of Israel, the poet now thunders his curse for those who do not obey this command to consider relentlessly that this has been:

> *Or may your house crumble, disease render you powerless, your offspring avert their faces from you.*[18]

Astonishing in its economy and power, this poem marks the radical difference between two worlds. It demands of those who have not known the 'other world' from within which the poem is written a consideration of what political philosophers from Arendt to Agamben would recognize as the question: consider if this is a man: that is to say, consider what happened to humanity in the laboratory for the systematic destruction of the humanity of the human in the concentrationary universe. Is it possible to take human beings and sustain them, still just within an organic, physiological life that is no longer *human* living? There is killing, mass murder and atrocity. But Levi is asking the world to consider a dimension of that sphere of horror which can only be spoken because it is the question posed by, and hence the burden carried by, the few who survived it to report on the other world to those whose warm homes and good friends insulated them from such experience and from such eternal knowledge of an abyss on which they trembled and others truly fell. As we know Levi did not believe he was a witness to the true horror and suffering: dying in the gas chambers and worse, the disintegrated living corpse, the *Muselmann*. He is a survivor of the concentrationary antechamber and its parallel, living hell of daily mortification that involved in its survival seeing what was the real destiny of those he might have joined but for rare kindness and luck.[19]

Primo Levi has become renowned as one of the most telling voices of testimony as well as the most measured of analysts of the world in which it became necessary to 'consider if this is a man, consider if this is a woman'. His most famous work, bearing that phrase as its title, was first published in Italian in a print run of only 2,000 copies on 11 October 1947. It was not re-issued until 1958 when Einaudi finally reprinted it. The English edition appeared in 1959 as did the first German edition, the German people being the most central addressee of Levi's writing.

Levi's 1946 poem serves here as an introduction to Alain Resnais's film *Night and Fog*. As a work of cinema, not literature, as itself an economical work of poetic montage and not testimonial narrative, as a work drawing exclusively on documents and not on attempted imaginative reconstruction, as a work commissioned by a French historical committee preserving the memories of the sufferings of political deportees from Occupied France to concentration camps of Germany or Poland and not focussed on the specific and extreme horrors of the genocidal massacre of European Jewish, Roma and Sinti citizens, *Night and Fog* might seem to stand in almost complete distinction to Primo Levi's poetry and literary masterpiece *If this is a Man* written in the immediate aftermath of his impossible 'return'.

In her essay, 'The Concentration Camps', written for the American leftist cultural periodical *Partisan Review* in 1948, the emergent political theorist Hannah Arendt states:

There are numerous such reports by survivors; only a few have been published, partly because, quite understandably, the world wants to hear no more of such things, but also because they all leave the reader cold, that is, as apathetic and baffled as the writer himself, and fail to inspire those passions of outrage and sympathy through which men have always been mobilized for justice, for 'misery that goes too deep arouses not compassion but repugnance and hatred' (Rousset).[20]

This is an important confirmation of the indifference or the inability to absorb witness testimony about which Levi had had nightmares in the camp. He dreaded the lack of interest expressed by the outside world as well as its incapacity for interest in a depth of 'misery' of things 'that, when suffered by men, transform them into "uncomplaining animals" (The Dark Side of the Moon, 1947)'.[21] That which was inflicted on men and women left those who remained human and suffered as such the systematic assault upon their humanness, suspended between human/not human in the eyes of an outside world that seemed unable to consider, with understanding, compassion and political sensitivity, 'if this [the bare survivor and the unwitnessed Muselmann] is a man.' Thus Arendt notes that the French writer and political deportee David Rousset and a German communist prisoner from Buchenwald, Eugen Kogon, who both wrote influential books on the vast German concentration camp system – Rousset giving us the term concentrationary: *l'univers concentrationnaire* – write 'assimilated recollections' for 'the world of the living'. They try to communicate and thus deliver not only books indispensable for understanding the camps, but for comprehension of 'the totalitarian regime as a whole'.[22]

In her subsequent three-part study *The Origins of Totalitarianism*, published in 1951, Hannah Arendt shifts from the suffering of those subjected to the system to the analysis of the system that created the suffering:

> What totalitarian ideologies aim at is not the transformation of the outside world or the revolutionizing transmutation of society, *but the transformation of human nature itself.* The concentration camps are the laboratories where changes in human nature are tested, and their shamefulnesss therefore is not just the business of their inmates and those who ran them according to 'scientific' standards; it is the concern of all men. Suffering, of which there has always been too much on earth, is not the issue, nor is the number of victims. Human nature as such is at stake, and even though it seems that these experiments succeed not in changing man, but only in destroying him, by creating a society in which the nihilistic banality of *homo homini lupus* is constantly realized, one should bear in mind the necessary limitations to an experiment which requires global control in order to show conclusive results.[23]

Primo Levi calls upon the world to contemplate the erosion of a man's humanity at the hands of other men, from the point of view of the surviving prisoner/inmate/concentrationee seeking to rebuild the solidarity between himself and those who lived in warm houses. Arendt, on the other hand, while accepting the fundamental premise that the concentrationary universe was a laboratory for the potential destruction of the human nature of its victims, urges a focus on the experimental, now tried and tested, system itself which was implicitly dependent on world domination, that is, an imperialism in which any 'other' could become victim of such alienation of their humanity. What do these poetic and political analyses imply for representation, iconic and otherwise in film? What would be the image of such an understanding of the concentrationary as a new and terrifying politics rather than as historical aberration enclosed in time and buried in the past?

IV

My copy of the American translation of David Rousset's *L'univers concentrationnaire* appearing as the much muted *The Other Kingdom* bears a single, impressed line drawing of barbed wire down the right side of the front cover. Thus by 1947, a visual trope – barbed wire – was being created for the specific nature of the camp in contrast to the typical image of the carceral with its prison bars, locked gates, enclosed buildings with barred windows. The barbed wire fence becomes a bridge through which to juxtapose two images that would evoke in a viewer the concentrationary universe. The first is from *Night and Fog* (Plate 26), and the second is the still from *Kapò* which I have already introduced (Fig. 11.4).

Iconographically, they appear to represent a similar event that is historically and geographically specific. Repeated, this imagery has become iconic. Is there a relation between the two images? Did one influence or resource the other? Is one a documentary source for the imaginative recreation by the other? Or is the second one a cinematic reiteration and indeed iconization of the other's contingency? Are they both in fact already 'citations' deployed to create cinematic encounters? Are they the chance, but indexical evidence of a terrible event, whose photographic reproduction as an image is as troubling as the event that the photograph captures? If this event is now a photographic sign, that can be repeated in representations such as films, what does cinematic recreation do: does the recycled image authenticate a sense of history or fall prey to the banalization of fiction? What is the event that the image can be either mobilized to document or be recreated to remember? Can what we see tell us what to know? What might we learn about the politics of representation from a comparison of apparently similar content but radically different conditions of production of these two images?

Both appear to represent death. By means of framing, both place the viewer in an encounter with a dead body – with the death of another, but from 'the other side' – of a barbed wire fence.

Let me spend time to start off with the still from *Night and Fog* (Plate 26). Taken on its own, we might first have to ask: are we confronting the self-immolation of a person against an electrified barbed wire fence as might be suggested from the fictional scene in *Kapò* with which I started? That would mean that the viewer is being invited to think about a decision to die made by the now dead man. We would be looking at 'his' death, dying as the result of his own action. Additional historical and cultural knowledge is required to read the signs offered by this photograph, where the black-and-white format already connotes history, the past, documentary evidence. The ceramic bulbs visible on the concrete pillar at the left indicate that the barbed wire fence is electrified, we imagine, to a degree sufficient to cause instant death in contact with its metal conductors. Contextual knowledge is also needed to understand the reasons why such a frightful death by electrocution might seem more desirable than remaining merely incarcerated behind the wire with the figures we read as prisoners because they are behind the wire, that we see in the fictionalized reconstruction of a camp in *Kapò*.

The image from Resnais's film is a cinematic use of a still photograph where its technical stillness underlines its signification: image of a *dead* person. It is, however, a 'quotation' of a photograph. Viewed in its context in Resnais's film, the photograph functions as a degraded remnant, seemingly documenting in its miserable physicality the death of an anonymous

Figure 11.5 Misidentified as *Dead German Kapo on Electrified Fence*, photograph from the Identification Service, Mauthausen, Spring, 1942, Fédération nationale des deportées, internés résistants et patriots

individual prisoner. Documentary research can establish, however, that the photograph belongs to the archives at the concentration camp of Mauthausen (Fig. 11.5). The Mauthausen-Gusen camp complex had been the site of the ordeal of Jean Cayrol, the surrealist poet and deportee invited to collaborate with Alain Resnais by writing the commentary to his montage of photographs and film clips. Is this fact important?

Mauthausen was an infamous major complex of concentration camps and slave labour camps in Austria near Hitler's home town of Linz that was set up in 1940 around an old fortress.[24] Its death toll was about 320,000 and at liberation there were 85,000 just-surviving prisoners. It was one of only two Grade III camps, which were specifically designated to create the most brutal and toughest regime for its inmates of *Vernichtung durch Arbeit: Extermination through Labour*. This meant that malnutrition combined with 12 hours of daily labour starved and exhausted the prisoners who were progressively reduced to the living dead known in Auschwitz as *Muselmänner*, and then killed off by gas van, lethal injection and eventually by Zyklon B in specially built gas chambers. This policy was specifically developed for those designated as the 'the incorrigible political enemies of the Reich' namely the intelligentsia of the home and occupied territories: the educated and higher social classes.[25] Hence it was where many political opponents, Spanish republicans and French resistance fighters were sent, including Jean Cayrol. It was a camp for the enactment of the *Nacht und Nebel* policy of punishment of prisoner and his family by untraceable disappearance. Many of the key images in *Night and Fog* are drawn from the Mauthausen archive (Shots 25, 30, 75, 77, 90, 98, 105, 121, 143, 147, 14, 151, 153, 195).[26]

Despite its adaptation from a huge castellated fortress, the memorial created at Mauthausen is symbolically barbed wire. Barbed wire is identified with the concentrationary in the way in which the cattle truck, after Lanzmann and the Holocaust memorial museums, has become the signifier par excellence of the transportation to genocide. It is now a generalizable political signifier.[27] Barbed wire was initially conceived in 1865 by the Frenchman Louis Jannin. The first patent was, however, registered in the United States in 1867 by Lucien B. Smith, and a second American, Joseph F. Glidden, patented a modified version in 1874. Initially used to constrain cattle in the open ranges of the American grasslands, this technology became a major implement for managing human movement during the First World War, notably across the no-man's-lands. But it was its use on prison walls to prevent escape and as the electrified boundary of Nazi concentration camps after 1933 that would raise this mundane agricultural instrument into its current iconicity as a symbol of oppression in the later twentieth century.

A much-used photograph of survivors at Buchenwald was taken by American war photographer Margaret Bourke-White for *Life* Magazine in

April 1945 (Fig. 11.6). It stands apart from the many that form the horrific archive of images of the liberation of such camps full of dying survivors and piles of corpses; all its figures are blessedly clothed and still alive enough to stand and confront us. Without any background, Bourke-White composed her image across the horizontal axis as a potentially limitless frieze of faces. The former prisoners stare out at the viewer from their other planet. The concentrationary universe is indicated by the striped prison garments and the barbed wire fence behind which these 'liberated' inmates now stand. Yet while they look at us, the spectators, the concentrationees are divided from us by a barbed wire fence that cuts horizontally across their vertically-striped garb as a barely visible barrier that is, none the less, an absolute division. What these men have seen and what they will never cease to carry as images burned into hunger and pain-dulled minds, our sight of them from this side of that frontier cannot imagine. The photograph makes them the metonyms of their own unimaginable trauma that is not shown; it is encrypted in their indecipherable expressions on the other side of these strands of wire. In the structure of the photograph, the wire indexes their suspension as survivors between two worlds, two deaths: the death their humanity suffered in that place and the relief of a death their bodies will later deliver – or that they, like Primo Levi, Paul Célan, Jean Amery and so many others, might actively seek by their own hands.

Figure 11.6   Margaret Bourke-White, *Survivors at Buchenwald, April 1945* (Getty Images)

At the moment of its creation, Bourke-White's photograph shared a terrible novelty with others much more horrific and abjecting. Bourke-White tells us that she was so appalled by what she was asked to record in Buchenwald that she hid behind the camera, allowing her aesthetic judgement of what would compose a fine photograph to protect her against what her eye alone might have to encounter.[28] Thus, I suggest that the aesthetic of this superbly constructed image allows the creation of a signifier for the very difficulty of saying what the boundary of the wire represents at the collision of the concentrationary universe with the incoming gaze of the uncomprehending visitors: the liberators and those who documented the moment of liberation with cameras.

Ten years later, Alain Resnais consolidated the iconic signification of barbed wire by setting up his opening tracking shots at Auschwitz-Birkenau to enable his camera to move firstly from high to low and then left to right (twice), so as to take the viewer through a virtual passage from the outside, everyday world to the interior of that infamous camp of both concentration and genocidal destruction. Such a cinematic gesture might now seem an obvious choice of shot. But it is not. When the Soviet Red Army liberated the Auschwitz I complex in January 1945, they designated a cameraman to film what they found. The Russians had anticipated a triumphant entry through a gate to meet the enclosed but jubilantly-freed prisoners, because they imagined the camp as a typical prison. Nothing of this sort occurred as only slowly and by lengthy explorations did the Soviet troops uncover the terrible reality of this vast, multi-sited factory-city of destruction, itself partially destroyed, littered with dead who had been shot as the SS fled, with some still walking prisoners or those who had died from cold, starvation and disease which menaced the 7,500 remaining inmates. Only in May 1945 did the Russians finally announce to the world what they had discovered at Auschwitz; they also tried to restage their arrival and liberation as they had anticipated it, using now recovered, but still displaced, former prisoners as the extras crowding behind the infamous *Arbeit Macht Frei* gate and joyously welcoming the arriving Soviet troops with an energy and returning human emotions impossible to summon while on the abyss of dying in ice-cold winter in January 1945. This false footage survives but was never shown as it so radically misrepresented the chaotic and horrifying historical reality the Russian troops actually encountered. None the less, it indicates the trope of the gate as figure of entry and exit in contrast to Resnais's insistence on the fineness, the semi-transparency but the absoluteness of the line of barbed wire that demarcated another universe within such proximity to the everyday.[29] *Night and Fog* registers the barbed wire as the material remains of the camp, but, as Max Silverman has noted, it also announces the fundamental premise of the film's trope of a disturbing proximity between the everyday and the horror of the camp, articulated by Jean Cayrol's repeated opening refrain:

Even a quiet landscape ...

Even a meadow with crows ...

Even a country road ...

Even a holiday resort with fair and steeple ...

can lead simply to a concentration camp. (Plates 2–7)

In Eyal Sivan and Michel Khelifi's controversial road movie, *Route 181* (2003) which travels, *Shoah*-style, along the Green Line posited in 1948 by the UN as the division between two putative states of Israel and Palestine, the filmmakers pause at an Israeli factory producing a recent and more lethal elaboration: razor wire. Burdened with the memories of *Night and Fog*, the viewer of *Route 181* cannot but gasp both at the existence of such a factory in Israel and at the manner in which the filmmakers placed it within the film precisely to agitate terrible memories. The factory owner reports that his production was in the doldrums during the 1990s, but now, with the infamous fence/wall and the extended encampments worldwide, business is booming.

Let me return to the still from *Night and Fog*. The flatness of the debased photograph of the dead prisoner on the barbed wire at Mauthausen (Plate 26) already prevents voyeurism while the apparent bleeding from the victim's opened mouth indexes a violent bodily trauma and makes the image teeter towards the horrific. What I want to point out is that this is a cropped image: in Resnais's film, we are looking at a *close-up* extracted from a larger original which occurs as a vertically formatted photograph produced by the Photographic Service of Identification at Mauthausen (Fig. 11.5).

The photograph has been re-identified, controversially, as being of a German Kapo who had been thrown onto the electrified wires as an execution. A wooden pillar is visible in front of the wire with a sign bearing the legend: *Hochspannung Vorsicht! Lebensgefahr – High Voltage Attention! Mortal Danger.* Scholars of the archive of concentrationary photography suggest that the post was temporarily placed there for the taking of the photograph, thus turning this image into a motivated, composed production. The photograph is dated to spring 1942. If this were the correct identification, it would open up several key questions: is the photograph indexical or are such images susceptible to projective readings based on the knowledge or ignorance of the viewer? Does it make a difference that this may be a staged document of an execution to be used as a warning within the camp as opposed to being the chance record of a chance suicide by a desperate inmate? Does it matter to the viewer that while the image clearly captures a moment of violence and death, the dead man might be a Kapo, that is, probably a common criminal placed near the top of the inverted pyramid of power within the camp and that the Kapo was surely responsible for inflicting the violence structural to the regime on other prisoners even though even he may have overstepped the SS rules and been punished by the SS? Or was the man thrown on the wires as warning to other Kapos for transgressions of kindness or lack of brutality? In fact, current opinion disowns this titling and suggests that the image is indeed an image of a prisoner having been thrown onto the wires by the SS, then photographed by the Photographic Service and (mis)labelled as representing a prisoner who has committed suicide or attempted to escape. That such images survive is a result of clandestine and very risky collecting of the evidence by Spanish Republican prisoners.[30]

We cannot know exactly what we are looking at. The point I need to establish is that the image may not be a representative photograph of the death of the ordinary Mauthausen concentrationee; if it is of a Kapo, a German prisoner, he has most likely been executed by the SS and is not attempting to escape the horrors of the camp in which as a Kapo he would have had a privileged if still tough existence. Using the same structure as Bourke-White, the viewer of this photograph, unlike that of the constantly moved, travelling viewer finding him/herself inside the camp by the opening of the film *Night and Fog*, is placed on the outside looking through the wire's horizontal banding. The cropped version of the photograph – a zoom-in to get closer to the dead figure on the wire – appears in Alain Resnais' s *Night and Fog* as shot 143, 14' 36" into the film, as the second shot of what Richard Raskin has called Sequence IX. If Rivette suggests it is not the use of documents *per se* but the montage that determines the value of *Night and Fog*, what has Resnais 'decided' with this crop and its positioning?

Sequence IX follows the prolonged introduction to the internal world of the camp and its insane order. It concludes with a black-and-white photograph, reverse shot through barbed wire looking towards a distant town [in fact, Lublin] (Plate 23), with a grand castle (Plate 24), accompanied by the voice-over speaking of 'the real world' of calm landscapes and previous times which appear in the distance, but not so far away. Verbally and visually, therefore, this sequence directly rhymes with the opening series of colour tracking shots tilting down, then panning from left to right, across the barbed wire boundary, each time revealing that the camera is, in fact, placed inside the perimeter of the camp looking through the screen of barbed wire that marks the fragile, fierce and absolute division between one world and the other, even while they lie in such utter proximity and apparent continuity (Plates 2–9).

Sequence IX follows with a repeat of the opening: a tracking shot at Auschwitz-Birkenau, in colour, locating the camera again at the edge of this divided space, but now it is situated inside one of the observation posts whose variable architectural styles have been described in Sequence IIb which marked the beginning of the concentration camp system as a matter of building enclosures whose visible signs are barbed wire fencing and the observation tower in various fanciful styles: alpine, garage, Japanese, no style. Thus two important visual signs are reconnected in this circular panning shot which is, however, now situated inside the lookout tower (Plate 25). Colour stock marks the present of the time of the filmmaking, which is signalled within the film as the time of remembering a past no longer visible even while its emptied ruins may be visited with all the uncanniness of unpopulated remains. Something of what cannot be shown is, none the less, indexed in the potentially murderous look-out point of surveillance that is momentarily the film's point of view while the voice-over, however, identifies, Levi-like, its subject-position as that of the prisoner:

> *For the inmate,* it [the distant view of the town shown in the previous shot] is an illusion. He belongs only to a closed, self-contained universe, hemmed in by the observation towers where soldiers keep watch, aiming at the prisoners, killing them occasionally out of boredom.

This dislocation between the viewing position, momentarily enacting murderous surveillance, and the evocation of the imprisoned, formally and semantically, calls for resolution. The reverse shot that such a logic of looking demands turns out to be the close-up in the black-and-white photograph of a human figure clutching barbed wires, eyes closed, mouth open, body limp (Plate 26). Thus across this edit, we have been switch-backed into a past that was invisible as the camera surveyed the green grass of the empty camp. From inside Majdanek's watchtower we have been transposed to a camp, not the extermination camp of Auschwitz-Birkenau of the opening colour sequence, but to KZ Mauthausen in Austria. It appears suddenly before us in this degraded, contextless, smudged, black-and-white, and cropped photograph which does not show us a prisoner casually shot for sport. In the manner in which this image appears, we might be tempted to read it as an image of a final act, as desperate as it is political. Are we invited, intended, able to read it as an image of a man claiming the right to have his own death in direct conflict with the arbitrariness of death for sport suggested by the voice-over? Such a self-willed death would be an act that is perverse and courageous in a place which was, Hannah Arendt would argue, defined by its terrible novelty of manufacturing death, or which, according to Adorno, changed all human dying since, there, death was no longer each person's unique human property, inalienable from its human subject. Sarah Kofman declares:

> Since Auschwitz all men, Jews (and) non-Jews, die differently: they do not really die; they survive death, because what took place – back there – without taking place, death in Auschwitz was worse than death.[31]

Ordinary death would have been a release from not only relentless physical torture, but from the psychological torture of incremental destruction of humanness. Thus Arendt argued that one of the horrors of the destruction of the human systematically practised in the concentrationary universe, following the initial alienation of juridical personhood, was the destruction of the moral personality. This itself rendered martyrdom senseless.[32] So is this a senseless death or is it a document of a claim to a *human* dying in the act of repossessing one's own death? Is it the film's logic that determines our answer? If this image is a document of an extremity of suffering that has led a man to kill himself, it is also, in its cruel way, a document of defiance of the disordering of relations between humanness and dying that Hannah Arendt identified as one of the distinctive dimensions of the concentration camp as realized totalitarianism. Whether subsequent historical research returns this particular photograph to its historical specificity as a political execution by the SS of one of their criminal lackeys, Resnais's placement of the image in his film, long before it had begun its work of iconization to become the image of a new kind of dying, is, to say the very least, incoherent and, at worst, a serious misappropriation that offers the spectator neither knowledge of nor a confrontation with historical reality.

What I am seeking to expose in this analysis of a tiny fragment of *Night and Fog* is a disjuncture of a profound order at the point at which the formal cinematic logic of *montage* – making a meaning otherwise not explicit by means of a suturing of two dissonant images through editing – and of *shot/reverse shot* – the production of anticipation in the viewer by creating a point of view that calls for its other in order to foreclose the threat of lack generated in the anticipatory first shot – deliver us to a confrontation with death in an image that does not obey either logic. In a short sequence of three shots without voice-over, accompanied by three notes played on plucked strings, we are moved from this shot from looking *through* the wire fence in close up at the face of the hanging body to a view inside the camp looking down its line at a fence from which is hanging another electrocuted body before returning to a position outside the fence once more looking at two bodies lying on the ground (Plates 27 and 28). Thus here, in *Night and Fog*, is exactly the repetition, the camera's return to the scene that Rivette so disowned in *Kapò*. Does a saving difference lie in Resnais's montage of found images of death in contrast to Pontecorvo's staged, hence falsified scene of death? Does it matter that these are dead *men* and not a woman? What can these images mean or do? Are we looking at death, or at murder, or at execution, or something beyond all three that was the reality of the concentrationary universe of which no survivor or later analyst could truly speak and which infects all iconic residues whatever their historical specificity? Is Resnais's visual track and its disordering or 'failing' of cinematic logics the only glimpse of the profound problematization of 'the limit' that is no longer death as had been known up to this point in history?

There are several other significant moments in *Night and Fog* in which the confrontation with death will be made through the medium of a close-up. For instance, in Shot 174, Resnais places a photograph of an inmate in the 'hospital' dead with staring eyes (Plate 29). In fact, this figure was not in the hospital at Auschwitz where the film places the viewer at that point in the film and the logic of the film might suggest. Research has established that this image is not even of a dead man; it shows a *dying* man in a photograph taken by Germaine Kanova of the French Service Photographique de l'Armée in Vaihingen on 13 April 1945 (Fig. 11.7). Vaihingen was a camp between Karlsruhe and Stuttgart that had been turned into a 'mouroir' – of all perversities, a twilight home for the sick and dying. The Germans had evacuated most of the camp to Dachau except for 700 untransportable prisoners too weak to move. They were left to starve and die. Vaihingen was liberated by French troops and this camp and its imagery were to the French

Figure 11.7   Germaine Kanova, *Dying Man, Vaihingen, 13 April 1945*, photograph, Etablissements cinématiques et photographiques des armées

public what Bergen-Belsen represented to the British and Buchenwald and Dachau to the Americans.[33]

Comparing the original, wide shot photograph by Kanova (Fig. 11.7) with a tightly cropped close-up used in *Night and Fog* allows another formal rhyme to emerge with the intense close-crop of an identity photograph from the Auschwitz Museum that is used in the film (Plate 20) to represent the shock of the prisoner's first encounter with the camp. Disrupting the alternating colour/present – black-and-white/past logic, at that point in the film, Resnais used shots filmed in Auschwitz I in black-and-white, with the camera tracking left to right towards the infamous gate bearing the legend *Arbeit Macht Frei*, creating an image to signify arrival from the outside world. Into this travelling shot he cut an intense, frontal close-up that confronts the viewer with the prisoner's staring shock as if in a mirror. The voice-over reports: 'First sight of the camp; it is another planet' (Plate 20). Later, the dreadful, moving film footage shot by British cameramen of the bulldozers of the British Army clearing a mass of diseased corpses at Bergen-Belsen will be punctuated by Russian footage of a single woman's dead face (Plate 37) and again in Shot 280, the mass will be intersected by a single face.

It is now conventional wisdom in photographic theory to align photography itself with death following Roland Barthes's reflections in *Camera Lucida* and the historical role of the photograph as a *memento mori* and a souvenir of the dead.[34] But here I want to draw out a construction within the film that marks a series of selections and decisions in which the viewer is confronted by means of tightly cropped close-ups with human faces either on the point of death or already dead, but in a manner *captured* by historical photography, because that manner of dying or having died is so radically different from all that had already become a part of photography's relation to mourning and memory, to a once living, now absent, but iconically sustained other. To see what the film shows requires us to open our eyes; to meet the staring but unseeing eyes of others *in extremis* transgresses the conventional protocols – death being a kind of sleep – and summons the viewer into an I-Thou moment based on the face as the site of humanity, identity and the moment of ethical relationship to alterity which has to undo the absolute division of life and death. Do these shocking punctuations of the film with radical close-ups of human faces, dying and dead, function critically as part of the relentless moving (in both physical and affecting senses) of the spectator between the invisible that the camera can revisit (in colour at the sites) without seeing or showing and the *photographic* evidence of sights and encounters by liberators or perpetrators who symptomatically took pictures of the most shocking extreme of a crime against humanity written on *faces*?

Because of the more or less absolute lack of photographic documentation of the process, *Night and Fog* cannot, however, *show* nor revisit the heart of the crime: industrialized mass racist murder which, for some critics of Resnais, should have constituted a specified focus within the film because of a genocide of two racially persecuted victim groups: Jews and the Roma and Sinti.[35] There is no footage of the process of extermination of Jewish Europeans at Treblinka, Sobibor, Chelmno, Belzec. As Joshua Hirsch has shown, the only filmed footage of any aspect of the entire and varied modes of Nazi mass murder of the Jewish Europeans is the two minutes of film made by Reinhard Wiener of a massacre in Liepaga, Latvia in August 1941.[36] How important is this single fact in terms of either documentation and evidence or the possible sources for reconstructive representations aiming to sustain a credible relation to a documented history that posits photography versus moving film?

But *Night and Fog* does address mass murder by several means that by the stage of the film in which the extermination process is introduced have become signatures of the film's formal poetics: the contemporary examination by means of the moving camera of the relics of the industrial installations in which mass murder and cremation occurred: the crematoria's ovens, and the single scene of a lengthy cinematic exploration of the interior and gouged ceiling of the gas chamber at Majdanek (Plate 35). Writing the accompanying text, Jean Cayrol had himself not seen this interior which is presented by a camera vertiginous in its movements that direct the gaze finally upwards and across the roughly textured and scored ceiling. The commentary knows what it cannot say: 'The only sign – but one has to know – is the ceiling scrabbled by fingernails. Even the concrete has been scratched up.' I only discovered the meaning of this phrase through repeated watchings, aided by the script, of Claude Lanzmann's *Shoah* in which Filip Müller, a Czech survivor of the several teams of *Sonderkommando* at Auschwitz I describes in detail the horrific and prolonged process of murder inflicted by Zyklon B poisoning which led the victims to struggle upward over one another to escape the heavy poison gas. Thus while the camera and its crews affirm that we can go to the place, we can never be in the place as it was.[37] There are only indexical signs scored into its fabric and the pan ends in a formal triangle of the bare, empty room's ceiling and corner. This grey-blue tinted shot, erasing the distinction between real-time, colour footage and archive image, jumps to one of the close-ups of a woman, dressed in striped prison garb and a woollen jumper visible beneath it, viewed from above, dull, opaque eyes staring in death (Plate 37).

Sequence XVIIIb (Shots 225–233) which starts at 21'47" into the film, prefaces this cinematic visit to the empty gas chamber marked by past death struggles that is punctuated by the close-up of a dead woman's face, but of a woman who has not been gassed to death and mashed in that deadly struggle against poison gas. Sequence XVIIIb represents a major dissonance. The film thus far has taken us into the concentrationary universe and its barbarous tortures, experiments, abuses of bodies, punishments and perversions. Now the film confronts another process that is exterminatory, not concentrationary: mass killing. Here, I note the emergence of a deeper, phallocentric political unconscious in Resnais's film that is shared, in part, with *Kapò*.

The system of the concentrationary universe is represented by *Night and Fog* by images of inmates who are largely men. At the point at which the process of mass execution and industrial murder has to be introduced, the images are predominantly of women: Sequence XVIIIb runs like this:

Shot 227: Medium shot: Women undressing under surveillance.

Shot 228 Close-up: Similar scene: women seen from behind seated on the ground.

Shot 229 Medium shot: A frieze/procession of naked women standing.

Shot 230 Close to medium shot: Four naked women running across the foreground with clothed soldiers in the background.

I do not intend to illustrate these images since that process would once again expose the subjects of the photograph to exactly what is troubling in the existence of such images and the repeated choice of such images in museums and illustrated books about the Holocaust, and indeed their usage in *Night and Fog*. We need to ask why such images exist, why they have been preserved and why they are so constantly re-used. This raises questions about who took the photographs and why. It also forces us to ask what determines their consistent selection to represent a process of killing that the photographs do not in fact record? Recent historical research into the locations and photographers of the particular selection of images used by Resnais (and so many others since) has corrected and specified both in ways that were not available to Resnais and his team in 1955. Thus we now know that Shot 229, showing a procession of naked women with children in the open air, is not an SS document but a photograph taken by a man called Hille, Bezercksoverwachtsmeister of the Gendarmerie on 14 October 1942 at Mizocz, Rovno, Ukraine as part of a series of seven of which five are extant. They represent the sequences in a punishment massacre of the women and children of the 1,700 inhabitants of the Mizocz ghetto in which a revolt had taken place on 13 October.[38]

The photograph in Shot 230, showing four naked women, clutching their breasts as they run naked before the photographer is also part of a different series taken of a massacre at Liepaga, Latvia on 15–17 December 1941 by Carl Strott who forced the women to run naked before his camera after undressing (he photographed this) and before being shot on the edge of a mass grave (he also photographed this where the women appear to be redressed in underwear).[39] The images all create a viewing position that is violently dominative of the women captured by the camera's gaze. The sadistic predatoriness of a sexualized gaze is overdetermined by racist ideology and the extraordinary, gendered conditions of wartime. Whether the photographer wished to document an atrocity out of outrage (like the filmmaker Wierner at the same place but months earlier discussed by Hirsch) or discontent or whether the pornographic occasion of looking at naked women during a long military campaign, or whatever other motivations we might have to contemplate, our encounter with the images momentarily aligns us with a perpetrator position – even a dissident one, and a masculine, heterosexual one, and possibly/probably a racist point of view, even while we begin to recoil once realizing what we are seeing. Whatever our own politics, the reading of the image prior to our taking a position in relation to what it shows requires a processing of its denotational signs: what are we seeing? Naked women and clothed men.

We might glimpse in these images the perverse actualization of the most famous of modernist paintings, which outraged its Parisian public with the juxtaposition of clothed men and a naked woman, Manet's *Luncheon on the Grass* (Paris, Musée d'Orsay, 1863) or of the valorized image of a classical processional frieze (Shot 229) in which nudity was one of the acceptable visual tropes. Both exemplify deep structures of sexual difference and sexuality that are being re-performed in the photographing of an event that represents the destruction of the very culture from which such tropes are being borrowed.

Yet again I notice that Resnais chose to move in. He cropped the original photograph of the Mizocz massacre, which locates the photographer on high ground looking down in a wide shot on the long procession of women with clothing scattered around them and a clothed, armed guard amongst them. It could be argued that Resnais's effective flattening of the image through the closer-cropping not only stymies the mastery provided by the wide-shot of the original; it allows the filmmaker to make visible at the centre of the image the face of one woman, then turned towards the photographer, introducing into the mass of passively lined up, profiled bodies, a moment of active dissonance, shattering mere voyeuristic appropriation of the naked women by the irruption of an appeal: the face as 'face' calling to the other beyond.[40]

Was it the auteur's thoughtlessness, in the face of the selective archive that contained such images of naked femininity approaching a horrible death, that has troublingly placed this overdetermined imagery of female nudity on view in this film about the concentrationary and at this point of the film, the exterminationary? Or could I defend Resnais by saying that such images were simply the only available archive of imagery with which to represent, within the terms of the film's narrative of its subject, the element of the mass killing? There is, of course, almost no documentation of the Taylorized industrial death in gas chambers that replaced this primitive process of murdering in the Ukraine by shooting. Clearly that is too simplistic.

If, as many critics rightly argue, there can be no representation of the 'core' of the Final Solution because no one remains to bear witness to it, or almost no one could safely document it, this 'place' is the gap, the abyss, that truly defies representation.[41] Our critical questioning, therefore, moves to the manner in which filmmakers 'frame' what cannot be seen, using sequences and montage of 'before' and 'after' images.

Before and *after* will involve showing ordinary people, dressed, walking and moving – such as we see in Shot 221 accompanied by the phrase: the round-up/deportations spread across the whole of Europe – and then, we should expect images of the aftermath. There is, however, no after-image; those killed in gas chambers were totally disappeared by being turned to ash in the crematoria. The aftermath is not a matter of massed unburied corpses; such images of corpses are of those of the abandoned dead at the last gasp of the *concentration* camps of Germany. They are not the sign of the exterminatory atrocity, but concentrationary disintegration during the military defeat.

The point of the mass exterminations is that following death by gassing, bodies were burnt in crematoria (and only rarely, when these malfunctioned, on pyres). The destroyed populations of moving people tramping to railway stations or being divided in selections on the ramps 'vanished' within hours of their arrival. No trace was left save the massed piles of orphaned belongings, sorted and stacked, documented in the aftermath of liberation of Auschwitz whose sheer mass alone testifies to a process which left no human trace or marker. If the *concentrationary* system produced corpses lying unburied and diseased in Bergen-Belsen, for instance, the *exterminatory* system left ash, charred fragments and 'Canada': the uncanny signs of now unthinkably invisibilized populations of millions. Nothing in the photographs of small groups of naked women huddled on the ground, or forced to line up and move towards the rifles that would kill them in remote ravines of the Ukraine or Latvia attests to the systematic deceptions, organizational logistics and brutal violence with batons, dogs and guns by which transport after transport of people were effaced from the earth between 7 December 1941 and 30 October 1944. Yet the existence, regular display, and even iconic function of the Mizocz photograph(s) and the Latvian sequence in so many museums and books including, and perhaps influenced by, *Night and Fog*'s strategic use of these images, argues for deeper explanation that links the exceptional with a powerful logic in western culture.

In a study of how western culture represents death, Elisabeth Bronfen has identified a recurring link between the aesthetic, femininity and death in which the conjunction of the first two terms serves as a means of disavowing the confrontation with the third term.[42] Bronfen argues that the aestheticized image of woman functions in a phallocentric culture as a means to disown a confrontation with human mortality. It is the beautiful or beautified images of the dead woman that makes death bearable *as, and by means of, an image.* It may thus be that this deeper cultural association between femininity and death, between aestheticized images and the disavowal of death, is what makes the repeatedly selected images of naked women in the killing fields into the bearable 'face' of the horror of mass murder in the Holocaust.[43] Thus while the section of *Night and Fog* in which Resnais attempted to encompass mass extermination thus appears to take the viewer to a confrontation with this core of horror, the images that he selected to narrate this process *doubly* disavow its reality. In doing so, they substitute for the kind of anxiety that so many other sequences in the film manage cinematically to induce (see Hebard in this volume), a sublimating pacification of anxiety before the abyss of death in general and these deaths in particular, which is generated by a deeply unconscious, phallocentric articulation of death with the feminine on the one hand, and death with sexuality on the other.

Resnais's film regularly used cropped images, zoned-in-on faces. This strategy brought the viewer closer to a visual confrontation with death in the image. Yet we can now see that a choice that feminized/aestheticized/eroticized that moment in which the viewer has to confront mass death also mobilizes other, unrelated, older tropes that momentarily derail the film's relentless movement of the viewer into seeing material traces in actual spaces of the violence. Resnais's sequencing and choices of images reveal not merely a historical discrepancy with regard to the nature of most terrible dying at the core of the Nazi racist exterminatory project. They also bind the film to a deeper cultural unconscious that displaces the threat of mortality by linking femininity and death, the very abjecting moment Rivette disowned in the film he countered to Resnais's thoughtful and critical montage.

V

Night and Fog can be shown, therefore, to be not dissimilar to *Kapò* in terms of choices made about the positioning of the viewer in relation to meeting death 'in the feminine'. Yet, clearly the two films were radically different projects. Is Rivette's distinction still intact?

Kapò is a fiction film, set in an imaginary camp whose set was specially constructed for the film in Yugoslavia. This fictional camp includes both instant extermination (Jewish deportees) and long-term concentration inmates (non-Jewish) and prisoners of war, as was the case in Majdanek and the Auschwitz complex. The former are mostly women who are the central characters of the fiction and the latter are Soviet soldiers.

Kapò is one of the earliest fictional projects to entangle in a confused and historically problematic way specifically Jewish experience during the genocidal assault and concentrationary life and death of non-racially persecuted prisoners during the Third Reich. *But it was not the first.* Shown during the pedagogic exhibition in Paris in 1954 which led to the commission of the film *Night and Fog,* former Auschwitz prisoner Wanda Jakubowska's *The Last Stage* was made on location in Auschwitz I in Poland in 1948 with other former Auschwitz prisoners, who were, by definition, all survivors of its regime. The film's story concerns the attempts made during the final months to destroy the final crematorium in order to prevent the SS plan to wipe out the remaining prisoners before the Russians arrived.

Jakubowska's *The Last Stage* is set in the women's camp for Polish prisoners – all the Jewish women prisoners are 'cleared out' in one fell swoop in the early part of the film. Her filmed scene of the departure of the trucks for the gas chambers at dusk is used by Resnais in Shot 155. *The Last Stage* focuses on the women working in the infirmary and a translator who are active in the resistance; they manage to smuggle out information about the planned total extermination of all inmates as the Germans face their defeat, thus defeating the plan itself. It is the story of the concentrationary world, but its dramatic narrative concerns resistance, solidarity, corruption and ultimate survival: heroic, but unrepresentative of that which defines Auschwitz on the one hand and the totalitarian system on the other. A gendered narrative becomes a

Figure 11.8 Still from *The Last Stop* (Wanda Jakubowksa, Poland, 1948). Arrival of Polish prisoners at Auschwitz I

means to confront the concentrationary. But because the film has a narrative structure, setting the scene of the Polish women's suffering at the brutal hands of SS doctors who kill newborn babies, following the initiation of newly arrived inmates, racist selections, brutal regime and dangerous work in the ultimately successful resistance, it must introduce and distinguish characters, dramatize emotions, develop relationships, and create suspense and tension. As the still shown in Fig. 11.8, bringing back into view the barbed wire, affirms, Jakubowska's film is indebted to a German-Expressionist filmic rhetoric. The director has used the resources of rich black-and-white film stock to create sinister night events such as the departure of trucks to the gas chambers or the arrival of trains – that scene also used by Resnais in his film (Plate 17) – but also creating specular moments of contemplative close-ups on beautifully lit women's faces.

The story of *Kapò* was created by Gillo Pontecorvo and his co-writer Franco Solinas (b.1927) who would later write Joseph Losey's *Monsieur Klein* (1976) and, with Pontecorvo, script both *Battle of Algiers* (1966) and the anti-slavery film, *Queimada* (1969) starring Marlon Brando. *Kapò* was Pontecorvo's second feature film and it was significant at its moment as a daring cinematic confrontation with the moral ambiguities of the concentrationary universe. The title *Kapò* points to an engagement with the internal, inverted and perverting power system within the concentration camp enacted mostly by those who were not Jewish. Kapos were usually common criminals set over intellectuals and at the lowest rung of being in the camps, the transient Jewish prisoners. The Kapo in Pontecorvo's narrative is, however, both a woman and Jewish. The leading character who becomes a Kapo does so by shedding her Jewish identity – that led her parents directly to a gas chamber – and by taking on the name of a deceased French political deportee.

The plot is this. Edith, a 14-year-old French Jewish girl sees her parents being rounded up in Paris and runs to join them. They are transported to a

Figure 11.9 Still from *Kapò* (Gilles Pontecorvo, 1958).
Death of Edith/Nicole (Susan Strasberg)

camp. The first night, she wanders off to the hospital and is found by an inmate who helps her by switching her Jewish identity with a just-deceased political prisoner named Nicole. Edith/Nicole must watch in silent horror while she sees her naked parents led with the rest of the transport to be gassed. With the help of a long-time prisoner, Edith/Nicole becomes a camp prostitute. She rises to being a Kapo, safe from hard labour and hunger and friendly with a 'decent' German officer. At the arrival of some Soviet communist prisoners of war, a love affair emerges with their leader Sascha. The brutal and brutalized Edith/Nicole is redeemed, however, at the end of the film by sacrificing her life. She agrees to switch off the electrification of the fences to allow a mass escape of prisoners, an action for which she knows she will be shot. The electrification of the fence has earlier been established by the infamous scene that I have already discussed, the scene leading to the tracking shot condemned by Rivette. Edith/Nicole dies in the arms of the German officer, revealing her true identity by reciting a Jewish prayer: the *Shema* (the title of Primo Levi's poem and the prayer sung by the Chorus in Schoenberg's *Survivor of Warsaw*) (Fig. 11.9).

Kapò acquired notoriety less for its being widely seen than for the condemnation by Jacques Rivette in 1961. If Adorno declared no poetry after Auschwitz, Rivette demanded 'No Thoughtless Fiction!' after *Night and Fog*. But how did a critique, which I hope to have shown is not so straightforward, come to have this force in French cinematic circles?

VI

In 1992, the film writer and journalist Serge Daney (1944–92) began a chapter of his cine-biography on 'The Tracking Shot in *Kapò*'. In his autobiographical reflection on his life with cinema, Daney identifies two primal scenes. One scene is reading the 1961 issue of *Cahiers du cinéma* that published Rivette's brief but devastating review of *Kapò*, a film Daney never watched as a result. The other was repeated high school screenings by a schoolmaster, the film critic Henry Agel, of those films he felt the students had to see in order to have their innocence about the world profoundly shattered. The memorable film was Alain Resnais's *Night and Fog.*

> Once, twice, three times, depending on Agel's whims and the number of sacrificed Latin lessons, I watched piles of dead bodies, hair, spectacles, and teeth. I listened to Jean Cayrol's despondent commentary recited by Michel Bouquet and to Hanns Eisler's music, which seemed ashamed of itself for existing. A strange baptism of images: *to comprehend at the same time that the camps were real and that the film was just.* And understanding

that cinema (alone?) was capable of approaching the limits of denatured humanity. I felt that the distances set by Resnais between the subject filmed, the subject filming and the subject spectator were, in 1959 – as in 1955 – the only possible ones. Was *Nuit et Brouillard* a 'beautiful' film? No, but it was just. It's *Kapò* that wanted to be beautiful and was not.[44]

Daney contrasts beauty with justness, aesthetics with ethics. But I suggested that 'beauty' or the aestheticization of death via the trope of the beautiful woman haunts both Pontecorvo's and Resnais's films irrespective of their differences as fiction and documentary. Daney's personal account of his coming to cinema, however, is also a theorization of the relations between a moment in the history of cinema – the moment of modern, post-war (French) cinema – and a moment in the history of the world, the modern world, in which humanity had to live after having been denatured, both of which moments collided around 1945, making the world afterwards no longer innocent but always in search of a *just* distance at which to see what must be seen, but to which the viewer must never be accommodated as a result of the manner of showing.

The vision, for example, represented by the innocent gaze of young Americans such as the 20-year old GI cameraman George Stevens exposed to the scenes of horror at Dachau in 1945 – Stevens would later become a film director and direct the filmed version of *The Diary of Anne Frank* in 1959 – is, according to Daney, different from that of anyone who came after because their vision was mediated by these images. For Daney, initial newsreels were the first gesture of cinema towards the scene at which the cameramen and women were first to arrive to see. But Daney then argues:

That is why the spectator who I was before *Nuit et Brouillard* and the filmmaker who tried to show the unrepresentable with this film, were linked by a complicit symmetry. Either it is the spectator who is suddenly 'missing from its place' and is stilled while the film continues, or it is the movie which instead of 'continuing', folds back onto itself and onto a temporarily definitive 'image' allowing the spectator to continue believing in cinema and the subject-citizen to live his life. Spectator stilled, image stilled; cinema entered adulthood. The sphere of the visible had ceased to be wholly available; there were gaps and holes, necessary hollowness and superfluous plenitude, forever missing images and always defective gazes. The spectacle and the spectator stopped holding all the balls. It is thus having chosen cinema – supposedly 'the art of the moving image' – I began my cinephagic life under the aegis of the *first image-stilled.*[45]

An earlier translation by Laurent Kretschmar in the internet journal *Senses of Cinema* offers a different rendering of Daney's key concepts: 'Stop of the spectator, stop on the image' which I personally prefer to the evocative concept of stilling.

Stop of the spectator/stop on the image: this double arrest is to do with ethics and politics. The double arrest, however, also means that the aesthetics of the practice can never be divorced from either. Held by neither medium nor content but by both, cinematic specificity concerns the dialectics of both showing and seeing and not showing and not seeing. According to Daney, a film, once encountered, watches the spectator watching thereafter. Thus the memory of the film haunts subsequent viewings of other films that are then questioned by that memory and its politics of the aesthetic. In the manner by which these stillings/arrests of image and spectator are enacted in films, pointing to what is invisible and unsayable by visible signs and spoken words, *Night and Fog* became for Daney, therefore, a monitory memory, working relentlessly on its viewers, interrogating from the screen all other films to come in terms of its own enunciation of a way to encounter the unexpected that must involve a dialectic of interruptions, discontinuities and internalized reflections on its own mechanisms of seeing and showing. Resnais's decisions to create abrupt dislocating jump-cuts, and to set up non-sequitur juxtapositions (recognizable as such through external documentary identification of the photographic sources he, none the less, uses *justly*) might then be read as precisely the signs of a modern cinema as a critical practice encountering a disorienting history that Daney appraises as that which cinema had to try to see but also had to try to show in a specific way that interrupted the desire to see all.

Rivette's interdiction on the tracking shot in *Kapò* contrasted with the double structure of arrests/stillings of image and spectator in *Night and Fog* served as an ethico-political talisman for all Daney's mature film criticism. It was also a way to understand something profound about the history of cinema and the cinema of history. Through having recognized the structure of arrested vision in Resnais's film as the opposite of Pontecorvo's feeding the anxious and curious eye with his tracking shot where he should have resisted: stopping the shot and stopping the spectator, Daney would not only guard against all the risks of the necrophilia and pornography of films that would come about the Nazis, the camps, the destruction. But this talisman raised the question of cinema, its modernity, or rather its modernism, and its most profound and difficult topic: death in its novel, modern, post-concentrationary form. How should that dehumanizing human event be represented? Or how do we represent it as a *human* event once it has become possible to denature not only humanity itself, but even human dying? What will happen to us when totalitarian killing (of both people and the human in those it did not kill outright) is represented in the *Kapò* manner? What happens when it is imagined, recreated, filmed, and then presented to the necrophiliac, pornographic, voyeuristic spectator precisely by building a track for the camera to move in for a second take of a beautiful actress's simulated dying? What happens when the viewer's hunger to see more, to see again, to be taken towards it and to find not the horror of a bleeding nose and lax-jawed death, but a beautiful image of a dead woman is serviced? How can such an apparatus as cinema register what happened to death in Auschwitz without repeating this feminization/aestheticization/disavowal? How can it speak, visually, the novelty of what Adorno declared was a dying worse than death? These questions resonate across the entire field of contemporary cinema with its ever-increasing spectacularization of violence and endless reproduction of deaths that are not ever allowed to resonate as human deaths yet make the spectator daily more accustomed to what is, as Zygmunt Bauman writes and everyday criminal codes speak it, human wastage or wasting humans.[46]

Instead of the tracking shot that inflicted a petrifying gaze on the fetish-object: a beautiful dead woman who serves as image to shield the hungry viewer from the truer horror, there is a film that offered Daney its opposite: a gaze that seemed not to see, wanted not to see and thus inadvertently, fearfully, showed death as an event. Daney's example is the 1959 Japanese film *Ugetsu* by Mizoguchi. Pontecorvo, courageous and political, did not, however, appear to tremble as did Mizoguchi who is appalled at violence, and this is inscribed in the film itself, triggering a stunned panoramic shot within which, almost missed, the character Miyaki is killed. The camera itself tries not to see, and thus enacts its own arrest denying the spectator a sight of death.

In the final sections of his article, part intellectual autobiography, part analysis of cinematic history straddling the moment of its modernist coming of age and its post-modernist default into necrophiliac infantilism, Daney registers the moment of a more recent dislocation between his intellectual formation around the primal scenes circa 1961 and the post-cinematic TV culture emerging circa 1980 – and in full force by 1992 – marked by the advent of digital technologies whose effects on these very deep questions of ethical indexicality and creative virtuality we are now to face for ourselves. Daney states: 'We had believed cinema, which means we had done everything not to believe it.'[47] Cinephilia had produced both a passion for cinema and a critical deconstruction of its potency through film studies. Two negative epiphanies mark a new moment for Daney.

The first was Marvin Chomsky's American TV series *Holocaust* screened in the United States and Europe during 1979. An actual visit in 1989 to Phnom Penh to see what an auto-genocide looked like led Daney to comment ironically that he there saw proof that cinema was no longer intimately linked to the history of men by the fact that, contrary to the Nazi torturers, who had *filmed* their victims (is this really true since we appear to have only a few minutes of actual filmed footage?), the Khmers left behind only photographs and mass graves. *Holocaust*, a TV mini-series, was the moment Hollywood and the Americans returned to tell the European story with actors, who were too well-fed, in a film heavy with generic humanism and sentimentalizing melodrama. 'The simulation-*Holocaust* was certainly no longer confronting the strangeness of a humanity capable of a crime against itself but it also remained stubbornly incapable of bringing back the singular beings – each with a story, a face and a *name* – who made up this history, who were the exterminated Jews.'[48] This series coincided with a wave of revisionism and Holocaust denial in French culture, a possibility no one of Daney's formation could imagine but into whose hands such easy and easing fabrications would easily feed.

As I suggested above, Daney works with a concept not only of watching cinema, but of being watched *by* cinema. Thus, in explaining the mere 20 years between his primal scenes and these moments of negative epiphany, he realizes that the questions which had watched him through cinema would no longer do so *through cinema*. Why not? Because something happened to cinematic formal self-consciousness, or even cinematic self-consciousness itself. The adultness of modernism appeared to Daney to be over. He explains: 'We must remain faithful to the face that once transfixed us. And every "form" is a face that looks at us.' Here Daney articulates one aspect that I have been tracking across the close-up as not only an image of a face, but the face as image, and ultimately image as face: the site of a confrontation not only with an anthropomorphic representation but with that which in the other calls to its viewer in their humanness, their ethicality and their politicality.

> That is why, even if I have feared them, I have never believed those at the *lycée* cine-club who were attacking the condescension of those poor 'formalist' fools, guiltily preferring the personal *jouissance* of the 'form' to the 'content' of films. But only the one who has been struck early enough by *formal violence* will end up realising – at the end of his life – how this violence also has an essence [alternative translation: content]. The form is desire …; the essence [content] but the background, when we are no longer here.[49]

Unexpectedly evoking the Adornian trope about formal violence with which I began, that is the necessary violence of the form as the means to produce the necessary affects relating to violence rather than a spectacle of violence or worse – redemption from it – Daney translates Rivette's indictment of the auteur's *attitude* into the question of *desire*. Desire is also traced into the cinematic experience at the level of form. This final thought takes Daney to his second negative epiphany. On television, Daney watched the Michael Jackson music video *We are the World! We are the Children!* (USA/Africa, 1985) which cosily assembled smiling and complacent musical celebrities to raise money for the starving children of Africa.

> The rich singers (*We are the world! We are the children!*) were mixing with the image of skinny children. Actually they were taking their place; they were replacing and erasing them. Mixing stars and skeletons in a typical fast editing where two images try to become one, the video elegantly carried out this electronic communication between North and South. Here we have, I thought, the present face of abjection and the improved version of my tracking shot in *Kapò*. These are the images I would like at least one teenager to be disgusted by and *ashamed* of. Not merely ashamed to be fed and affluent, but ashamed to be seen as someone who has *to be aesthetically seduced* where it is only a matter of conscience – good or bad – of being human and nothing more.[50]

It is thus at the level of the electronic digital mixing of one image with another that:

> I realized that all my history is there. In 1961, a movement of a camera aestheticized a dead body and 30 years later a dissolve makes the wealthy and the starving ones dance together. Nothing has changed, neither me, forever incapable of seeing in all this a carnivalesque dance of death, medieval and ultramodern, nor the predominant conceptions of consensual beauty. The form has changed a bit though. In *Kapò* it was possible to be upset at Pontecorvo for inconsiderately abolishing a distance he should have 'kept'. The tracking shot was immoral for the simple reason of putting us – him the filmmaker and me the spectator – in a place where we did not belong ... because he deported me from my real position as spectator-witness forcing me to be part of the picture. What was the meaning of Godard's formula if not that *one should never put himself where one isn't nor should he speak for others.*[51]

A tracking shot in 1961 required work; rails, dollies and so forth served to position the spectator of the movie in a place of mastery and desire completely at odds with the ethical and political imperative of the topic of the film. At the level of decisions that have to be judged and costed, Pontecorvo's shot is very different from the instant dissolve at the touch of the fingertips on a digital console by someone incapable of realizing what the meaning of the action might be beyond its alluringly aesthetic effect. This, says Daney, is what revolts him about a *world without cinema* ... 'meaning without this sense of belonging to humanity through *a supplementary country called cinema*'.[52] Cinema involved a kind of work and a work of construction for which one could hold the filmmaker ethico-politically responsible. Without that kind of cinema, what was intimated as its corruption by Rivette and learnt as a critical posture by Daney becomes commonplace editing effect against whose contaminating proximities and mixings there appears to be little critical defence.

For Daney, the camps – the concentrationary universe – was a historically formed limit not only inherited from actual historical occurrence but from its mediation into culture, memory and consciousness through a self-conscious cinema represented by Resnais's *Night and Fog*. Its disclosure through an iconic and, I am suggesting, ultimately Adornian film such as *Night and Fog*, marked the end of childhood innocence by what it showed and, as importantly, how it showed it, where it left/kept the viewer by means of its own stops on the image, its abrupt dislocations of the power of its own endlessly moving camera, its own loss of words, and, I have been suggesting, by the uneven particularity of its face-to-face confrontation with death. Even where it is betrayed, as I have argued, by pre-scripted troping of death disavowed by the image of the feminine, the film exposes itself struggling with an impossible historical reality.

The loss of that self-knowledge of a cinema with limits, effaced by a shift from the hegemonic potentiality of a critical cinema to the digital ease of entertainment and spectacle, the seduction of the digital dissolve chronically refusing the stop on the image and rendering impossible the arrest of the spectator, perhaps should be taken seriously, despite the dangers of falling into classic 'oldfogeyism', becoming boringly grumpy old cinephiles. Theodor Adorno's serious anxiety about politically committed art (Pontecorvo being such an *engagé* by the very fact of choosing to make a movie about the moral ambiguities of the camp world already in the later 1950s) committing moral abominations seems relatively easy to discern compared to what confronts us now when we have to ask how we might find our moral compass and even political guiding principle: what are the equivalences for 'the tracking shot' in the instant dissolves we find in *We Are the Children*?

In a world intensely aware of a half-century and more running deeper and deeper in blood, atrocity, genocides, traumatic civil war, political and criminal terror, how will we find critical terms to discriminate about the manner in which cinema or visual representation can induce thought, or, in Adorno's terms, *compel a change of attitude* through a visceral induction into thoughtful awareness through a formal configuration of the image? Can we discern the value of the *art* that Daney calls 'cinema' in contrast to that which makes a spectacle out of pain, or suffering or horror? Furthermore, in responding to suffering, are we risking making trauma a new genre of entertainment? Has cultural criticism got the terms to help us see where we should not seek to look?

Our histories demand cultural forms and critical practices that can live the paradox Adorno began to delineate when reality became such that it radically disempowered all metaphysics and even challenged representation itself while, none the less, demanding of art the representational space of encounter that is cruel and painful enough to arrest us into knowledge of what continually threatens *human* life.

Notes

1. Theodor Adorno, 'Commitment', [1962] in Andrew Arato and Eike Gebhardt (eds), *The Essential Frankfurt School Reader* (Oxford: Basil Blackwell, 1978), p. 312.
2. Adorno is referencing Sartre's three-act play about the effects of war on people's humanity: *Morts sans Sepulture* (1946).
3. Theodor Adorno, 'Commitment', p. 312.
4. Theodor Adorno, 'Commitment', p. 312.
5. Theodor Adorno, 'Commitment', p. 313.
6. Theodor Adorno, 'Commitment', p. 314.
7. Theodor Adorno, 'Commitment', pp. 314–15.
8. Gilles Deleuze, *Cinema I: The Movement Image*, trans. Hugh Tomlinson and Barbara Habberjam (Minneapolis, MN: University of Minnesota Press, 1987), p. 88.
9. Mary Ann Doane, 'The Close-up: Scale and Detail in Cinema', *Differences: A Journal of Feminist Cultural Studies* 14/3 (2003), p. 107.
10. Mary Ann Doane, 'The Close-up: Scale and Detail in Cinema', pp. 97–104.
11. Jacques Rivette, 'De l'Abjection' *Cahiers du Cinéma* 120 (juin 1961), pp. 54–55. Reprinted in Antoine De Baecque (ed.), *Théories du Cinéma* (Paris: Cahiers du cinéma, 2001) pp. 37–40. Also available at http://simpleappareil.free.fr/lobservatoire/index.php?2009/02/24/62-de-l-abjection-jacques-rivette. Jacques Rivette, 'On Abjection', trans. David Phelps with the assistance of Jeremi Szaniawski at http://www.dvdbeaver.com/rivette/OK/abjection.html (accessed 10 August 2009).
12. Jacques Rivette, 'On Abjection', n.p.
13. These are reproduced in Richard Raskin, Nuit et Brouillard *by Alain Resnais* (Aarhus: Aarhus University Press, 1987), p. 30. This essay could not have been written without the research and reconstruction of the shooting script provided by Richard Raskin to whom I am deeply indebted.
14. Jacques Rivette, 'On Abjection', n.p.
15. Jacques Rancière, 'The Future of the Image', in *The Future of the Image*, trans. Gregory Elliott (London: Verso, 2007), p. 3.
16. Jacques Rancière, 'The Future of the Image', p. 6.
17. In researching this poem, I discovered Dustin Ellis Howes, '"Consider if this is a Person": Primo Levi, Hannah Arendt and the Political Significance of Auschwitz' *Holocaust and Genocide Studies* 22/2 (Fall, 2008), 266–92. While sharing the idea that Levi and Arendt are exploring a similar issue from different perspectives, and while acknowledging the importance of treating Levi as a comparable philosophical thinker, I do not entirely follow Howes' argument that Levi is asking if there can be a shareable humanity between survivor and non-participant. I understand the demand to 'consider'

as a demand to confront the processes specific to the camps that Arendt identifies as the experimental destruction of the humanness of the prisoners.

18. All quotations of the poem are from Primo Levi, *Collected Poems*, trans. Ruth Feldman and Brian Swann (London: Faber and Faber, 1992), p. 9. Reprinted with permission.

19. Primo Levi, *Conversazioni e interviste* (Turin: Einaudi, 1997), p. 216; discussed at length in Giorgio Agamben, *The Remnants to Auschwitz: The Witness and the Archive*, trans. Daniel Heller-Roazen (New York: Zone Books, 1999).

20. Hannah Arendt, 'The Concentration Camps', *Partisan Review* XV (1948), p. 743.

21. Hannah Arendt, 'The Concentration Camps', p. 743.

22. Hannah Arendt, 'The Concentration Camps', p. 744.

23. Hannah Arendt, *The Origins of Totalitarianism* (New York: Schocken Books, 1951), p. 459.

24. For an important, distinctive and important contemporary documentary about Mauthausen, see *KZ* (2006, Rex Bloomstein).

25. It is important to register the various forms of class war enacted within the National Socialist system which targeted intellectuals as both potential political resistance and as members of privileged elites. Hannah Arendt comments on this class hatred in the running of the concentration camps, initially by the SA, within Germany during the 1930s while Jean Amery writes tellingly of the specific mode of torture inflicted on the intellectual by the regime of brute labour within the camps in his book *Jenseits von Schuld und Sühne* (1964) translated into English by Sidney and Stella P. Rosenfeld as *At the Mind's Limits: Contemplations by a Survivor on Auschwitz and its Realities* (Bloomington, IN: Indiana University Press, 1998).

26. All shot numbers refer to Richard Raskin's identification numbers in the shooting script he recreated in Richard Raskin, Nuit et Brouillard *by Alain Resnais* (Aarhus: Aarhus University Press, 1987).

27. In Wikipedia, for instance, the regime of the socialist totalitarian state, the GDR, was defined by the dual entities of *Mauer* – the Wall – and *Stacheldracht* – barbed wire.

28. Margaret Bourke-White, *Portrait of Myself* (New York: Simon and Shuster, 1963), pp. 160, 259–60. See also Barbie Zelizer, *Remembering to Forget: Holocaust Memory Through the Camera's Eye* (Chicago, IL: University of Chicago Press, 1998).

29. Max Silverman, 'Horror and the Everyday in Post-Holocaust France: *Nuit et Brouillard* and Concentrationary Art', *French Cultural Studies* 17/1 (2006), pp. 5–18.

30. I am grateful to Danièle Baron, archivist, FNDIRP for this clarification. Email correspondence 23/3/2011.

31. Sarah Kofman *Smothered Words*, [1987] trans. Madeleine Dobie (Evanston, IL: Northwestern University Press, 1998), Kofman is citing Theodor Adorno, 'Meditations on Metaphysics: I After Auschwitz', in *Negative Dialectics* (London: Routledge, 1973), p. 362.

32. Hannah Arendt, 'Social Science Techniques and the Study of Concentration Camps', *Jewish Social Studies* 12/1 (1950) reprinted in *Essays in Understanding 1930–1954: Formation, Exile and Totalitarianism*, ed. Jerome Kohn (New York: Schocken Books, 1994), p. 240.

33. Clément Chéroux, *Mémoire des Camps: Photographies des camps de concentration et d'extermination 1933–1999* (Paris: Marval, 2001), p. 152; Serge Lampin, 'Vaihingen, le camp du dernier repos', *Le Patriote résistant* 604 (1990), 14–15. The full photograph is reproduced on p. 155.

34. Roland Barthes, *Camera Lucida: Reflections on Photography* [1980], trans. Richard Howard (London: Flamingo, 1984) and Andrea Liss, *Trespassing Through Shadows: Memory, Photography and the Holocaust* (Minneapolis, MN: University of Minnesota Press, 1998).

35. The exception is the four photographs taken in August 1944 by Auschwitz *Sonderkommando* member 'Alex' discussed by Georges Didi-Huberman in his study, *Images in Spite of All: Four Photographs from Auschwitz*, trans. Shane B. Lillis (Chicago, IL: University of Chicago Press, 2008). These were images taken secretly and at great risk by a hidden hand-held camera of women undressing before entering the gas chamber and then the bodies being burned in the open air (when the crematoria did not function or were overwhelmed with the numbers of the dead). Resnais includes one of these images, cropped and in close-up in Shot 240, 23'37" (Plate 38).

36. Joshua Hirsch, *After-Image: Film, Trauma and the Holocaust* (Philadelphia, PA: Temple University Press, 2004), p. 1.

37. In Lanzmann's *Shoah*, his camera moves in and around the ruined foundations of crematoria at Birkenau, while Müller speaks in a manner not dissimilar from that in *Night and Fog*. For the description of the gas chamber, see Claude Lanzmann, *Shoah: The Complete Text* (New York: Da Capo Press 1995), pp. 113–17. See Filip Müller, *Eyewitness Auschwitz: Three Years in the Gas Chambers* [1979], trans. Suzanne Flatauer (Chicago, IL: Ivan R. Dee, 1999).

38. Photographs in the United States Holocaust Memorial Museum WIS#17875-79 (File # 431.863). Hille gave the photographs to the Czech lawyer for whom he worked as a doorman after the war, who handed them to the Czech government. They thus entered the public domain and Hille's statements were confirmed in 1961 by Josef Paur also of the Gendarmerie.

39. Yitzhak Arad, *The Pictorial History of the Holocaust* (Jerusalem: Yad Vashem and New York: Macmillan Publishing Co., 1990), figs. 201–203, pp. 192–3.

40. The trio of a woman cradling her child's head, a woman looking away and this appealing face form the core of the prolonged painterly contemplation of how we can look back in the work of French-Israeli artist Bracha Ettinger. See Griselda Pollock, 'The Graces of Catastrophe: Matrixial Time and Aesthetic Space Confront the Archive of Disaster', in *Encounters in the Virtual Feminist Museum: Time, Space and the Archive* (London: Routledge, 2007), pp. 165–97.

41. Here we must reference, however, Georges Didi-Huberman's significant essay on the four surviving photographs taken by members of the Sonderkommando outside Crematorium V at Auschwitz-Birkenau in August 1944, 'Images Malgré Tout', in Clément Chéroux (ed.), *Mémoire des Camps*, pp. 219–41. See also Nicholas Chare, *Witnessing Abjection* (London: I.B. Tauris, 2011).

42. Elisabeth Bronfen, *Over her Dead Body: Femininity, Death and the Aesthetic* (Manchester: Manchester University Press, 1992).

43. Griselda Pollock, 'Dying, Seeing, Feeling: Transforming the Ethical Space of Feminist Aesthetics', in Diarmuid Costello and Dominic Willsdon, (eds) *Life and Death of Images* (London: Tate Publishing, 2008), pp. 213–35. Also see 'Photographing Atrocity: Becoming Iconic?' in Geoffrey Batcher, Nancy K. Miller and Jay Prosser (eds), *Picturing Atrocity: Reading Photography in Crisis* (London: Reaktion Books, 2011).

44. Serge Daney, 'The Tracking Shot in *Kapò*', in *Postcards from the Cinema*, trans. Paul Douglas Grant (Oxford and New York: Berg, 2007). First published in *Trafic* 4 (1992), p. 20.

45. Serge Daney, 'The Tracking Shot in *Kapò*', p. 25.

46. My comments here resonate with Judith Butler's recent questioning on mournable dying in Judith Butler, *Precarious Life: The Power of Mourning and Violence* (London: Verso, 2004) and with Zygmunt Bauman, *Wasted Lives: Modernity and its Outcasts* (Cambridge: Polity Press, 2004).

47. Serge Daney, 'The Tracking Shot in *Kapò*', p. 30.

48. Serge Daney, 'The Tracking Shot in *Kapò*', pp. 32–3.

49. Serge Daney, 'The Tracking Shot in *Kapò*', p. 33.

50. Serge Daney, 'The Tracking Shot in *Kapò*', pp. 33–4.

51. Serge Daney, 'The Tracking Shot in *Kapò*', p. 34.

52. Serge Daney, 'The Tracking Shot in *Kapò*', p. 35.

Bibliography

About, Ilsen 'La Photographie au service du système concentrationnaire national-socialiste (1933–1945)', in Clément Chéroux (ed.), *Mémoire des camps: photographies des camps de concentration et d'extermination nazies (1933–1999)* (Paris: Marval, 2001), pp. 29–53.

About, Ilsen, Matyus, Stephan and Winkler, Jean-Marie (eds), *La Part visible des camps. Les photographies du camp de concentration de Mauthausen* (Vienna-Paris: Bundesministerium für Inneres-Editions Tiresias, 2005).

Adorno, Theodor W., 'Commitment' [1962], in Andrew Arato and Eike Gebhardt (eds), *The Essential Frankfurt School Reader* (New York: Continuum, 1992), pp. 300–18.

———, 'Meditations on Metaphysics: I After Auschwitz' in *Negative Dialectics* (London: Routledge, 1973), pp. 361–73.

———, *Minima Moralia: Reflections from Damaged Life*, trans. E.F.N. Jephcott (London: Verso, 1978).

Agamben, Giorgio, *Enfance et histoire: Destruction de l'expérience et origine de l'histoire*, trans. Yves Hersant (Paris: Payot, 1989).

———, *Homo Sacer: Sovereign Power and Bare Life* [1995], trans. Daniel Heller-Roazen (Stanford, CA: Stanford University Press, 1998).

———, *The Remnants of Auschwitz*, trans. Daniel Heller-Roazen (New York: Zone Books, 1999).

———, 'What is a camp?' *Means without End: Notes on Politics*, trans. Vincenzo Binetti and Cesare Casarino (Minneapolis, MN: University of Minnesota Press, 2000).

———, *States of Exception* [2003], trans. Kevin Attell (Chicago, IL: University of Chicago Press, 2005).

Amery, Jean, *Jenseits von Schuld und Sühne* (1964) trans. Sidney and Stella P. Rosenfeld as *At the Mind's Limits: Contemplations by a Survivor on Auschwitz and its Realities* (Bloomington, IN: Indiana University Press, 1998).

Soviet Government Statements of Nazi Atrocities, Anon. (London: Hutchinson, 1946).

Antelme, Robert, *The Human Race*, trans. Jeffrey Haight and Annie Mahler (Marlboro, VT: The Marlboro Press, 1992).

Arad, Yitzhak, *The Pictorial History of the Holocaust* (Jerusalem: Yad Vashem and New York: Macmillan Publishing Co., 1990).

Arendt, Hannah, 'The Concentration Camps', *Partisan Review*, XV: 7 (1948), 743–63.

———, 'Social Science Techniques and the Study of Concentration Camps', *Jewish Social Studies* 12/1 (1950), 49–64.

———, *The Origins of Totalitarianism* (New York: Schocken Books, 1951).

———, *The Human Condition* (Chicago, IL: University of Chicago Press, 1958).

———, *Essays in Understanding 1930–1954: Formation, Exile, Totalitarianism* (New York: Schocken Books, 1994).

Armes, Roy, *The Cinema of Alain Resnais* (New York: A.S. Barnes, 1968).

Avisar, Ilan, *Screening the Holocaust: Cinema's Images of the Unimaginable* (Bloomington, IN: Indiana University Press, 1988).

Barnouw, Erik, *A Tower In Babel: A History of Broadcasting in the United States*, Vol. 1 (New York: Oxford University Press, 1966).

Barnow, Dagmar, *Germany 1945: Views of War and Violence* (Bloomington, IN: Indiana University Press, 1996).

Barthes, Roland, *Camera Lucida: Reflections on Photography* [1980], trans. Richard Howard (London: Flamingo, 1984).

———, *The Rustle of Language*, trans. Richard Howard (New York: Hill and Wang, 1986).

———, *Oeuvres Complètes*, Vol. 2., ed. Eric Marty (Paris: du Seuil, 2002).

Bartov, Omer, Grossman, Atina and Nolan, Mary (eds), *Crimes of War. Guilt and Denial in the Twentieth Century* (New York: The New Press, 2002).

Baudry, Jean-Louis, 'Ideological Effects of the Basic Cinematographic Apparatus', *Narrative, Apparatus, Ideology*, ed. Philip Rosen (New York: Columbia University Press, 1986), pp. 281–98.

Bauman, Zygmunt, *Modernity and the Holocaust* (Cambridge: Polity Books, 1989).

———, *Wasted Lives: Modernity and its Outcasts* (Cambridge: Polity Press, 2004).

Beckett, Samuel, *The Unnamable* in *Molloy; Malone Dies; The Unnamable*, trans. the author (London: Calder and Boyars, 1959).

Benjamin, Walter, 'Theses on the Philosophy of History', in *Illuminations*, ed. Hannah Arendt, trans. Harry Zohn (New York: Schocken Books, 1968), pp. 253–64.

———, 'On some motifs in Baudelaire', in *Illuminations*, ed. Hannah Arendt, trans. Harry Zohn (New York: Schocken Books, 1968), pp. 157–202.

————, *The Origin of German Tragic Drama* [1963], trans. John Osborne (London: NLB, 1977).

————, *The Arcades Project*, trans. Howard Eiland and Kevin McLaughlin (London: The Belknap Press of Harvard University Press, 1999).

Bergson, Henri, *La Pensée et le mouvant. Essais et conférences Œuvres*, ed. André Robinet (Paris: PUF, 1959; 1970 edn).

Bersani, Leo and Dutoit, Ulysse, *Arts of Impoverishment: Beckett, Rothko, Resnais* (Cambridge, MA: Harvard University Press, 1993).

Bhabha, Homi K., *The Location of Culture* (New York: Routledge, 1994).

Blanchot, Maurice, *The Writing of Disaster*, trans. Ann Smock (Lincoln, NE: University of Nebraska Press, 1986).

Bloomstein, Rex, *KZ* (2006).

Boguslawska-Swiebocka, Renata and Ceglowska, Teresa, *KL Auschwitz. Fotografie dokumentalne* (Warsaw: Krajowa Agencja Wydawnicza, 1980).

Bourke-White, Margaret, *Portrait of Myself* (New York: Simon and Shuster, 1963).

Brandt, Willy, 'Mut zur Wahrheit', *Der Abend*, 14 November, 1956.

Brayard, Florent, *La 'Solution finale de la question juive': la technique, le temps et les catégories de la décision* (Paris: Fayard, 2004).

Brayard, Florent (ed.), *Le Génocide des juifs entre procès et histoire 1943–2000* (Paris-Brussels: IHTP-Éditions Complexe, 2000).

Bronfen, Elisabeth, *Over her Dead Body: Femininity, Death and the Aesthetic* (Manchester: Manchester University Press, 1992).

Browne, Nick, 'The Spectator-in-the-Text: The Rhetoric of *Stagecoach* [1975–76]', in Bill Nichols (ed.), *Movies and Methods*, Vol. 2 (Los Angeles, CA: University of California Press, 1985), pp. 458–75.

Browning, Christopher, *The Path to Genocide: Essays on Launching the Final Solution* (Cambridge: Cambridge University Press, 1998, new edn. 1992).

————, *The Origins of the Final Solution: The Evolution of Nazi Jewish Policy, September 1939–March 1942* (Lincoln, NE: University of Nebraska Press, 2004).

Burke, Peter, *Eyewitnessing: The Uses of Images as Historical Evidence* (Ithaca, NY: Cornell University Press, 2001).

Butler, Judith, *Gender Trouble: Feminism and the Subversion of Identity* (New York and London: Routledge, 1990).

————, *Precarious Life: The Power of Mourning and Violence* (London: Verso, 2004).

Camus, Albert, *Essais*, eds Roger Quillot and Louis Faucon (Paris: Gallimard, 1965).

Cantor, Jay, 'Death and the Image', *TriQuarterly* 79 (1990), 173–98.

Caplan, Jane and Wachsmann, Nicholaus (eds), *Concentration Camps in Nazi Germany* (London and New York: Routledge, 2010).

Caruth, Cathy, 'The Obscenity of Understanding: An Evening with Claude Lanzmann', in Cathy Caruth (ed.), *Trauma: Explorations in Memory* (Baltimore, MD: Johns Hopkins University Press, 1995), pp. 200–20.

————, *Unclaimed Experience: Trauma, Narrative, and History* (Baltimore, MD: Johns Hopkins University Press, 1996).

Caruth, Cathy (ed.), *Trauma: Explorations in Memory* (Baltimore, MD: Johns Hopkins University Press, 1995).

Cayrol, Jean, *Lazare parmi nous* (Paris: Seuil, 1950).

————, 'Nous avons conçu *Nuit et Brouillard* comme un dispositif d'alerte', *Les Lettres françaises* 606 (9 February 1956).

————, *Il était une fois Jean Cayrol* (Paris: Seuil, 1982).

————, 'De la mort à la vie', in *Nuit et brouillard* (Paris: Fayard, 1997), pp. 45–114.

————, *Oeuvre Lazaréenne* (Paris: Seuil, 2000).

Chamberlin, Brewster S., 'Todesmühlen. Ein früher Versuch zur Massen-"Umerziehung" im besetzten Deutschland 1945–1946', *Vierteljahrheft für Zeitgeschichte* 3 (1981), pp. 420–36.

Chambers, Ross, *Untimely Interventions: Aids Writing, Testimony and the Rhetoric of Haunting* (Ann Arbor, MI: University of Michigan Press, 2004).

Chare, Nicholas, *Auschwitz and Afterimages: Abjection, Witnessing and Representation* (London: I.B. Tauris, 2011).

Chéroux, Clément (ed.), *Mémoire des camps. Photographies des camps de concentration et d'extermination nazis (1933–1999)* (Paris: Patrimoine photographique-Marval, 2001).

Colombat, André-Pierre, *The Holocaust in French Film* (Metuchen, NJ: Scarecrow Press, 1993).

Comolli, Jean-Louis, 'Fatal rendez-vous', in Jean-Michel Frodon (ed.), *Cinema and the Shoah. An Art Confronts the Tragedy of the Twentieth Century*, trans. Anna Harrison and Tom Mesand (New York: SUNY Press, 2010), pp. 47–62.

Cooke, Miriam and Woollacott, Angela (eds), *Gendering War Talk* (Princeton, NJ: Princeton University Press, 1993).

Cornaton, Michel, *Les Camps de regroupement de la guerre d'Algérie* (Paris: Harmattan, 1998).

Crimp, Douglas, 'Mourning and Militancy', in Russel Ferguson, Martha Gever, Trinh T. Minha, and Cornell West (eds), *Out There: Marginalization and Contemporary Cultures* (Cambridge, MA: MIT Press, 1990), pp. 233–45.

Damisch, Hubert, 'Montage du désastre', *Cahiers du cinéma*, 599 (2005).

Daney, Serge, 'Le Travelling de *Kapò*', *Trafic* 4 (1992), 5–19.

————, 'The Tracking Shot in *Kapò*', in *Postcards from the Cinema*, trans. Paul Douglas Grant (Oxford and New York: Berg, 2007), pp. 17–38.

Davis, Colin, *Haunted Subjects: Deconstruction, Psychoanalysis and the Return of the Dead* (Basingstoke and New York: Palgrave Macmillan, 2007).

Dawidowicz, Lucy, 'Visualizing the Warsaw Ghetto: Nazi Images of Jews Refiltered by the BBC', *Shoah: A Review of Holocaust Studies and Commemorations*, 1/1 (1978), 5–6, 17–18.

de Certeau, Michel, *L'Écriture de l'histoire* (Paris: Gallimard, 1975).

————, *Heterologies: Discourse on the Other*, trans. Brian Massumi (Minneapolis, MN: University of Minnesota Press, 1986).

————, 'The Historiographical Operation', in *The Writing of History* (New York: Columbia University Press, 1988), pp. 56–114.

de Man, Paul, 'The Rhetoric of Temporality', in *Blindness and Insight: Essays in the Rhetoric of Contemporary Criticism* (Minneapolis, MN: University of Minnesota Press, 1971).

Deguy, Michel (ed.), *Au sujet de Shoah: le film de Claude Lanzmann* (Paris: Belin, 1990).

Delage, Christian, 'Cinéma, enfance et histoire', in Antoine de Baecque and Christian Delage (eds), *De l'histoire au cinéma* (Paris-Brussels: IHTP-Éditions Complexe, 1998), pp. 61–98.

————, 'L'image comme preuve: L'expérience du procès de Nuremberg', *Vingtième Siècle. Revue d'histoire* 72 (2001) 63–78.

————, 'La couleur des camps', *Les Cahiers du judaïsme* 15 (2003), 71–80.

————, 'Les camps nazis: l'actualité, le documentaire, la fiction. À propos du *Criminel* (*The Stranger*, Orson Welles, USA, 1946)', *Les Cahiers de la Shoah* 7 (2003), 87–109.

————, 'Samuel Fuller à Falkenau: l'évènement fondateur', in Christian Delage and Vincent Guigueno (eds), *L'Historien et le film* (Paris: Gallimard, 2004), pp. 46–58.

————, 'L'image dans le prétoire. Usages du document filmé chez Fritz Lang and Stanley Kramer', *Études photographiques* 17 (2005), 45–66.

————, '*Nuit et Brouillard*: a Turning Point in the History and Memory of the Holocaust', in Toby Haggith and Joanna Newman (eds), *Holocaust and the Moving Image: Representations in Film and Television since 1933* (London: Wallflower Press, 2005), pp. 127–39.

Delage, Christian and Guigueno, Vincent (eds), *L'Historien et le film* (Paris: Gallimard, 2004).

Delbo, Charlotte, *Aucun de nous reviendra: Auschwitz et après I* (Paris: Minuit, 1970).

————, *Auschwitz and After*, trans. Rosette C. Lamont (New Haven, CT and London: Yale University Press, 1995).

Deleuze, Gilles, *Cinema 1: The Movement Image*, trans. Hugh Tomlinson and Barbara Habberjam (Minneapolis, MN: University of Minnesota Press, 1987).

———, *Cinéma 2: L'Image-Temps* (Paris: Minuit, 1985)/*Cinema 2: The Time-Image*, trans. Hugh Tomlinson and Robert Galeta (London, Athlone Press, 1989).

Deleuze, Gilles and Guattari, Félix, *Anti-Oedipus: Capitalism and Schizophrenia*, trans. Robert Hurley, Mark Seem and Helen R. Lane (Minneapolis, MN: University of Minnesota Press, 1983).

Delfour, Jean-Jacques, 'La Pellicule maudite: sur la figuration du réel de la Shoah', *L'Arche* 508 (2000), 14–17.

Delporte, Christian, 'Les medias et la découverte des camps (presses, radio, actualités filmées)', in François Bédarida and Laurent Gervereau (eds), *La Déportation: Le système concentrationnaire nazi* (Paris: Musée d'Histoire contemporaine-BDIC, 1995), pp. 205–13.

Derrida, Jacques, *Of Grammatology*, trans. G. Spivak (Baltimore, MD: Johns Hopkins University Press, 1976).

———, *Spurs: Nietzsche's Styles*, trans. B. Harlow (Chicago, IL: University of Chicago Press, 1979).

Derrida, Jacques and Stiegler, Bernard, *Echographies of Television: Filmed Interviews*, trans. Jennifer Bajorek (Cambridge: Polity Press, 2002).

Didi-Huberman, Georges, 'Pour une anthropologie des singularités formelles. Remarque sur l'invention warburgienne', *Genèses: Sciences sociales et histoire* 24 (1996), 145–63.

———, 'Le Lieu malgré tout' [1995], in *Phasmes: Essais sur l'apparition* (Paris: Minuit, 1998), pp. 228–42.

———, *Devant le temps: Histoire de L'Art et l'Anachronisme de l'Image* (Paris: Editions de Minuit, 2000).

———, 'Montage des ruines', *Simulacres* 5 (2001), 8–17.

———, 'Images Malgré Tout', in Clément Cheroux (ed.), *Mémoires des Camps: photographies des camps de concentration et d'extermination nazis 1933–1999* (Paris: Marval, 2001).

———, *L'Image survivante. Histoire de l'art et temps des fantômes selon Aby Warburg* (Paris: Minuit, 2002).

———, 'De ressemblance à ressemblance', in Christophe Bident and Pierre Vilar (eds), *Maurice Blanchot. Récits critiques* (Tours-Paris: Éditions Farrago-Léo Scheer, 2003), pp. 143–67.

———, *Images malgré tout* (Paris: Minuit, 2003)

———, *Images in Spite of All: Four Photographs from Auschwitz*, trans. Shane B. Lillis (Chicago, IL: University of Chicago, 2008).

Doane, Mary Ann, 'The Close-up: Scale and Detail in Cinema', *Differences: A Journal of Feminist Cultural Studies* 14/3 (2003), 89–211.

Donadey, Anne, '"Une Certaine idée de la France": The Algeria Syndrome and Struggles over "French" Identity', in Steven Ungar and Tom Conley (eds), *Identity Papers: Contested Nationhood in Twentieth-Century France* (Minneapolis, MN: University of Minnesota Press, 1996), pp. 215–33.

Doneson, Judith, *The Holocaust in American Film* (New York: Jewish Publication Society, 1987).

Douglas, Lawrence, 'The Shrunken Head of Buchenwald: Icons of Atrocity at Nuremberg', in Barbie Zelizer (ed.), *Visual Culture and the Holocaust* (New Brunswick, NJ: Rutgers University Press, 2000), pp. 275–99.

————, 'Film as Witness: Screening *Nazi Concentration Camps* before the Nuremberg Tribunal', in *The Memory of Judgment: Making Law and History in the Trials of the Holocaust* (New Haven, CT: Yale University Press, 2001), pp. 11–37.

Drame, Claudine, 'Représenter l'irreprésentable: les camps nazis dans les actualités françaises de 1945', *Cinémathèque* 10 (1996), 12–28.

Dreyfus, Jean-Marc, 'Censorship and Approval: The Reception of *Night and Fog*', in Ewout van der Knaap (ed.), *Uncovering the Holocaust: The International Reception of Night and Fog* (London and New York: Wallflower, 2006), pp. 35–45.

Dulong, Renaud, *Le Témoin-oculaire. Les conditions sociales de l'attestation personelle* (Paris: Éditions de l'EHESS, 1998).

Dümling, Albrecht, 'Musikalischer Kontrapunkt zur filmischen Darstellung des Schreckens. Hanns Eislers Musik zu *Nuit et Brouillard* von Alain Resnais', in Manuel Köppen (ed.), *Kunst und Literatur nach Auschwitz* (Berlin: Erich Schmidt, 1993), pp. 113–23.

Eisler, Hanns, *A Rebel in Music*, trans. Marjorie Meyer (New York: International Publishers, 1978).

Ek, Richard, 'Giorgio Agamben and the Spatialities of the Camp: An Introduction', *Gografiska Annaler B Human Geography* 88/4 (2006), 363–86.

Elsaesser, Thomas, 'Freud as Media Theorist: Mystic Writing-pads and the Matter of Memory', *Screen* 50/1 (2009), 100–13.

Evans, Martin, *The Memory of Resistance: French Opposition to the Algerian War, 1954–1962* (Oxford: Berg, 1997).

Farocki, Harun, *Respite* (2007).

Felman, Shoshana, 'The Return of the Voice: Claude Lanzmann's *Shoah*', in Shoshana Felman and Dori Laub (eds), *Testimony: Crises of Witnessing in Literature, Psychoanalysis and History* (New York: Routledge, 1992).

Fleckner, Uwe, '"Der Leidschatz der Menschheit wird humaner Besitz". Sarkis, Warburg und das soziale Gedächtnis der Kunst', *Sarkis. Das Licht des Blitzes – Der Lärm des Donners* (Vienna: Museum moderner Kunst-Stiftung Ludwig, 1995), pp. 33–46.

Fleury-Vilatte, Beatrice, *Cinéma et culpabilité en Allemagne, 1945–1990* (Perpignan: Institut Jean Vigo, 1995).

Foucault, Michel, *Surveiller et punir* (Paris: Gallimard, 1975).

———, 'Film and Popular Memory', trans. M. Jordin, *Radical Philosophy* 11 (1975), 24–9.

Freud, Sigmund, *Interpretation of Dreams* [1900], trans. Joyce Crick (New York: Oxford University Press, 1999).

———, *The Complete Letters of Sigmund Freud to Wilhelm Fliess, 1887–1904,* trans. and ed. Jeffrey Moussaieff Masson (Cambridge, MA: The Belknap Press of Harvard University Press, 1985).

———, 'The Uncanny', [1918] *Standard Edition of the Complete Psychological Works of Sigmund Freud*, ed. and trans. James Strachey, Vol. 17 (London: Hogarth Press, 1962).

———, *Inhibitions, Symptoms and Anxiety* [1926], ed. James Strachey, trans. Alix Strachey (New York: W.W. Norton, 1959).

Friedlander, Saul, 'Trauma and Transference', *Memory, History, and the Extermination of the Jews of Europe* (Bloomington, IN: Indiana University Press, 1993), pp. 117–38.

———, 'Trauma, Memory, and Transference', in Geoffrey H. Hartman (ed.), *Holocaust Remembrance: The Shapes of Memory* (Oxford: Blackwell, 1994), pp. 252–63.

Friedlander, Saul (ed.), *Probing the Limits of Representation: Nazism and the 'Final Solution'* (Cambridge, MA: Harvard University Press, 1992).

Frieß, Jörg, 'Das Blut ist geronnen. Die Münder sind verstummt? Die zwei deutschen Synchronfassungen von Nuit et Brouillard', *Filmblatt*, 28, (Autumn 2005), 40–57.

Frodon, Jean-Michel (ed.), *Cinema and the Shoah: An Art Confronts the Tragedy of the Twentieth Century*, ed. and trans. Anna Harrison and Tom Maes (New York: SUNY Press, 2010).

Fuller, Samuel, *A Third Face: My Tale of Writing, Fighting and Filmmaking*, eds. Christa Lang Fuller and Jerome Henry Rudes (New York: Bantam Books, 1962).

———, *The Big Red One* (1980), trans. Géraldine Koff d'Amico (Paris: Christian Bourgois, 1991).

Gadjigo, Samba, H. Falukingham, Ralph, Cassirer, Thomas, and Sander, Reinhard (eds), *Ousmane Sembene: Dialogues With Critics and Writers* (Amherst, MA: University of Massachusetts Press, 1993).

Gauthier, Guy, *Le Documentaire, un autre cinéma* (Paris: Armand Colin, 1995; 2005 edn).

Genette, Gérard, *Narrative Discourse: An Essay in Method*, trans. Jane E. Lewin (Ithaca, NY: Cornell University Press, 1980).

Gervereau, Laurent, *Les Images qui mentent. Histoire visuel au XXe siècle* (Paris: Le Seuil, 2000).

Geyer, Michael, 'The Politics of Memory in Contemporary Germany', in Joan Copjec (ed.), *Radical Evil* (New York: Verson, 1996), pp. 169–200.

Ginzburg, Carlo, *The Judge and the Historian: Marginal Notes on a Late-Twentieth-Century Miscarriage of Justice*, trans. Antony Shugaar (London: Verso, 1999).

———, *History, Rhetoric, and Proof: The Menachem Stern Jerusalem Lectures* (London/Hanover: University Press of New England, 1999).

Gladstone, Kay, 'The Origins of British Army Combat Filming during the Second World War', *Film History* 14 (2002), 326–8.

Godard, Jean-Luc, *Jean-Luc Godard par Jean-Luc Godard*, ed. Alain Bergala (Paris: Cahiers du Cinéma, 1998).

Gordon, Avery, *Ghostly Matters: Haunting and the Sociological Imagination* (Minneapolis, MN: University of Minnesota Press, 1996).

Guattari, Félix, 'Everybody Wants to be a Fascist', *Semiotexte* II, 3:86 (1977), reprinted in Félix Guattari, *Chaosophy Collected Essays and Interviews*, ed. Sylvère Lotringer (Cambridge, MA: MIT Press, 1995).

Guerzoni, Benedetta, '*The Memory of the Camps,* un film inachevé. Les aléas de la dénonciation des atrocités nazies et de la politique britannique de communication en Allemagne', *Les Cahiers du judaïsme* 15 (2003), 61–70.

Haggith, Toby and Newman, Joanna (eds), *Holocaust and the Moving Image: Representations in Film and Television since 1933* (London: Wallflower Press, 2005).

Hanssen, Beatrice, *Walter Benjamin's Other History: Of Stones, Animals, Human Beings, and Angels* (Berkeley, CA: University of California Press, 1998).

Hartman, Geoffrey H., *The Longest Shadow: In the Aftermath of the Holocaust* (Bloomington, IN: Indiana University Press, 1996).

Hebard, Andrew, 'Disruptive Histories: Toward a Radical Politics of Remembrance in Alain Resnais's *Night and Fog*', *New German Critique* 71 (1997), 87–113.

Heck, Thomas and Gossens, Peter, '*Nacht und Nebel.* Ein Film wird übersetzt', in Axel Gellhaus (ed.), *Fremde Nähe. Celan als Übersetzer* (Marbach: Deutsche Schillergesellschaft, 1997).

Heidegger, Martin, *The Question Concerning Technology and Other Essays*, trans. W. Lovitt (New York: Harper Colophon Books, 1977).

Henderson, Mae, 'Toni Morrison's *Beloved*: Re-membering the Body as Historical Text', in Hortense Spillers and Marjorie Pryse (eds), *Comparative Identities: Race, Sex and Nationality in the Modern Text* (New York: Routledge, 1991).

Hewitt, Leah, *Remembering the Occupation in French Film: National Politics in Postwar Europe* (Basingstoke: Palgrave Macmillan, 2008).

Hilberg, Raul, *The Destruction of the European Jews* (New Haven, CT: Yale University Press, 2002).

Hirsch, Joshua, *Afterimage: Film, Trauma and the Holocaust* (Philadelphia, PA: Temple University Press, 2004).

Hirsch, Marianne, *Family Frames: Photography, Narrative, and Postmemory* (Cambridge, MA: Harvard University Press, 1997).

———, 'Surviving Images: Holocaust Photographs and the Work of Postmemory', *The Yale Journal of Criticism* 14/1 (2001), 5–37.

Hirsch, Marianne and Spitzer, Leo, 'Gendered Translations: Claude Lanzmann's *Shoah*', in Miriam Cooke and Angela Woollacott (eds), *Gendering War Talk* (Princeton, NJ: Princeton University Press, 1993), pp. 3–19.

Howes, Dustin Ellis, '"Consider if this is a Person": Primo Levi, Hannah Arendt and the Political Significance of Auschwitz', *Holocaust and Genocide Studies* 22/2 (2008), 266–92.

Hughes, Robert (ed.), *Film: Book Two – Films of War and Peace* (New York: Grove Press, 1962).

Insdorf, Annette, *Indelible Shadows: Film and the Holocaust* (New York: Random House, 1983).

———, *L'Holocauste à l'écran* (Paris: Le Cerf, 1985).

Institut Lumière, *Nuit et Brouillard* collection and Archives nationales, CAC (Centre of Contemporary Archives) of Fontainebleau 1989/0538 article 945.

Joly, Martine, 'Le cinéma d'archives, preuve de l'histoire?', in Jean-Pierre Bertin-Maghit and Béatrice Fleury-Vilatte (eds), *Les Institutions de l'image* (Paris: Éditions de l'EHESS, 2001), pp. 201–12.

Kaes, Anton, 'Holocaust and the End of History: Postmodern Historiography in Cinema', in Saul Friedlander (ed.), *Probing the Limits of Representation: Nazism and the Final Solution* (Cambridge, MA: Harvard University Press), pp. 206–22.

Kahan, Claudine and Mesnard, Philippe, *Giorgio Agamben à l'épreuve d'Auschwitz* (Paris: Kimé, 2001).

Kansteiner, Wulf, 'Genealogy of a Category Mistake: A Critical Intellectual History of the Cultural Trauma Metaphor', *Rethinking History* 8/2 (2004), 193–222.

Kaplan, Brett Ashley, *Unwanted Beauty: Aesthetic Pleasure in Holocaust Representation* (Urbana, IL: University of Illinois Press, 2007).

Kertész, Imre, 'Discours prononcé à la reception du prix Nobel de littérature à Stockholm, le 10 décembre 2002', trans. N. and C. Zaremba, *Bulletin de la Fondation d'Auschwitz*, 80–81 (2003), 169.

Kessel, Joseph, 'Images vues au tribunal de Nuremberg (1945)', *Les Cahiers du judaïsme* 15 (2003), 97–9.

Klüger, Ruth, *Still Alive: A Holocaust Girlhood Remembered* (New York: The Feminist Press, 2001).

Koch, Gertrude, 'The Angel of Forgetfulness and the Black Box of Facticity: Trauma and Memory in Claude Lanzmann's film *Shoah*', trans. Ora Wiskind, *History and Memory* 3/1 (1991), 119–32.

Kofman, Sarah, *Smothered Words* [1987], trans. Madeleine Dobie (Evanston, IL: Northwestern University Press, 1998).

Kogon, Eugen, *Der SS Staat* [1950], trans. Heinz Norden as *The Theory and Practice of Hell: The German Concentration Camps and the System Behind Them* (New York: Farrer, Strauss and Giroux, 1950).

Korman, Gerd, 'The Holocaust in American Writing', *Societas* 2 (1971), 250–70.

Kramer, Sven (ed.), *Die Shoah im Bild* (Munich: Text + Kritik, 2003).

Krantz, Charles, 'Resnais's *Night and Fog:* A Historical and Cultural Analysis', in Sanford Pinsker and Jack Fischel (eds), *Literature, the Arts, and the Holocaust* (Greenwood, FL: Penkevill, 1987), pp. 112–13.

Kristeva, Julia, *Pouvoirs de l'horreur: Essai sur l'abjection* (Paris: Seuil, 1980). Trans. Leon S. Roudiez as *Powers of Horror: An Essay on Abjection* (New York: Columbia University Press, 1982).

LaCapra, Dominick, *Representing the Holocaust: History, Theory, Trauma* (Ithaca, NY: Cornell University Press, 1994).

———, 'Lanzmann's *Shoah*: "here there is no why"', *Critical Inquiry* 23/2 (1997), 231–69.

———, *Writing History, Writing Trauma* (Baltimore, MD: Johns Hopkins University Press, 2000).

Lampin, Serge, 'Vaihingen, le camp du dernier repos', *Le Patriote résistant* 604 (1990), 14–15.

Lang, Berel, 'The Representation of Limits', in Saul Friedlander (ed.), *Probing the Limits of Representation: Nazism and the 'Final Solution'* (Cambridge, MA: Harvard University Press, 1992), pp. 300–17.

Langbein, Hermann, *Hommes et femmes à Auschwitz* [1972], trans. Denise Meunier (Paris: Fayard, 1975; new edn, 1997).

Lanzmann, Claude, 'Seminar with Claude Lanzmann', *Yale French Studies* 79/96 (1991), 82–99.

———, 'Why Spielberg Has Distorted the Truth', *Guardian Weekly*, 3 April 1994, 14.

———, *Shoah: The Complete Text* (New York: Da Capo Press, 1995).

Laqueur, Walter, *The Terrible Secret: Suppression of the Truth about Hitler's 'Final Solution'* (New York: Henry Holt & Co., 1998).

Lardeau, Yann and Weiss, Emil, *A Travelling is a Moral Affair* (Paris: M.W. Productions, 1986).

Lauterwein, Andréa, 'Les deux mondes, Paul Celan et Anselm Kiefer', unpublished PhD thesis. Paris III, Dept. of German, December 2002.

Le Forestier, Laurent, 'Fuller à Falkenau: l'impossible vision?', *1895. Revue de l'Association française de recherché sur l'histoire du cinéma* 47 (2005), 184–93.

Lefebvre, Jean-Pierre, 'Paul Celan traducteur des camps (on five verses of the poem "Engführung")', in 'Les Camps et la littérature. Une littérature du XXe siècle', *La Licorne*, 1999, no. 51.

LeSueur, James D., *Uncivil War: Intellectuals and Identity Politics during the Decolonization of Algeria* (Lincoln, NE: University of Nebraska Press, 2005).

Levi, Primo, *Survival in Auschwitz: The Nazi Assault on Humanity*, trans. Peter Woolf (New York: Collier, 1961).

———, *If This Is a Man*, trans. Stuart Woolf (London: Abacus, 1987).

———, *The Drowned and the Saved*, trans. Raymond Rosenthal (New York: Random House Vintage Books, 1989).

———, 'Retour à Auschwitz' (1982), transcription Marco Belpoliti, trans. Catherine Petitjean, in Primo Levi and Leonardo Debenedetti, *Rapport sur Auschwitz* (1945–1946), trans. Catherine Petitjean (Paris: Kimé, 2005).

———, *Collected Poems*, trans. Ruth Feldman and Brian Swann (London: Faber and Faber, 1992).

Levi, Primo and Debenedetti, Leonardo, *Rapport sur Auschwitz* (1945–1946), trans. Catherine Petitjean (Paris: Kimé, 2005).

———, *Auschwitz Report*, trans. Judith Woolf (London/New York: Verso, 2006).

Levinas, Emmanuel, *Totality and Infinity: An Essay on Exteriority*, trans. Alphonso Lingis (Pittsburgh, PA: Duquesne University Press, 1969).

———, *Totalité et infini: Essai sur l'extériorité* (The Hague: Martinus Nijhoff, 1971).

Liebman, Stuart, 'Les premières constellations du discourse sur l'Holocauste dans le cinéma polonais', in Antoine de Baecque and Christian Delage (eds), *De l'histoire au cinéma* (Paris-Brussels: IHTP-Éditions Complexe, 1998), pp. 193–216.

———, 'La libération des camps vue par le cinéma: l'exemple de *Vernichtungslager Majdanek*', trans. J.-F. Cornu, *Les Cahiers du judaïsme* 15 (2003), 49–60.

Lindeperg, Sylvie, *Clio de 5 à 7. Les actualités filmées de la Libération: archives du futur* (Paris: CNRS éditions, 2000).

———, Nuit et Brouillard: *Un Film dans l'Histoire* (Paris: Odile Jacob, 2007).

———, '*Night and Fog*: Inventing a Perspective', in Jean-Michel Frodon (ed.), *Cinema and the Shoah*, trans. Anna Harris and Tom Maes (New York: SUNY Press, 2010), pp. 63–84.

Lindeperg, Sylvie and Wieviorka, Annette, *Univers concentrationnaire et génocide. Voir, savoir, comprendre* (Paris: Mille et Une Nuits, 2008).

Liss, Andrea, *Trespassing Through Shadows: Memory, Photography and the Holocaust* (Minneapolis, MN: University of Minnesota Press, 1998).

Lowy, Vincent, *L'Histoire infilmable: Les camps d'extermination nazis à l'écran* (Paris: L'Harmattan, 2001).

Lubline, Warren, 'The Trajectory of *Night and Fog* in the USA', in Ewout van der Knapp (ed.), *Uncovering the Holocaust: The International Reception of Night and Fog* (London: Wallflower Press, 2006), pp. 149–64.

Lyotard, Jean-François, 'The Différend, the Referent, and the Proper Name', *Diacritics* 14/3 (1984), 3–14.

Matard-Bonucci, Marie-Anne and Lynch, Édouard (eds), *La Libération des camps et le retour des déportés* (Brussels: Éditions Complexe, 1995).

Mbembe, Achille, *On the Postcolony* (Berkeley, CA: University of California Press, 2001).

Mesnard, Philippe, 'La mémoire cinématographique de la Shoah', in Catherine Coquio (ed.), *Parler des camps, penser les génocides* (Paris: Albin Michel, 1999), pp. 473–90.

Michael, Robert, 'A Second Look: *Night and Fog*', *Cinéaste* 13/4 (1984), 36–7.

Monaco, James, *Alain Resnais* (New York: Oxford University Press, 1979).

Mondzain, Marie-José, 'La Shoah comme question de cinéma', in Jean-Michel Frodon (ed.), *Le Cinéma et la Shoah: Un art à l'épreuve de la tragédie du 20e siècle* (Paris: Cahiers du Cinéma, 2007), pp. 29–36.

Monicelli, Francesco and Saletti, Carlo (eds), *Il racconto della catastrofe. Il cinema di fronte a Auschwitz* (Verona: Società Letteraria-Cierre Edizioni, 1998).

Moorehead, Caroline, *Sidney Bernstein: A Biography* (London: Jonathan Cape, 1984).

Mouchard, Claude, ' "Ici"? "Maintenant"? Témoignages et œuvres', in Claude Mouchard and Annette Wieviorka (eds), *La Shoah: Témoignages, savoirs, œuvres* (Saint-Denis: Presses Universitaires de Vincennes-Cercil, 1999), pp. 225–60.

Müller, Filip, *Eyewitness Auschwitz: Three Years in the Gas Chambers* [1979], trans. Suzanne Flatauer (Chicago, IL: Ivan R. Dee, 1999).

Mulvey, Laura, 'Compilation film as "deferred action": Vincent Monnikendam's *Mother Dao, the Turtle-Like*', in Andrea Sabbadini (ed.), *Projected Shadows: Psychoanalytic Reflections on the Representation of Loss in European Cinema* (London/New York: Routledge, 2007), pp. 109–18.

Murphy, David, 'Fighting for the Homeland? The Second World War in the Films of Ousmane Sembene', *L'Esprit Créateur* 47/1 (2007), 56–67.

Murrow, Edward R., 'They Died 900 a Day in "the Best" Nazi Death Camp', *PM*, 16 April 1945. http://www.jewishvirtuallibrary.org/jsource/Holocaust/murrow.html (accessed 8 September 2009).

Narboni, Jean and Simsolo, Noël, *Il était une fois … Samuel Fuller. Histoires d'Amérique*, transcription and trans. Dominique Villain (Paris: Cahiers du Cinéma, 1986), pp. 114–15.

Neumann, Gerhard and Weigel, Sigrid (eds), *Lesbarkeit der Kultur. Literaturwissenschaften zwischen Kulturtechnik und Ethnographie* (Munich: Wilhelm Fink, 2000).

Niney, François, *L'Épreuve du reel à l'écran. Essai sur le principe de réalité documentaire* (Brussels: De Boeck Université, 2000; 2002 edn), pp. 253–92.

Niney, François (ed.), *La Preuve par l'image? L'évidence des prises de vue* (Valence: Centre de Recherche et d'Action culturelle, 2003).

Nora, Pierre, 'Between Memory and History: Les Lieux de Mémoire' [1984]. *Representations* 26 (Spring 1989), 7–25.

——, *Les Lieux de Mémoire,* 7 vols (Paris: Editions Gallimard, 1984–1992).

Nouss, Alexis, 'La traduction mélancolique (on Paul Celan)', in Ginette Michaud (ed.), *Psychanalyse et traduction: voies de traverse*, Études sur le texte et ses transformations, Canadian Association for Translation Studies, McGill University, 9/2 (1998).

Okrah, Kwadwo Asafo-Agyei, 'Sankofa: Cultural Heritage Conservation and Sustainable African Development', *The African Symposium: An Online Journal of the African Educational Research Network* 8/2 (2008).

Owens, Patricia, 'Humanity, Sovereignty and the Camps', *International Politics* 45 (2008), 522–30.

Pagnoux, Elisabeth, 'Reporter photographe à Auschwitz', *Temps modernes* 613 (2001), 84–108.

Perec, Georges, *W ou le Souvenir d'Enfance* (Paris: Denoël, 1975).

Peterson, Judith, 'A Little-known Classic: *Night and Fog* in Britain', in Ewout van der Knapp (ed.), *Uncovering the Holocaust: The International Reception of Night and Fog* (London: Wallflower Press, 2006), pp. 106–28.

Petrie, Jon, 'The Secular Word "HOLOCAUST": Scholarly Myths, History, and Twentieth Century Meanings', *Journal of Genocide Research* 2/1 (2000), 31–63.

Pollock, Griselda, *Encounters in the Virtual Feminist Museum: Time, Space and the Archive* (London/New York: Routledge, 2007).

——, 'The Graces of Catastrophe: Matrixial Time and Aesthetic Space Confront the Archive of Disaster', in *Encounters in the Virtual Feminist Museum: Time, Space and the Archive* (London: Routledge, 2007), pp. 165–97.

——, 'Dying, Seeing, Feeling: Transforming the Ethical Space of Feminist Aesthetics', in Diarmuid Costello and Dominic Willsdon, (eds) *Life and Death of Images* (London: Tate Publishing, 2008), pp. 213–35.

——, 'Photographing Atrocity: Becoming Iconic?', in Geoffrey Batchen, Mick Gidley, Nancy K. Miller, Jay Prosser (eds), *Picturing Atrocity: Reading Photography in Crisis* (London: Reaktion Books, 2011).

Rancière, Jacques, 'L'historicité du cinéma', in Antoine de Baecque and Christian Delage (eds). *De l'histoire au cinéma* (Paris-Brussels: IHTP-Éditions Complexe, 1998), pp. 45–60.

————, 'Is History a Form of Fiction?' in *The Politics of Aesthetics: The Distribution of the Sensible* [2000], trans. Gabriel Rockhill (London: Continuum, 2004).

————, *La Fable cinématographique* (Paris: Le Seuil, 2001).

————, 'S'il y a de l'irreprésentable?', *Genre Humain* 36 (2001), 81–102; reprinted as 'Are Some Things Unrepresentable?', in Jacques Rancière, *The Future of the Image*, trans. Gregory Elliott (London: Verso, 2007), pp. 109–38.

————, *The Future of the Image*, trans. Gregory Elliott (London: Verso, 2007).

Raskin, Richard, Nuit et Brouillard *by Alain Resnais: On the Making, Reception and Functions of a Major Documentary Film, Including a New Interview with Alain Resnais and the Original Shooting Script*, Foreword by Sascha Vierny (Aarhus: Aarhus University Press, 1987).

————, *A Child at Gunpoint: A Case Study in the Life of a Photo* (Aarhus: Aarhus University Press, 2004).

Rastier, François, 'Primo Levi: prose du témoin, poèmes du survivant', in François-Charles Gaudard and Modesta Suárez (eds), *Formes discursives du témoignage* (Toulouse: Éditions Universitaires du Sud, 2003), pp. 143–60.

————, *Ulysse à Auschwitz: Primo Levi, le survivant* (Paris: Le Cerf, 2005).

Revel, Jacques, 'Un exercice de désorientation: *Blow up*', in Antoine de Baecque and Christian Delage (eds), *De l'histoire au cinéma* (Brussels: Éditions Complexe, 1998).

Rivette, Jacques, 'De l'Abjection', *Cahiers du Cinéma* 120 (1961), 54–5. Reprinted in Antoine De Baecque (ed.), *Théories du Cinéma* (Paris: Cahiers du cinéma, 2001), pp. 37–40.

Robin, Régine, 'Une mémoire menacée: la Shoah' in *La Mémoire saturée* (Paris: Stock, 2003), pp. 217–375.

Roseman, Mark, *The Villa, The Lake, The Meeting: Wannsee and the Final Solution* (London: Penguin Books, 2002).

Rothberg, Michael, *Traumatic Realism: The Demands of Holocaust Representation* (Minneapolis, MN: University of Minnesota Press, 2000).

————, *Multidirectional Memory; Remembering the Holocaust in the Age of Decolonization* (Stanford, CA: Stanford University Press, 2009).

Rousset, David, *L'Univers concentrationnaire* (Paris: Editions de Pavois, 1946); translated as *The Other Kingdom*, trans. Ramon Guthrie (New York: Reynal and Hitchcock, 1947), and reissued in 1951 as *A World Apart*.

————, *Les Jours de notre mort* [1947] (Paris: Hachette-Littératures, 1993).

Rousso, Henry, *Le Syndrome de Vichy, de 1944 à nos jours* (Paris: Seuil, 1987).

Salgas, Jean-Pierre, 'Shoah, ou la disparition', in Denis Hollier (ed.), *De la littérature française* (Paris: Bordas, 1993), pp. 1005–13.

Santner, Eric L., *Stranded Objects: Mourning, Memory and Film in Postwar Germany* (Ithaca, NY: Cornell University Press, 1990).

———, 'History beyond the Pleasure Principle: Some Thoughts on the Representation of Trauma', in Saul Friedlander (ed.), *Probing the Limits of Representation: Nazism and the 'Final Solution'* (Cambridge, MA: Harvard University Press, 1992).

Sanyal, Debarati, 'A Soccer Match in Auschwitz: Passing Culpability in Holocaust Criticism', *Representations* 79 (2002), 1–27.

Saxton, Libby, *Haunted Images: Film, Ethics, Testimony and the Holocaust* (London/New York: Wallflower Press, 2008).

Schneider, Michael, *Den Kopf verkehrt aufgesetzt oder die melancholische Linke* (Darmstadt: Luchterhand, 1981).

Schwartz, G., *Die nationalsozialistischen Lager* (Frankfurt: Campus, 1990).

Server, Lee, *Samuel Fuller: Film is a Battleground. A Critical Study, with Interviews, a Filmography, and a Bibliography* (Jefferson/London: McFarland, 1994).

Silverman, Max, 'Horror and the Everyday in Post-Holocaust France: *Nuit et Brouillard* and Concentrationary Art', *French Cultural Studies* 17/1 (2006), 5–18.

———, 'Interconnected Histories: Holocaust and Empire in the Cultural Imaginary', *French Studies* 62/4 (2008), 417–28.

Sofsky, Wolfgang, *The Order of Terror: The Concentration Camp* [1993], trans. William Templer (Princeton, NJ: Princeton University Press, 1997).

Söllner, Alfons, 'Hannah Arendt's *The Origins of Totalitarianism* in its Original Context', *European Journal of Political Theory* 3/2 (2004), 219–38.

Sontag, Susan, 'Fascinating Fascism', in *Under the Sign of Saturn* (New York: Vintage Books, 1980), pp. 78–83.

———, *On Photography* (London: Penguin, 1977); *Sur la photographie* (1973), trad. Philippe Blanchard (Paris: Christian Bourgeois, 1983; 1993 edn).

———, *Regarding the Pain of Others* [2003] (London: Penguin, 2004).

Spivak, Gayatri Chakravorty, *The Post-colonial Critic: Interviews, Strategies, Dialogs*, ed. Sara Harasym (New York: Routledge, 1990).

Stora, Benjamin, *La Gangrène et l'oubli: la mémoire de la guerre d'Algérie* (Paris: La Découverte, 1998).

Struk, Janina, *Photographing the Holocaust: Interpretations of the Evidence* (London: I.B. Tauris, 2004).

Strzelecki, Andrzej, *The Evacuation, Dismantling and Liberation of KL Auschwitz* (Oswiecim: Auschwitz-Birkenau State Museum, 2001).

Swiebocka, Teresa (ed.), *Auschwitz. A History in Photographs*, trans. Jonathan Webber and Connie Wilsack (Oswiecim/Warsaw/Bloomington, IN: Auschwitz-Birkenau Museum/Ksiazka I Wiedza/Indiana University Press, 1993).

Teskey, Gordon, *Allegory and Violence* (Ithaca, NY: Cornell University Press, 1996).

Traverso, Enzo, *Le Passé, modes d'emploi. Histoire, mémoire, politique* (Paris: La Fabrique, 2005).

van der Knapp, Ewout (ed.), *Uncovering the Holocaust: The International Reception of* Night and Fog (London: Wallflower Press, 2006).

van der Kolk, Bessel and van der Hart, Onno, 'The Intrusive Past: the Flexibility of Memory and the Engraving of Trauma', in Cathy Caruth (ed.), *Trauma: Explorations in Memory* (Baltimore, MD: Johns Hopkins University Press, 1995), pp. 159–64.

Van Wert, William F., 'Point/Counterpoint in *Hiroshima mon amour*', *Wide Angle* 2/2 (1978).

Vaughan, Dai, *Portrait of an Invisible Man: Working Life of Stewart McAllister, Film Editor* (London: British Film Institute, 1983).

Vidal-Naquet, Pierre, *Les Assassins de la mémoire. 'Un Eichmann de papier' et autres essays sur le révisionnisme* (Paris: La Découverte, 1991).

Wachsmann, Nikolaus, 'The Dynamics of Destruction: the Development of Concentration Camps, 1933–1945' in Jane Caplan and Nikolaus Wachsmann (eds), *Concentration Camps in Nazi Germany* (London/New York: Routledge, 2010), pp. 17–43.

Wajcman, Gérard, 'De la croyance photographique', *Temps modernes* 613 (2001), 47–83.

Warburg, Aby, 'L'art du portrait et la bourgeoisie florentine: Domenico Ghirlandaio à Santa Trinità. Les portraits de Laurent de Médicis et de son entourage' (1902), trans. S. Muller, *Essais florentins* (Paris: Klincksieck, 1990).

Weigel, Sigrid, 'Scholems Gedichte und seine Dichtungstheorie. Klage, Adressierung, Gabe und das Problem einer biblischen Sprache in unserer Zeit', in Stephen Mosès and Sigrid Weigel (eds), *Gershom Scholem. Literatur und Rhetorik* (Cologne/Weimar/Vienna: Böhlau, 2000), pp. 16–47.

Weinberg, David, 'France', in David S. Wyman (ed.), *The World Reacts to the Holocaust* (Baltimore, MD: Johns Hopkins University Press, 1996).

Weiss, Emil, *Falkenau, vision de l'impossible* (Paris: M.W. Productions, 1988).

Welles, Orson, *Moi, Orson Welles. Entretiens avec Peter Bogdanovitch* (1992), trans. Évelyne Châtelain (Paris: Belfond, 1993).

Wende, Waltraud Wara (ed.), *Geschichte im Film. Mediale Inszenierungen des Holocaust und kulturelles Gedächtnis* (Stuttgart/Weimar: Metzler, 2002).

Wiesel, Elie, *The New Leader*, 5 August 1963.

———, *Night*, trans. Stella Rodway (London: Penguin, 1981).

Wieviorka, Annette, 'Indicible ou inaudible? La déportation: premiers récits (1944–1947)', *Pardès* 9–10 (1989), 23–59.

———, *Déportation et genocide: entre la mémoire et l'oubli* (Paris: Plon, 1992).

———, *L'Ère du témoin* (Paris: Plon, 1998).

————, *Auschwitz, 60 ans après* (Paris: Robert Laffont, 2005).

Williams, Christopher, *Realism in Cinema* (London: Routledge Kegan Paul, 1980).

Williams, Linda (ed.), *Viewing Positions: Ways of Seeing Film* (New Brunswick, NJ: Rutgers University Press, 1995).

Wilson, Emma, 'Material Remains: *Nuit et Brouillard*', *October* 112/1 (Spring 2005), 89–110.

————, *Alain Resnais* (Manchester: Manchester University Press, 2006).

Wormser, Olga and Michel, Henri, *Tragédie de la Déportation. 1940–1945. Témoignages de survivants des camps de concentration allemands* (Paris: Hachette, 1954).

Young, James, *Writing and Rewriting the Holocaust: Narrative and the Consequences of Interpretation* (Bloomington, IN: Indiana University Press, 1988).

Zelizer, Barbie, *Remembering to Forget: Holocaust Memory through the Camera's Eye* (Chicago, IL: University of Chicago Press, 1998).

Zumbusch, Cornelia, *Wissenschaft in Bildern. Symbol und dialektisches Bild in Aby Warburgs Mnemosyne-Atlas und Walter Benjamins Passagen-Werk* (Berlin: Akademie Verlag, 2004).

Notes on Contributors

Georges Didi-Huberman is a philosopher and art historian who currently teaches at the Ecoles des Hautes Etudes, Paris. He has published over 30 books on the history and theory of images, in a range of fields that spans the Renaissance to contemporary art and which focuses notably on problems of iconography from the nineteenth century and their uses in artistic practices in the twentieth century. His notable publications include *Images in Spite of All: Four Photographs from Auschwitz*, trans. Shane B. Lillis (Chicago: University of Chicago Press, 2008); *Devant le temps. Histoire de l'art et anachronisme des images* (Paris: Minuit, 2000); *L'Image survivante. Histoire de l'art et temps des fantômes selon Aby Warburg* (Paris: Minuit, 2002).

Kay Gladstone is a Senior Curator (Acquisitions and Documentation) in the Film Archive of the Imperial War Museum. Recruited by the IWM in 1972 to catalogue the foreign language film collection, he later interviewed on audio tape most of the surviving members of the Army Film and Photographic Unit and curated several displays on the history of combat filming; his article 'The AFPU – The origins of British Army combat filming during the Second World War' was included in *Film History* 14/3–4 (2002). In 1984 he introduced at the Berlin Film Festival the first public screening of the never-completed British documentary *Memory of the Camps*; his paper 'Separate Intentions: the Allied Screening of Concentration Camp Documentaries in Germany in 1945–46: Death Mills and Memory of the Camps' was published in *Holocaust and the Moving Image: Representations in Film and Television since 1933* (Wallflower Press, 2005). He has written on amateur film in *Mining the Home Movie: Excavations in Histories and Memories*, edited by Karen L. Ishizuka and Patricia R. Zimmermann (University of California Press, 2007), and from 2007 to 2010 represented the IWM on the core management team for the AHRC database *Colonial Film: Moving Images of the British Empire* (www.colonialfilm.org.uk).

322 | *Notes on Contributors*

Andrew Hebard is an Assistant Professor of English and American Literature at Miami University of Ohio. He has most recently published in *American Quarterly* and *African American Review* and has just finished a book manuscript titled '*An Empire of Letters': The Poetics of Sovereignty in the United States*. The book examines the relation between literary conventions and situations where the American state suspended its own laws to regulate racially marked populations.

Joshua Hirsch is the author of *Afterimage: Film, Trauma, and the Holocaust* (Temple University Press, 2004). He received his PhD in Film and Television from UCLA in 2001, and has taught film studies at the University of North Texas and other universities.

Sylvie Lindeperg is a historian. She is a Professor at the Université de Paris I-Panthéon Sorbonne. She is the author of *Les Ecrans de l'ombre. La Seconde Guerre mondiale dans le cinéma français* (CNRS Éditions, 1997); *Clio de 5 à 7. Les actualités filmées de la Libération* (CNRS Éditions, 2000); *Nuit et Brouillard. Un film dans l'histoire* (Odile Jacob, 2007); *Univers concentrationnaire et génocide. Voir, savoir, comprendre*, in collaboration with Annette Wieviorka (Mille et Une Nuits, 2008). With Jean-Louis Comolli she is the co-author of the film *Face aux fantômes* (Ina et Ciné-Cinéma, 2009).

John Mowitt is Professor in the Department of Cultural Studies and Comparative Literature at the University of Minnesota. He is the author of numerous texts on the topics of culture, theory and politics, most recently *Re-Takes: Postcoloniality and Foreign Film Languages* (2005) and the co-edited volume *The Dreams of Interpretation: a Century Down the Royal Road* (2007), both from the University of Minnesota Press. He recently collaborated with the composer Jarrod Fowler to transpose his book, *Percussion: Drumming, Beating, Striking* (Duke University Press, 2002), from a printed to a sonic text. His current project, *Radio: Essays in Bad Reception* is forthcoming from the University of California Press. He is also a senior co-editor of the journal *Cultural Critique*, a leading Anglophone academic publication in the field of cultural studies and critical theory.

Griselda Pollock is Professor of Social and Critical Histories of Art and Director of the Centre for Cultural Analysis, Theory and History at the University of Leeds. Known for her critical work on gender, class, race and sexuality in the fields of art history and feminist cultural theory, *Differencing the Canon: Feminist Desire and the Writings of Art's Histories* (Routledge, 1999) and *Encounters in the Virtual Feminist Museum: Time, Space and the Archive* (Routledge, 2007), she has been working on issues of trauma and cultural memory for over 15 years with a special focus on the Holocaust, aesthetics and psychoanalysis. Her forthcoming studies include *After-Affect/After-Image: Trauma and Aesthetic Inscription* and *Theatre of Memory: Charlotte Salomon's Leben? Oder Theater?* She is the editor of the series *New Encounters: Arts, Cultures, Concepts* with I.B. Tauris (*Conceptual Odysseys* (2007); *Digital and other Virtualities*, with Antony Bryant (2010)). With Max Silverman she is editing the series *Concentrationary Cinema, Concentrationary Memories and Concentrationary Imaginaries*.

Debarati Sanyal is Associate Professor of French at the University of California-Berkeley. She is the author of *The Violence of Modernity: Baudelaire, Irony and the Politics of Form* (2006) as well as numerous articles on the Second World War, post-war France and Holocaust memory. She also co-edited '*Noeuds de Mémoire*: Multidirectional Memory in Postwar French and Francophone Culture' (Yale French Studies, 2010) and is completing a book titled *Dangerous Intersections: Allegory, Complicity and Memory in Postwar France*.

Libby Saxton is Senior Lecturer in French and Film Studies at Queen Mary, University of London. Her research interests include the interactions between film and continental thought, especially philosophies of ethics; post-war French cinema; representations of the Holocaust and the Franco-Algerian War; and the relationship between film, memory and testimony. She is author of *Haunted Images: Film, Ethics, Testimony and the Holocaust* (Wallflower, 2008), co-author, with Lisa Downing, of *Film and Ethics: Foreclosed Encounters* (Routledge, 2009) and co-editor, with Simon Kemp, of *Seeing Things: Vision, Perception and Interpretation in French Studies* (Peter Lang, 2002). She is currently co-editing, with Axel Bangert and Robert Gordon, a book entitled *Holocaust Intersections: Genocide and Visual Culture at the New Millennium* (forthcoming with Legenda, 2012).

324 | Notes on Contributors

Max Silverman is Professor of Modern French and Director of the Centre for French and Francophone Cultural Studies at the University of Leeds. His most recent work is on post-Holocaust culture, colonial and postcolonial theory and cultures, and questions of race, memory and violence. He is currently writing a monograph on connections between the Holocaust and colonialism in the French and Francophone cultural imaginary and directing a four-year AHRC-funded project (in collaboration with Griselda Pollock) entitled *Concentrationary Memories and the Politics of Representation*. He has recently co-edited, with Michael Rothberg and Debarati Sanyal, a special issue of *Yale French Studies* entitled '*Noeuds de mémoire*: Multidirectional Memory in Post-war French and Francophone Culture'. With Griselda Pollock he is editing the series *Concentrationary Cinema, Concentrationary Memories and Concentrationary Imaginaries*.

Emma Wilson is Professor of French Literature and the Visual Arts at the University of Cambridge and a Fellow of Corpus Christi College. Her publications include: *Sexuality and the Reading Encounter: Identity and Desire in Proust, Duras, Tournier and Cixous* (Oxford University Press, 1996); *French Cinema since 1950: Personal Histories* (Duckworth, 1999); *Memory and Survival: The French Cinema of Krzysztof Kieslowski* (Legenda, 2000); *Cinema's Missing Children* (Wallflower, 2003); *Alain Resnais* (Manchester University Press, 2006); and *Atom Egoyan* (University of Illinois Press, 2009). Her latest book, *Love, Mortality and the Moving Image*, is forthcoming.

Index